BIOGRAPHICAL MEMOIRS OF FELLOWS III

Published for THE BRITISH ACADEMY
by OXFORD UNIVERSITY PRESS

Oxford University Press, Great Clarendon Street, Oxford OX2 6DP

Oxford New York
Auckland Bangkok Bogotá Buenos Aires Cape Town Chennai
Dar es Salaam Delhi Hong Kong Istanbul Karachi Kolkata
Kuala Lumpur Madrid Melbourne Mexico City Mumbai Nairobi
São Paulo Shanghai Singapore Taipei Tokyo Toronto

British Library Cataloguing in Publication Data
Data available

ISBN 0–19–726320–8
ISSN 0068–1202

Typeset in Times
by J&L Composition, Filey, North Yorkshire
Printed in Great Britain
on acid-free paper by
CPI Bath

The Academy is grateful to Professor P. J. Marshall, CBE, FBA
for his editorial work on this volume

Contents

GERALD AYLMER

Gerald Edward Aylmer
1926–2000

GERALD AYLMER, historian of seventeenth-century England, was born on 30 April 1926 at Stoke Court, Greete, Shropshire, the only child of Captain Edward Arthur Aylmer, DSC, RN, and his wife Phoebe (née Evans). His father was Anglo-Irish. The Aylmers—the name derives from the Anglo-Saxon Aethelmar, latinised as Ailmerus—had taken part in the Anglo-Norman conquest of Ireland. Sir Gerald Aylmer was Chief Justice of Ireland in the second quarter of the sixteenth century. After him came many high-ranking naval and military officers. Admiral Matthew Aylmer commanded the British Fleet during the War of the Spanish Succession and was made an Irish peer. The fifth Lord Aylmer fought in the Peninsular War and was Governor-General of Canada. The sixth was an admiral who had been with Nelson at the Nile. General Sir Fenton Aylmer won the Victoria Cross in India. Gerald's mother was descended from self-made South Wales business people, but there were two more admirals on her side of the family.

Gerald's great-uncle Willie, Lord Desborough, was the father of the First World War poet, Julian Grenfell, and a celebrated athlete: President of the MCC, the Lawn Tennis Association, the Amateur Fencing Association, and the 1908 Olympic Games. He stroked an eight across the Channel, climbed in the Alps, shot in India and Africa, twice swam Niagara and was elected an Honorary Fellow of Balliol. Another forebear was Rose Aylmer, whose beauty was celebrated in W. S. Landor's famous elegy:

Proceedings of the British Academy, **124**, 3–21. © The British Academy 2004.

Ah, what avails the sceptred race!
Ah, what the form divine!

It might have been thought that, to Gerald, a firm believer in social
equality, and one who himself declined public honours, this remarkable
ancestry would have been irrelevant; and indeed he spoke rather dis-
paragingly of some of his forebears, such as the fifth Lord Aylmer, who,
at the age of 73, was sworn in as a special constable during the Chartist
demonstration of 1848, only for the first woman he met to say to him,
'Much harm, *you'll* do, you old fool.'[1] In his last book, Gerald drily
records that, if Samuel Pepys had had his way, Matthew Aylmer, then a
captain, would have been hanged for dipping his colours to a Spanish
admiral; in which case, he, Gerald, would never have existed.

Yet Gerald, who duly attended great-uncle Willie's old college and
gave his son Tom the ancient family name of Bartholomew, was far from
indifferent to his lineage. Just as many agnostics (Gerald among them)
retained the moral earnestness of their Christian forebears, so this self-
confessed egalitarian possessed the same integrity, sense of honour, and
devotion to public service as his aristocratic ancestors. Gerald had all the
gentlemanly qualities. He was honest, brave and courteous. Unshakeable
in his adherence to principle, he was sensitive to constitutional niceties
and had a sharp eye for injustice. A naturally passionate man, he kept a
tight rein on his feelings; when occasionally allowed to escape, they
were always expressed in a controlled and decorous manner. He was
un-self-regarding to an almost ridiculous extent. As a member of the
Historical Manuscripts Commission, he once received a complimentary
copy of the Commission's latest publication, a calendar of the correspondence of the nonconformist divine Philip Doddridge. Gerald wrote
back, expressing his thanks, but adding that, 'at £40, I do wonder whether
it is a justifiable perquisite of office for all Commissioners to receive such
a publication'. His scrupulosity was of a kind which seemed almost
archaic in an age when self-interest and personal gratification were widely
regarded as acceptable motives for action.

Gerald's rock-like dependability was all the more remarkable, because
his childhood was unsettled. His father, as a naval officer, was constantly
on the move, until settling in Dorset on retirement. When his parents were
posted abroad, Gerald lived with his grandmother. He was sent to
Beaudesert Park, a preparatory school in Gloucestershire, a sadistic insti-

---

[1] Lieut. Gen. Sir Fenton J. Aylmer, VC, *The Aylmers of Ireland* (1931), p. 264.

tution, where he was terrified and unhappy; then to Winchester, another harsh place, where daily cold baths were compulsory and the lavatories had no doors. A schoolfellow recalled him as 'large, fair, flabby and the least physically co-ordinated person I have ever known'. But he also noted 'a certain ponderous authority' and 'a hyper-active conscience'; and he added that 'he continually says things which widen my world'.[2]

Winchester was, for Gerald, a place of intellectual emancipation; it was there that he developed his scholarly interests and his increasingly left-wing views. He had always been notable for his independence of mind. At the age of four, he was overheard playing in a stream with his slightly older cousin. The cousin, as befitted a future admiral, was giving the orders. Gerald protested, in a manner which those who knew him in later years would have immediately recognised: 'You see, Iwan,' he told his cousin, 'some people have different thinks from others.' Gerald's thinks were indeed different, though he never lost hope that others might be brought round by reason. In April 1939, when he was thirteen, he wrote a letter to Adolf Hitler, warning him that any further act of aggression on his part would mean war; a youthful admonition which the Führer would have been well-advised to heed. At Winchester Gerald became convinced that social conditions in Britain were in urgent need of reform. He discovered Kingsley Martin's *New Statesman*, a powerful influence on his intellectual development thereafter, along with the writings of William Temple, who was a distant relation and had officiated at the marriage of his parents, and of R. H. Tawney, who would later become his graduate supervisor.

Throughout his life, Gerald was greatly moved by poverty and took a deep interest in African affairs and the problems of the Third World. In the 1950s, he and his wife were activists in CND, on the moderate, pragmatic wing; they went on three Aldermaston marches and Gerald spoke in Trafalgar Square. In the 1980s he was depressed by the way in which British politics seemed to have gone into reverse; in his last book, he compared the year 1979, when Mrs Thatcher became prime minister, to 1660, when hopes of a better world were quenched by the restoration of Charles II. In 1991 he gave a paper at St Peter's College, defiantly entitled 'Why I am still a Socialist', though the 'socialism' he expounded was of an exceedingly moderate kind. He accepted that capitalism was unequalled as a means of maximising wealth in the developed countries, but he felt that the profit motive and the market could in themselves never

---

[2] Thomas Hinde [Sir Thomas Chitty], *Sir Henry and Sons: a Memoir* (1980), p. 144.

provide adequately for health, education, welfare, culture and the arts, leave alone the preservation of the environment, the needs of the Third World and the interests of future generations.[3]

Gerald had originally been destined for the Navy, but after a few years at Winchester that career came to seem patently inappropriate. In 1944 he went up to Balliol College on a history exhibition. But it was wartime and, after one term at Oxford, he volunteered for the Navy, where he served for the next three years, as an ordinary and then an able seaman; by necessity rather than choice, for he would have liked to have been an officer. In retrospect, he was grateful for the experience. Years later, in a Presidential Address to the Royal Historical Society, arguing that the religiosity of seventeenth-century parishioners could not be measured by the quantity of communion wine consumed, he remarked that 'anyone who has served on the lower deck of the Royal Navy before the abolition of the rum ration will appreciate the fine distinction between "sippers" and "gulpers" ' (*Trans. Royal Hist. Soc.*, 5th ser. 37 (1987), 230).

The more ribald aspects of Gerald's naval career have been immortalised by his shipmate, the jazz singer George Melly. On shore leave in Gibraltar, Gerald was arrested when trying to crawl across the Spanish border: 'pissed as a newt and covered in mud, he . . . spent the night roaring out in a police cell that his father was an admiral'. Melly recalls his 'deep booming voice and magnificent laugh', his 'love of gossip' and their shared enthusiasm for the poems of W. H. Auden. He also remarks that there was 'a kind of dogged nobility about him, an admirable probity'. It was Gerald who helped to get Melly off the potentially serious charge of distributing anarchist literature on board one of His Majesty's ships, by discovering that parallel sentiments were expressed by George Bernard Shaw in works which were freely available in the ship's library.[4]

In 1947 Gerald returned to Balliol. One of his tutors was Christopher Hill, who became a life-long friend and whose view of the seventeenth century profoundly influenced his own. Gerald retained his intellectual independence, but much of his later work was essentially a response to issues which had originally been posed by Hill. Gerald is said to have been a 'self-contained, slightly reserved, hard-working' undergraduate. He took a First in Modern History in 1950 and then spent a year as Jane

---

[3] MS of unpublished paper given at St Peter's College on 19 Feb. 1991.

[4] George Melly, *Rum, Bum and Concertina* (1977), pp. 132, 118. Gerald appears (on the far right) of a photograph illustrating Melly's later article, 'The navy lark: what a gay time we had', *Sunday Times*, 3 Nov. 2002.

Eliza Procter Fellow at Princeton University, an experience which gained him new friends, notably Richard S. Dunn, historian of West Indian slavery and editor of the papers of William Penn, and, thanks to the teaching of Professor W. F. Craven, left him with an enduring interest in American history. Right into his retirement, Gerald continued to teach the colonial period to undergraduates. He was fascinated by 'the interaction of the New World environment with the social and mental heritage which the settlers took with them from the Old'; and in the early history of Massachusetts he saw a small-scale indication of the way in which a continuing Puritan commonwealth might have evolved in England (*Trans. Royal Hist. Soc.*, 5th ser., 36 (1986), 11).

On his return from the USA, Gerald took up a Junior Research Fellowship at Balliol. There, under the supervision of R. H. Tawney, whom he had met in 1950, through Archbishop Temple's daughter, a friend of his aunt, he completed his thesis, 'Studies on the Institutions and Personnel of English Central Administration, 1625–42' (1954). This work, which he characteristically described as 'a preliminary survey', 'limited, tentative, inconclusive', filled two volumes and 1208 pages. 'There are no short cuts in administrative history,' he remarks on p. 1143. 'The way has been long, the path narrow and the gate strait.' In response to the anguished protest of his examiners, the Modern History Board locked the stable door by prescribing that future D.Phil. theses should be subject to a word-limit. The story that the thesis had to be carried to the Examination Schools in a wheelbarrow is apocryphal, but it reflects the awe which Gerald was already inspiring in others.

In 1955 Gerald married Ursula Nixon, an illustrations editor at Oxford University Press, whose father, an army officer, was also Anglo-Irish. 'It was the cleverest and most fortunate thing he ever did,' remarked Christopher Hill. For the next forty-five years Gerald and Ursula were a true partnership: both possessed the same enormous energy, and the same generosity of spirit, but otherwise were very different in temperament, Ursula's practicality, common sense, warmth and outspokenness admirably complementing Gerald's discretion and initial reserve. She was closely involved in all his scholarly projects and an invaluable copy-editor. Gerald always wrote lucidly, but he could be ponderous and made frequent use of the exclamation mark; Ursula did much to lighten his prose style. They adopted two children, Tom and Emma.

Gerald spent the next eight years as an assistant lecturer (1954) and lecturer (1962) at Manchester University. It was a star-studded department, where he made lasting friendships, particularly with Gordon Leff,

Donald Pennington and Penry Williams. But he deplored the professorial autocracy and the lack of contact with the students, who were taught impersonally in large lecture classes. He attempted to teach in smaller groups; and, with Ursula, invited students to cider parties. He published an article, suggesting that those below the rank of professor should be allowed to take part in university government.[5] One of his professors referred to him as 'a trouble-maker'.

While at Manchester, Gerald published his thesis, condensed and rewritten, as *The King's Servants. The Civil Service of Charles I.* It was a magisterial study; and almost overnight it made Gerald a famous historian. Two years later, Eric James, who had taught Gerald at Winchester, and was now Vice-Chancellor of the newly created University of York, invited him to come as the first Professor of History, at the age of 36. It was an inspired choice.[6] Gerald's fifteen years at York were his heroic period. He created a new department, with a novel syllabus, new methods of examining, a relatively democratic system of government and an exceptionally gifted staff. Gerald had an eye for talent and made a series of imaginative appointments. York rapidly became what Manchester had once been: the nursery from which Oxford recruited its college tutors and other universities their professors. Gerald was an inspiration to his junior colleagues, respecting their opinions and working hard to foster their careers. He and Ursula were generous with hospitality and even financial help.

When problems arose, his attitude was philosophical. In January 1974, he wrote to a friend about

> next term's probable student troubles. Will the demands of student militants (e.g., to be able to change university syllabuses and examination requirements, not to mention the teaching that is on offer, as they go through the course) seem as self-evidently right and reasonable in a generation or two's time as (say) the working class having the vote, or equal rights for women seem to most of us today? Or is student power, as I would maintain, an aberrance rather than a progressive force? The trouble is that, as a liberal, one is conditioned to questioning one's own position and wondering whether one may not, after all, be wrong, which one's opponents, like other totalitarians, never stop to do.

Throughout his time at York, Gerald remained head of department, with control of finance, appointments and promotions, but the chairmanship and other offices rotated. At the regular departmental meetings,

---

[5] 'University government—but by whom?', *Universities Quarterly*, 13 (1958–9).

[6] Though his first choice had been Lawrence Stone, whose appointment appears to have been subsequently vetoed by the new university's advisers.

Gerald sat unobtrusively; only on rare occasions did a subsequent missive indicate that things had moved in a direction of which the founder disapproved.

Meanwhile he was consolidating his authority as a seventeenth-century historian. His textbook, *The Struggle for the Constitution 1603–88* (1963; 4th edn., 1975), written with admirable simplicity, established itself as an introductory guide to the constitutional conflict which he regarded as the central theme of the period. *The Interregnum: the Quest for Settlement*, which he edited in 1972, was a superior essay in a genre which would become increasingly popular with publishers over the ensuing decades, the collective volume comprising articles by different contributors all relating to a single theme. *The Levellers in the English Revolution* (1975) was a judicious selection of Leveller writings, prefaced by a fifty-page introduction which remains the best short survey of the subject. He edited a microfilm edition of *The Clarke Manuscripts at Worcester College, Oxford* (1979) and, with John Morrill, published *The Civil War and Interregnum: Sources for Local Historians* (1979). He was involved in the ambitious project of the Cornmarket Press to reprint all the Thomason Tracts; it got as far as thirty-four volumes of *Fast Sermons* and nineteen of the newspaper, *Mercurius Politicus*. He enlisted the present writer to help him in planning a multi-volume *Regional History of England*, but the venture collapsed when the publisher took fright.

Above all, his research into the administrative history of the mid seventeenth century was proceeding apace. He declined Eric James's invitation to become a Pro-Vice-Chancellor and in 1973 brought out the second volume in his trilogy, *The State's Servants. The Civil Service of the English Republic, 1649–1660*. Never given to hyperbole, Gerald now confessed to 'middle-aged caution', and the conclusions he drew from his vast mound of evidence were more tentatively expressed than ever. But he conclusively demonstrated that the republic's administration was infinitely more efficient than that of the old monarchy.

After fifteen years at York, it was time for a move. In 1977 he was tempted by the Directorship of the Institute of Historical Research. But Oxford exerted an irresistible pull. He seriously considered the headship of one college and was runner-up for another. So when his friend and former York colleague, the German historian, T. W. (Tim) Mason, persuaded the Fellows of St Peter's to offer Gerald the succession to Sir Alec Cairncross, he was already accustomed to the idea of returning to Oxford, and, though given only half an hour in which to decide, readily agreed.

There followed a particularly difficult period in Gerald's life. In 1979 St Peter's was still struggling for parity with other Oxford colleges. Established in 1929 as a sort of Low Church answer to Keble, it had become a full college only in 1961. It was strong in some subjects, but its endowment was small; its site was cramped; and its shortage of living accommodation, combined with the absence of a long academic tradition, did not make it easy to attract the ablest students. Gerald had every sympathy with the college's simplicity and unpretentiousness, but his Mastership was dominated by the need to acquire the resources with which to build more accommodation and endow tutorial fellowships. Courting benefactors is not work which everyone finds congenial. For Gerald, who tended to agree with Francis Bacon that the ways to enrich are many and most of them foul, it was at times even distasteful. Yet he launched the Fiftieth-Anniversary Appeal and, with the aid of his colleagues, secured the support of some notable benefactors. During his time as Master, the college greatly enlarged its student accommodation and made plans for a Law Centre, specialising in intellectual property.

Gerald's presence at St Peter's did a great deal for its academic image. Here was a major scholar who led by example, kept the College in touch with the world of learning, and was prepared to teach undergraduates and supervise researchers, while keeping up his own work. He published articles every year and produced for the OPUS series a judicious synthesis of the period in which he was most interested, *Rebellion or Revolution? England 1640–1660* (1986). Academic performance at St Peter's improved, though not as much as he would have liked; and, since results at other colleges were improving too, the college's relative position did not greatly change. As Master, Gerald was much respected by the junior members, who admired his fairmindedness, his firmness on such matters as noise and idleness, and his readiness, if it seemed necessary, to take their side against the Fellows. The junior members were the beneficiaries of the personal kindness and hospitality which he and Ursula so readily dispensed. His many graduate students were particularly devoted to him. Gerald was also deeply concerned for the college staff; the achievement in which he took most pride was that of having persuaded the Governing Body to raise their wages by twenty-four per cent in a single year.

Relations with the Fellows, however, were much less happy. Some individuals presented him with awkward personal problems; others proved temperamentally incompatible. Gerald showed much patience and forbearance. But after York, where he had the advantage of having appointed all his colleagues, he found it harder to adjust to being a newcomer and only *primus inter pares*, among fellows whom he had not chosen and who were quick to question his judgement. He was a man of strongly held principle, who did not believe in concealing or finessing what he regarded as ethical issues, even though others saw them merely as practical problems. The emotional temperature rose; and there were some painful moments.

Yet when he retired from St Peter's in 1991, two years early, in order to have more time for his historical work, the achievement was plain for all to see. The college had outgrown its denominational origins, enhanced its endowment, extended its buildings, and made some excellent elections to the Fellowship. Within the university, Gerald was President of the local branch of the Association of University Teachers and a strongly committed Curator of the Bodleian ('the only University position that I have the slightest wish to hold', he wrote in a letter of 1985). The Keeper of Western Manuscripts recalled that 'his contributions to meetings [of the Curators] were marked by the same scrupulous fairness and generosity of spirit which characterized everything that he said and did. Proposals which came from the university administration he always measured by their effects on the library staff, and those which originated within the library by their effects on readers.' Gerald also contributed to the scholarly amenities of Oxford by helping to postpone the total disappearance of Thornton's bookshop, acting, with a colleague, as honest broker and negotiating its sale to a new owner.

In the historical profession at large, he was now an elder statesman. He was given honorary degrees by the universities of Exeter and Manchester. His extensive knowledge of public and private archives made him a natural choice as a Commissioner for Historical Manuscripts in 1978 and he chaired the Commission from 1989 to 1997. He was a friend and mentor to the Commission's successive Secretaries and kept a watchful eye open for the migration of seventeenth-century manuscripts. During his chairmanship, the reorganisation of local government called for repeated representations to government departments and meetings with ministers.

His strong faith in the value of collective biography made him an equally inevitable member of the Editorial Board of the History of Parliament Trust, for thirty years (1968–98). He chaired the Board between 1989 and 1997, a period which saw the appointment of a new general editor, the move to its own premises in Woburn Square and the extension of its activities to include the House of Lords (a development which he had long urged).

He was elected to the British Academy in 1976 and became an inde-fatigable attender at section meetings, taking new elections very seriously. Between 1984 and 1988 he was President of the Royal Historical Society, giving four Presidential Addresses on 'Collective mentalities and seven-teenth-century England', in which he analysed the reactions of different groups—puritans, royalists, radicals and neutrals—to the Civil War and its aftermath. His discussions of these problems of allegiance and moti-vation drew upon a wide range of reading and were notable for their breadth of imaginative sympathy.

All these responsibilities meant innumerable journeys to London and long hours poring over agenda papers. To these tasks, he brought the qualities he showed throughout his life: scrupulous attention to business, self-deprecating modesty and constant concern for the welfare of the staff who kept these different organisations going. He was endlessly helpful to younger scholars and to foreign visitors. He made lecture tours to the USA, USSR, India and China. A diligent correspondent, he maintained his many friendships, while becoming guide and mentor to the young and not-so-young from many parts of the world. Under his and Ursula's pro-tective wing, lame ducks could always find shelter. The title of his Festschrift, *Public Duty and Private Conscience in Seventeenth-Century England* (1993), alluded to his qualities as a man as much as to his historical interests.

When he retired, he and Ursula, though retaining a base in Oxford, moved to a handsome house near Ledbury, Herefordshire, filling it with an equally handsome collection of the books needed for his research. He continued with his historical work, publishing many articles and handing in the text of the final volume of his trilogy, *The Crown's Servants: Government and Civil Service under Charles II 1660–85*, only three days before his sudden and unexpected death in the John Radcliffe Hospital on 17 December 2000, when what should have been a routine operation went tragically wrong. Gerald would have appreci-ated the irony that his premature demise qualified him for inclusion in *The Oxford Dictionary of National Biography*, for which the cut-off point was 31 December 2000, and to which he had himself contributed a number of articles. He was buried in Llangrove, near Ross-on-Wye, Herefordshire, where he and Ursula used to have a cottage, which they often lent to their friends, and where Gerald did some of his best work. His widow saw the manuscript of *The Crown's Servants* through the press, choosing the illustrations, correcting the proofs and compiling the index.

Gerald's large oeuvre can be conveniently divided into five main categories. First, there are the occasional studies which were stimulated by the institutions, people and places he encountered. Like many historians, he sought to make sense of his own experience by locating it within a longer temporal dimension. Perhaps his rootlessness as a child explains the tenacity of his local and personal loyalties and his desire to express them in his scholarly work. He discharged his debt to Winchester with an article on 'Seventeenth-Century Wykehamists' for *Winchester College: Sixth Centenary Essays* (1982). He commemorated his formidable Oxford friend, John Cooper, by editing, with John Morrill, a collected volume of his papers (1983), prefacing it with a sympathetic essay on 'J. P. Cooper as a scholar'; he also took over, expanded and completed Cooper's chapter on 'The Economics and Finances of the Colleges and the University, *c*. 1530–1640' for volume iii of the *History of the University of Oxford* (1986). He repaid his old tutor with an essay in Christopher Hill's Festschrift on 'Unbelief in Seventeenth-Century England'. He marked his long association with York by publishing a note on the location of the office of the secretary to the Council of the North, and by editing, with Canon Reginald Cant, a handsome collective *History of York Minster* (1977), to which he also contributed an essay on 'Funeral monuments and other post-medieval sculpture', rich in biographical comment on the persons commemorated.[7] He did much research into his adopted county of Herefordshire, giving close attention in *The King's Servants* to such local families as the Harleys and the Pyes, writing an article on the Interregnum rulers of the county (1972) and, with Canon John Tiller, editing and contributing to a collective volume on *Hereford Cathedral: a History* (2000). In the last decade of his life he turned to the history of his ancestral Ireland, with a study of 'The first duke of Ormond as patron and administrator'.

Above all, there was his hereditary link with the Navy. Towards the end of his D.Phil. thesis, Gerald declared his belief that the distinctive qualities of British government and society, its openness and its parliamentary democracy, long depended on the power of the Fleet to guard the narrow seas; and that in turn reflected the quality of naval administration; the victories of Drake and Nelson were won in the ordnance office and the naval dockyards. That was one great argument for studying

---

[7] On monuments to successive archbishops of York, he remarks: 'While his predecessor Sterne is portrayed in the process of waking and getting up, Lamplugh is fully on his feet, as if anticipating the General Resurrection. One can but hope such confidence is not misplaced.'

administrative history. Gerald contributed a chapter on 'Navy, State, Trade and Empire' to the first volume of the *Oxford History of the British Empire* (1998), in which he noted, in passing, 'the emergence of a naval tradition betwen the 1680s and the 1720s', the lifetime of his ancestor, Admiral Matthew Aylmer. He served on the Council of the Navy Records Society; and he planned a book on *The Royal Navy and the English State: Henry VIII to George III*, though in a letter of July 1989 he conceded that his was 'more likely to be a posthumous fragment'. Out of his studies in naval history came a particularly original piece on 'Slavery under Charles II; the Mediterranean and Tangier' (*English Historical Review*, 114 (1999)). This showed that English naval administrators in the later seventeenth century regarded it as perfectly acceptable to enslave Turks and Greeks captured at sea and force them to row in the galleys and to quarry stones with which to build the mole at Tangier. 'The slave *bagnio* or compound in downtown Tangier,' he remarks, 'must have been something like a concentration camp.'

The second category of Gerald's writings stems from his interest in seventeenth-century radicalism, the aspect of the period with which, like Christopher Hill, he was most warmly in sympathy. His book on the Levellers was accompanied by articles on their social origins, on Edward Sexby's attempt to export their ideas to the radicals of Bordeaux and on the relationship, if any, of their theories to those of John Locke. Gerald vigorously defended the existence of the Ranters against Professor J. C. Davis's contention that they were a contemporary fantasy. He discovered a previously unknown pamphlet by Gerrard Winstanley, *Englands Spirit Unfoulded*, in which the Digger leader rather surprisingly urged his readers to take the Engagement of loyalty to the Commonwealth. He wrote sensitively about Winstanley, commenting on 'his marvellously vigorous and evocative prose, his passionately sincere concern for the underdog, and his consuming vision of a better world'. He confessed that, though unmoved by the communism of Plato, More and Marx, he found 'a disturbing force and even relevance in Winstanley's vision'. This did not stop him from tracing, in another article (1982), the emergence in seventeenth-century England of the new definition of property as absolute individual ownership. But he continued to admire seventeenth-century radicalism for 'its amazing range, vitality and eloquence, which were not to be equalled, still less surpassed for many a long year' (*Trans. Royal Hist. Soc.*, 5th ser., 38 (1988), 25).

Thirdly, there are his general interpretative writings on the seventeenth century, notably the two text-books, *The Struggle for the Constitution* and

Rebellion or Revolution? In the opening paragraph of the former, he maintained that 'English seventeenth-century history has a special claim to be studied more thoroughly than most other periods'; this was because it saw the establishment of parliamentary government, which would become a model for many other parts of the world; because the American and French Revolutions followed the pattern of the English Revolution; and because England was almost unique in having no revolution in modern times because it had had one in the seventeenth century. He modified his view of the period in later years, in response to the writings of so-called 'revisionist' historians, who pointed out that the traditional governing classes picked up the reins again after 1660 and that Charles II moved back to monarchical absolutism in the last years of his reign. But he did not abandon it; confessing that he had come to realise that he 'was—after all—an old Whig (and one with some residual Leveller leanings too)' (*The Crown's Servants*, p. 5).

Fourthly, there are his essays in comparative history. Although never claiming any expertise outside the history of England, Ireland and colonial America, Gerald was always keen to set his findings into a larger picture. He wrote the article on 'Bureaucracy' for the companion volume to *The New Cambridge History* (1979); and in the early 1980s, he founded a discussion group of historians and historical sociologists, drawn from all over the country, with interests stretching from the fifth to the twentieth centuries. They met annually at St Peter's to discuss the history of state formation in England.[8] This was the origin of his article on 'The peculiarities of the English state' (1990). In an unpublished paper of 1995, he said that what he got out of these meetings, apart from the strong impression that the English state had been formed by the tenth century, was a growing conviction that more European comparisons were needed. He became closely involved in the European Science Foundation's project on 'The origins of the modern state in Europe', which led to the publication of a number of collective volumes.

Finally, there is the work for which Gerald Aylmer will be longest remembered, namely his trilogy on seventeenth-century office-holders. Based on a huge range of published and unpublished sources, and presented within a carefully considered analytic framework, these volumes are likely to remain an invaluable resource so long as seventeenth-century

[8] For a brief account of the group, see Derek Sayer, 'Gerald Aylmer and DGOS: In Memoriam', *The Journal of Historical Sociology*, 15 (2002). Many of the participants are listed in a footnote to Gerald's article, 'Centre and Locality: the Nature of Power Elites', in Wolfgang Leonard (ed.), *Power Elites and State Building* (1986).

England is studied. Gerald did not invent administrative history. On the contrary, it already had a distinguished pedigree, stretching from the six volumes of T. F. Tout's *Chapters in the Administrative History of Medieval England* (1920–31) to G. R. Elton's *The Tudor Revolution in Government*, which appeared in 1953, when Gerald was working on his D.Phil. thesis. But Tout and Elton were more interested in institutions than in people, whereas Gerald's concern was with the office-holders themselves as much as with the posts they held. In his view, administrative history required 'an approach which is at once rigorous in its handling of the source materials and human in its concentration on the part played by single individuals or small groups of men' (*Annali della Fondazione Italiana per la Storia Amministrativa*, 1 (1964), 20). His achievement was to bring to the history of bureaucracy the prosopographical approach, the study of collective biography, pioneered in Britain by L. B. Namier in *The Structure of Politics at the Accession of George III* (1929), and put to brilliant use by Ronald Syme in *The Roman Revolution* (1939).

Two other influences impelled Gerald to the study of bureaucracy. The first was the tradition of sociological work on the subject, from Max Weber onwards. Gerald regarded history as a social science (*The Struggle for the Constitution*, p. 17). He believed that administrative history was capable of being treated more exactly than many other forms of history and he saw his work as a step towards a sociology of institutions. He was particularly stimulated by the controversy which had been aroused in left-wing circles by the American political writer, James Burnham, author of *The Managerial Revolution* (1941), and by the Yugoslav dissident, Milovan Djilas, whose *The New Class* appeared in English translation in 1957.[9] These authors suggested that the true wielders of power were not the owners of property, but the managers and officials who controlled the state apparatus and the means of production. Gerald himself believed that 'larger plans for the improvement of our society are inseparable from the mechanics of government and from the personnel and methods of administration' (*The State's Servants*, p. 1).

The second and more immediate context was the controversy about the origins of the English Civil War which dominated the historiography of the 1940s and 1950s. In his Raleigh lecture of 1948, J. E. Neale had pointed to a deterioration of political morality and an enhanced compe-

---

[9] In 1959 Gerald met and had discussions with Djilas's exiled colleague, Vladimir Dedijer, Marshal Tito's biographer and former comrade-in-arms, who was then a Simon Research Fellow at Manchester University.

tition for office in the last years of Elizabeth I. A few years later, H. R. Trevor-Roper attributed the rise of the gentry, not to land management and entrepreneurial skills, as urged by R. H. Tawney and Lawrence Stone, but to the profits of royal office. In his view, the Civil War was a back-woods reaction by those gentry who felt themselves excluded from the pickings to be had at court. The controversy was marked by rhetorical brilliance and personal acrimony, but the evidence adduced on either side was distinctly impressionistic. Gerald's achievement was to move the dis-cussion into a new phase by placing the subject of office-holding on a firm statistical base. He also provided a much-needed injection of scholarly humility.

When the *The King's Servants* appeared in 1961, it was its relevance to current controversy which attracted most attention. The book showed beyond any doubt that the Civil War was not a conflict of 'ins' and 'outs', rising and declining gentry. Although some families founded their fortune on office, it was 'impossible to identify the rising with the office-holding gentry'. At most, the profits of office may have amounted to a thirteenth of the gentry's total income. This was nothing less than a total demolition of Trevor-Roper's thesis, and it was all the more effective for being carried out courteously and unpolemically.

The book's achievement, however, transcended this local context. It offered a definitive account of the structure of royal administration and a profusion of carefully presented statistical and biographical facts about the officials of Charles I—their social origins, their mode of entry and terms of service, their sources of income and their political allegiance. Gerald showed how offices were acquired, not by merit, but by one of the 'three Ps'—patronage, patrimony or purchase. Posts were regarded as private property, rather than as an opportunity for public service, and, if below the very highest offices, were usually held for life. Salaries were slight and officers depended upon fees, perquisites and other indirect profits of office. The distinction between accepted practice and 'corrup-tion' was not easy to draw. Office-holding was thus 'a conservative vested interest', acting as a brake on royal action.

With *The State's Servants*, Gerald reached the part of the story in which he had always been most interested, namely the administrative impact of the English Revolution, to which *The King's Servants* had been merely the necessary prologue. In its organisation, this second volume closely resembled its predecessor. It began with a lucid description of the administrative structure, in this case one of immense complexity, because of the proliferation of committees during and after the Civil War. Then came a discussion of the officials themselves, their mode of appointment, terms of service, remuneration and length of tenure. This was followed by a social analysis of selected administrators, together with miniature biographies of representative individuals. Finally, there was an assessment of the impact of the bureaucracy upon the population at large.

Though surrounded by characteristically Aylmerian qualifications, the conclusions were clear. The Revolution led to considerable changes. Fewer offices were held by members of the upper classes and careers became more open to the talents. Sinecures, absenteeism and venality were reduced. Fees were regulated and salaries increased. The result was a higher standard of professionalism and administrative probity. There were scandals, but, given the immense sums of money which changed hands during these years, through land confiscation and heavy taxation, the lack of evidence for large-scale corruption is striking. Though stressing that the reforms of the Interregnum were incomplete, Gerald suggested that the effect of Charles II's restoration was to delay serious administrative reform for 150 years.

The Crown's Servants was shorter than its two predecessors but organised in much the same way, though with the additional feature of a group portrait of office-holders at ten-year intervals. Once again, it was founded on a huge range of sources. Once again, there was a fascinating range of biographical detail, linked by sagacious commentary. But the book's overall impact was less dramatic than that of the two previous volumes, partly because some of Gerald's findings had been anticipated in articles by Sir John Sainty in the 1960s, partly because his own conclusions were very unemphatically presented, but chiefly because the situation he describes was itself rather confused. In many respects Charles II's regime saw a reversion to the practices of the pre-1640 era, but in others it continued the reforming work of the Interregnum. 'Charles II's servants were more upper-class, less puritan, less self-made, and less committed to ideals of public service than the men of 1649–60' (p. 269). But in some areas of the administration there was a shift away from life tenure, a trend towards higher salaries in lieu of fees and perquisites and a move to greater professionalism. By the end of the reign, the administrative foundations for Britain's rise to world power had been laid, though the necessary fiscal reconstruction would occur only after 1688.

These three books were supported by a great many articles on aspects of the subject, including an essay on 'Place Bills and the Separation of Powers' (1965) and a Prothero lecture of 1979, which surveyed the 'extraordinary patchwork' of eighteenth-century administration, a mixture of 'old and new, useless and efficient, corrupt and honest'. Like all Gerald's work, his writings on administrative history were marked by clarity, scrupulosity and even-handedness.

Few historians leave a more solid achievement behind them, and scarcely any of those who do take on administrative responsibilities. Gerald was able to do so much because he was a ferociously hard worker. He did not work out of neurotic compulsion, but from self-indulgence. His work was meat and drink to him, and he loved it. At the same time, he had an overwhelming sense of duty and self-discipline. Even when out for a walk he would set himself targets: a distance to be covered, a landmark to be reached. I remember, on a car journey through Herefordshire, catching sight of him. It was an appalling Sunday afternoon, with strong winds and drenching rain. There, on the rough bank on the side of the bleak Ledbury bypass, in a raincoat and with his khaki bush hat pulled over his eyes, undaunted by the weather and the fast-moving traffic, was Gerald, head down, striding into the wind and rain; he had decided on a walk and it was to be taken, regardless of the weather.

As he grew older, his great height and craggy body made him look like a gnarled old tree. At meetings, he would sit with his head bent over his papers, in a posture which only his exceptionally long neck could have made possible, apparently asleep or lost in private reverie. Then, suddenly, his deep voice would break the silence with an observation of magisterial profundity, which revealed how thoroughly he had been pondering the issue in question, and, as often as not, decisively resolved the matter. He delivered his public utterances with his chin on his chest, his eyes halfclosed and his visage expressive of some strange internal agony. But what he said invariably carried authority.

He never used the past to show off, but treated historical figures with the same courtesy and consideration that he extended to colleagues, students and strangers, always giving them the benefit of the doubt until proved wrong. Neither did he ever affect a posture of omniscience, but constantly reminded his readers of the limits to what was or could be known. In a letter of 1982, he wrote, 'as you know, I have a slight antiintellectual streak, agreeing with Richard Cobb that the cleverest people don't always make the best historians. Very clever people are more likely to be tempted to impose their own interpretations on the facts than less bright people (such as myself) who are unlikely to have novel interpretations to which they wish or need to make the facts relate.' As President of the Royal Historical Society he could refer casually to 'historians of greater intellectual penetration, as well as wider and deeper scholarship than myself' (*Trans. Royal Hist. Soc.*, 5th ser., 39 (1989), 18). When he dissented from other scholars, it was always 'with the greatest respect'.

From anyone else, this might have been humbug, but Gerald's modesty was genuine. It sprang from a deep awareness of the imperfections of human nature and a certainty that the passage of time will make all our hopes and works obsolete. In particular, he knew that historical writing could never be more than provisional. At the end of his D.Phil. thesis, he observes that history is a collective endeavour: each writer depends on the work of those who have gone before; and the most to be hoped is that our work will in its turn be useful to those who come afterwards. The only certainty is that posterity will find it, in one way or another, inadequate. He reproduced these sentiments in *The King's Servants*, adding the dispiriting observation that 'rare indeed is the historical wine which improves with keeping'.

Fortunately, Gerald did not succumb to the gloom which this philosophy might have induced. For all his *gravitas*, he was excellent company. He could be very witty, with a splendidly ironic sense of humour, a warm laugh and a keen eye for the grotesque. He was very convivial and loved good food and drink. He inspired affection in an extraordinarily diverse range of people.

He has been commemorated by the establishment of an annual Gerald Aylmer Lecture at the University of York and an annual Gerald Aylmer seminar organised by the Royal Historical Society and The National Archives.

KEITH THOMAS
Fellow of the Academy

Note. The letters by Gerald Aylmer quoted in this memoir are in the writer's possession and will eventually be deposited in the Bodleian Library. Details of most of the works cited can be found in the 'Select Bibliography' by William Sheils of Gerald Aylmer's writings up to 1990, in John Morrill, Paul Slack and Daniel Woolf (eds), *Public Duty and Private Conscience in Seventeenth-Century England: Essays presented to G. E. Aylmer* (Oxford, 2003). The same volume contains three biographical essays: Christopher Hill, 'Gerald Aylmer at Balliol'; Gordon Leff, 'Gerald Aylmer at York'; and Austin Woolrych, 'Gerald Aylmer as a scholar'.

The entry on 'Aylmer, Gerald Edward (1926–2000)' in *The Oxford Dictionary of National Biography* (2004) is by Penry Williams. There are obituaries in *The Daily Telegraph*, 29 Dec. 2000; in *The Guardian*, 29 Dec. 2000 (by Austin Woolrych); in *The Independent*, 30 Dec. 2000 (by Barrie Dobson); in *The Times*, 10 Jan. 2001; in *The*

Bodleian Library Record, 17 (2001) (by Mary Clapinson); in *The Journal of the Society of Archivists*, 22 (2001) (by Christopher Kitching); and in *History Workshop Journal*, 52 (Oct. 2001) (by Patricia Crawford).

In compiling this memoir I have been greatly helped by Mrs Ursula Aylmer and by many of Gerald Aylmer's friends and colleagues, including Dr Lawrence Goldman, Dr Christopher Kitching, Dr Anne Laurence, Professor Henry Mayr-Harting, FBA, Professor John Morrill, FBA, Professor Paul Slack, FBA, Mr William Thomas and Mr Francis Warner.

SPENCER BARRETT

William Spencer Barrett
1914–2001

SPENCER BARRETT (he disliked his first given name) was born on 29 May 1914, educated at Derby School, and won a scholarship to Christ Church, Oxford, where he received high praise from tutors including A. J. Ayer and D. L. Page. Although he gave his life to classics, at school Barrett had been equally good at mathematics, as one might have guessed from his extra-curricular activities as well as the tenor of his classical work. He duly obtained a First in Mods and Greats, and won a wide range of university prizes. After a year's teaching at Christ Church he moved to Keble in 1939, participating for a while in the attenuated academic life of wartime Oxford. The college, which at that time was also inhabited by MI5 secretaries, became the Barretts' first family home when Spencer married Peggy Hill; their son and daughter were born in this period. A snapshot from his early years: once he had cause to write to the very senior Cyril Bailey, editor of Lucretius. He started the letter 'Dear Dr Bailey', but it came back to him with 'Dr' firmly deleted; 'Dear Bailey' would have been correct, despite their disparity in age. From 1942 (without needing to leave Oxford, since the group functioned in the School of Geography) Spencer also worked as a civilian officer for Naval Intelligence, acquiring his preferred sleeping hours, 4 a.m. to 12 noon—since his material had to be ready for collection at 8 a.m., it was more convenient to stay up for most of the night than to rise at crack of dawn. As a result, his post-war tutorials were usually given in the afternoon or evening, though he would agree to 12 noon if pressed.

Proceedings of the British Academy, **124**, 25–36. © The British Academy 2004.

Quite a number of classical scholars worked in the same Naval Intelligence division. The formidable W. S. Watt, later Professor of Latin at Aberdeen University (for whom, see below, pp. 359–72), became a particular friend to Spencer Barrett; among others were A. N. Sherwin-White (St John's College, Oxford) and A. F. Wells (University College, Oxford). One of their tasks was to produce handbooks on different countries, bringing together information which might be useful (in the broadest sense, including 'to maintain the high standard of education in the Navy') to naval commanders operating in that area. Many of these volumes came to rest in Hertford College Library, since the Professor of Geography, who led the group, was a Fellow of that college. Stephanie West (the present Librarian) has found the volume on Persia valuable for her own work on Herodotus. Spencer's family think that they remember him speaking about Madagascar in such a context, but we have not been able to confirm this—perhaps the volume was never finished.

He liked to remark that there were strong links between Christ Church and Keble, going back to the latter's foundation; nonetheless it was strange that Spencer Barrett became so devoted to a college where, as a firm and scrupulous atheist, he could not make the declaration allowing him to hold the title of Fellow—in all other respects he was treated as a Fellow—until the Keble Statutes changed in 1952. Following the sudden death of Austin Farrer in 1968, it fell to Spencer, as Acting Warden, to preside over another change of statute: henceforth the Warden of Keble need not be an Anglican clergyman. Characteristically he ensured that the immediate election should be conducted under the old statutes. He had a great respect for tradition; for example, making a pointed version of the Latin grace, so that non-classical scholars reading in Hall could get their pauses right. When it became increasingly hard to find recipients of closed awards in theology who would commit themselves to serving in particular dioceses, Spencer felt real sadness that the wishes of the original donors could no longer be fulfilled.

Spencer Barrett immersed himself in very many aspects of college life. His favourite projects usually had a mathematical component, and often made allowance for alternative courses of future events: for example, would it be worth double-glazing the new building on the assumption that the price of heating oil doubled? He worked out the salary scales, redesigned the Porters' Lodge and made a model of a proposed stairway in the Warden's Lodgings. A car was returned to the garage with a precise statement of the speedometer's degree of inaccuracy. When an Inspector of Taxes queried whether a calculator was an allowable working expense for a classicist, Spencer shot him down in flames with a demonstration that, in order to understand a particular line of Pindar, one had to know how Mount Etna would appear to a sailor passing at a certain distance from the shore. Of course the amount of money at issue was insignificant—but that was not the point.

My first encounter (as an undergraduate from another college) with Spencer Barrett was at his Euripides *Hippolytus* lectures in 1959. The Pusey lecture room was always packed. Full and immaculate hand-outs suggested a finished commentary (no doubt anyone else would long since have sent the typescript to the Press). Certain small points immediately struck us; it seemed that we had not been taught Greek correctly at school. *Sigma* on the blackboard was shaped like a half-moon, *iota* written adscript where we had been taught to write it subscript, *zeta* pronounced as 'sd' (e.g. in Hippolytus' mother, the Amasdon). None of this, as I recall, was explained, but it all carried a mysterious authority. Always there was something to wonder at, whether an emendation to the text by one John Milton, 'a scholar who was also a poet', or the occasion when a minor British scholar who had previously always been condemned, got something right where the great Wilamowitz got it wrong. Above all we were struck by the rigour of Barrett's argumentation: erroneous opinions must be refuted by multiple hard evidence, not set aside by hazy impressions. Once I was emboldened to write to him, proposing an emendation which to an eighteen-year-old seemed unquestionably right. No reply—ah well, perhaps I had hoped for too much. Then, six months later, a reply came, explaining at some length where my letter had spent the intervening period, pointing out that my emendation was the wrong tense but adding kindly that one incidental remark of mine had been useful to him.

In 1960 E. R. Dodds retired from the Regius Professorship of Greek, and Spencer Barrett could have been considered a plausible successor. Oral tradition—at least in Keble—suggests that this was indeed so, hinting that things might have been different if only his *Hippolytus* had been published by then. Certainly Barrett was invincible in his specialist areas, but he did not have Hugh Lloyd-Jones's wide interest in ancient Greek literature of all types and periods, from Homer to Nonnus in the fifth century AD. He would probably not have enjoyed the extra burden of administration which went with the chair; his work as Acting Warden of Keble after Austin Farrer's death was very conscientious but very slow, and it was with relief that he handed the college over to Dennis Nineham. The personal Readership (quite a rare distinction in 1966) which he was granted by Oxford University suited him better. Another well-merited recognition was his Fellowship of the British Academy (1965).

The Oxford University Press must have been driven to distraction by Spencer's perfectionism; several times they announced a publication date for *Hippolytus*, but had to postpone because there was something with which he was not entirely happy. Finally, however, in 1964, the great book, which had dominated family as well as professional life for so long, saw the light of day. I did notice one unfavourable review, which predicted 'a patient literature of refutation' in the periodicals (this did not materialise!). Spencer himself expressed intense irritation about another reviewer—not a native English speaker. On *Hippolytus* 18, Barrett observed that the Greek word for 'dog', when applied to a hound, is ordinarily feminine; the unhappy reviewer informed the world that, according to Barrett, the Greeks normally employed bitches for hunting! Undergraduates did not find the book altogether easy to use, but it was quickly realised that, for any scholar working seriously on Greek Tragedy, Barrett's *Hippolytus* was essential reading.

The fullest and most penetrating discussion of Barrett's *Hippolytus* was that of Professor Hugh Lloyd-Jones in the *Journal of Hellenic Studies*, 85 (1965), 164–71; for example, on p. 165 (starting from the use of secondary literature)

> Barrett cites enough evidence to support his argument, and no more; he has the finest and most delicate appreciation of that evidence's value. The minutest points are treated, and yet the reader is never bored, so lively and so lucid is the editor's presentation and so compelling the continuous activity of the keenest and sharpest critical intelligence. Sometimes ruthless logic is pushed too far. Euripides was a poet and not a scholar, and cannot have taken half the trouble to write the play that Barrett has taken to explain it [!]; in some places he is credited with a degree of rationality hardly to be demanded of the most rational of logicians. But the occasional annoyance caused by what some readers may think pedantry or fussiness is a small price to pay for the privilege of contact with a mind of such remarkable acuteness.

Individual components of the work are judged as follows: (p. 165) Barrett 'is a textual critic of the highest order, possessing learning, ingenuity and judgement, each in high degree. He stands as far from the conservatism of those who cling desperately to the most absurd readings of the manuscripts as from the radicalism of the wild emenders'; (p. 165) '. . . the author's extraordinary familiarity with the Greek language. He knows classical Greek poetry by heart, and his knowledge is made more effective by his firm grasp of Greek grammar, both morphology and syntax'; (p. 166) 'The treatment of metre is throughout masterly; the handling of the lyrics compares well with that of Wilamowitz, undemonstrable theorising is absent, and the book is rich in the detailed metrical observation that aids textual criticism.'

Lloyd-Jones is not uncritical: for example on p. 166:

> No mortal can have everything, and this commentary will not inspire the reader with delight in the *Hippolytus* as work of art . . . More serious is a tendency to water down the tragic dilemma by lecturing Hippolytus for 'puritanism', 'priggishness' etc., at times almost giving the impression that the whole trouble might have been avoided if Hippolytus had shown more common sense. Barrett truly says (pp. 391 f.) that the downfall of Hippolytus 'springs from a defect that it is the reverse side of his very virtue; his cult of purity, for all its beauty and nobility, is bound up with an intolerant rejection of an essential part of human life'. Hippolytus' utterance at 1364–7 causes the editor to rebuke him for 'blindness to the defects of his narrow puritanism'; and the farewell of Artemis at 1437–9 prompts him to complain that 'for all its beauty the love of Hippolytus for Artemis lacks something essential'. That is the attitude of a monotheist [Spencer would have described himself as an atheist, but perhaps we see here the difference between a monotheistic atheist and a polytheistic atheist!]. The ancient Greeks were not Christians and did not insist on having everything; and they knew that there are some good things that one cannot have without sacrificing others.

Lloyd-Jones concludes (p. 171), 'If some of [the above remarks] indicate disagreement, that should not obscure the reviewer's admiration of what seems to him a truly great achievement.' Those who know Sir Hugh will be aware that he does not bestow such praise lightly.

Apart from *Hippolytus*, Spencer Barrett's most important publication was a sixty-five-page discussion of Sophocles' *Niobe* (and other plays on the same theme) in Richard Carden's book, *The Papyrus Fragments of Sophocles*, 'with a Contribution by W. S. Barrett' (he insisted on that wording). The two papyri to which he devotes most attention (neither ascribed to Sophocles by any positive external evidence such as coincidence with an already-known quotation) both describe the killing of Niobe's children by Apollo and Artemis. The damaged nature of the text calls forth his own views about the staging of such a spectacular scene. One of the papyri is in five fragments, which Spencer himself had examined in the minutest detail. Although one would not have described him as a papyrologist, to an outsider he seemed to possess all the techniques of a professional. Indeed the majority of Greek authors in whom he took a special interest depend to a considerable extent on ancient papyri for their text; Spencer would often go up to London at a weekend, coming back to say that he had managed to read a few more letters from a papyrus of Bacchylides or Stesichorus. I was surprised—since he had never spoken to me about this—to find out that he had played quite a part in the recovery of Menander's comedy *Dyscolos* from papyri. Among other writings, note his contribution (on Pindar, *Olympian* 13) to '*Dionysiaca*', *Studies by former pupils presented to Sir Denys Page*, his Christ Church tutor.

Spencer Barrett's Readership reduced his college teaching by more than a half and opened the way for a new appointment at Keble, as a result of which I had the privilege of being his colleague for fourteen years. The division between Greek and Latin teaching was absolute—for this purpose the New Testament was deemed to be written in Latin. In his later years he pretended not to know Latin, which was nonsense, of course. Not to mention his youthful epyllion on Delos, of which only the first line survives ('Latonam perhibent, genitor quo tempore divum'), the editors of *Classical Quarterly* tried long and hard to extract from his head a substantial article on Seneca's tragedies, one of which he had used with the greatest caution in the preface to *Hippolytus* as possible evidence for Euripides' earlier, lost, play on the same theme. Apparently he sent some suggestions to an editor of Seneca, with disappointing results. An indication of Spencer's high repute in Latin too was the pleasure expressed by Robin Nisbet on learning that his emendation 'Sidone' for 'sidere' in Horace, *Odes* 3. 1. 42 had won Barrett's approval.

Admissions-time at Oxford (now much changed) as it was in the 1970s, brought out certain Spencerian characteristics in their purest form. The system at its most complicated decreed that a minor award (Exhibition) at a lower-choice college outweighed ('trumped') a mere commoner place at a higher-choice college; similarly a major award (Scholarship) trumped an Exhibition. There always seemed to be a battle royal between Keble and Pembroke, in the persons of Spencer Barrett and Godfrey Bond. One soon learned that it was fatal to betray, by word, gesture or expression, the slightest interest in, say, a Balliol candidate, since Pembroke, despite having used their full advertised quota of awards, would inevitably then produce an extra award and whisk away the promising youngster. The system also led to log-jams in which everybody's decision depended upon everybody else's decision. Gordon Williams (a Fellow of Balliol, later Professor at St Andrews and Yale) told me of an occasion in his time when one college had announced a decision, and it fell to Keble to make the next move. Before he would do this, Spencer Barrett called for a Greek lexicon, to ascertain whether or not the candidate's use of a particle in his Greek prose was correct—if Spencer himself did not know the answer, this was surely a matter of pure chance! Another complicated part of the system was arranging interview times so that candidates could get from one end of Oxford to the other, visiting five or six colleges. Although under no obligation whatever, Spencer used to organise the timetable; this clearly appealed to the mathematical and puzzle-solving side of his nature (he regularly entered *The Times* crossword competition and reached the final stages without ever winning). Anyone interviewed at the maximum number of colleges was hailed as a *perihodonikes* (an athlete who had competed with success in all the major Greek games).

Keble did not obtain very many top-flight undergraduates in classics; Spencer's *annus mirabilis* was 1963, when three obtained a First in Mods (two of these, Brian Bosworth and Richard Hawkins, went on to become professional academics). He confessed that, in social terms, he sometimes found less able ones to be more interesting. Certainly he made a great impression on his pupils of all ranges of ability, and was viewed by them with much affection. Proof of this comes from his retirement party held in 1981. One participant has computed that two thirds of all his Keble pupils, from 1939 to 1981, were present on that occasion—an extraordinary statistic. Spencer himself regularly came back from retirement in Bristol for college reunions, until shortly before his death in 2001; he remembered all his pupils in detail, and was able to pronounce that a candidate in Mods in 1995 had obtained the second best First of any Keble classicist since 1939.

In many ways Spencer Barrett may seem to have been an old-style Oxford classics don. He did not move very far from homebase. As far as I am aware, he did not lecture outside England (although he was certainly invited to speak in America) and not very often outside Oxford. He did not even visit Greece until middle age, and that was partly to confirm some details of the topography of Trozen (thus, not Troezen, in Euripides' time) about which, essentially, he had already made up his mind. His published work, though superb in quality, was modest in quantity, considering that he had such a long career. One could not imagine him leaving his college for a chair at another university. There were no honorary degrees for him (and no sign that he felt the lack of them), no international fame as a lecturer. Yet he was fully abreast of continental scholarship. When he presided at a meeting of the Oxford Philological Society at which Eduard Fraenkel gave a personal memoir of Wilamowitz, he described the occasion as 'the living scholar to whom I owe most talking about the dead scholar to

whom I owe most'. Conversely there is evidence of the high esteem in
which Spencer Barrett was held by scholars in his field, for example in
France and Germany.

Graduate studies at Oxford were relatively undeveloped in his time, but,
to the extent that he was involved in these, he demanded the very highest
standards. One pupil despaired of meeting these after a single session; in
another case, as an examiner, he not only pointed out the candidate's error
but even charted in detail the path through the secondary literature which
had led to the erroneous conclusion. On the other hand Annette Harder in
her edition of Euripides' *Kresphontes* and *Archelaos* thanks W.S.B. for
'long discussions in Keble College' of her Groningen dissertation. Spencer
was never fully reconciled to the introduction of literature into Greats, and
resolved not to examine in that Final Honours School. In fact he did not
often examine in Mods, partly, perhaps, because his perfectionism made
him such a slow marker—something which causes difficulties for fellow-
examiners. In one Mods year, however, he was deputed to mark the Juvenal paper, outside his normal range. The problem, as he recalled, was
solved when he discovered the existence of a candidate called Nisbet—it
was only necessary to read Nisbet's script first.

As well as laicisation of the Wardenship, Keble underwent a radical
change in Spencer Barrett's time, in the admission of women (1979).
Spencer was in favour—as indeed was almost everyone else. But his stated
reason was idiosyncratic, though quite logical: so that, after retirement, he
should not have to return to a college which was unfamiliar to him. A story
which he used to tell against himself must belong to the intervening two
years. Spencer was always much concerned that there should be free space
in the Fellows' car park when (as a consequence of his unusual sleeping
hours) he arrived early in the afternoon. Once seeing a young woman lean-
ing her bicycle against the forbidden wall, he went up to her: 'Excuse me,
are you a member of this college?' To which the reply was 'No, but I spend
quite a lot of time here, and so I can probably help you.'

When retirement came, in 1981, Keble elected Spencer Barrett to an
Honorary Fellowship (rather than an Emeritus Fellowship). The higher
accolade was fully deserved on the double criterion of exceptional academic distinction and exceptional service to the college. He was greatly
moved by the farewell gathering of his former pupils: 'One does one's job,
and then' (with a gesture towards the company) 'this'. Roman obituaries
sometimes include a section which opens 'He did not see . . .'. Dying in
2001, Spencer did not know of Keble's decision to cease admitting undergraduates to read classics, classics and modern languages and classics and

English with effect from 2004. This knowledge would undoubtedly have distressed him very much.

The dinner given to Spencer by his Senior Common Room colleagues was perhaps one of Peggy Barrett's last public occasions—and she did very well, since Alzheimer's disease was already beginning to take a hold. Spencer continued to live in Oxford for several years; after Peggy was transferred to a nursing home he used to take her out for a drive in the car, which she seemed to enjoy, though by the end she hardly knew who he was. Thereafter he moved down to Clifton, close to the family of his son John who was teaching mathematics at Clifton College.

During our years of tutorial collaboration at Keble there was little or no overlap in our research interests (incidentally Spencer did not much like the term 'research', preferring to speak of 'doing my own work'). But during the 1980s the present writer was working on a Greek project, editing with a commentary Callimachus' fragmentary poem, *Hecale*. Spencer took a keen interest in this, eventually accepting the dedication of the book. If a problem gripped his imagination, Spencer would spend an extraordinary amount of time and trouble on it. One such arose in Callimachus' *Hecale*. The question was, did some papyrus scholia on Thucydides quote just a part (already known from another source) of one line from the *Hecale*, or two complete hexameters? Pfeiffer had taken the former view, Wilamowitz the latter. It seemed to me that Wilamowitz had much the more convincing arguments. The thing to do was to telephone Spencer about 11 p.m., when he was at his brightest and best. He did indeed immerse himself in this problem. First he consulted a (not very good) photograph of the papyrus in the Ashmolean Museum, and, with the help of graph paper, traced what could be read of the crucial letters. A papyrological specialist was shortly due to visit Cairo, where the original lay in the Egyptian Museum, and had asked whether anyone had particular questions on which he might be able to give a verdict. It was Spencer who formulated, with the utmost precision, the question which needed answering. In due course the hoped-for reply came from Cairo, 'If you are to read . . . which I think you can . . .' Furthermore Spencer emended one letter (which would have to be deemed a scribal error) in the Thucydides-scholion, making sense of the two lines of Callimachus (the earliest Athenians celebrated dramatic festivals in honour of Dionysus of the Marshes, not Dionysus of the Black Goatskin). Finally, he had to discuss the width of the column in the Thucydides-scholion. All of this (mostly verbatim from Spencer) can be followed in Callimachus, *Hecale*, ed. Hollis (Oxford, 1990), pp. 271–5 on fr. 85.

Although having served as Spencer Barrett's colleague on the most amicable terms for many years, I never lost a sense of awe at his scholarship. One question often arose in my mind—how many times had he been proved definitely to be wrong on an academic matter? Of course it may seldom fall to classical literary scholars to be proved beyond all doubt either right or wrong. In the early 1960s a papyrus fragment of Greek elegy came to light. Its style rather suggested the early third century BC, before the influence of Callimachus became so strong; authorship unknown (Hermesianax of Colophon is one possibility). The text is describing a series of mythological scenes, but what is the connection between them? Unfortunately the first part of the Greek lines had been lost. It was Spencer Barrett who provided a most unexpected solution to the problem, by restoring the verb 'I will tattoo'. Thus the mythological scenes and objects are to be tattooed on various parts of a miscreant's body. This seems to bring the text into the territory of a recognisable Hellenistic genre, the curse-poem. Once, many years later, I was walking with Spencer round the quad at Keble when he said 'They have found the other part of that papyrus—it confirms my restoration'. It seems that the finder (or a subsequent owner) of the papyrus may deliberately have torn it in two, perhaps in the hope of making more money from a double sale.

Apart from tragedy, Barrett's main interests lay in Greek lyric: Stesichorus, Bacchylides and above all Pindar, on whom he delivered notable lectures. For many years he had some borrowed papyri of Pindar at home. As time went on and nothing was heard of them, I was deputed to enquire about their well-being, which I did with some caution. All he said was, 'People are quite wrong in thinking that they contain remarkable new readings'; but this sufficed and they were safely retrieved with the help of John Barrett. A former pupil, not particularly academic, once lamented to him how difficult he found Pindar; Spencer's reply came out uncensored: 'Oh no, very easy.' Everyone always believed that some great work on Pindar would emerge, whether a commentary or a critical text. Spencer was concerned that a publisher might not be willing to arrange the lines on the page as he himself desired and believed to be correct. In fact his own typescript was always so meticulous and so pleasing to the eye that it would only have needed photocopying.

Spencer was to have twenty years of retirement. His intellect remained as sharp as ever, but his energy decreased. Of the papers recovered after his death, none seemed to have been written very recently. There are eleven boxes of these papers, collected—some of them from the floor of his Bristol flat—by his daughter, Mrs Gillian Hill (Spencer found a pleasing symmetry in the fact that his wife had been surnamed Hill before her marriage, his daughter after hers). She, as a professional archivist, also made a first attempt at cataloguing the papers. Of course it was necessary for them to be examined by a scholar of the highest calibre and interests similar to those of Spencer Barrett; much gratitude is due to Martin West for the many hours which he has already devoted to this work, and for consulting James Diggle. Hopes that we might find the authoritative Barrett text of Pindar have been fulfilled only in part. There is indeed a text, incorporating some of his own ideas, but no accompanying apparatus criticus. That is surprising, since one can hardly imagine Spencer making one without the other, but, if the app. crit. was mislaid in a removal of household belongings, it has clearly been lost for ever. As one might expect, there are very detailed metrical investigations, for example of final syllables in Pindar. Not everything is suitable for publication, but in the opinion of Martin West, it should be possible to make up a medium-sized volume of papers by Spencer Barrett on Greek lyric and tragedy. And the text of Pindar without apparatus criticus might still be of considerable value to a very promising young scholar who is preparing an Oxford Classical Text of Pindar.

Looking for a brief quotation to express the nature of Spencer Barrett's scholarship, I hit upon the following extract in W.S.B.'s contribution to Richard Carden's *Papyrus Fragments of Sophocles*, pp. 198–9. It is a matter of setting arguments against an impression: 'If that impression was right, my arguments here must be rejected; if the arguments are valid, the impression was wrong. I have not much doubt myself that the arguments should prevail.' No less important to Spencer were the personal relationships with his pupils, characterised by lasting affection and respect. Two examples come to mind, both showing that differences of religious belief were no barrier. An early pupil receiving the degree of Doctor of Divinity in the Sheldonian was touched to find that Spencer had specially come up from his retirement in Bristol so as to be present at the ceremony. The second example concerns a pupil who read Classical Mods followed by Theology Finals (later he became a Chaplain Fellow of Keble). He was about to be ordained, on which occasion it is the custom to send out cards to friends and associates, saying 'Please pray for x . . .'. What to do about Spencer, who could not reasonably be expected to pray? The easiest course was simply to omit him from the circulation list. Instead John Davies sent a card to Spencer, adding in the top left-hand corner 'For Information'. Spencer himself was delighted with the neatness of this solution.

Spencer Barrett's last visit to Keble was to attend the memorial service for a long-standing colleague, the historian Douglas Price. Just recently alterations had been made to Spencer's design for the Porters' Lodge, and I was a little worried about how he would take these. His only comment was 'Ah, so they have done what I originally recommended'. He died on 23 September 2001, aged 87. At a well-attended memorial meeting in Keble on 1 June 2002, there were speeches by representatives of the Barrett family, colleagues (including Peter Parsons, Regius Professor of Greek) and pupils. One of his granddaughters, who had read Biology at Keble in the 1990s, played the viola beautifully. In the Keble Senior Common Room there is a drawing of Spencer. Sadly, he himself (according to his family) did not like it. Although never having been taught by him myself, I can imagine him just so when in tutorial mode, explaining gently but firmly why the Greek language does not allow us to understand a line of Pindar or Euripides in Professor So and So's manner.

ADRIAN HOLLIS
Keble College, Oxford

CHARLES CARTER

Charles Frederick Carter,
1919–2002

CHARLES CARTER was born on 15 August 1919. His father, Frederick William Carter, was a distinguished electrical engineer who became an FRS; his mother, Edith Mildred Cramp, was an active member of the Society of Friends. Perhaps his father passed on a mathematical ability and a skill in solving practical problems. From his mother's influence, he was a Quaker, and his continued devotion to the Society had a major influence on his life.

As a day boy at Rugby School he acquired a competence in mathematics sufficient for direct admission to Part II of the Maths Tripos at Cambridge in 1938. When he completed Part II in 1940 with First Class Honours he had not been long enough in residence to qualify for a degree.

He registered as a conscientious objector and sought exemption without conditions from military service. That was not granted and he spent three months in Strangeways Prison. He then worked with the Friends Relief Service until he returned to Cambridge in 1943. Charles met Janet Shea in the spring of 1943. Though not then a Quaker, she was working with the Friends Relief Service. They were engaged shortly before she lost a leg after a collision with a Fire Service lorry. In her collection of essays *Conversations with Myself* (2001), Janet wrote that careful thinking had made Charles decide that he should return to Cambridge for another three terms to complete his degree course so that he would be better equipped to take care of a handicapped wife.

He enrolled in Part II of the Economics Tripos in 1943, and at the end of the academic year was awarded a First in Economics and a Distinction

Proceedings of the British Academy, **124**, 39–47. © The British Academy 2004.

in Statistics. He was informed at the time that it was his outstanding performance in Statistics that got him his First. Charles and Janet were married during the Christmas vacation of his last year. They were a devoted couple for fifty years, loving parents of three children, and both matter of factly engaged in good works.

Carter's supervisor at St John's was Guillebaud, Alfred Marshall's nephew, and of course he was expected to study Marshall's *Principles*. Carter responded creatively to Marshall's analytical rigour and to his insistence that economic laws and reasonings were 'merely part of the material which Conscience and Common Sense have to turn to account in solving practical problems, and in laying down rules which may be a guide in life' (eighth edition, p. vi).

The young Carter was not impressed by Keynes's view (*Essays in Biography*, p. 175) that Marshall was too anxious to do good. Over twenty years later, in the Preface to his *Wealth* (Watts, 1968), Carter wrote that it had occurred to him that 'it might assist humility if people could be encouraged to think more exactly not just about the statistical measure of wealth, but the purposes which that wealth serves', and in the last chapter that 'the richer a country becomes, the less need it has to be ruled by economic thinking'.

In 1945 Carter was appointed Lecturer in Statistics at Cambridge, and in 1947 became a Fellow of Emmanuel College. He wrote many papers in his six years at Cambridge on a range of post-war economic problems. His main publications—*The Measurement of Production Movements* (1948, with Reddaway and Stone), papers on 'The New Index of Industrial Production' (London and Cambridge Economic Service, February 1948), 'The Real Product of the UK 1946–50' (LCES, August 1951), and 'Index Numbers of the Real Product of the UK' (*Journal of the Royal Statistical Society*, Vol. 1, 1952)—provided a better foundation for the attempted explanations of the roles of increased capital and labour in economic growth, and that of a rather large residual becoming known as 'technical progress'. Shortly after he left Cambridge, he and Andrew Roy wrote *British Economic Statistics* (1954) which examined the statistics used or available for the formulation of economic policy in the United Kingdom, and suggested significant improvements in the provision of statistics and in their use.

Two notes written during his time at Cambridge are of special interest. Apart from a demonstration 'in mathematical terms' of the relations between marginal and average cost and his 'simple diagrammatic exposition for those who find it easier to think in geometry' in his *Science of*

Wealth (Arnold, 1960), those two notes—on 'The Dual Currency Problem' and (with Harry Johnson) 'Unrequited Imports and the terms of Trade', in *The Economic Journal* in 1948 and 1950 respectively—were his only explicitly mathematical publications. The first, which he wrote at the request of Professor D. H. Robertson, was, he said, highly unoriginal and a sketchy and unrigorous mathematical treatment; the second was 'a correction of Professor Pigou's confusing mathematical argument'. Pigou's response was that 'Mr Carter is an expert mathematician and I have no doubt that the workings in the note are correct.' In his review of Samuelson's *Foundation of Economic Analysis* (*Economic Journal*, 1950), he wrote that the book lacked the lucidity and sense of unifying principle that one looks for in a work on foundations and that the maths in the volume—often obscure and wrong—would ensure minimum readership by non-mathematicians, and irritate 'even hardy econometricians'. It is a pity that he did not respond to the challenge of writing a shorter, more lucid version, but his interest in solving pressing economic problems of the moment was too strong. Also like Marshall, and, I suppose, like Keynes, 'he always felt a slight contempt from the intellectual or aesthetic point of view of the rather "potty" scraps of elementary algebra, geometry and differential calculus which make up mathematical economics' (Keynes, *Essays in Biography*, p. 157).

The *Economic Journal* of March 1950 published Carter's review article of Shackle's *Expectations in Economics*, and of December 1953 his 'Revised Theory of Expectations'. He approved Shackle's rejection of the idea that businessmen make decisions on the basis of a mathematical outcome of a particular line of action—one of the besetting sins of economists is 'to try to make rugged Marshallian entrepreneurs and slick city financiers dance to the dream-music of a mathematician'—but thought the Shackle theory unrealistic in focusing attention on two possible outcomes—a potential gain and a potential loss—and logically flawed in that it is impossible to devise a means of compounding two pure rankings (or one ranking and a numerical index) to make another unique ranking. Carter's view of realistic postulates was influenced by the analysis of his own processes of thought in reaching decisions on the management of investment funds, first at St John's and then as Director of the Friends' Provident Life Office.

In 1952 he became Professor of Applied Economics at Queen's University Belfast and a year later he was appointed a member of the United Nations Expert Committee on Commodity Trade, and later in that year the UN published its report *Commodity Trade and Development*.

In 1954 he became Chairman of the Science and Industry Committee established following the Belfast meeting of the British Association for the Advancement of Science at which there was concern that Britain's eminence in science was not matched by its performance in the application of science in industry. 'What Britain invents other countries exploit', was a frequent complaint, and Carter and I were entrusted by the Committee to find out why. We soon found that Britain was more eminent in scientific discovery than in the *invention* of new products and processes, and that British firms were not very good at making the transition from inventions to the use of inventions whether British or foreign. Our three volumes, which presented the results of our investigations and our proposals for improvement—*Industry and Technical Progress, Investment in Innovation, Science in Industry, Policy and Progress*—were published by Oxford University Press in 1957, 1958 and 1959. It was fashionable at that time for scientists to assume that more basic research would increase the opportunities for applied research which would increase the opportunities for engineering applications and so on. From our examination of the statistical relationships between scientific research and engineering development, and economic growth, and case studies of innovations—the introduction of new or improved processes and products—we were able to produce a much more realistic model of innovations which involved non-linear interaction between research, capital expenditure criteria, production and marketing. 'The Characteristics of Technically Progressive Firms' (*Journal of Industrial Economics*, March 1969) provided a statistical analysis of the characteristics, and we provided a check list that would enable firms to improve their performance in making innovations and, of special importance in Britain, in fully exploiting them. We also published a critical paper on 'Government Scientific Policy and the Growth of the British Economy' which proposed major changes in government procedures and policy. Carter was later a member of the Ministry of Technology's Advisory Council, though the establishment of that Ministry was not on our list of recommendations, and a member of the Government's Council for Scientific and Industrial Research from 1959–63.

Arising from those investigations, Carter wrote many analytical and policy papers such as 'How Much Research?' (*Federation of British Industries Review*, June 1960), 'Policy for Backward Industries' (*Manchester Statistical Society*, 1960–1), 'The Economic Use of Brains' (*Economic Journal*, 1962), 'The Problem of Scientific Research in Ireland' (*Irish Banking Review*, September 1962), and 'The Distribution of Scientific Effort' (*Minerva*, Winter 1963).

While at Belfast Carter was involved in programmes for economic growth on both sides of the Irish border. The prevailing mood in Northern Ireland did not favour such a light treatment of the border, but his Quaker convictions and detachment from institutional religion, quiet seriousness of purpose and obvious integrity, enabled him to calm local suspicions. After his move to Manchester he became a member of the Republic of Ireland's Capital Investment Advisory Committee (1956) and its Commission of Higher Education (1960–7). Then, as an indication of the acceptance in the North of his open-minded desire to find a solution to the Irish problem (he published with D. P. Barrett, *The Northern Ireland Problem* in 1962), he was from 1977–87 first Chairman of the Northern Ireland Planning Council.

He became Stanley Jevons Professor of Political Economy and Cobden Lecturer at the Victoria University of Manchester in 1959. His *Science of Wealth* (Arnold, 1960) is an elementary text book of economics 'for those whose only acquaintance with economics would be a subsidiary course taken for a single year, and in particular for those students of technology or science who wish to get a general idea of the working of the industrial-business world on which they may depend for a living.' The balance between description and analysis is ideal, and a third edition was published in 1973. His publications while at Manchester from 1959 to 1963 were restricted by his activities as editor of the *Economic Journal* from 1961. His attitude to the role of mathematics, as quoted earlier, certainly influenced his judgement on what should be published in the *Journal*, a judgement not always appreciated by mathematical economists.

While at Manchester he gave oral evidence to the Robbins Committee on Higher Education. In the written 'Proposals for Reform in University Education' (*Manchester School*, September 1963), he and I proposed to recapture some of the virtues of a free market in education by giving students—subject to appropriate tests of competence—a right to a government grant, free of any test of needs, equal to half the fee, and further needs-tested grants and loans, repayable during the first twenty years of working life, equal to the difference between grants and the total costs of fees and maintenance. We proposed also that each university receive separate grants for teaching, research and capital. The research grants would be administered by the Council of the Department of Scientific and Industrial Research, the Medical Research Council, and proposed Research Councils for the Social Sciences and the Humanities.

The proposal to separate teaching and research grants was strongly criticized at the time by many in the universities who maintained that it failed to comprehend the intimate relations between teaching and research. In 1963 Carter was a member of the Heyworth Committee which recommended the establishment of a Social Science Research Council. In 1971, after his transfer to the new University of Lancaster, he wrote, with G. Brosnan and others, *Patterns and Policies in Higher Education*, and then in 1980 in the first year of his retirement from Lancaster, an excellent book on *Higher Education in the Future*.

In 1962 the University Grants Committee had appointed a Planning Board to establish the University of Lancaster, with Sir Noel Hall, Principal of Brasenose College, Oxford, as Chairman. The Board made its plans for the nature of the University and its buildings on a greenfields site, and then sought a Vice-Chancellor. Charles Carter was the Board's choice. I was a Visiting Professor in Australia at the time, and when I returned Sir Noel gave me an account of Carter's virtues. He added that although an outstanding economist Carter would not become a Fellow of the British Academy. (Hall got that wrong: Carter became a Fellow in 1970 during his time at Lancaster.) As a member of the Planning Board, and a colleague at Manchester, I was asked to persuade him to agree to be Vice-Chancellor. To my surprise persuasion was not needed. I knew of his dissatisfaction with academic governance at Belfast and Manchester, though I did not know of the strength of the Quaker presence in Lancaster and the region. How far that affected his ready acceptance of the position of Vice-Chancellor I did not know. Perhaps it was significant that the colours he chose for the university were red and (quaker) grey.

The speed with which he established the university was remarkable. In 1966 the first buildings on the campus were opened, and in 1968 the students started to move into their new college residences which provided also for teaching rooms and staff, but in the meantime the first 260 students had been admitted in October 1964 in temporary premises in Lancaster little more than a year after he became Vice-Chancellor. The university motto *Patet Omnibus Veritas* fitted his conviction that the door to higher education should become much wider, and the sooner the better.

He soon proved himself to be a superb administrator. When grants for residential buildings were less than expected he borrowed the necessary funds, and had buildings designed suitable for letting to visitors during student vacations. He attracted academic and research staff of high quality, and he was influential in providing for more student choice of the nature of their degree studies than was the case at Belfast and Manchester and similar universities.

He had a strong belief in the good sense of students if given responsibility, and he provided for formal student participation in university affairs. He was greatly disappointed when in the early seventies revolting students brought the university to a stop. To the surprise of many he promptly called the police and introduced a code of discipline.

He overcame rather dismissive views of teacher training colleges held at that time by many university staff, arranged for cooperative measures with teachers' colleges in the region, and made provision for the admission of students whose 'learning from experience' had prepared them for a university education. (He was later Chairman of the Learning from Experience Trust.)

His skill in assessing the teaching and research qualities of potential members of staff, and his encouragement of research activities led to a rapid growth of the university's rated performance in research. In the UGC's research rankings, Lancaster was ranked 16 out of 55 by 1989, and 14 in 1992.

He was so disciplined, and dealt with analytical, administrative and drafting problems so quickly, that he was able to maintain a great range of other activities. His *Wealth* (Watts) was published in 1968 to draw attention to the failure of the economists to relate their analyses of economic growth to a 'clear ultimate purpose'. After outlining economists' accounts of the factors in economic growth, he then analysed the relations between wealth and individual happiness and between wealth and the quality of civilisation. It should be a text in all courses in economics and politics. He edited the *Economic Journal* until 1970 and then became Secretary General of the Royal Economic Society. He continued to be a Director of the Friends Provident Life Office and remained on the Commission on Higher Education of the Republic of Ireland until 1967. His new activities included the Northwest Economic Planning Council (1965–8), chairing the Post Office Review Committee (1976–7) which showed how telecommunications could be detached from postal services and led to the creation of BT, and chairing the new Northern Ireland Economic Planning Council (1977–87). He was knighted in 1978 for public services. From 1966 he was a member of the Joseph Rowntree Memorial Trust, and from 1969 a member of the Sir Halley Stewart Trust. His Swarthmore Lecture of the Society of Friends was entitled *On Having a Sense of All Conditions* (1971). He gave many other lectures including 'Problems of Economic Growth' (published in *Essays in Modern Economic Development*, ed. R. L. Smyth, 1969), an evening lecture at the British Association meeting in Aberdeen in 1963, in which he gave his estimate of £100,000 million as Keynes's contribution to economic growth.

Carter retired from the University of Lancaster in 1979 at the age of sixty, after an outstanding performance as Vice-Chancellor. He was able to give greater attention to the Northern Ireland Planning Council, to the Joseph Rowntree Memorial Trust (where he was involved in quiet initiatives to find a solution to the Northern Ireland conflicts, and later in a project on relations between central and local governments), and to the Sir Halley Stewart Trust, of which he was Chairman from 1986–97.

He had been Chairman of the Centre for Social Policies, which in 1978 was amalgamated with Political and Economic Planning to form the Policy Studies Institute. He became Chairman of the Research Committee of PSI and Editor of *Policy Studies* to which he contributed a range of papers on 'the state of the nation'. In 1971 he edited *Industrial Policy and Innovation* and contributed a chapter on 'Reasons for not innovating'. The Technical Change Centre publication *Knowns and Unknowns in Technical Change* (1985) included his paper on 'Innovation and Public Attitudes' in which he suggested amendments to the Carter and Williams conclusions in the years 1957–9. These were to put greater emphasis on the quality of education available to an elite of high-flyers, and the complications of government interventions. In 1989, his Presidential Address at the Annual Conference of the British Association for the Advancement of Science was also on the complexities of innovation. That he was also President in 1990 and Joint President from 1991–7 was an indication of his capacity to conduct orderly committee discussions and to formulate proposals that resulted in agreed decisions without great waste of time. In committees he was at his best as chairman. When a meeting was badly chaired he could get irritable and become tactless in discussion.

At PSI he initiated a proposal for what proved to be an excellent publication on *Britain in 2010* and he contributed working papers on macro and production issues and changes in consumption patterns. In a paper read to the Manchester Statistical Society in 1989, he looked further into the future—to 2015.

At the Rowntree Memorial Trust and the Halley Stewart Trust he was able to further his belief that wealth should be put to the service of those in greatest need, and he was disappointed that even Labour governments were so reluctant to introduce ethical taxation policies. In 1980 he had given the Eileen Younghusband Lecture on 'Personal Social Services in an Unsuccessful Economy', and in 1990 wrote a chapter on 'Constraints' in *The State and Social Welfare*, by Thomas and Dorothy Wilson

(Longmans, 1991). At the Joseph Rowntree Foundation he chaired a committee that explored relations between central and local government, and that led to the publication (also in 1991) of *Members one of Another: The Problems of Corporate Actions.*

Given his great range of activities it was not surprising that some people regarded him as formidable, even unapproachable. That he was rather shy and had a life purpose that made him guard against wastes of time explain that reputation, which was undeserved. He was very approachable and caring with his students and (most of) his colleagues. He had an impish sense of humour, and never thrust his austere religious views on others. I worked with him for some time before I realised that he was a Quaker—I had brothers who were 'conscientious objectors' but not Quakers. I enjoyed his company, and we remained close friends after he went to Lancaster as Vice-Chancellor and I to Sydney.

After he retired from the University of Lancaster he moved to Seascale in Cumbria. There he cultivated his garden—for part of his time—and a first-rate gardener he proved to be. Cumbria was a long way from London, but he could work on trains and enjoyed travelling in them and consulting Bradshaw, though his memory was such that he rarely needed to do so. He died on 22 June 2002. Charles Carter maintained his presence among the Whitehaven Quakers, and was for several years their Treasurer. He was 'born into the Society of Friends' and never strayed from it, and its opposition to war and active concern for the underprivileged. His *Wealth* ended with a quotation from William Penn: 'So absurd a thing is man, after all his proud pretences to wit and understanding', and he preceded that with his affirmation that what he considered 'essential is the belief in self-fulfilment, and its advance to a higher level of achievement, through co-operation with or in union with a greater universal purpose. Those who cannot accept this belief will, I think, find it hardest to suggest a way in which we can avoid being mastered by our own affluence.'

BRUCE WILLIAMS
The University of Sydney

JOHN ERICKSON

John Erickson
1929–2002

JOHN ERICKSON made his mark as a historian, scholar, soldier and military analyst in the period of the twentieth century which witnessed the major upheaval in international relations caused by the Second World War—especially in Europe—and the clash between Soviet Communism and the Western group of nations which became known as the Cold War.

John Erickson was born in South Shields, Tyne and Wear, on 17 April 1929, the son of the late Henry Erickson and Jessie, née Heys, in a family with seafaring antecedents, English and Scandinavian, which equipped him for a life devoted to European history, politics and languages, and eventually military affairs. His father, who died in 1981, served with the Royal Navy during the Second World War in wartime convoys, including those to the Soviet Union. His son's education in South Shields High School may have included an early introduction into European languages during the war years which proved very useful to him in later life. On leaving school in 1947 at the age of eighteen he was called up to do National Service, initially in the King's Own Scottish Borderers, and then in the Intelligence Corps. He was posted to the British Army in Austria, where with the rank of sergeant, he interpreted in Anglo-Soviet military liaison meetings of the Allied Control Commission in Vienna. Later in his service he was assigned to the Allied War Crimes Tribunal located in Austria, part of whose responsibilities was the search for German and Austrian, as well as Russian, Yugoslav and other Balkan collaborators with the Axis Powers and their arrest and trial on charges of war crimes. His involvement in the Allied War Crimes effort gave him an early opportunity to

Proceedings of the British Academy, **124**, 51–68. © The British Academy 2004.

work with our Soviet and Yugoslav allies, and to foster an intense hatred of Nazism and all its works. Perhaps this experience also gave impetus to his growing interest in the history of those nations who had fought against it during the Second World War.

On completing his National Service in 1949 Erickson enrolled in St John's College, Cambridge, to study Slavonic and other East and Central European languages, including German, Russian and Serbo-Croat. He acquired a deeper interest in East European history, and following his first-class BA degree in 1952 he remained at the college to work for a Ph.D. His subject was the European revolutions in 1848. Sadly, he and his examiner were unable to agree on his treatment of the topic, and Erickson withdrew his doctoral thesis in 1956. He was then offered a Research Fellowship at St Antony's College, Oxford, on military history, primarily that of the Soviet Army since its foundation in 1918, which he gratefully accepted. Erickson had the good fortune to study under an acknowledged expert on the Eastern Front, David Footman, and the Warden of the College, Sir William Deakin. The latter was the Head of the first official British Military Mission to serve with Marshal Tito's Yugoslav Partisans in 1943; from him Erickson obtained first-hand information about the Resistance to the Axis occupation forces in Yugoslavia during the war. Erickson began to assemble his own expert data-base from British, American, French and German records on the Soviet-German war, and to make valuable use of his Fellowship travel grants to visit some of the Central and East European countries involved. These included Germany and Austria, Poland, Czechoslovakia, Yugoslavia and Hungary; he was not able to travel to the Soviet Union at this stage in his research. Erickson developed a special admiration for Poland and the Poles— whose language he successfully learnt—particularly in the light of their record in resisting aggression throughout the whole of the conflict in Europe from 1939 to 1945.

While he was at St Antony's College he met a visiting Yugoslav student, a Serbian girl named Ljubica Petrovic. Her father, Dr Branko Petrovic, had served in the Yugoslav Resistance during the Second World War; he, and a brother and other family members were captured and executed by the Germans in September 1943. John and Ljubica were married in Oxford on 18 July 1957. They had a very happy and fruitful marriage. They had two delightful children Amanda-Jane born on 20 August 1962, and Mark, born on 16 April 1964—both in Manchester. It was indeed a very successful union: Ljubica dedicated herself to helping her husband in his career and his study of the war, the Soviet Union and Yugoslavia, collaborating in his research and especially in the editing of his books and articles and providing expert handling of photographs and other source material. She co-authored a number of his publications and was his invaluable supporter as well as a devoted wife and mother. In the years ahead the family enjoyed many holidays and travels to Ljubica's native Yugoslavia.

When he was in Oxford Erickson completed his first major book on the Soviet Armed Forces: *The Soviet High Command, 1918–1941* in 1960 and published it in 1962. This work of over 650 pages opens with an account of the foundation, on 23 February 1918, of the Red Army of Workers and Peasants under the orders of the revolutionary Communist government established in Russia after the defeat of the Imperial Army in the First World War, and the arrival in Russia from abroad of the Bolshevik Party leaders led by Vladimir Il'ich Lenin in 1917. The book describes in detail the birth-pangs of the new army in fighting foreign enemies and a civil war in Russia between the Communist forces and those of the old Tsarist regime which came to be known as the White Armies. Erickson successfully combined in this first book his deep understanding of Russia and the revolution which had swept the country. He describes how the new Army was organised and led by Communist activists under Lenin's collaborator Leon Trotsky helped by numbers of professional officers of the Imperial Army sympathetic to the Bolshevik cause. Erickson's treatment of the civil war demonstrates the ad hoc nature of the creation of the new Army and underlines his ability to assess the roles of the various elements which the Bolsheviks used to establish their new instrument of state power.

After the civil war and the introduction of Soviet communist rule over the whole of the vast country, Erickson's book describes the emergence of the Soviet Union as an isolated and impoverished state ruled by a dictator of Georgian Caucasian origin, ruthless and conspiratorial in temperament, Josef Stalin (born Dzhugashvili) who was to dominate its policies and its armed forces for the best part of thirty years. The book traces the development of the Red Army during this period, which exhibited some improvements in organisation, training and fire-power in the 1920s and 1930s. But these were cut short in 1937 to 1939 by Stalin's decimation of the Army's High Command in the military purges of those years. Among those eliminated were three of the five Marshals of the Soviet Union (Russia's highest rank) and many thousands of commanders and political commissars. Some were simply executed; others condemned to die after show trials or secret court hearings, or given lengthy prison terms in concentration camps. Erickson presents the details in two significant chapters: 'The Killings' and 'Exeunt Omnes'. He shows how when the Red Army did go into action in the war against Finland in 1939–40 and in the early phases of the German invasion of the Soviet Union in 1941, most of the senior commanders and staff officers were woefully unable to carry out their tasks. This army was accurately described by one distinguished American military historian, David Glantz, as 'The Stumbling Colossus'.[1]

Erickson recounts how unprepared and confused the Red Army was when the German attack came on 22 June 1941. He quotes a message from a command post in the Western Special Military District to the Commissariat of Defence in Moscow saying: 'We are being fired on: what shall we do?' He traces the rapid advance of the main German Army Groups into Soviet territory leading to the virtual collapse of the Soviet forces deployed in the frontier areas in full military detail, including the relevant order-of-battle information, and underlines the low morale of the retreating Russians. For in a matter of weeks the German armies were at the gates of Leningrad, in the main cities west of Moscow and in the western areas of the Ukraine. Few Soviet commanders in the field were able to withstand the German onslaught: many were killed or executed for their failures. Erickson singles out one Soviet General who seemed to keep his nerve: namely the Chief of the General Staff, Army-General, later Marshal, Georgi Zhukov, whom Stalin sent first to consolidate the defence of Leningrad and then to take over the preparations for the protection of Moscow. Erickson shows in impressive detail how Zhukov and his best army commanders, including the future Marshal Rokossovski, held the line before Moscow and launched the successful counter-offensive on 6 December 1941 which, though slow in pace, forced the German army to retreat. Zhukov's victory at Moscow, described in precise and convincing terms, brings Erickson's first book on the Second World War to a fascinating conclusion.

When completing *The Soviet High Command* in Oxford Erickson was offered in 1958 what turned out to be his first regular teaching post: a lectureship in the Department of History in St Andrews University in Scotland, an appointment recommended by the then Principal, Sir Malcolm Knox. Three years later he left St Andrews for Manchester University. In 1961 he joined the Department of Government there, first as a lecturer, then as a senior lecturer and finally as a Reader in Politics.

---

[1] David Glantz: *The Stumbling Colossus* (Kansas, 1998).

It was during his fruitful years in Manchester that Erickson achieved his rightful place among scholars working in the field of Soviet military history and contemporary developments in the Soviet Armed Forces— including Soviet historians and senior serving officers in the Soviet forces. It was clear that Erickson's *The Soviet High Command* became known and widely read in Russia: a book which Soviet experts found well-written, accurate and unbiased. Among his admirers apparently were Academician A. M. Samsonov, the Head of the Department of Military History of the Soviet Academy of Sciences, and Lieutenant-General S. P. Platonov, Head of the Military-Historical Directorate of the Soviet General Staff. They and their colleagues probably sought opportunities to meet this Western military historian who had published such detailed accounts of the evolution of the Red Army before and during the Soviet-German war. Even more significant for them, Erickson's writing demonstrated a genuine admiration for the Soviet armed forces, for those who organised and commanded them, and for the ordinary soldier, sailor and airman who carried out their operations.

Their opportunity to meet and collaborate with Erickson came in 1963. In the previous year the highly respected American war reporter and author, Cornelius Ryan, who had made his name in a major book and film on the Allied landings in Normandy in 1944, was preparing a study of the capture of Berlin by the Russians in April–May 1945 to be called *The Last Battle*. In the course of his negotiations with the Soviet authorities about a visit to Moscow in order to study Soviet military documents, reports and diaries of important participants in the battle for Berlin, Ryan expressed a wish to meet and interview them if possible. The Soviet military historians, primarily Academician Samsonov, agreed, and asked Ryan: 'Please bring John Erickson as your adviser and interpreter; he knows more about our Armed Forces than we do, and we are very anxious to meet him!' Ryan, it is said, agreed at once (although he and Erickson had never met) and the two set off for Moscow in April 1963.

The 1963 visit to Moscow gave Erickson too the opportunity to meet and interrogate Soviet military leaders who were not only participants in the Berlin operation but in many of the major battles of the war on the Eastern front. He had already read many of their published works, but was now anxious to read their own war diaries, their battle reports and their individual accounts of the conduct of the war by the Soviet leadership, including their Supreme Commander-in-Chief, Stalin. Naturally he attended all the meetings organised by the Russians for Ryan, acting mainly as his interpreter. But as his relationship with his Soviet hosts

developed favourably, he was able to borrow or copy documents never
released before to foreign scholars which helped him in his on-going studies. He was already planning to write two further volumes on the war in
the East: *The Road to Stalingrad, 1941–1943* and *The Road to Berlin,
1943–1945* with military details drawn from both official Soviet materials
and personal memoirs.

Erickson's first interviews in Moscow were with participants in the
Berlin campaign. Among the first was Marshal Vasili Sokolovski who had
been Deputy Commander-in-Chief of Marshal Zhukov's First Beloruss-
ian Front in 1945, and after the war Commander-in-Chief of Soviet
forces in East Germany and Chief of the General Staff from 1952 to 1960
and was the author of a book on the Berlin campaign. Erickson and
Ryan interviewed him on 17 April 1963 and found him helpful and ready
to enlarge on the archive material that he and his team of military historians had brought with them. Sokolovski told them that his book had
contained the first evidence made available to the Russian people that
Hitler had died in Berlin in 1945. Erickson records that he found the
interview with the then commander of the Eighth Guards Army,
Colonel-General Vasili Chuikov and in 1963 a Marshal of the Soviet
Union, Commander-in-Chief of the Soviet Ground Forces and part-time
Head of Civil Defence extremely interesting—and emotional—as the
Russian commander recalled the capture of the city and the enormous
number of Soviet casualties that the war entailed. Equally worthwhile
was his talk with Marshal Ivan Koniev, commander of the First
Ukrainian Front in 1945 and Commander-in-Chief of the forces of the
Warsaw Pact from 1955 to 1960. Koniev read out (with his spectacles
perched on the end of his nose) extensive passages from his personal war
diaries, stressing that he had held Front commands since the beginning of
the war. Erickson also had a rarely granted interview with Marshal
Konstantin Rokossovski, whom he regarded as the Red Army's best tactical and strategic commander, who expressed disappointment at not participating directly in the storming of Berlin. He had criticised Marshal
Zhukov, the High Command and Stalin for their conduct of the early
stages of the war, including their tactical decision-making in the defence
of Moscow in 1941. Other senior Soviet war leaders whom Erickson saw
were Marshal Andrei Yeremenko, one of the most experienced Front
commanders and a veteran of the battle of Stalingrad, and the Head of
Soviet Artillery, Chief Marshal Nikolai Voronov, as well as some distinguished middle-ranking officers of Army, Rifle Corps and Divisional levels. Erickson subsequently stressed that although this visit to Moscow

was short, it enabled him to add personal experience to his growing archive of documentary and other historical evidence on which to base his further research and writings.

Erickson returned to Manchester University in 1963 to resume his teaching in the Department of Government. Under this heading he ventured for the first time into the field of military–political relations in Britain, collaborating with Professor J. N. Wolfe in editing a book entitled *The Armed Services and Society* which was published in 1969. His work in this area also involved studying cost-efficiency techniques designed to produce the most efficient Armed Forces for democratic Britain without antagonising the professional career officers. But Erickson's main work was in Soviet military history. He returned to the preparation of his major war history of the Eastern front: *The Road to Stalingrad*, and *The Road to Berlin* on which he worked during the next decade.

While these books were under way, Erickson found himself in increasing demand for expert advice on the Soviet Union in journals, newspapers and at conferences in Britain and overseas. A book on Panslavism in 1964 was followed by *The Military-Technological Revolution* which he edited, written by a number of other scholars including Raymond L. Garthoff, Thomas W. Wolfe and the Soviet military analyst Major-General Nikolai Talensky in 1966. In 1967 he collaborated with the late Professor Leonard Schapiro and Peter Reddaway in a reappraisal of Lenin as a war leader during the Russian revolution, and paid his first high-level teaching visit to the United States in that year. He was a Visiting Professor at the Russian Research Center in the University of Indiana, and in 1968 visited the University of Michigan at Ann Arbor to contribute to an important book edited by Richard Pipes on the origins of the Red Army. He also taught at Berkeley, Princeton, Harvard and Chicago during many visits to the United States at this stage in his career. Erickson's appetite for academic and technical studies proved insatiable. A personal visit to his home in Manchester would find him and his wife Ljubica engulfed in stacks of papers, books, documents and draft studies which demonstrated how hard-working a scholar he was and how sought-after an expert he had become on the Soviet armed forces past and present—including among Soviet officers and military historians in Moscow.

In 1967 Erickson took a major decision to leave Manchester and seek a post in the University of Edinburgh. In 1968 the Ministry of Defence under Denis Healey's inspired leadership encouraged and financed a number of universities to establish posts of 'Higher Defence Studies', and the University of Edinburgh appointed Professor Harry Hanham, later to be Vice-Chancellor of Lancaster University, to the position in Edinburgh. He then asked Erickson to join him there as a lecturer in Higher Defence Studies.

In this capacity, while continuing to write his books and articles on Soviet military affairs, he developed growing contacts with scholars and government officials around the world. He launched extended pro- grammes for students at the university, mostly postgraduates, and also British and American serving officers working on these subjects. He widened the range of his expertise into the more contemporary aspects of events, including Soviet–American strategic relationships, Sino-Soviet relations, and the Warsaw Pact—as it was in the 1970s—and the naval and air elements in the East–West balance in military power. Erickson, ably assisted by Ljubica, his wife, and a closely knit team of followers in Edinburgh University, concentrated on the growth of the strength of Soviet and NATO Armed Forces. He was also able at this time to com- plete and publish his *Road to Stalingrad 1941–1943* book in 1975 and to begin work on his second volume on the war on the Eastern front, *The Road to Berlin 1943–1945*. The latter included a masterly account of the largest tank battle ever fought: the Battle of Kursk in central European Russia in July 1943, culminating in the Soviet offensive along the whole of the Eastern front from Leningrad (liberated in January 1944) to the campaign on the Black Sea coast. This massive offensive shattered the German and Axis armies in Russia and opened the way for the final advance of the Red Army to the German capital which was taken in May 1945. In 1969 Erickson paid his second visit to the Soviet Union as a member of a BBC documentary team preparing programmes on that country to be broadcast on Radio 4. The team interviewed Ivan Maisky, the wartime and pre-war Soviet ambassador to London, and Yuri Gagarin, the first man in space and cosmonaut, as well as some historians writing on international affairs.

Erickson's increasing interest in the balance of forces between the two alliances drew him to pay further attention to the problems of arms con- trol in the 1960s and 1970s. This coincided with greater interest on the part of Western and Eastern governments and ministries of defence. Here the Centre for Higher Defence Studies in Edinburgh University showed increasing promise as an academic base where international study and debate of defence and arms control issues could take place in a realistic atmosphere. This growth in the Centre's potential role coincided with the first high-level super-power negotiations between Moscow and Washing- ton on the limitation, agreed by treaty, of both sides' strategic (nuclear) forces. The first of these treaties was the Strategic Arms Limitation Treaty (SALT I) signed in 1972, followed by SALT II signed in 1979. Simultaneously the two governments signed an Anti-Ballistic Missile Defence Treaty (ABM) in 1974. In a sense these agreements turned the intercontinental strategic nuclear element of the armed forces of both countries into a separate strategic 'umbrella' whose size, modernisation and development could be 'controlled' through negotiation between the powers concerned. The main remaining arms control problem which particularly exercised Erickson appeared in Europe. Here both NATO and the Warsaw Pact were anxious to modernise their Intermediate Range Nuclear Missile Forces (IRBM) and to deploy them in accordance with evolving military doctrines—partly in order to strengthen their conventional capabilities and to avoid nuclear conflict. Soviet modernisation deployment came first: in 1977 with the SS-20 missile deployed forward in Europe. This, along with the establishment of upgraded Theatre of Military Operations headquarters in the East, gave the Soviet Forces a head-start over NATO. The American equivalent, the Pershing-2 missile and the Ground-Launched Cruise missiles (GLCM) systems were not deployed until 1983. These developments made the extension of the strategic nuclear weapons talks into the European theatre extremely difficult. The new deployments of forces and weapons aroused deep suspicions of intentions to resort to war on both sides, and the continuation of negotiations on arms control stalled in the early 1980s. At the strategic level the ongoing talks—the Strategic Arms Reduction Talks (START)—successor to SALT came to a halt in 1984. Moreover, President Reagan's Strategic Defence Initiative (SDI) announced in 1983 alarmed the Soviet leaders apparently to the point where they became convinced that the United States was deliberately bypassing the SALT and ABM treaties. As early as 1980 it could be said that military diplomacy between the East and the West was virtually at a standstill. Another negative factor was the Soviet invasion of Afghanistan in December 1979 and the shooting down of a Korean civil airliner over the Pacific in 1983. All these elements led to a reluctance in Western governments to continue negotiations or even discussions with the Soviet Union.

This complex and worrying scenario helped to influence Erickson's forthcoming role in attempts to re-establish an informed academic dialogue between East and West on arms control issues. The earliest initiative came in Edinburgh through a process which became known as the Edinburgh Conversations. Thanks to the initiative of the late Lord Ritchie Calder, then the Chairman of the Scotland–USSR Society, who paid a

visit to Moscow in 1980, initially to discuss some of the existing con-
tentious issues between the West and the Soviet Union, including the
Soviet invasion of Afghanistan, human rights, nuclear weapons and disarmament. The tone of the meetings was said to be vigorous and even hostile, and Lord Ritchie Calder returned to Scotland sure that no further
meetings could be held. To his amazement, it was reported, that shortly
afterwards he received a message from his Russian hosts asking him to
bring a group of Scots able and willing to continue the discussions on
terms acceptable to both sides. Lord Ritchie Calder welcomed the suggestion, and after consulting senior figures in Edinburgh University, including
the Principal and Vice-Chancellor, Dr John Burnett, and Erickson, he
arranged for ten Scottish academic representatives to visit the Soviet
Union to plan the discussions. Erickson, who had been in Washington to
brief senior American military officers on other issues when Lord Ritchie
Calder was in Moscow, accompanied the Scottish group and took part in
talks with the Soviet Deputy Chairman of the Foreign Affairs Committee
of the Communist Party, Vadim Zagladin. It was agreed that three Soviet
officials would visit Edinburgh in February 1981 in the hope of organising
a meeting in the city in the autumn of that year.

It was obvious in Edinburgh that if these talks were to succeed the key
figure on the British side must be Erickson. He called a meeting of the
university representatives with the Russians to exchange views on what
might be the main subjects for debate. They put forward international
law, physics, computer engineering, genetics, medicine and history, and
also laying down an information base. Other topics might be awareness of
the problem of disinformation and deciding how the discussions might
exert influence on the policymakers and prepare a mechanism for resolv-
ing differences about facts, for example, on how much in terms of military
power, each side had. On the following day, the three Soviet representatives met the Principal and Vice-Chancellor of the university, Dr Burnett.
It was agreed that a meeting on the theme 'Survival in the Nuclear Age'
of three or four days should be held in Edinburgh University in the
autumn of 1981, that the sessions should be informal but with prepared
papers provided where appropriate, and that numbers should be restricted
to not more than ten on each side. Dr Burnett stressed that the 'Conversations' would not be concerned exclusively with nuclear-military matters,
but that wider ranges of topics involving survival should be brought into
the agenda.

These contacts and discussions led to the first set of the Edinburgh
Conversations which was held in Edinburgh from 5 to 7 October 1981.

From the start it was accepted by both sides that Erickson would be a central figure in keeping the talks going, realistic and worthwhile in content, and carried on in an atmosphere of mutual trust. First of all, he held the vital post of Professor of Higher Defence Studies in the university which gave him the status (especially in Russian minds) for directing a debate of this kind. He clearly enjoyed good relationships with the most senior officials in the university, including the Principal and Vice-Chancellor, and with other academics, government servants and trade-union leaders, and this became ever more evident as the Conversations proceeded. More significantly he was already *the* accepted Western academic expert on the Soviet Armed Forces, past, present and future, the author of two major books on the history of the Second World War on the Eastern Front, and a scholar consulted by all NATO and many neutral governments and universities on the facts and figures of the East–West military balance. The Russians whom the group planned to meet were, in many cases, well known to Erickson already as was the range of published and some unpublished material for which Soviet military analysts were responsible. Moreover, these Russians shared the West's admiration for his knowledge, fair-mindedness and skill in communicating his views, verbally and in print.

Erickson also had other advantages when dealing directly with the Russians. His Russian was fluent and wide-ranging; he also spoke other European languages including French, German and Norwegian, and from Eastern Europe: Polish, Czech and Serbo-Croat. He had a fantastic memory for military detail ranging from strategic decision-making to precise information on the order-of-battle of East European and Soviet armies, navies and air and air-defence formations and units and the growing deployments of Strategic Missile Troops within the Soviet Union and abroad. He was equally knowledgeable on weapons systems of various kinds, their capabilities and their weaknesses. He also understood the problems of morale, discipline and society within the armed forces which he was studying. Deeper still, he had developed a kind of instinctive understanding of how the Russian mind worked on the issues being discussed, how the Russians argued their case, and how and when to stand back and listen and when to press an opposing view vigorously. And all these advantages benefited the Conversations alongside his unique qualities as an interpreter which won the respect of both groups. When the sessions were under way, it was Erickson who was responsible for checking draft reports of the debates and the accuracy of other interpreters' versions of what had been said. Perhaps above all, Erickson's contributions to the whole process clearly indicated that he had a personal and professional dedication to the success of the Conversations, stressing always the academic nature of the talks and refusing to give them any kind of governmental or official status. Nor would he allow propaganda elements to enter his contributions, although he did agree to, and take part in, press conferences. At one of these, in the Second Edinburgh Conversations session in October 1982, a Soviet journalist asked him: 'Are you a member of The Peace Movement?' He replied: 'No, I'm not. I am a member of the movement for peace.'

The first set of Edinburgh Conversations was, as planned, held from 5 to 7 October 1981 in Edinburgh. The British delegation was headed by Lord Ritchie Calder and Dr John Burnett, with Erickson as the main contributor to the discussions. The Soviet group was led by Professor Vitaly Kobysh of the Department of International Information of the Communist Party. The British group was joined by a distinguished retired General, Sir Hugh Beach, who was an acknowledged expert on the military and military–political aspects of the organisation and policy-making processes of the NATO armed forces and on arms control. He had been a much-admired Commandant of the Army Staff College in Camberley, where he contributed greatly to the quality of the work of the college's students. The Soviet delegates, like their British counterparts, debated the concept of 'limited nuclear war', and agreed on the principle of 'no first use of nuclear weapons' should war break out. Those present also ruled out defining Europe as a 'Theatre of War', especially as a 'Theatre of Nuclear Weapons'. Media coverage in Scotland was favourable, as were the official comments in the Soviet press.

It was agreed at this session that the second set should be held in Moscow from 25 September to 2 October 1982. Erickson led the group from Scotland, which included Professor Iain McGibbon of the Department of International Law at the university, Dr John Loraine of the Centre of Human Ecology and representatives of the Scottish Trade Union movement. On arrival in Moscow this group was joined by delegates flying from London who included Dr Burnett, a son of Lord Ritchie Calder, Nigel Calder, General Sir Hugh Beach, and a very distinguished soldier, Field Marshal Lord Carver, whose last post had been Chief of the Defence Staff. During the Second World War he had been, at the age of 27, the youngest brigadier in the British Army serving in the Middle East. The Soviet delegation had a new leader, Gennadi Yanaev, then the Deputy President of the Union of Soviet Friendship Societies, and later to become famous (or infamous) in 1991 as one of the leaders of the unsuccessful coup d'état against Gorbachev. However, he carried out his duties as head of the Soviet group in the Edinburgh Conversations with good sense and some humour during the 1980s. The main military representative in the Soviet team was Major-General Konstantin Mikhailov, an artillery officer with many years of service in the General Staff working on arms control. Another member of the Soviet team was Academician Georgi Arbatov, Director of the Institute of US and Canadian Studies, a Deputy of the Supreme Soviet, and a well-known presenter of the Soviet point of view on international affairs. His military advisor was Lieutenant-General Mikhail Mil'stein, a veteran of the Second World War and a respected military analyst and historian. Apparently at the request of the Russians, an American representative was added to the British team: the person chosen was Colonel Lynn Hansen, an Air Force officer with experience of arms control policies and a former student of Erickson in the Centre of Higher Defence Studies at Edinburgh University. Lynn Hansen was to remain in the delegation until the end of the Conversations; he then continued his work on arms control with the rank of ambassador.

As the Conversations got under way it became clear that a procedural problem had arisen which took all Erickson's Soviet expertise to solve. It was a Russian and Soviet tradition to enter negotiations with a draft communiqué compiled before the talks began which their delegates presented as the accepted basis for the final conclusions of the negotiations. This principle was unacceptable to the British side: among other issues it led to increasing delays in the completion of the sessions involved, and to some degree of acrimony in some of the exchanges between the delegations. Erickson, with some assistance from his colleagues, succeeded in persuading the Russians to agree to a more balanced procedure although as the Conversations progressed they did try to reinstate their ideas without much success.

Meanwhile the second set of the Conversations on the Soviet side was dominated by accusations of 'intransigence' by the Americans in 'failing to stop the arms race' and by calls on the British side for new thinking on war, as nuclear hostilities could solve nothing in the problems faced by the world. In the final agreed communiqué all participants were united in their view that the Soviet/United States talks on strategic arms limitation and reduction (SALT/START) and on limiting medium-range nuclear systems in Europe should aim to achieve the speediest possible results. A particularly moving moment during the visit to Moscow came when Field Marshal Lord Carver laid a wreath at the Tomb of the Unknown Soldier on 27 September in Red Square. This was much appreciated by the Russians present, but had a special poignancy for Erickson in view of the murder of his father-in-law and other members of Ljubica's family in Yugoslavia during the Second World War.

The third set of Conversations took place in Edinburgh from 17 to 22 September 1983. Sixteen days before the conference was due to open a diplomatic crisis emerged following the shooting-down of a Korean civil airliner over the Pacific by the Soviet Air Defence forces with loss of 269 lives. Retaliatory diplomatic action was taken by Britain and the United States, and some hostility was expressed in both countries to the continuation of the Conversations with the Russians. The university authorities decided, however, that academic discussions should resume, and the British welcomed their Soviet counterparts in Edinburgh on 17 September. Erickson and the university Principal explained to the press that in their view these academic non-governmental talks should continue. The Americans agreed and sent a senior negotiator and former Director of their Arms Control and Disarmament Agency, Professor Eugene Rostow. The British added Vice-Admiral Sir Ian McGeoch, a former Flag-Officer Scotland, to their group. Given the existing international crisis atmosphere, this set of the Conversations broke no new ground and press comment was muted. The challenge was regarded by Erickson as an important one, and he used his authority and his friendly relationships with all concerned to keep the delegations together—and talking.

During this set of negotiations both sides agreed that it would be sensible for a small group of senior members of the teams to visit their opposite numbers prior to the main sessions of the Conversations in order to agree on the agenda in advance. This was done before the fourth set held in Moscow from 15 to 22 September 1984. At the main meeting the British team was strengthened by the addition of Nicholas Soames, a British Member of Parliament, and what was of special interest to the Russians, a grandson of Winston Churchill, and also by Admiral Sir James Eberle, a distinguished sailor and then Director of the Royal Institute of International Affairs. The Americans added Ambassador Max Kampelman, to their delegation. The session was taken up with an energetic exchange between Ambassador Kampelman and Georgi Arbatov (who had clashed previously on East–West issues including arms control) but the heat was taken out of the atmosphere by an intervention by Admiral Eberle which, it was said, 'levelled the score'. Erickson disliked the way in which Arbatov presented the Soviet case, and spent much time balancing the two versions of the dialogue to the satisfaction of both

sides. A press conference which was chaired jointly by Erickson and
Gennadi Yanaev apparently went well, and Erickson was described by
one of his colleagues as much more relaxed than in previous days.

The fifth set of the Conversations, preceded by a preparatory visit held
in Moscow to decide the agenda, took place in Edinburgh from 12 to 17
April 1986. This meeting took place against the background of an
American air strike against targets in Libya, which was carried out on 16
April by bombers which had taken off from airfields in Britain. The
Conversations, however, continued, and the atmosphere was said to be
unaffected by the Libyan crisis. Gennadi Yanaev would only say that the
attack could not contribute to world stability, but there was no formal
discussion on the subject.

The sixth set was held in Moscow from 27 September to 5 October
1987 following an agenda meeting in February that year which turned out
to be one of the most important preparatory sessions prior to a full
Conversation. The main reason was that in March 1985 Mikhail
Gorbachev, a younger member of the Politburo, had succeeded to the
post of General Secretary of the Communist Party of the Soviet Union
and had begun the process of reforming the Party and the Government
under the general headings of *Perestroika* and *Glasnost*. Although the
exact translation, let alone meaning, of these Russian terms was far from
clear either in Moscow or abroad, one Soviet diplomat interpreted the
former as 'refurbishment' of government, society and the relationship
between the Party leadership and the people. *Glasnost* was stated to mean
'limitation of censorship', leading, eventually perhaps, to freedom of
speech or writing. Not unnaturally, both Westerners and Russians called
on Erickson to give his views on the messages coming out from the
Kremlin at the preparatory and the full meetings of the groups. Erickson
commented that he was very impressed by the new policy of *Perestroika*
and the probable link with 'reconstruction' or 'refurbishment', but there
was danger that such interpretations could cause confusion among people on both sides. The time had now come to inject new ideas on military
and technical issues. He also stressed that the Edinburgh Conversations
should stick to the pattern of no formal agenda and simply go on
allowing for a free exchange of views and ideas on a few themes.

This set of the Conversations saw the addition to the British team of
Field Marshal Sir John Stanier, a former Chief of the General Staff, to
present the British thinking on the military issues to be discussed, and Sir
Clive Rose, a former Ambassador to NATO. Once again the main business was redrafting the communiqués put forward by the Soviet side on

arms control, the nuclear balance in Europe, the importance of the meetings between the leaders of the Soviet Union and the United States in
Reykjavik opening up real steps towards nuclear disarmament and arms
control, and visible lowering of military tensions in the balance of power
in the world. As before, Erickson was at the centre of this process, and his
contribution helped to bring this set to a successful conclusion.

In December 1987 Erickson visited the United States and learnt that
the Americans involved would like the Conversations to continue. In
Scotland the holder of the post of Principal and Vice-Chancellor of the
University had changed, but Sir John Burnett (who was knighted in that
year), agreed to carry on as a British Co-Chairman of the Conversations,
and, after the preparatory agenda meeting was held in September 1988,
he led the British team in Edinburgh for the seventh—and final—meeting, which opened on 4 December 1988. The Western delegation, led by
Sir John Burnett, included Erickson, General Sir Hugh Beach, Lynn
Hansen, and Colonel David Glantz, editor of the American *Journal of
Soviet Military Studies*. The Soviet team was headed by General
Mikhailov and Professor Vladimir Trukhanovski, a former ambassador
and a famous historian.

The agenda for the seventh set of the Conversations, though basically
similar to that of its predecessors, was strongly influenced by changes in
the political and military relationships between the Western powers and
the Soviet Union brought about by the new leadership in the Soviet
Union under Mikhail Gorbachev. The themes discussed at the meetings
included interpretations by both sides of the new policies put forward by
Gorbachev on 'Common Security: Perspectives and Possibilities'. Discussion centred on the impact of his *Perestroika* concept, the defence-orien-
tated doctrine of 'sufficiency' in the military strengths of NATO and the
Warsaw Pact, and his offer in a speech at the United Nations to reduce
the strength of the Soviet Armed Forces by 500,000 men—a proposal
that was welcomed by all participants. There appeared to be general
agreement that, in spite of the significant lowering of tension between
Gorbachev's Soviet Union and the West the issues involved deserved a
further Conversation in 1989, and in April of that year Erickson went to
Moscow to discuss arrangements. Meetings were held for the first time in
the Ministry of Foreign Affairs, and an agenda was agreed, but after the
British delegation's return to Edinburgh, diplomatic relations deteriorated between Britain and the Soviet Union, hopefully, temporarily. The
British side decided that since the overall international situation had
improved to the point where state-to-state relations had overtaken the

achievements of the Edinburgh academic links, the Conversations should be brought to a close. The university leadership agreed, and Erickson notified the American and Soviet participants to this effect. The termination of the Conversations was an amicable one. There can be no doubt that they contributed significantly to the retention of worthwhile contacts between East and West during a period of very tense diplomatic and military relationships, and that the key figure in their origins and continuation was Erickson, whose reputation as a diplomat, especially in a liaison capacity, was added to that of a historian, analyst, teacher and scholar in an admirable way.

In the concluding stages of the Edinburgh Conversations Erickson's career in the university moved further ahead. He was appointed a University Endowment Fellow in 1988, while retaining his post as Director of the Centre of Higher Defence Studies which enabled him to continue his teaching, his writing and research into Soviet military history. He also accepted the offer of the Presidency of the British Association of Civil Defence and Emergency Planning Officers in 1985 which he held for one year. Meanwhile Erickson had been elected a Fellow of the Royal Society of Edinburgh in 1982, a Fellow of the British Academy in 1985 and a Fellow of the Royal Society of Arts in 1991. It would take too long to list all his books, let alone his articles, lectures and attendance at conferences as well as his appearances on television and talks on the radio. But some of his writings cannot be omitted. His editorial role was enhanced, for example, in the book *Barbarossa: the Axis and the Allies* which was published in Edinburgh in 1994. In 1996 he contributed a chapter based on Soviet military archives on the Battle for Berlin (printed in Russian as *posledny shturm*) in the book *The End of the War in Europe* edited by Gill Bennett in London.[2] In the same year he wrote with Ljubica *The Soviet Armed Forces 1918–1992: A Research Guide to Soviet Sources*. Of particular value and artistic quality as well as historical importance was his book published in London with Ljubica, *The Eastern Front in Photographs*, a beautifully prepared volume which brings to light the essence of the war in the east as seen by the camera. Perhaps his last completed book which came out in 2000 was *From Barbarossa to Stalingrad and Berlin*. When he died on 10 February 2002, other works remained unfinished: among them a study of the Soviet Home Front provisionally entitled 'Blood, Bread and Steel', and a history of the Russian General Staff. John Erickson's and Ljubica's decision to leave his archive of Soviet military records

---

[2] Gill Bennett (ed.), *The End of the War in Europe* (1996).

which they had built up together over many years to the National Library of Scotland, is a gift of characteristic generosity to all interested in the evolution of international relations following the end of the Second World War. In the words of one of this country's outstanding soldiers, scholars and teachers, Professor Sir Michael Howard, in praise of Erickson: 'Nobody deserves more credit for the ultimate dissolution of the misunderstandings that brought the Cold War to an end and enabled the peoples of Russia and their western neighbours to live in peace. The magnificent archive that he has left to the University of Edinburgh is a fitting memorial.'

One of the most attractive elements in Erickson's life and character was the quality of his capacity for friendship. Whatever he was engaged in professionally he never allowed the hardest workload or the most complex challenge to interfere with his search for happy relationships with his colleagues, his personal generosity, or his readiness to help and encourage other scholars. Mention has already been made of his long and happy marriage to Ljubica and his devotion to their children Amanda-Jane and Mark. In parallel came his admiration for Ljubica's homeland, Yugoslavia, in whose defence, as already mentioned, her father, Dr Branko Petrovic lost his life as a patriot during the war. Erickson and his wife spent most of what spare time they could find on holiday there, especially with the children. It was with deep sadness that they witnessed the break-up of the Federal Republic of Yugoslavia—and some resentment that the NATO Alliance had unfortunately played a part in that country's dissolution.

Finally, a more personal memory: the writer of these lines had the good fortune to know Erickson for over fifty years, and enjoyed the privilege of sharing some work with him on Soviet political and military affairs. With all the burdens of his achievements he remained unswervingly loyal to his friends, was always delightful company, the recounter of many witty and relevant anecdotes and a generous listener to others. He will be remembered professionally as surely the earliest explorer into the once-great fortress of Soviet military power and the scholar with the expertise to explain it to the West. He carried out this task with understanding, clarity and humanity that have never been matched.

MALCOLM MACKINTOSH
Formerly Assistant Secretary, Cabinet Office

RAYMOND FIRTH   *Hugh Firth*

Raymond William Firth
1901–2002

RAYMOND FIRTH drew his first breath in Auckland on 25 March 1901, and his last in London, on 22 February 2002, nearly 101 years later. He became an anthropologist, working chiefly in the Pacific, Malaysia and London, in the fields of economics, religion and kinship. He held permanent teaching posts at Sydney (1930–2) and at the London School of Economics (1932–40, 1944–68). During the Second World War he served in Naval Intelligence; he became secretary of the Colonial Social Science Research Council in 1944–5, and was a founding member of the Association of Social Anthropologists of the United Kingdom and Commonwealth in 1946. He was elected to the British Academy in 1949 as an economist, later helping to create the Social Anthropology section. He was elected corresponding or foreign member of the American Academy of Arts and Sciences, of the American Philosophical Society, of the Royal Society of New Zealand, and of New South Wales, and of the Royal Danish Academy of Sciences and Letters. In retirement he held eight visiting posts at American and Pacific universities. He was knighted in 1973 and received Honorary Doctorates from Oslo, Michigan, East Anglia, Australian National University, Chicago, British Columbia, Exeter, Auckland, Cracow and London. He was appointed Companion of the New Zealand Order of Merit in 2001. In 2002 he was awarded the Leverhulme Centenary Medal of the British Academy but did not live to receive it in person.

Firth was a patient and generous teacher whose many graduate students remained loyal throughout their lives; he was an able and

Proceedings of the British Academy, **124**, 71–88. © The British Academy 2004.

purposeful administrator of great integrity: no one alive can remember him doing a mean or malicious or self-interested act. In anthropology he was resolutely humane and empirical: his aim was always to convey the variety and complexity of people's experience, and to show how his theory was based on that understanding. He had many academic friendships outside anthropology, was well-read in several disciplines, and was affable and generous with his learning. Without being puritan, in later life he took his pleasures somewhat austerely, with a preference for romanesque architecture, for example, and early music. He married Rosemary Upcott, daughter of a distinguished official in the Treasury, in 1936. Their son Hugh was born in 1946.

* * *

Firth's father Wesley was a Methodist by religion and a builder by trade. His children (Raymond; Gretta, 1905–7; Cedric, 1908–94) were born in Remuera, now part of Auckland City. The family moved to Mauku in 1910 and Firth attended primary school three miles away: he walked there barefoot (boots reserved for Sundays) until his father gave him a horse for transport in 1911. In 1914 he became the first pupil from that school to win a Junior National Scholarship and in 1915 moved to Auckland Grammar School, staying during term with friends of his parents. His further schooling was supported by a Senior National Scholarship, he went on to Auckland University College. In his notes on his early life Firth was at pains to remark that he never got a first prize, and that he came low down in the order for his university scholarship. He attended full-time, unusually, because his father 'believed firmly in unfettered education'. Whatever he thought at the time, Firth (in his seventies or eighties when he wrote the notes) seems to say that he became a scholar and researcher of such eminence against all odds, not merely social and geographical ones. He records only one triumph at this stage: in 1919 his economics paper was marked at 35 per cent and he scraped through, while the examiner failed nearly all the other candidates. The examiner was J. M. Keynes, and the bare pass felt like a distinction.

If his academic performance fell short of brilliance it was not from lack of energy and curiosity. In his school days Firth had travelled widely in New Zealand (school trips on SS *Clansman*) and was captivated by landscape and people. In 1920 he took up geology and began to learn Maori, taking conversation lessons from the Auckland court interpreter. His MA thesis (economics and history) was on the kauri gum industry.

The fossilised resin of the ancient forests of *Agathis australis* had been used for a variety of purposes by the Maori; it became a commodity after European settlement, exported as an ingredient in varnishes until superseded by synthetics in the 1920s. To do this work Firth visited the kauri forests and interviewed the gum-diggers. It got him a First Class, it was published, and was the basis of his first article, published in the *New Zealand Journal of Science and Technology*.

In 1923 he began to teach at Auckland Grammar School and at a Methodist Sunday school while reading for the University Diploma in Social Science. He was drawn more and more to the study of the Maori, and gave early papers to the Anthropology and Maori Race section of the Auckland Institute. His horizons were expanding: he could have become a schoolteacher–scholar, a Methodist figure-head, a pillar of New Zealand society. Instead he began to prepare himself for a wider world. He broke his early engagement to a local woman, daughter of friends of his parents; his father arranged for him to take lessons to diminish his Kiwi accent, and in 1924 he went to study in England: still no scholarship, but a Free Passage awarded by the Senate of Auckland University, and an allowance of £250 p.a. from his generous and committed father. He arrived in London in September and began reading for a thesis on the economies of Polynesia. This (as with many graduate students) was gradually transformed. In fact, on his first day he failed to meet his designated economics supervisor, and having told the School Secretary (Jessie Mair, future wife of Beveridge, mother of Lucy Mair) that he was also interested in a secondary way in anthropology, she sent him to Seligman's office, and Seligman introduced him to Malinowski. In the course of 1925 he narrowed the field to Maori, and under the influence of Seligman and Malinowski and his fellow graduate students, changed to 'a more anthropological approach'. In 1926 the Rockefeller Research Fund committee (administering funds entrusted to LSE) made an award to Malinowski to employ Firth as a research assistant at £2 10*s*. a week, for twenty hours' work. He got his Ph.D. in 1927, and planned fieldwork of an anthropological kind.

He arrived in Sydney in November of that year, meeting Radcliffe-Brown and Hogbin, and decided on Tikopia as his research base. It took him two months to arrive there, and he stayed for fifty weeks. On his return to Australia he was appointed Lecturer in the University of Sydney and remained there for two years. They were the 'golden years' of his early life: congenial company, an active and provocative intellectual life in the university and amongst Sydney's advanced thinkers. In particular he liked and admired Radcliffe-Brown for his pioneering analytical work on Australian Aborigines' kinship systems, and for his glamorous slightly avant-garde social persona. He also realised that Radcliffe-Brown thought more clearly and reasoned more cogently than Malinowski. When Radcliffe-Brown left Sydney for Chicago in 1931, Firth remained as Acting Professor, Acting Chairman of the Department and (the beginning of a long association) Acting Editor of *Oceania*. In 1932 Malinowski offered him a lecturership at the London School of Economics. Firth left Sydney and arrived at LSE in January 1933. In London he led the life of a busy and energetic young academic. He taught, he published, he gave lectures to outside bodies such as the Workers' Educational Association. On Saturday afternoons he played badminton with Beveridge (Director of LSE), Hayek and others, followed by tea at the Waldorf. Or he week-ended, visiting Lucy Mair's family (she was by then a lecturer at LSE) which unconventionally often included Beveridge. He went on holiday in Wales with Evans-Pritchard; on walking tours in the Cotswolds with Michael Postan the economic historian; he spent part of the summers walking in the Dolomites and touring continental Europe, he and others from the Department using a pension near Malinowski's house in Oberbozen as their base.

Malinowski died in 1942. He had been a dominating influence, in work and play, on the young Firth—as teacher, host, employer, patron, colleague. Malinowski could be domineering; he could make appallingly unfunny jokes; he never understood economics—his reading in the sociology of economic life led him to a reactive development of idiosyncratic concepts that lacked the clarity necessary to interest economists in his work. Firth respected the ethnographer for the rest of his life (so far as completeness is concerned the Tikopia corpus is a response to the challenge of Malinowski's works on the Trobriands); his practice as a teacher in seminars seems to have evolved from Malinowski's graduate seminars, although Firth was more concerned perhaps to give each member an opportunity to contribute, his own role was therefore less dominant and less volatile. Firth also maintained the international character of the graduate body at LSE: they welcomed students from all parts of the world, most of whom returned to become prominent in their own countries. In a speech on indigenous anthropologists in 2001, Firth was able to cite the work of eight from Polynesia alone; and of those eight at least half had been students at LSE during Firth's or Malinowski's reign.

He met Rosemary Upcott in 1935. Busy, sociable, polemical, to some extent in the public eye, their engagement was noted in the *Evening Standard* (6 Jan. 1936) 'Dr Raymond Firth, lecturer in social anthropology at the London School of Economics, who has often expressed pronounced views on marriage and divorce, is engaged . . .'. Before their marriage Rosemary had enjoyed an *amitié* with Edmund Leach, then a young engineer. He had gone to work in China for four years, and had developed an interest in anthropology. On his return Rosemary introduced him to Raymond and to LSE where he became a graduate student in 1937. That became a four-sided friendship when Leach married Celia Buckmaster in 1940, and it was of such strength it survived the many intellectual and academic provocations made mostly by Leach in later years.

In 1939 (having failed to get funding for research in China) the Firths learned Malay and arrived in Kelantan via Penang in August. They stayed in the fishing village of Pernpok until the fall of France, when they returned to England via Australia, New Zealand, Panama and Halifax. Crossing the Atlantic their convoy was attacked by the German pocket battleship the *Admiral Scheer*. The sole escort vessel *Jervis Bay*, an armed merchant cruiser, conducted a heroic diversionary action and was sunk with the loss of 190 men. But during the battle, as night fell, most of the rest of the convoy managed to escape; and, although the *Rangitiki* had been reported lost with all hands, they arrived eventually at Milford Haven.

Firth moved at first to Cambridge, where LSE had removed to safety, but in early 1941 he joined the Admiralty's Naval Intelligence division, producing the Handbooks for the Pacific Islands. He also went to the United States in 1942, to assist in the American effort to map and describe the new theatre of war. At this time he prepared *Malay Fishermen, their Peasant Economy* for publication. He turned to London and to Naval Intelligence at Chatham House in 1943, maintaining some academic activity. In June 1944 he was appointed secretary to the new Colonial Social Science Research Council (CSSRC), set up following the Hailey Report of 1938 to provide an empirical basis of knowledge for colonial development after the war. He was employed half-time by the Colonial Office and half-time by the Admiralty.

Later that year he was offered the chair of Anthropology at LSE, in succession to Malinowski, and accepted pending the end of the war. He returned full-time to LSE in December 1945, joining Audrey Richards as a member (rather than functionary) of the CSSRC. At this time Evans-Pritchard was elected to the Chair of Social Anthropology at Oxford. Firth was on the Board, which at one stage offered the position to him.

Firth declined: he had just been appointed to LSE; he believed that Evans-Pritchard was the most suitable candidate.

In 1947 Firth was invited to advise the Australian National University on the creation of a Research School in Pacific Studies, and in March 1948 visited Canberra with Sir Keith Hancock and J. F. Foster as well as the scientists Sir Howard Florey and Sir Marcus Oliphant. The discussions continued into 1949, and in 1950 Firth visited the USA to discover the range of Pacific studies there. He visited ANU again in 1951, was acting Director of the Research School of Pacific Studies, and was invited to become permanent director. He agonised; and after consultation with Rosemary (who had said she would do what he wanted), eventually accepted. Rosemary was then very upset, so Firth changed his mind and declined the appointment. He was able nonetheless to make a field trip to Tikopia (with James Spillius) in March 1952. He was invalided out in September, suffering from acute pneumonia, but was able to visit his family in New Zealand after a convalescence in Australia. In effect the Canberra offer was Firth's last serious temptation to leave LSE, although he was offered a chair at Harvard in the following year. He had become Fellow of the British Academy in 1949, and was President of the Royal Anthropological Institute in 1953–4: he was immersed in teaching and administering in London, making relatively short trips to seminars or to lecture for at most a month or so at (among others) UNESCO, the universities of Chicago and New York, and at Burg Wartenstein. He made a short study of kinship in east London in the early fifties. A six months' fellowship at Palo Alto in 1959 was of particular importance to him: he was able to have his family with him for part of the time; he became more deeply understanding of American anthropology, and made enduring friendships with the social scientists who were also in fellowship. But London became the permanent base for his work. He and Rosemary led a busy life outside the School, going to the theatre, opera and concerts. For instance, in March 1961 they went to plays on six evenings: Shakespeare, Shaw, Marlowe, Fry, Sophocles; he recorded no frivolous entertainment in his diaries.

In his last years at LSE he was able to visit Auckland again, to see his father (who died in 1977, aged 104), and to make a short field-trip to Kelantan (1963), visiting Singapore, Auckland, Montreal and Ann Arbor (1967). After his retirement he made more extensive visits. He was visiting professor at Hawaii for the academic year 1968–9: Alice Dewey, the head of department, had been his student. He spent periods of four to six months as visiting professor at British Columbia (Cyril Belshaw was his former student there), at Cornell, City University of New York, ANU and University of California, Davis. These were all appointments with serious teaching obligations: in each of these places he was welcomed and fêted, but made a point of showing that he was an active and up-to-date anthropologist: not a relaxed panjandrum collecting his laurels, but a serious contributor to the work of his hosts and their students, giving good measure for the honour they did him.

The most striking example of this was in 2001 at the party held in the New Zealand High Commission in London to celebrate his one hundredth birthday. He received the Polynesian Society's Nayacakalou Medal, named for a Fijian anthropologist and politician who had at one time been Firth's doctoral student. Firth, thanking the Society's representative, said that he understood that previous recipients had given a lecture in return. He did not intend to give a lecture, but if he were to, his title would be 'The Creative Contribution of Indigenous People to Their Ethnography'. He expressed doubts about the claim that indigenous people could have an anthropology that was the product of their own culture (an 'indigenous epistemology'): 'I am firmly convinced that the routes to knowledge are not exclusive, but universally shared.' Ethnography was a different matter. Not only had all anthropologists always been indebted to local experts in all social matters, but some anthropologists were natives of the societies they studied: he cited eight of special interest to members of the Polynesian Society, pointing out that they had sometimes perhaps controversially used their insights to 'attempt to redress asymmetry in the current society'. But 'for me ethnography and social anthropology in general as they have developed have been the creation of both alien Western and indigenous contributors' (*Journal of the Polynesian Society*, September 2001, 241–5). Even from a younger person it would have been a remarkable performance: knowledgeable about the personnel, sharp on the issues, restrained, good-humoured—and touched with pride that so many of the people concerned had been his pupils, or Malinowski's.

* * *

Firth visited Tikopia for nearly twelve months in 1927 and again for a few months in 1952, with James Spillius. He made a further one month visit in 1966. The island is quite small (about 3 sq. miles) and then had a population of 1,278 (1,750 in 1952). His main publications derived from this fieldwork were *We the Tikopia*, mainly on kinship and social organisation

(1936, and various subsequent editions); *Primitive Polynesian Economy* (1939, 2nd edn. 1967); *The Work of the Gods in Tikopia* (1940, 2nd edn. 1967); *Tikopia Ritual and Belief* (1967); *Rank and Religion in Tikopia* (1970), and *History and Traditions of Tikopia* (1970). His visit with Spillius resulted in *Social Change in Tikopia: a restudy after a generation* (1959), which included an important account of Tikopia responses to natural disaster. They had suffered hurricanes in January 1952, and consequent famine. Firth showed that Tikopia maintained neighbourly and ceremonial exchanges—in extremis at a token level—above consumption: civility, in short, is more important than naked self-interest, a counter-example to set against fictional (*Lord of the Flies*) and ethnographic (*The Ik*) suggestions that civilisation is a shallow veneer over 'savagery'. His more specialised publications, with co-authors, include *Tikopia String Figures* (1970, with Honor Maude), *Tikopia Songs* (1990, with Mervyn Maclean, including a tape cassette), and *A Tikopia–English Dictionary* (1985, with Ishmael Tuki and Pa Rangiaco). He was especially proud of this last volume, which attested his command of the language, used an extensive system of cross-referencing that indicates the semantic range of words and encapsulated connections amongst Tikopia concepts and institutions. These books and monographs stand alongside innumerable articles and notes and published letters of which the last were 'Tikopia dreams: personal images of social reality' (2001) and 'Linguistic and social patterns of separation and reunion' (posthumously, in 2003).

This may seem to be a rather extensive publication on a rather small number of people, and Firth was aware that his work was cited and sometimes criticised by colleagues whose command of the corpus was scarcely complete. His reply was succinct: we should not imagine that a thousand people living in a territory one eightieth the size of Rutlandshire had less life, less activity, less work to do and fewer dilemmas than smart but callow graduate students lounging around in the LSE canteen. In fact the seven main volumes are vivid, fresh and are not repetitive (Firth marked items in his field notebooks to show that he had used them in published work). He was especially concerned to show that Tikopia lived complex lives, faced moral and political dilemmas, wondered what to do in changing circumstances, and did not always do the same tasks or fulfil their obligations in standard repetitive ways. That concern was not compatible with a terse mode of writing, and his style of anthropology (sharply distinct from that of many of his contemporaries) seemed to demand expansiveness.

Firth's work in Kelantan (fieldwork 1939–40; *Malay Fisherman: their Peasant Economy*, 1946; 2nd edn. rev. and enlarged, 1961; reissue 1998) is not so extensive: his wife Rosemary undertook the research on domestic organisation and kinship matters (published as *Malay Housekeeping*, 1943; 2nd edn. 1963) and war curtailed fieldwork. But it was a detailed account of economic activity which expanded his range: Malay fishermen were dependent on markets and market operators, had relations of debt and credit. They had a peasant rather than a primitive or modern economy, and Firth knew that his analysis of the bargaining between fishermen and their merchants was pioneering. His third main area of ethnographic inquiry was in London. In the 1950s he made a study in the east end of London which was well received: his short book *Two studies of kinship in London* (1956) was an inspiration to Wilmot and Young who founded the Institute of Community Studies, and developed Firth's ideas, not always on lines of which he approved. Further work on kinship in north London resulted in a monograph with Anthony Forge and Jane Hubert, as well as useful papers on research methods describing how they had conducted these innovative inquiries.

Firth also published work in economic anthropology more generally. *Primitive Economics of the New Zealand Maori* (1929) was his Ph.D. Thesis, written before he went to Tikopia. He edited *Capital, Saving and Credit* (1964, with Basil Yamey) and *Themes in Economic Anthropology* (1967). He was always attached to the categories of Western economists, and used 'labour', 'capital', 'property' freely in his analyses of non-Western economies. He never argued (as for example Polanyi and Sahlins did) that different kinds of economy were based on different principles and needed different kinds of economics. He was at pains to describe how concepts of proven worth such as 'property' might vary from place to place and from time to time. That in turn might lead economists to a more nuanced understanding of their matter. In his last years he was much concerned that economists had begun to write about culture, and that some anthropologist should comment sharply on their works.

In 1972 Firth gave the inaugural Radcliffe-Brown lecture 'The Sceptical Anthropologist? Social Anthropology and Marxist views on society' (*Proc. Brit. Acad.*, 58) in which he argued that Marx's views on primitive society and economy were 'amorphous'. Engels and Lafargue, he said, represented an 'out-dated arid evolutionary position'. Marx's account of pre-capitalist economic formations, crucially under-informed, was no use at all as an account of primitive, Asiatic or communalist societies; but even myths might be useful, though perhaps only as points of contestation or departure. He was politely scornful of the mainly French anthropologists who argued that 'kinship . . . serves as both infrastructure and superstructure': the point was not to find equivalents of Marx's fundamental categories in this or that primitive society, but to ask Marxist questions about real people doing real things. In particular, Firth thought that anthropologists' attention might be drawn to aspects of non-western society that their traditional training had hitherto led them to ignore. For instance, it was no harm to explore occasions of conflict and contradiction rather than to be set on discovering cohesion and harmony. In the sometimes bitter arguments about the role of social anthropology in imperial and colonial domination he took the line that British anthropologists had (within the limits of their training and avocation) been as impartial and balanced as it was reasonable to expect: they were not colonial officers, but more like the factory and health inspectors whose reports on conditions in nineteenth-century England had informed the work of both Marx and Engels, and whose competence, accuracy and freedom from bias were essential to socialist or any other kind of analysis.

Firth's lecture showed great learning not only in the canons of Marxist literature, but in the fragmented and often tiresome writings of the *groupuscules marxisants* of the 1960s. But he remained Firthian: he was interested for example in the attempts, by Salisbury among others, to measure objective labour value in non-monetary economies, and to compare the anthropologists' assessments (based on time spent) with 'the natives'. He was interested in what could be tested, and in what that might contribute to our understanding of human action. His combination of learning with empiricism brought to bear on manageable conceptual issues was typical of his work. It was as if he thought that an attack on high theoretical systems was futile: it was more sensible to put major or all-encompassing intellectual constructs to one side, and to examine the bricks to understand their strength and usefulness; so, not Marxism–Leninism, but labour-value and the actual forms of production in Asia.

His account of property rights in Tikopia is classic. 'Enquiries as to land ownership in Tikopia elicit a description in one of four different ways', indicating a series of overlapping and reversionary rights. Ownership in any of its four versions was not exclusive: people might borrow land, especially but not exclusively for seasonal crops, with only retrospective token acknowledgement of an 'owner's' rights. The topic is introduced in *We the Tikopia* and discussed rigorously in *Primitive Polynesian Economy*—in the chapter firmly and provocatively entitled 'Property and

Capital in Production'. He did not look for analogues of the components of western economic systems: he took the concepts, and showed that they were complex, flexible, and more varied than western economists believed.

Another example of Firth's determined occupation of the middle range is his remarks on Marcel Mauss's *The Gift*. Mauss had proposed three obligations: to give, to receive, to make a return. Firth denied that they were in fact 'universally mandatory'. Empirical investigation showed that each of the three contained 'significant areas of choice and uncertainty', and showed too that people did not in fact always meet their obligations. Mauss, concerned to establish why people everywhere sought to make a return for gifts received, had proposed that all gifts partake of an archetypical gift which he thought he had discovered as a survival in Polynesia. They spoke of *hau*, the 'spirit of the thing given', which sought always to return to its origin and which made recipients of gifts uncomfortable if this need of *hau* was unrequited. Most sceptics might take a radical line, arguing against the possibility that a universal phenomenon could be explained by Polynesian ethnography. Firth, however, showed that *hau* did not mean what Mauss claimed it did, and that it was much more limited in effect than Mauss had thought. If you wanted to explain the need to return a gift you had to look at the sanctions others could apply to a defaulter—loss of status, loss of future gifts, loss of ritual or religious standing. Firth seems never to have had a root-and-branch instinct, but undermined the grandiose propositions of his predecessors and contemporaries with empirical reasoning.

A final example, from Firth's explorations in religious and conceptual anthropology, is in his article 'Twins, Birds and Vegetables' (*Man*, NS I i. 1966). Lienhardt had reported that Dinka occasionally said that some men were lions, and appeared to mean that they were essentially lions who took human form. Similarly, Evans-Pritchard had written about Nuer that they said 'twins are birds'. The question was what they meant or thought: Evans-Pritchard maintained that the identification was not metaphorical, but was part of a 'complex analogical representation which requires to be explained in more general terms of Nuer religious thought'. Firth proposed that in each case the 'are' implied an identification of men and lions, twins and birds, and that the evidence in neither man's work was sufficient to explore the possible meanings. He was constructive: Tikopia evidence (reviewed at some length and with acute precision) suggested that there were at least three ways in which people might identify themselves or others, or things, with spiritual beings, and he proposed

that lions were one kind, twins another. If you examined the psychological and social patterns to distinguish the kinds of identification, you
might then suggest what consequences that might have for general analysis of, for example, totemism. Evans-Pritchard replied perhaps rather eva-
sively in the correspondence pages of *Man*: if Firth had shown him the
article in advance he would have been able to discuss Nuer ideas in detail,
and to make suggestions about Firth's reading of his work; as matters
stood he could only correct some matters of fact. Firth's reply was 'that
in dealing with such a delicate and difficult matter as description of belief
we need as much evidence as possible, both of what the people concerned
say and of what they have been observed to do. When the people themselves do not state their beliefs in direct terms, the indirect evidence
needs to be even more carefully marshalled, with the investigator's
generalisations supported by concrete data.'

Firth, by inclination and ability, worked always with middle-range
ideas. When many of his contemporaries spoke of structure or structuralism, he spoke of organisation. His friends at the time saw him as
bridging the alleged abyss between Radcliffe-Brown's structuralism and
Malinowski's functionalism, but in later life Firth denied this: he had
not sought to mediate. He had achieved a distinct position which arose
he said from his training in economics and from his experience of
Tikopia. Structures may very well exist, but they are inaccessible to
observation. What could be seen and conveyed to others were the
week-to-week or year-to-year arrangements that men and women made
to meet obligations and to satisfy social and material needs. Social
organisation required coordination and agreement; it depended on
imprecise rules ('room for manœuvre' as his colleague Lucy Mair called
it), and it required time. Social organisation is the 'systematic ordering
of social relations by acts of choice and decision'. Such acts followed
on from others; situations differed one from another, were never exactly
replicated, and the choices and decisions were not always the same—
they might be, for instance, cautious or tentative solutions to dilemmas.
Firth thought that structure was the outcome of repeated acts of
organisation: it consisted of precedents, each of them an approxima-
tion to some set of expectations about how people should do things
properly. It was not a permanent and constraining univocal controller,
but set conventional more or less fragile limits to the range of things
people might choose from, and was itself affected by the organisational
choices made each and every day, week, year. Firth diminished structure: it was a distillate of past practice, was never precise enough to

eliminate the need for choice and could hardly be permanent or positively constraining. You might think Firth could have abandoned 'structure' altogether: 'organisation' is sufficiently explanatory. But that would have required him to make a full-scale assault on an item of high and imprecise theory: that was not his style, and he was content to elaborate the intermediate range. Firth laid the foundations of this pattern or habit of thought in the 1920s, and although he developed and expanded it in successive works, he maintained it against persuasive fashion for seventy years.

Firth characteristically used the past tense in his ethnography:

> ... at the time of an incision ceremony in Rofaea, Pa Niukapu made a double journey to Matafana and back after dark in pouring rain to see how his children were. He knew they were sleeping with their grandmother, in no discomfort, but he wished to be assured of their well being. As he was a mother's brother of one of the initiates he had to return again to Rofaea to sleep. (Firth, *We the Tikopia*, 1936)

It is vivid, located in time and space and weather, conveying the contingency of action and the intersection of motives and proscription. By describing several rituals, boat-building parties, feasts—and indeed, how Tikopia coped in the aftermath of a hurricane—he was able to build up a picture of what was distinctive in economy, politics, kinship, religion; to suggest its fluidity and adaptability. If you compare the account Evans-Pritchard gives of a similar sort of event, the differences are marked and clear:

> Each village acts independently in arranging for its boys to be initiated. After the operation the boys live in partial seclusion and are subject to various taboos. ... Only age-mates of the father of the initiate in whose homestead the feasting takes place attend it: others keep at a distance lest they see the nakedness of their kinswomen and mothers-in-law. (Evans-Pritchard, *The Nuer*, 1940)

The two passages deal with initiation, but in very different ways. Evans-Pritchard described the general and habitual practice of 'Nuer', in the ethnographic present tense. His actors were villages or age-sets. He wished to insert his account of the ritual practice into an account of a structure of relations among age-mates (which is itself part of a structure of lineages and tribes). And his use of the ethnographic present here and elsewhere allowed him to elide implicitly into an account of what he claimed were enduring principles of social structure. Firth wrote in the past tense, and was concerned with knowledge, with motives and experience: named people in named places, expressing purpose and doing things within a framework of permission and prohibition.

Evans-Pritchard and Firth had been friends since Firth's arrival at LSE. Firth drank his first glass of wine with Evans-Pritchard (at l'Escargot in Soho in September 1924); they went on holiday together. The first sign of a rift occurred after Firth had supported Evans-Pritchard in the election to the Oxford Chair of Social Anthropology in 1946. As early as 1937 Firth had proposed (in a memorandum to the Colonial Office on 'the utilisation of anthropological services') 'the appointment in each territory of a specific Government Anthropologist'. Post-war, he and Audrey Richards, members of the CSSRC, argued that research to support HM Government's efforts at development in the colonies should be based in universities in the colonies. The researchers would have a secure local base; the universities would acquire multi-disciplinary teams with local members as well as semi-attached expatriates who would be in close touch with local administrators. The model in Richards's mind became the Institute for Social Research at Makerere, of which she was the first Director (1950–6). Firth had made extensive tours in West Africa (July–October 1945) and in Malaya and Singapore (July–October 1947) to review the possibilities, and was wholly supportive.

Evans-Pritchard took another view: the research should be based in Britain. Young researchers would be trained, for example, in 'pure' anthropology in British universities, and would then do fieldwork overseas, returning after a year or two to write up their theses. In 1948 Evans-Pritchard persuaded the newly-created Association of Social Anthropologists (of which he was Chairman, Firth Hon. Secretary) to send a deputation to the Colonial Secretary mandated to argue for the Britain-based scheme. They were well-received, but the government opted for the proposal from Richards and Firth. Firth referred to this as 'a mild contretemps', and he bore no lasting malice. It was, however, the first step towards a deterioration of relations. They were on mismatched good terms: Evans-Pritchard acknowledged Firth's personal qualities and kindnesses, but increasingly mistrusted his anthropology. Firth had been active in securing Evans-Pritchard's election to the British Academy, and Evans-Pritchard wrote 'This, I fancy, could only be your doing, and it is chiefly for that reason I am accepting. This adds to your many acts of generosity, none of which I forget' (13 June 1956). But at the same time he found Firth's anthropology lacking in grand ambition. Moreover, the LSE Department under Firth acquired a character as pragmatic, involved with government, busy in the world in ways which were inimical to pure anthropologists. Evans-Pritchard disapproved, and wrote that Firth 'had chosen mammon'. For his part Firth acknowledged Evans-Pritchard's intellectual gifts, with reservations. He can hardly have been comfortable with an anthropology that was conceived to reveal 'a structure of relations among relations'. The ideas in Evans-Pritchard's *Witchcraft, Oracles and Magic* were not wholly original—they were 'perhaps more commonly shared than he imagined'; he had not done justice to Margaret Mead; he paid scant regard to the work of his juniors in the discipline. Firth was uncomfortable with Evans-Pritchard's religiosity, and with the personality cult that grew up in the coterie that surrounded him. Oxford anthropologists in the 1950s and 1960s did cultivate the idea that their work was æsthetically and intellectually on a higher plane than anthropology elsewhere. In spite of these faults he regarded Evans-Pritchard as the most brilliant man of their generation, and admired him for it. But Firth seems to have received rather few acts of generosity or good will after the mid-1950s.

Edmund Leach, too, disapproved of the changing nature of the LSE Department. Leach had been a graduate student in 1938–9, and again in 1946–7; thereafter a lecturer. But he left for a post in Cambridge in 1953, expressing his dissatisfaction. It is clear that Leach thrived on controversy, perhaps especially with friends and colleagues in nearest proximity, and that he was an enthusiast for new ideas and schemata. Firth recognised and admired his qualities, but responded always with *distinguos*. To take an example from towards the end of Leach's life: in 1987 at the conference of the Association of Social Anthropologists Leach maintained that all ethnography was 'fiction': human creativity determined the presentation of fieldwork to a scholarly audience, and to pretend that it was in any sense objective was a fundamental mistake. Firth's off-the-cuff response was measured. (The story that Firth began his reply 'You may well speak for yourself but not for other ethnographers' does not correspond to the memory of those present, and is uncharacteristically waspish.) Ethnographers were human, he said, and it was necessarily true that their creativity was involved in their writings. But not all creativities were the same: anthropologists were trained quite differently from novelists or poets. They were obviously influenced by assumptions current in their own societies, indeed he had pointed this out himself in 1969. If you wished to distinguish good ethnographers from bad ones, you did so by reference to the reality they gave an account of. All this he delivered in calm and unprovoked terms, knowing quite well that Leach at any rate for part of the time did indeed think that the true excitement of anthropology lay in spinning fine theories derived as it might be from topology, from structuralism, from communication theory or, in this case, from relativistic postmodernism. To Leach's perpetual and exhilarating exuberance Firth responded as the bourgeois who refused to be *épaté*. In its own way this was as provoking to Leach as Leach had hoped to be to Firth.

Firth's principled refusal to abandon the middle range exasperated the fireworks men and women of the three decades 1950–80. Marxists, as well as structuralists and postmodernists and the many other more aleatory -ists of the time, all got the treatment: learned, calm, gentle, empirical, coupled with acute caution about highfalutin theory. They thought and said that Firth was atheoretical, and Leach (typically) wrote that Firth's aspiration to write anthropological theory was like a clown's desire to play Hamlet. It is certain that Firth was less flashy than some of his pyrotechnical contemporaries; certain too, that they could not recognise that what Firth did was firmly theoretical (if it didn't flash for them it wasn't theory). His emphasis on organisation, on motives and dilemmas, his proposal that structure was the outcome of continuously renewed organisation were important elements of an established and thoughtful theoretical position. It is at present a matter of speculation whether Firth noted that, twenty years later, many British anthropologists applauded Bourdieu's invention of the concept *habitus*, giving special emphasis to human motives and dilemmas, and proposing that structures grew out of perpetually modified acts of conformity and convention.

Firth was brought up a Methodist, abandoning his ancestral religion sometime in the 1920s, perhaps between his first glass of wine (1924) and his lecture on *The Soul* to the Sydney Free Thought Society in 1932. He told Peter Loizos that fieldwork in Tikopia had changed him profoundly: Tikopia had no Methodist restrictions, and still managed to live relatively orderly lives, and had a sense of morals and made moral judgements.

He became a 'practising humanist' and a member of the Rationalist Press Association. He nevertheless wrote constantly about religion. Evans-Pritchard had been received into the church of Rome in Benghazi in 1944, and came eventually to declare that people without faith could not really understand religion. Firth's response was that losing a faith (as he had done) might be as good a key to understanding as acquiring one (as Evans-Pritchard had). In his three volumes on Tikopia religion, and in his numerous lectures and articles—the nine most significant in Firth's estimation collected in *Religion: a Humanist Interpretation* (1966)—Firth asserted that religious activity, concerned with gods, was therefore concerned ultimately with ineffable ideas. But it also served more mundane purposes: it purported to answer otherwise unanswerable questions, and thus brought psychological comfort and reassurance to believers. Religion often encapsulated moral ideas, regulating conduct. Ritual mobilised economic goods, and a church could be 'a sociological force of great impact'. Both ritual and a church can stimulate artistic creativity of a sublime order as well as violence and oppression. All this was susceptible to analysis by sociologists and social anthropologists. In short, religions were not mysterious: Firth was interested in what religionists in all their variety found mysterious, but thought that this would be discovered and described using plain language, common sympathy and respect, together with scrupulous ethnography. Of course, no understanding was perfect; but in essence understanding religions was no different from understanding economies or polities. He thought both that religions were human creations, made from specific intellectual, experiential, æsthetic resources, and that Durkheim's grand dictum that societies created their gods in their own image was 'oversimplified'.

In this he was true to himself and to his tried methods of analysis. Although he had no faith and thought that the prohibitions of Methodism were tiresome, he retained to some extent the style of his early Christianity-moulded childhood. Then, he said, he had found immense happiness in simple things: a party could be a real party with only tea and lemonade. His tastes in later life were less austere, but he enjoyed himself seriously. And perhaps because of his awareness of his lost faith he treated religious issues rather reverently; certainly his language became more portentous.

Firth was a centenarian. His contemporaries, who witnessed his formative years, predeceased him; we can know little of that time, or of the personal course he ran to become the man we knew. His early married life, with many absences abroad, was perhaps not always easy. But he and Rosemary achieved an intellectual and emotional conjugality 'in argument and agreement' and she was 'the most important personal influence' on his life, for more than sixty years (Rosemary died in 2001). From his writing we can see that his general approach to anthropology was formed fairly early: he was an organisation man from the 1930s, both in his theory and in his administrative activities. He maintained the intellectual position of the empiricist, the theorist of the middle range, firmly, calmly, sensibly for the next seventy years. In administration he was a consistent and fair-minded advocate for anthropology at home and abroad. In the School he built a serious and humanely engaged international department of great renown. His students were intensely loyal, but he never asked them to become Firthians.

J. H. R. DAVIS
Fellow of the Academy

Note. In writing this memoir I have been greatly assisted by John Drury, Hugh Firth, Jean La Fontaine, Peter Loizos, David Mills, and David Parkin. They are not responsible for errors, but they have added greatly to its depth and range.

Firth's papers are mainly deposited in the archives of the London School of Economics; a complete bibliography is retained by the School.

HROTHGAR JOHN HABAKKUK   *B. J. Harris*

Hrothgar John Habakkuk
1915–2002

AN OUTSTANDING ECONOMIC HISTORIAN, greatly admired Principal of Jesus College Oxford for seventeen years, and a distinguished Vice-Chancellor of Oxford University, Hrothgar John Habakkuk was born on 13 May 1915 in Barry, Glamorgan. His very rare name, which was to cause spelling problems for generations of undergraduates, he owed to a seventeenth-century ancestor's choice of surname, in which he had given free rein to the Welsh sense of affinity with Old Testament Prophets. Hrothgar, as he was always known by his friends before the 1970s, derived from the chance that his father, Evan Guest Habakkuk, happened to be reading *Beowulf* at the time of his son's birth, and this forename was also to cause trouble, not only with its spelling. Later on, as will transpire, he experienced the sea change of becoming 'Sir John' and 'John' as a response to the euphonics of a knighthood and to spare the anxieties over how to handle 'Hrothgar' of a public which was increasingly unfamiliar with the *Beowulf* story. His mother, Anne, was by all accounts a strong and determined, not to say formidable, woman—in this most rationalist of families she told her son when he not unreasonably objected to going to Sunday school, that it was far better than mooning around the house reading the newspaper, and packed him off to good effect: well over three-quarters of a century later he remembered clearly that it was his Band of Hope teacher who first introduced him to St David.[1] Anne's mother, Hrothgar's maternal grandmother, died in 1884 when her daughter was eighteen months old, and this catastrophe—along with cheap

---

[1] H. J. Habakkuk, sermon in Jesus College, Oxford, on St David's Day, 2000.

Proceedings of the British Academy, **124**, 91–114. © The British Academy 2004.

American grain—drove his maternal grandfather, a Welsh-speaking Montgomeryshire farmer, to work in the Aberfan colliery. Hrothgar's paternal grandfather, a mining engineer, was killed in a mining accident in 1887. These family misfortunes gave Hrothgar an abiding sense that life is precarious and that chance may bring some unforeseen disaster. This— and of course the experience of coming to maturity in the 1930s—goes a long way towards explaining the streak of caution and circumspection in both his scholarship and his university administration.

The move off the land and down the Aberfan mines was not an unmit- igated downward slide for the family, as it provided the setting and means for Anne to become a pupil teacher at the age of thirteen, to go on to teacher training, and to become a school teacher in Barry. She always bit- terly regretted that the general public-service rule of the times compelled her to abandon her teaching career on marriage. This undoubtedly was a powerful influence on Hrothgar's determination, when he had the oppor- tunity, to further the education of women. The importance of education was the central lesson of his childhood. His father had been obliged to leave school at fourteen, but later through the support of an uncle was able to go to the university college at Aberystwyth, although not able to afford to stay long enough to get an honours degree. After a spell of school-teaching, Evan Guest then became a local government official, as Secretary to the Education Committee of Barry Council and clerk to the governors of Barry County School and of its sister girls school. This parental combination of learning and teaching furnished an upbringing in which books, serious discussion and argument, and a nonconformist ethic tempered with the agnosticism fostered by rationalist thinking, were the main formative influences. His great schoolfriend, Bryan Hopkin— later Chief Economic Adviser to the Treasury—on his first visit to the Habakkuk home was disconcerted when Hrothgar asked him what he thought was the most important common element in the world's religions, not a subject which figured in the Hopkin household's normal discourse (nor a subject which much occupied Hrothgar's mind in later life).

Alongside his family, Barry and Barry County School were the impor- tant formative factors in his early years. Barry, he later pointed out, as an entirely new town was very special in having a precise birthday: 14 November 1884 when the excavation of the dock and the construction of the Barry Railway began. Hrothgar's father, although born on a farm, was brought to live in Barry in 1886, and he was brought there because after his father was killed in a mining accident his mother remarried to a miner, who then came to work as a coal-tipper in the Barry dock. This was John Hughes, Hrothgar's step grandfather, still working as a tipper in the 1920s when his step grandson talked with him at the docks.[2] Barry in the 1920s still felt like a pioneer town, its oldest inhabitants all incomers from the Welsh hinterland or from across the Severn (there was a regular paddle-steamer service between Weston-super-Mare and Cardiff), and something of the feeling of excitement, novelty, and intensity of living on a frontier in a boom town had survived the First World War, even though Barry had lost for ever its pre-1914 atmosphere of headlong expansion as the largest coal-exporting port in the world. Barry was being reinvented as a seaside resort with the beaches of Barry Island, but the docks and coal remained the core of the town's economy. Hrothgar recalled that an east wind on a Monday was still a major menace—the coal dust from the coal-tips played havoc with the washing on the clothes lines. The atmosphere was not all grime and hard work: a community was being forged by very active music, literary, and dramatic societies, sports clubs, and lively local politics. There is no record of any sporting interest—beyond a recollection of the town's devastation when the local doctor's horse, Little Titch, came last in the Derby—but Hrothgar did recall taking part when he was only ten years old in fierce arguments over the merits of candidates in a local council election; his performance as Orsino in *Twelfth Night* was long remembered; and he sang with gusto the school song, 'To our town where mighty Severn opens to the Ocean Blue . . .'

The institutions which shaped the community were the churches and chapels, more than forty of them, and the schools. The influence of the former is problematic, while that of Barry County School is unambiguous. It is true that in his St David's Day sermon Habakkuk spoke in personal terms of religion 'as we experienced it' in the interwar years. He sang the great Welsh hymns, took to heart the message that 'we are pilgrims through a barren land', and witnessed the fervour and austerity of Welsh nonconformity at first hand. He experienced religion, however, as a moral code and system of ethics, not as something entailing faith, doctrine, theology, and worship; it provided a set of rules for the conduct of life. These rules were replete with prohibitions: 'there were a great many "thou-shall-nots" . . . there was no talk of self-fulfilment and a great deal about duty, obligation, and conformity'.[3] Undoubtedly these rules did much to shape Hrothgar's own work ethic and sense of duty; but at the

---

[2] H. J. Habakkuk, MS notes of a speech given at the launch of D. Moore, ed., *Barry: the centenary book* (Barry, Glamorgan, 1984).
[3] Habakkuk, sermon on St David's Day, 2000.

same time their narrowness and joylessness contributed to his youthful rebellion against what he felt to be the parochialism of life in Barry.

Barry County School, on the other hand, was the gateway to the wider world. His father, as secretary to the governors, may have sat at a table in the playground collecting the admission fees from new boys, but Hrothgar got into the school entirely through his own success in the competitive scholarship examination. Barry had a notably progressive local education authority, and the County School had an outstanding head-master, Major Edgar Jones, 'the Thomas Arnold of Wales'. Both the history masters, David Williams and Ifor Powell, later became university lecturers and professors, and they started a Barry tradition of schooling distinguished academic historians, which over the twentieth century included David Joslin (Cambridge Professor of Economic History, 1965–70), Sir Keith Thomas, FBA, and Martin Daunton, FBA as well as Hrothgar himself. His contemporary schoolfellows included Glyn Daniels, future Cambridge Professor of Archaeology, as well as Bryan Hopkin. He and Hrothgar in 1931 won two of the four 'Geneva Scholarships' offered each year by the Welsh League of Nations Union to sixth-formers, scholarships which financed their attendance at a Summer School in Geneva devoted to the League of Nations and international relations. This cemented the Habakkuk–Hopkin axis and sharpened their interest in, and knowledge of, international affairs.[4] Together they won scholarships to St John's, Cambridge, in 1933, Hopkin to read Economics, Habakkuk History.

Hrothgar, already a teenage socialist who had been active in the school debating society, spent much time as a Cambridge undergraduate discussing politics, and went to many meetings with Bryan Hopkin— whose friendship doubtless kept him abreast, also, of the new economics of Keynes and Joan Robinson. Hrothgar was strongly anti-communist, having been greatly impressed by a talk in the local chapel early in 1933, given by Gareth Jones (son of headmaster Edgar Jones) who had just spent the winter in the Ukraine: he spoke of the catastrophic famine caused by forcible collectivisation that he had seen at first hand. Hrothgar was also influenced by his dock-side conversations with his step grandfather, who greatly disliked the local communists and thought they were dishonest rogues. At Cambridge he used to argue with his brilliant contemporary John Cornford, the communist poet and womaniser later killed in the Spanish Civil War, whose irresponsibility shocked Hrothgar

---

[4] Bryan Hopkin, *A Short Account of My Life* (privately printed, 2003), p. 7.

almost as much as his politics. 'What I most hated about the communists,' he wrote in the last month of his life, 'was their millenarian element—the belief that a million or so deaths were well worth the coming of the age of prosperity and peace which they would inevitably bring about. I used to argue with Cornford whom I now think was much less sensible and well informed than my father's stepfather.'[5]

Hrothgar's experience of 'red Cambridge' was exhilarating, but limited: he had no contact with the famous Cambridge spies, though he did know George Barnard, also at St John's, 'the chief local commissar of the student Communist Party'—who ended up as Professor of Mathematics at Essex University and President of the Royal Statistical Society.[6] The academic experience was decisive in shaping his life. Hrothgar distinguished himself in the Tripos, and what he remembered years later were the lectures of the Professor of Economic History, J. H. Clapham, packed with information, a descriptive treatment of Britain's economic history from before the Conquest to the end of the nineteenth century, replete with anecdotes and curious facts; but above all he recalled the sheer ebullience and intellectual excitement of Munia Postan's lectures, darting about from nineteenth-century movements of capital and labour to fourteenth-century agrarian crises, and grounded in the latest continental teachings of figures—Sombart and Bloch, for example—who were virtually unknown in Cambridge. It was, Hrothgar recalled in his address at the memorial service for Sir Michael Postan, 'an entirely fresh vision of economic history'.[7] All the same when he decided in 1936 to stay on at Cambridge to do historical research he at first proposed as his field, for reasons he failed to recall, not any economic history, but Dutch Arminianism in the seventeenth century. He rapidly dropped that idea, and Clapham, who was to be his supervisor (but not for a Ph.D., for which he never registered, it not being the done thing at that time for high-fliers) suggested that he should research the industrial revolution in South Wales. He rejected that topic also, partly because he regarded the history of South Wales as parochial, and perhaps partly because in his socialist phase he was out of sympathy with the great industrial capitalists like the coal owner David Davies, the creator of Barry. Looking back in

---

[5] H. J. Habakkuk to Sir Bryan Hopkin, 21 Oct. 2002. For a sympathetic, not to say adulatory, view of Cornford see Eric Hobsbawm, *Interesting Times* (2002), esp. chap. 8.

[6] Hobsbawm, *Interesting Times*, p. 116. Habakkuk had picked up this reference, sign of the enduring alertness of his mind, and his voracious reading: HJH to Hopkin, 21 Oct. 2002.

[7] H. J. Habakkuk, address at the memorial service for Sir Michael Postan, 13 Feb. 1982 (*Peterhouse Record*, 1981/82)

retirement it was a decision he rather regretted, maybe a lost opportunity. For the rest of us it was a decision which cleared the way for Hrothgar to become the pioneering historian of English landownership, although he claimed that this happened completely by accident. Postan returned to Cambridge one day from the newly formed Northampton Record Office (virtually the single-handed creation of Joan Wake), where he had been immersed in manorial records, bubbling over with enthusiasm for the richness of the sources there, and announced that Hrothgar positively had to seize the opening for creating a completely new field of historical enquiry, the history of the eighteenth-century Northamptonshire gentry from their private family records.

When reminiscing in his eighties about this momentous step he claimed it was taken entirely under the almost hypnotic influence of Postan's supremely confident and exuberant pronouncements. An interest in landowners, however, was not without some roots in Hrothgar's own youth, for he remembered as a boy speculating about the vivid contrast between the new Barry of the coal-tips and the old Barry of neighbouring Porthkerry Park, 'the almost feudal estate of Lord Romilly', where he often went walking. And he claimed that an interest in the effects of the marriages of Welsh heiresses to English and Scottish husbands was a question 'which occurred naturally to a schoolboy in Glamorgan in the 1920s when the Marquess of Bute, the Mackintosh of Mackintosh, the Earl of Dunraven, and the Earl of Plymouth were still great names'.[8] In later life he wondered whether it had not been a mistake to plunge into the landownership subject at the deep end, into the vast piles of extremely wordy and abstruse title deeds—which were also physically difficult to handle—that formed the bulk of the available family records, when it might have been better to start with the more easily accessible printed private estate acts (a series starting in the later eighteenth century) with their random national coverage and their evidence about the legal deficiencies in the circumstances and powers of individual landowners which they were concerned to remedy.[9] It is certainly true that his pathbreaking contributions to the history of landownership all came to derive fundamentally from close scrutiny of legal instruments—marriage settlements, wills, conveyances, and the like—where later historians would tend to use

---

[8] Habakkuk, speech at launch of *Barry: the centenary book*. H. J. Habakkuk, 'Marriage and the Ownership of Land', in R. R. Davies, R. A. Griffiths, I. G. Jones, and K. O. Morgan, eds. *Welsh Society and Nationhood: Historical Essays Presented to Glanmor Williams* (Cardiff, 1984), p. 182.
[9] Video-interview with Sir John Habakkuk by N. B. Harte, 17 March 2001, for the Economic History Society series (to be deposited in LSE).

other sources, such as family or business correspondence, and estate accounts, as their starting points. Thus it came about that Hrothgar was launched into research where the key to understanding the documents was some familiarity with the technicalities not simply of the laws of real property, but of obsolete laws of real property. For the rest of his life he was enthralled—though not continuously—by this austere discipline: in his retirement in the 1980s, it is recorded, 'a colleague remembers seeing him in the Law Library [of the Bodleian], poring over abstruse works on land law, with, on his face, a look of beatific contentment'.[10]

The last four years of the 1930s were spent in preparing for his dramatic arrival on the academic scene (if overshadowed by other events), with the publication in 1940 of two substantial pieces, one an acutely perceptive treatment of an established subject, the chapter on 'Free Trade and Commercial Expansion, 1853–70' in the *Cambridge History of the British Empire*, and the other the highly original article on 'English Landownership, 1680–1740', which opened up an entirely new field of study. In 1938 he became a Fellow of Pembroke College, and it is possible that his venture into imperial economic history arose out of lectures and tutorials [sc. supervisions in Cambridge] he was giving on nineteenth-century subjects. Although it was an excursion into territory to which he never returned, this chapter has all those qualities of clarity, lucidity, logical exposition, and judicious employment of economic theory, which were to become the hallmarks of his scholarship. Moreover it contains distinct anticipations of concepts such as informal empire, and multilateral settlements of international payments, which were only to be fully articulated, many years later, by other historians.[11] This capacity for initiating or anticipating future lines of enquiry and interpretation, cultivated by his mentor Postan, was also to be characteristic of Hrothgar's most influential work.

The bulk of his research time, however, was spent on the Northamptonshire records. Some of the time was in Lamport Hall, where Joan Wake was busy establishing a private enterprise county record office. Here Hrothgar was startled by the abrupt and hectoring manner with which Joan Wake treated a scruffily dressed old man who kept on asking for her help in deciphering the medieval Latin script of documents he was

[10] Keith Thomas, Address at the Memorial Service for Sir Hrothgar John Habakkuk, 8 Feb. 2003 (printed by All Souls College, Oxford), p. 13.
[11] H. J. Habakkuk, 'Free Trade and Commercial Expansion, 1853–1870', in J. Holland Rose, A. P. Newton, and E. Benians, eds., *Cambridge History of the British Empire*, vol. 2, *The New Empire, 1783–1870* (Cambridge, 1940), pp. 751–805.

studying, telling him he ought to try to master some elementary palaeo-
graphical skills before wasting her time. Curious to find out who the victim of this bullying was, Hrothgar stole a glance at the visitors' register,
only to see the cryptic signature 'Spencer'. The hapless researcher was
none other than the donor of most of the records Joan Wake had collected, engrossed in looking at his own family papers and enjoying her
badinage. This episode doubtless led eventually to Hrothgar's gaining
access to the Althorp muniments that had not yet been transferred to
Lamport Hall, and to his legendary encounter with the law. It seems that
in the early days of the blackout in the autumn of 1939, while hurriedly
completing the research for his landownership article, he was working far
into the evening when a policeman saw a light in the muniment room and
a figure crouched by the safe. Asked what he thought he was doing, he
replied that he was studying eighteenth-century landownership. Naturally
such an implausible activity aroused the suspicions of a rural constable,
who then demanded to know his name. On being told it was Habakkuk,
he remarked 'And I suppose your first name is Jehovah', to which the
innocent reply was 'No, it's Hrothgar', which confirmed the constable's
sense that he was being mocked. So Hrothgar was marched off to the
police station, where his attempt to establish his identity by citing the
equally improbably named Munia Postan as his referee simply prolonged
his detention, until straightforward Sir John Clapham could be contacted
to vouch for him.

The seminal landownership article marked out both a lifelong interest and the starting point for a group of followers who have developed
the modern history of the subject in the same way that followers of
Postan developed the history of medieval landownership and tenure. In
this article he announced the social and economic significance of
Orlando Bridgeman's invention of the legal device of trustees to preserve contingent remainders—the essential feature of what became
known as 'strict settlements' of landed families' estates, as distinct from
the more easily overturned and unreliable instruments that family
lawyers had been using before the Interregnum to provide for the line of
possession and succession to estates. The purpose of these new-style
trustees, normally created in the dispositions for succession to the family estates contained in the deed of settlement made on the marriage of
the heir to an estate (hence known as 'marriage settlements') or in his
will, was to protect the rights to succeed of specified children, most
probably as yet unborn, or of more remote relatives, and thus to prevent
the owner for the time being (or tenant-for-life) from selling off the fam-

ily estate, or frustrating these 'remainders' through any other action. The relatively rapid adoption of this new form of settlement, which by the end of the seventeenth century had become normal practice in all landed families, Habakkuk argued, was a major factor in halting a previous tendency for landed estates to be broken up or subdivided through sales and inheritance patterns, and in establishing a new tendency for estates to be preserved intact from generation to generation, with younger sons and daughters provided for in portions secured as charges on the family estate, rather than in mini-estates or parcels of land carved out of father's property. Coupled with the new willingness of the courts to uphold the 'equity of redemption', which made lenders on mortgage more wary in calling in debts from landowners, these developments in land law, consolidated during the Restoration, played a major part in favouring the growth and security of large estates. At the same time, the argument ran, the greater landowners were better able to cope with the rising taxation of the Marlborough wars, especially with the new land tax, than either the country gentry or more especially the smaller freehold landowners—what remained of the former English peasantry. Hence the sixty years after 1680 witnessed the rise of the landed aristocracy at the expense of both gentry and peasantry. Thus was sketched a neat counterpoint to the coming doctrine of the rise of the gentry as the key feature of the century 1540–1640, although Tawney's classic article was not published until a year after Habakkuk's.[12]

Over the following half century the Habakkuk thesis of the rise of the great estates generated great interest, stimulating ever more rigorous research as more and more landowners' archives became accessible, and sustaining a large volume of publications, many of them increasingly controversial. In contrast to the sometimes vitriolic controversy over the 'rise of the gentry' the debate over the 'rise of the great landowners' developed rather slowly, and came to focus on the nature and effects of marriage settlements. Hrothgar enlarged on his views of marriage settlements in his 1949 paper to the Royal Historical Society, in which speculation on the effects on the wealth and landholdings of the recipients of the portions that brides brought to their marriages, through using them to acquire more land (somewhat to the neglect of the contrary effects on the fortunes of the brides' fathers), led to the further thesis that the class

---

[12] H. J. Habakkuk, 'English Landownership, 1680–1740', *Economic History Review*, 10 (1940), 2–17. By later standards it was an essay, or sketch, since it contained no footnotes or references. R. H. Tawney, 'The Rise of the Gentry, 1558–1640', *Econ. Hist. Rev.* 11 (1941).

of greater landowners was in effect 'raising itself up by its own boot-straps'.[13] Critical comments on his thesis came from C. Clay, J. V. Beckett, and Lloyd Bonfield, and with the arrival of feminism and gender history debate homed in on marriage settlements and was dominated by notable exchanges between Lawrence Stone and Eileen Spring.[14] Hrothgar took on board those findings of fresh research in the archives which he considered helpful, and as was his invariable habit paid little attention, at least in print, to the more combative and aggressive arguments, with the result that he was sometimes thought to be arrogant in not deigning to engage in controversy—quite the opposite of the truth, for he was by disposition courteous as well as diffident. Over the years Hrothgar modified and altered his views about marriage settlements, and about the rise of the great estates, absorbing some of the findings of other scholars, and refining and sharpening his own analysis of their impact, until in his final statement much of the 1940 thesis was stood on its head.[15] Constant development of his thinking, rather than reiteration of a static position, was another of his strengths.

That is to jump ahead. The Second World War abruptly interrupted many careers. Hrothgar had a short spell with the code-breakers in Bletchley, but spent most of the war in the Board of Trade. It would indeed have been too good to be true if temporary civil servant Habakkuk had been involved with the crazy project known as, and misspelt as, Habbakuk. This was to have been an alternative to the Mulberry harbours: a floating airstrip 2000 feet long, weighing 2.2 million tons, and made of frozen sea-water mixed with sawdust. It appealed strongly to Lord Mountbatten, but alas, Hrothgar was not the controller of sawdust, and the codename was adopted because the Old Testament book refers to 'a work which you will not believe though it be told to you'.[16] It is only a little less astonishing to find that Hrothgar finished the war drafting briefs on the trade treaty negotiations which accompanied the Bretton Woods

---

[13] H. J. Habakkuk, 'Marriage Settlements in the Eighteenth Century', *Transactions of the Royal Historical Society*, 4th ser. 32 (1950), 28.

[14] The best guides to this literature are in Lloyd Bonfield, 'Marriage Settlements and the "Rise of Great Estates": The Demographic Aspect', *Econ. Hist. Rev.* 2nd ser. 32 (1979), and idem, '"Affective Families", "Open Elites" and Family Settlements in Early Modern England', Econ. Hist. Rev. 2nd ser. 39 (1986), esp. 342, n. 7. The most recent statement of Eileen Spring's position is in Eileen Spring, *Law, Land, and Family: Aristocratic Inheritance in England, 1300 to 1800* (Chapel Hill and London, 1993).

[15] See below, pp. 110–11.

[16] D. Lampe, *Pyke, The Unknown Genius* (1959), pp. 128–62.

conference on postwar international currency mechanisms.[17] This may well have sharpened his interest in the historical background of the pre-1914 operation of the gold standard and convertible currencies, but apart from that—and the cementing of his friendship with Postan (also a wartime civil servant, in the Ministry of Economic Warfare)—it is not easy to discern direct influences on his later academic career of his wartime experiences.

That is, if one excepts his meeting with Mary Richards, whose own wartime experiences, while waiting to go up to Girton, were in working with deprived children at the East End settlement, Cambridge House, where in 1944 she met Hrothgar who was also living there. It is reported that they first held hands on VE Day. Mary then took up her place at Girton, and they did not marry until after she graduated, in 1948. This was indeed the decisive event in Hrothgar's personal life, the foundation of a partnership of more than fifty years. Mary complemented Hrothgar: she came from the other side of the Bristol Channel; her upbringing was in an Anglo-Catholic family (her father was a priest, and she went to a convent school) and she remained an active Anglican; and although he wrote about technology Hrothgar never moved beyond writing with pen and ink, with numerous additions and amendments pinned and paper-clipped to his manuscripts, while Mary was fluent on a typewriter, and later taught herself word-processing on a computer. So she became Hrothgar's essential support, not only in their family life bringing up four children, but also in his professional life. Her assistance when he was editor of the *Economic History Review* was especially valuable, since his spelling was pretty unreliable. She was an excellent hostess when he was Principal of Jesus, and Vice-Chancellor, 'a great believer in breaking up little groups at parties; though not everyone responded with equal enthusiasm to her cheerful invitation to "come across the room and meet the mathematicians"'.[18] In his retirement it was Mary who urged him on to finish his great book on landowners, and who typed, revised, and indexed it. He was bereft when she died—mercifully, that was only a few months before his own death.

While Mary went to Girton, Hrothgar returned to Pembroke College, as director of studies in history and university lecturer in economics, his lectures on British economic history being directed at both economists and historians. He shared with Postan a Special Subject on the British Economy, 1886–1938, a virtually contemporary subject well-suited to the

---

[17] Video-interview of Habakkuk by Harte.
[18] Keith Thomas, Memorial Address, p. 6.

home of Marshallian and Keynesian economics and a reminder that Hrothgar, as well as Postan, had no narrow chronological limits to his interests. His collaboration with Postan was close: in 1946 he became assistant editor of the *Economic History Review*, Postan having been sole Editor since 1934, and in 1950 began a ten-year period as Joint Editor with Postan, inaugurating the continuing *Review* practice of joint editorship. This intensely active postwar period in Cambridge, which left precious little time for his own writing, saw his reputation advance to the point where his election to the Chichele Chair of Economic History at Oxford, in 1950, was an obvious choice, even though his publication record then stood at no more than three articles. Thereafter, although retaining certain Cambridge features in his work, he became devoted to Oxford, with the passionate loyalty of an adopted son.

He spent seventeen highly productive years in the Chichele chair, regularly publishing an article a year while vigorously developing economic history at Oxford, especially through his graduate seminar; previously the subject had been left to London, Cambridge, Birmingham, Manchester, and Glasgow. He introduced the practice of having a full minute of each seminar paper and discussion, and as his first graduate student and seminar secretary I found this exercise an invaluable way of getting to grips with the take-off into self-sustained growth, trade cycle theory, Kontratiev cycles, and other mysteries. He continued to build his reputation in the Postan manner, through a string of articles, rather than through writing the large books favoured by his initial supervisor, Clapham; but it was the publication of his first book, in 1962, *American and British Technology in the Nineteenth Century*, which not only consolidated his position as one of the leading figures on the international stage (alongside Postan he had been involved in the creation of the International Economic History Association in 1959), but also created a whole school of (mainly) American economic historians, who have paralleled in their vigour and significance the school of (mainly) British historians of landownership which grew out of his 1940 article. A posthumous article by Rothbarth in 1946 had initiated the academic discussion of the effects of labour scarcity on the American economy, but it was Habakkuk's book which launched this American cottage industry, and which drew upon economic theories dealing with the choice of techniques.[19] This book was the fruit of lectures

---

[19] H. J. Habakkuk, *American and British Technology in the Nineteenth Century: the Search for Labour-Saving Inventions* (Cambridge, 1962). E. Rothbarth, 'Causes of the Superior Efficiency of USA Industry as Compared with British Industry', *Economic Journal*, 56 (1946), 383–90.

given in visits to Harvard, Columbia, and Berkeley, in which he speculated on the links between factor endowments and the frequently contrasting prevailing technologies in the two economies. It remains the most brilliant example of Hrothgar's historiographical methodology, the 'marriage of history and theory' expressed in the elegant prose of a master of the logical deduction of theoretical explanations from concrete empirical observations. The starting point was the observations of British visitors to the USA in the 1850s that in specific industries, woodworking and small arms manufacture, the Americans were commonly using more advanced and more automatic machinery than their British counterparts. The general explanation Hrothgar offered was in terms of labour scarcity, specifically the comparative scarcity and high cost of unskilled labour in America attributable largely to the abundance of 'free' land which attracted labour into farming; alongside this he argued for a secondary scarcity of capital to account for the 'flimsy' and short-life nature of much American machinery and infrastructure (particularly noticeable in railway equipment) in comparison with British emphasis on solid and immensely durable machines. He toyed with cultural explanations, that something about American society produced more innovative and adventurous entrepreneurs than did Britain, only to reject them in favour of structural economic differences. This book confirmed his distinction as an economic historian of international importance, and was swiftly followed by his election as a Fellow of the British Academy in 1965 and as a foreign member of both the American Academy of Arts and Sciences and the American Philosophical Society.

Hrothgar did not make any further contributions to this technology debate and its close connections with the mechanics of the operation of the nineteenth-century Atlantic economy, beyond a 1962 article on the somewhat fortuitous complementarity of building cycles in Britain and America.[20] The large body of literature generated by the technology book was analysed by Peter Temin in the festschrift for Hrothgar's seventieth birthday, paying generous tribute to him for having 'transformed the concept of labour scarcity . . . into a serious research topic'.[21] It was Peter Temin, however, who—no doubt quite unintentionally—had scared Hrothgar away from having anything more to do with the subject.

[20] H. J. Habakkuk, 'Fluctuations in House-building in Britain and the United States in the Nineteenth Century', *Journal of Economic History*, 22 (1962), 198–230.

[21] Peter Temin, 'Labour Scarcity and Capital Markets in America', in F. M. L. Thompson, ed. *Landowners, Capitalists, and Entrepreneurs. Essays for Sir John Habakkuk* (Oxford, 1994), pp. 257–73.

Already faintly alarmed by the rise of cliometrics, Temin's 1966 article 'Labor Scarcity and the Problem of American Industrial Efficiency in the 1850s', which contained a formal theoretical presentation of Habakkuk's argument and a highly algebraic appendix that mounted a mathematical proof of inconsistencies and paradoxes in the Habakkuk treatment of labour scarcity, convinced Hrothgar that the practice of economic history, at least in the United States, had moved beyond his intellectual reach.[22] Reflecting in old age, he claimed that the invitation in 1967 to become Principal of Jesus College came in the nick of time to prevent a serious collapse in his self-confidence as an economic historian; at the time it would have seemed more like a welcome change from the sometimes rather uncongenial life of All Souls.

He had, after all, other irons in the fire besides his interest in theories to explain the choice of technologies. Landownership, in England and in comparison with European countries with different property systems, had remained a strong interest in many of the articles he wrote while Chichele Professor. These ranged from the market in monastic lands in the sixteenth century through to the land market in the late eighteenth century, passing on the way the impact of the Civil War, Interregnum, and Restoration on landed estates, and developing theories about changing relationships between the rate of interest and the price of land which came to occupy a prime place in his thinking alongside the marriage settlements.[23] He was also developing a third main interest, in historical demography and the relationships between population movements and economic growth (and decline). It would be an exaggeration to claim that he founded a third group of disciples, for historical demography had many other influential contemporary leaders. But his 1953 article 'English Population in the Eighteenth Century' was as stimulating and pathbreaking as his dramatic entries into the other two fields. When it was reprinted in 1965 the editors of the volume commented: 'It may be said to have marked the revival . . . of interest in the unsolved questions concerning population growth in the eighteenth century, and it influenced subsequent work by raising the possibility that this growth might after all have been due to changes in fertility to a much greater extent than had

---

[22] Peter Temin, 'Labor Scarcity and the problem of American Industrial Efficiency in the 1850s,' *Jnl. Econ. Hist.* 26 (1966), 277–98.

[23] There is a complete bibliography of his works in Thompson, ed. *Landowners, Capitalists, and Entrepreneurs*, pp. xi–xiii.

previously been thought possible.'[24] In 1953 the received view was that population growth in the second half of the eighteenth century was caused by a falling death rate brought about by medical and public health improvements. The notion that eighteenth-century medical improvements were considerable enough to have reduced mortality had been recently demolished, but a declining death rate resulting from improving living conditions and nutrition remained the favoured explanation. Habakkuk did not produce any new demographic evidence, but simply by reasoning power and logic advanced arguments for supposing that a rising birth rate, consequent on a fall in the age at marriage or more likely a decline in the proportion of women who never married, could have been the mainspring of population growth. What mattered to him as an economic historian was whether economic developments produced population changes, or vice versa, and he satisfied himself that something like the run of abundant harvests, and cheap bread, of the 1730s and 1740s could well have produced earlier marriages and increased fertility.

He sharpened this argument in his 1958 article on 'The Economic History of Modern Europe', in which changes in fertility and nuptiality figured as the key mechanisms of population growth and in some circumstances the triggers of economic change while in others possibly its main consequences; and this thesis was developed to cover alternating and contrasting demographic trends over several centuries in the Arthur Pool Memorial lectures he gave in Leicester University in 1968.[25] Demographers, however, were sceptical of inference and hypothesis unsupported by new hard evidence, and generally remained attached to death rate explanations. Even those disposed to look at changes in fertility as the chief agent of change were doubtful about some of his unsupported speculations on their origins in rational calculations by parents about the eventual size of surviving families in the light of their supposed knowledge of infant mortality. As the most expert of the book's reviewers commented; 'In a field of study where new knowledge and new means of testing old hypotheses are both growing apace, it may prove to wear less well than some of Mr Habakkuk's earlier and excellent discussions of

[24] H. J. Habakkuk, 'English Population in the Eighteenth Century', *Econ. Hist. Rev.* 2nd ser. 6 (1953), 117–33; reprinted in D. V. Glass and D. E. C. Eversley, eds. *Population in History* (1965), editors' note, p. 269.

[25] H. J. Habakkuk, 'The Economic History of Modern Europe', *Jnl. Econ. Hist.* 18 (1958), 486–501. The Arthur Pool Memorial Lectures were published as idem, *Population growth and economic development since 1750* (Leicester, 1971).

demographic, economic, and social structural history.'[26] Nevertheless, when the new evidence eventually arrived, from a vast exercise in cooperative research in parish registers, family reconstitution, and back projection, it was Hrothgar's birth rate thesis which was broadly confirmed, albeit with modifications and refinements of both the chronology and the causal chain which he had originally proposed.[27]

By 1981 he had long moved on from both technology and demography, increasingly occupied with university administration and politics from his position as Principal of Jesus. At All Souls he had been rather out of sympathy with the lack of academic seriousness of some of his colleagues, and frankly dismayed by the decision that the pioneer historian of the making of the English landscape, W. G. Hoskins, had been deemed not good enough to become a Fellow. Since early days in Oxford Hrothgar had been in demand for public service, serving on the Grigg Committee on Departmental [Whitehall] Records, 1952–4, the Advisory Council on Public Records, 1958–70, and then on the Social Science Research Council, 1967–71, and the National Libraries Committee, 1968–9. This committee work with colleagues from other disciplines and different professions proved to be an excellent preparation for becoming an energetic and successful head of house, a position he regarded as 'the height of human felicity'.[28] If he had previously rather moved away from his Welsh origins, he rediscovered and acknowledged them from the Jesus perspective, at once recognising in the portrait of the Founder, Hugh Price, a reminder of the elderly Vale of Glamorgan farmers he had known as a boy. To coincide with his translation he published an article in the *Welsh History Review*, and in 1975 became President of University College, Swansea.[29] He would have ranked his greatest achievement as Principal the acceptance of the 'Jesus scheme' in the early 1970s, under which five men's colleges were allowed to admit women undergraduates on a trial basis; this turned out to be a decisive move in Oxford's painfully slow recognition of women's education, so that within a generation only

---

[26] E. A. Wrigley, review of *Population Growth and Economic Development*, *Econ. Hist Rev.* 2nd ser. 26 (1973), 728.

[27] E. A. Wrigley and R. S. Schofield, *The Population History of England, 1541–1871* (1981, second edition Cambridge, 1989).

[28] Keith Thomas, Memorial Address, p. 12.

[29] H. J. Habakkuk, 'The Parliamentary Army and the Crown Lands', *Welsh History Review*, 3 (1966–7), 403–26. He explained that he chose to examine the acquisitions of a group of Welsh soldiers 'because my introduction to the history of the Civil Wars I owe to David Williams [one of the history masters at Barry County School], who endowed this period with a magic which, for me, it has never lost'.

one single-sex college was left in Oxford, that being a women's college. From a purely college standpoint Hrothgar's cultivation of good relations with old members, crowned with the Edwin Stevens benefaction which enabled Jesus to house all its students for all of their three years in residence, would be his most memorable legacy.

Sometimes rather intimidating to undergraduates whom he would engage in intellectually taxing conversation at parties (where Mary would provide welcoming and less demanding small talk), Hrothgar was so clearly tolerant, liberal, and fair-minded that the student eruptions of 1968 caused him very little trouble. He took in his stride the attendance of a goldfish at Governing Body meetings, it being the solemnly elected President of the JCR, but was understandably exasperated when an ex-public-schoolboy made the absurd claim that the College's charges were forcing him to live at 'subsistence level', a state which Hrothgar had seen at first hand both in the breadlines of South Wales in the 1930s and in India in the 1960s. In 1973 he became the first Vice-Chancellor of Oxford University from Jesus College for 275 years, and one of the early holders of the four-year term of office that had recently been introduced as one of the reforms recommended by the Franks Commission (1966). 'As Vice-Chancellor,' it was remarked, 'he had the great advantage of usually being the most intelligent person in the room, as well as the one who had most closely studied the papers.'[30] Little wonder then that as a committed and skilful exponent of academic democracy he persuaded the endless committees of university governance to reach sensible, liberal, decisions on the issues of his time: a student sit-in at the Examinations Schools; a tied vote over a proposed honorary degree for Bhutto of Pakistan; above all, the beginnings of the still-continuing slide in university funding which came as a shock after the post-Robbins (1968) euphoria. He was equally enchanted with the ceremonial dimension of vice-cancellarial life, developing into a much sought-after speaker with a fund of good stories from Barry and Cambridge days, and apparently relishing the experience of official limelight: 'we have quantities of photos', Mary wrote, 'of topping out a building in construction (Hrothgar's face contorted with passionate eloquence), or robed for some ultra-dignified occasion'.[31]

Unlike many of his successors he actively enjoyed being Vice-Chancellor. As he neared the end of his term the Senior Proctor

---

[30] Keith Thomas, Memorial Address, p. 11.
[31] Mary Habakkuk to the author, 2 May 1993. He told some of these stories in the video-interview with Harte.

commented that 'when we took over we expected to find a tired man, haggard, in the autumn of his office. We were left wondering if this was autumn, what on earth spring could have been like.'[32] 'Spring', as an interview in the *Times Higher Education Supplement* recorded in 1974, had seen him confessing to finding the administrative duties as Vice-Chancellor 'rather fun', even regarding the need for cheeseparing after the recent cuts in government funding 'almost with relish'.[33] There were moments, though, when the 'fun' was of the adrenalin-coursing, con-frontational variety. There was once a demonstration in the Broad chant-ing 'Habakkuk out! Habakkuk out!', and with 500 booing students outside the Clarendon Building he and the University Registrar stood grasping their umbrellas ready to do battle. Then the students invaded the Indian Institute, the Vice-Chancellor and Registrar with a posse went to Hertford College, got ladders, and climbed into the upper floor of the Institute, charging downstairs and evicting the invaders. Prudently the Vice-Chancellor had been restrained from climbing the ladder; he insisted in the face of noisy demonstrations that nineteen students who had been identified among the invading force should be brought before the Proctors and be sent down for a year. Thus was order restored.[34]

Energetic, resourceful, companionable, with a spring in his step that belied his sixty years, widely respected for the cogency and vigour of his defence of the idea of a 'liberal university', in 1976 he was elected as the first Oxford chairman of the Committee of Vice-Chancellors and Principals (later to rename itself Universities UK). He articulated for a wide audience his passionate, radical, and closely reasoned attachment to the independence of the institutions which embodied and protected the freedom of the world of learning, scholarship, research, and teach-ing, most notably in his great speech to the meeting of the International Association of Universities in Moscow in August 1975. He warned the 900 delegates from eighty-six countries that the role of universities as centres for the 'unfettered exchange of ideas' was under increasing threat from the interference of governments using their control of the purse-strings, with the increasing demands that universities should concentrate on activities relevant to national needs meaning that society could easily lose sight of the unique function of universities as centres of learning and free inquiry. He foresaw that the university population would con-

[32] Quoted in Keith Thomas, Memorial Address, p. 12.
[33] *Times Higher Education Supplement*, 7 June 1974, p. 7.
[34] Video-interview with Lady Habakkuk by Pat Thane, 7 March 1997, Girton College Cambridge archive.

tinue to expand in the next twenty-five years, perhaps at a slower pace than before, until something approaching half of the age group were receiving a university education, many no doubt on courses less specialised than traditional honours degrees. He concluded that if, through this expansion

> the university is compelled to conform to the views which happen to be fashionable or dominant at the moment, if it is induced to direct too many of its resources to meeting the immediate needs of society as these are interpreted by the state at a particular point of time—then we shall find that the ability of the university to perform its central function has been impaired, and its capacity to produce creative and original work weakened.[35]

Hrothgar received a knighthood in the 1976 New Year's Honours, and chose to be known as Sir John. Americans, in particular, who had difficulty in coming to terms with either the spelling or the pronunciation of Hrothgar, had for some time been in favour of the manageable John. When he retired as Vice-Chancellor in 1977 (in the event he returned temporarily for a few months in 1978) it was reported that 'Sir John's final view from the top is gloomy', because of the squeeze on university finances and the implication that the government did not expect or want student numbers to grow.[36] Personally and as a historian he was far from gloomy. When he became Vice-Chancellor he thought 'the trouble is that my subject is going econometric. By the time I finish being Vice-Chancellor it will be completely beyond me.'[37] He had been working on the recent history of the steel industry, but he was never satisfied with this and it remained an unpublished manuscript when he died. In 1977, keen to resume activity as a scholar, it is true that he kept well clear of econometrics. Instead he returned directly to his academic starting point, English landownership; he became President of the Royal Historical Society, and in November 1977 delivered his first presidential address, 'The Land Settlement and the Restoration of Charles II'.[38] Remarkably, while the paper must have been written while he was still a full-time Vice-Chancellor, it dealt with an entirely fresh aspect of a subject on which he had published in the 1960s. The detailed exposition of the steps by which Charles and Hyde avoided any commitment to confirm the purchasers of

---

[35] *THES*, 22 Aug. 1975, p. 1.
[36] *THES*, 30 Sept. 1977, p. 31.
[37] *THES*, 7 June 1974, p. 7.
[38] H. J. Habakkuk, 'The Land Settlement and the Restoration of Charles II', *TRHS*, 5th ser. 28 (1978), 201–22.

confiscated crown, bishops', capitular, and delinquent lands, and manoeuvred the resumption of most lands without compensation, except for purchasers of incomes in possession on church lands, however, did not greatly modify the accepted view of the Restoration land settlement. The three succeeding presidential addresses (1978–80) were devoted to 'The Rise and Fall of English Landed Families, 1600–1800'. In the main these were reworkings of some of his earlier contributions, in no clear sequence: (I) dealt with heiresses and the rise of large estates; (II) with private estate acts and sales by indebted landowners; (III) returned to the sale of monastic lands, and the development of a market in land in the early seventeenth century. However, they did contain the delightful quotation

> Helmsley, once proud Buckingham's delight
> Fell to a scrivenor and a City knight.

The scrivenor was the banker Charles Duncombe, typical new man of the 1690s, ancestor of the earls of Feversham, and the estate became Duncombe Park.[39]

In his final three years at Jesus he was also kept busy as Chairman of the Oxfordshire Health Authority, and then having retired as Principal of Jesus in 1984 Hrothgar, back at All Souls, gave the Ford Lectures the following year. Spurred on and assisted by Mary, these, much expanded and revised, were published in 1994 as *Marriage, Debt, and the Estates System: English Landownership, 1650–1950*. This great work of nearly 700 pages of text and more than 50 pages of endnotes is not so much a distillation of a lifetime's reflections on large questions concerning the social and economic dimensions of the history of England's long dominant landed class, as a cornucopia of a lifetime's accumulation of facts, quarried from an enormous range of archival and printed sources, about the marriages, debts, purchases, and sales of the landed aristocracy. It has to be said that this magnum opus attracted a mixed reception.[40] Reviewers were impressed by the extraordinary wealth of the material Hrothgar had collected over the years, by the clarity of his exposition of the inner work-

---

[39] H. J. Habakkuk, 'The Rise and Fall of English Landed Families, 1600–1880: II', *TRHS*, 5th ser. 30 (1980), 216.

[40] H. J. Habakkuk, *Marriage, Debt, and the Estates System: English Landownership, 1650–1950* (Oxford, 1994). Major reviews were by J. V. Beckett, 'Family Matters', *Historical Journal*, 39 (1996), 249–56; David Spring, in *Albion*, 27 (1995), 517–20; Lloyd Bonfield, in *American Historical Review*, 101 (1996), 483–4; Barbara English, in *Agricultural History Review*, 44 (1996), 114–16.

ings of the English landed family and his mastery of the technicalities of the legal arrangements these involved, and by his readiness to revise some of his own earlier arguments. Thus it no longer seemed that the landed aristocracy were 'raising themselves by their own bootstraps', but rather that the operation of marriages and inheritances was constantly recirculating lands that were already within the 'estates system', with families taking it in turns as it were from generation to generation to be gainers or losers, and from time to time estates passing out of the hands of great landowners and swelling the ranks of landed gentry through purchases by new men. While some welcomed the book as the definitive account of strict settlements, their functioning in preserving the 'estates system', and the significance of that system (of gentry and magnate estates) for agriculture and much of industry and urban development, others were disappointed and even sharply critical. The criticisms were directed chiefly at the methodology of piling instance upon instance and largely leaving them to speak for themselves, and at the supposed superior air of being above the fray conveyed by Hrothgar's aversion from direct engagement with the debates and controversies—sometimes vociferous—which had been largely generated by his own work.

The book is densely packed, by no means a straightforward or easy read even for those well-acquainted with the field, and it requires close attention. That reveals that Hrothgar had taken on board all the modifications and alterations to his initial positions that he regarded as reasonable, and as for those arguments with which he disagreed—for example on the scale and consequences of aristocratic indebtedness, on the openness of the elite, on the rise of affective marriage, or on the treatment of the womenfolk of landed families—he simply allowed them to be flattened by implication through the massive weight of the evidence he presented. He demonstrated, for instance, with the chapter and verse of specific cases in which actual numbers were recorded in the deeds, that in eighteenth-century settlements it was normal for a widow's jointure (income for life) to equal about one-quarter of her husband's total income (as well as being ten per cent of the portion she brought on her marriage). This, he argued with some plausibility, was a reasonable substitute for a widow's common law right to dower of one-third of a husband's income, since enforcing dower and collecting it in rents had always involved legal and administrative costs, and a degree of uncertainty. He did not present this in the context of an academic debate not because he regarded himself as above the fray, but because he did not subscribe to the fashion for combative and aggressive scholarship. In his own modest words, 'I have not striven to identify the points on which my conclusions differ from those of other scholars.'[41]

The reservations about the methodology of the book were more serious. He had certainly moved a long way from the days when the 'marriage of history and theory' had been the touchstone of his research. There is precious little theory in this book, except for lawyers' theory on the interpretation and impact of legal instruments. Indeed, with its evidence drawn from deeds, settlements, private acts, and genealogies, rather than from letters, journals, diaries, or estate accounts, it is in a sense more of a lawyer's book than a social or economic historian's book, and the material is often described in the lawyer's language of a particular case illustrating a general point. It is also true that Hrothgar's pronounced distrust of econometrics and quantification meant that he declined to do any counting and produced no tables or graphs, so that the evidence is presented in a literary rather than a statistical framework. What had happened was that in the historian's continual tension between being a 'lumper' or a 'splitter' the accumulation of evidence had pushed Hrothgar more and more into the splitters' camp. What the evidence indicated was the great diversity of the experiences, and the behaviour, of landed families in their marriages, their children, heirs, and heiresses, their debts, their extravagances and economies, their purchases and sales of lands, and their good or bad luck. The certainties which he had seen in 1940 had been dissolved by his increasingly detailed knowledge of the workings of the estates system. The 'diversity of experience,' he had come to feel, 'makes the identification of representative behaviour and of dominant trends particularly difficult.' Despite the literally thousands of examples he had assembled, Hrothgar modestly concluded

> I do not, however, know enough about a sufficiently large number of families to specify the basis on which a . . . representative sample should be selected. I have therefore proceeded by example. As I am well aware, examples, even if tiresomely numerous, are not proof. And the method is particularly dangerous when, as in the case of the landed elite, behaviour was so diverse that it is possible to find an instance to illustrate the most implausible generalization. All I can hope is that this work will make it easier to test hypotheses in a more systematic fashion.[42]

The result was a triumphant demonstration of the strengths of a perhaps somewhat old-fashioned historical empiricism, worthy of his ori-

---

[41] Habakkuk, *Marriage, Debt, and the Estates System*, p. vii.
[42] Ibid. p. x.

ginal supervisor, Clapham, and provided future researchers with a vast body of data and, though buried in the fifty pages of endnotes, a quite extraordinary guide to the sources, and the literature, of the history of landownership. Moreover, some trends were established. There was change over time, essentially the result of demographic changes which saw a reduction in the infant mortality of the landed classes from the mid-eighteenth century, and a significant increase in life expectancy from the early nineteenth century, which together produced trends towards fewer failures of male heirs, more surviving daughters and younger sons, and longer delayed succession by eldest sons, all of which in turn had serious implications for the amount of family support, and hence debt, which an estate had to carry. Change as a result of major alterations in strict settlements did not come until the 1882 Settled Land Act—which Hrothgar somewhat cavalierly described as a conservative, technical, measure of land law reform unconnected with the contemporary liberal and radical attacks on the 'land monopoly'—an Act which brought 'to an end the effectiveness of the strict settlement as a device to fuse a particular family into a particular estate, which had been its primary function since the seventeenth century'.[43] The unchallengeable powers of sale conferred on tenants-for-life by this Act were used over the following decades to bend before the pressures of agricultural depression, death duties, and war, and the final chapter of the book is devoted to the decline of the landed interest from the 1880s to 1950. Circumspect to the end Hrothgar declined to accept the more extreme versions of the disappearance of landed estates, and concluded that 'the greater part of English agricultural land is still held in the form of units which are still recognizably estates'. He had explained 'La Disparition du paysan anglais' in 1965; fittingly the final sentence of the great book is simply 'There is no English peasantry.'[44]

This was his last published work, though he continued to relish conversations about the long-term rate of interest and claimed merely to be waiting, with some impatience, for medievalists to supply him with rather more evidence for ruling rates of interest in the early middle ages than a single observation of the rate at which Simon de Montfort's forfeited lands were valued in 1265, before he could complete a monograph on the subject. He greatly enjoyed his years as a Distinguished Fellow of All Souls in the 1980s and 1990s, carrying on working in libraries well after

---

[43] Ibid. p. 646.

[44] Ibid. p. 704. H. J. Habakkuk, 'La Disparition du paysan anglais', *Annales*, 20 (Paris, 1965), 649–63.

the big book had been finished, keeping up with seminars where his interventions were as crisp and sharp as ever, and above all relishing conversations and gossip (never malicious) with friends, colleagues, and visitors. His relaxations remained what they had been in his prime, a long walk every Sunday, often on Port Meadow, and reading Victorian novels and poetry.[45] In the final years his brisk, jaunty, step was stilled, but the quizzical look from under the bushy eyebrows and the wonderful voice of reason never left him. He moved to Somerset to be with his daughter Alison and to be near Mary, who had to go into a nursing home. He was bereft when she died in August, and barely three months later he himself died, on 3 November 2002. He was perhaps the last of the generation of historians who began to make their mark before the Second World War, one who rose to the summit of his profession through the exciting and innovative quality of his scholarship in three separate areas of historical enquiry, and who was a notable guardian of the institutions of the 'liberal university' through his unruffled reasonableness. A Memorial Service was held in the University Church of St Mary the Virgin, Oxford, on 8 February 2003.

F. M. L. THOMPSON
Fellow of the Academy

Note. I am grateful to Hrothgar's children, especially David and Alison, for providing me with information about his life, and letting me have copies of the MSS of his major speeches. My debt to Keith Thomas's Address at the Memorial Service is inadequately acknowledged in the footnote references.

---

[45] *THES*, 7 June 1974, p. 7. He never recorded any hobbies in *Who's Who*.

RICHARD HARE

Richard Mervyn Hare
1919–2002

RICHARD HARE left behind at his death a long essay titled 'A Philosophical Autobiography', which has since been published.[1] Its opening is striking:

> I had a strange dream, or half-waking vision, not long ago. I found myself at the top of a mountain in the mist, feeling very pleased with myself, not just for having climbed the mountain, but for having achieved my life's ambition, to find a way of answering moral questions rationally. But as I was preening myself on this achievement, the mist began to clear, and I saw that I was surrounded on the mountain top by the graves of all those other philosophers, great and small, who had had the same ambition, and thought they had achieved it. And I have come to see, reflecting on my dream, that, ever since, the hard-working philosophical worms had been nibbling away at their systems and showing that the achievement was an illusion.

Yet his imagination could also be less modest: a gaggle of moral philosophers is trapped beneath the earth in a smoke-filled chamber; they talk at cross purposes, and refuse to take the way out into the open air that he alone has discovered. It was his ambition to have united elements from Aristotle, Kant, and Mill in a logically cogent way that solved the fundamental problems of ethics (though with unfinished business); and he usually believed himself to have achieved this. For much of his career, his 'prescriptivism' formed an important part of the curriculum, certainly in Britain. His disappointment was not to have persuaded others (an occasional 'we prescriptivists' was always uncertain of reference), and to have

---

[1] *Utilitas*, 14 (2002), 269–305. I shall draw on this pervasively for biographical information, in which it is far richer than its title suggests.

Proceedings of the British Academy, **124**, 117–137. © The British Academy 2004.

left no disciples; he once told John Lucas that this made his life a failure.[2] Yet he leaves behind generations of pupils grateful for the transmission not of a doctrine but of a discipline; and posterity, while unlikely to ratify the logical validity of his theory, will admire it for its uniting of apparent opposites: freedom and reason, tradition and rationalism, eclecticism and rigour.

I

Richard Mervyn Hare was born at Backwell Down, outside Bristol, on 21 March 1919. He was to be known professionally as 'R. M. Hare', and personally as 'Dick Hare'. His father, Charles Francis Aubone Hare, was director of a firm, 'John Hare & Co.', making paint and floorcloth; his mother was Louise Kathleen Simonds, of a brewing and banking family. The family firm was hit by the recession of the 1920s, when it was liquidated or merged. His father died of the strain when Dick was ten, and his mother, who tried carrying on as director, died five years later. He was then cared for chiefly by guardians and relatives on his mother's side (one of whom, Gavin Simonds, became Lord Chancellor). He was sent to school first at Copthorne in Sussex, and then, from 1932 to 1937, as a classical scholar at Rugby. He was awarded a scholarship to Balliol College in 1937, where he read two years of Greats before the outbreak of war.

Despite a largely classical education (which left its mark in the forceful felicity of his prose), Dick's mind was already turning towards moral philosophy. He ascribed this to two things: the need to define an attitude towards fighting, and a feeling of guilt at living in moderate comfort. He spent much time while still at Rugby working with the unemployed, and finally decided not to be a pacifist, but to join the OTC. When war broke out, he characteristically volunteered for service in the Royal Artillery, and circumvented the results of a medical test in order to be permitted active service overseas. He was eventually put on a ship for India in autumn 1940. He had a year (which he described as one of the happiest of his life) training Punjabi soldiers, and enjoying some adventures (twice finding his own way back through the jungle, once after losing his guns to the Japanese). He was finally taken prisoner when Singapore fell in February 1942. He then suffered a long

---

[2] Obituary in *Balliol College Annual Record 2002*, pp. 30–2.

march up the River Kwai to near the Three Pagodas Pass, with a group of officers whose task was to work as coolies building the railway from Siam into Burma. So he knew too well the 'violent untiring labours' that Aristotle associates with virtue in an ode to a dead friend that was dear to Dick's heart. He writes in his autobiography, 'I prefer to pass over our sufferings during the eight months we were there';[3] he rarely mentioned them (except when more fortunate critics of his views rashly imputed to him the exemption from other experience that can be the privilege of an Oxford fellowship). He was eventually imprisoned with fellow officers in Singapore, whence he was released after exactly three and a half years when the war ended.

Astonishingly, those years already bore philosophical fruit. While on leave in 1940, he wrote twenty pages setting out 'my philosophy'. When Singapore fell, he looted a ledger from Changi jail, and started writing a monograph called 'An Essay in Monism'. He carried this on his back during the march, and completed it just before being released. He later dismissed it as 'containing mostly rubbish';[4] and it is indeed largely homemade (with some influence from Whitehead, Eddington, and—indirectly—Russell's neutral monism), though already characteristic in its lucidity and confidence. It remains virtually unknown, and connects with his maturer thinking in ways that deserve mention.[5] A central notion, initially put to work in relating mind and matter without dualism, is *rhythm*: 'Goodness is Rhythm *willed from within* by a Person'; 'Beauty is something we perceive, whereas Goodness is something we do.' Hare already adopts the dichotomy, fundamental to his later philosophy, between cognition and will: 'We say that a man cognises something when he is consciously affected by it; we say that he wills something when he consciously causes it . . . Cognition is the passive, will the active function of personality.' There is also already an emphasis upon the importance, which he later took for granted, of the word 'ought'. Criticising 'materialists' (among whom he counts utilitarians) for letting 'the word "ought" slip out of their vocabulary', he remarks, 'Both the Greeks of the Fourth Century BC and we in our own times have seen how quickly people like Thrasymachus spring up, and with what dire results, once men have

---

[3] 'A Philosophical Autobiography', 283.
[4] D. Seanor and N. Fotion (eds.), *Hare and Critics: Essays on Moral Thinking* (Oxford, 1988), p. 201.
[5] It is now accessible among a mass of typescripts lodged in Balliol College Library by John Hare, by whose kind permission I draw on them here.

forgotten the meaning of "ought".'[6] Very much later he was to regret his
inability to convey more than 'feebly and aridly' supplementary reflections such as these: 'The quality of mutual love and affection between
people, without which our life would have few joys, cannot be had without the right dispositions; and these dispositions, therefore, are the condition of both happiness and morality.'[7] Here, within a chapter on 'sin',
he is happy to follow Plato: 'Successful tyrants—that is, those who use
other people solely as means to their own selfish ends—have been few in
history, and it is open to question whether any of them have been happy.
For no man can be truly happy by himself; most human happiness is a
function of our association with other men . . . Such association is barred
to the man who has made other men hate him. The person of a tyrant is
inevitably stunted.'

The writing of 'An Essay in Monism' was an heroic exercise in detachment. Did Dick's sufferings do more to colour his later ethics? His reticence leaves the question open, but the evidence is that the after-effect was
profound.[8] Lucas states this well: 'There were no external supports for
morality in a Japanese prisoner-of-war camp. Moral principles could not
be argued about with one's captors, only affirmed in the face of them by
an act of will: "Here stand I, I will no other." There was an existentialist
strain to Dick's moral philosophy.'[9] And David Richards writes, 'I was
struck in our correspondence by how important to him his terrible war
experience was (thus, his feeling for the limits of reasonable discussion
with fanatics).' The fanatic, in Hare's usage, is the man so committed to
some ideal that he is willing to sacrifice even his own interests to it; hence
appeal to the interests of others is not going to move him. (If that was
Hare's interpretation of the motives of his tormentors, it was surely a
generous one.) After visiting Japan many years later, he spoke appreciatively of the courtesy of his hosts and the elegance of their customs; being
rational, he nursed no resentment against a nation. When he wanted an
example of counter-suggestibility put to sadistic purposes, he would cite
the schoolmaster who tells his charges to be silent as he leaves the room

---

[6] This illustrates how a philological training could produce an attitude anticipatory of Oxford
'ordinary language' philosophy. It was in the early years of that, within his unpublished essay
'Practical Reason' (1950), that Hare was to write, 'It is on the difference in meaning between the
sentences "What shall I do?" and "What am I going to do?" that the case against determinism
largely rests.'

[7] Preface to *Moral Thinking: Its Levels, Method, and Point* (Oxford, 1981), p. vii.

[8] See also note 42 below.

[9] *Balliol College Annual Record 2002*, p. 31.

with the intention that they should disobey him and get beaten.[10] For illustrating a conceptual point, he preferred a prep school to a slave-camp; he was too English to dine out, or support a thesis, upon horrors endured. Yet a heroism infuses both the content and the manner of his mature philosophy. A postcript to 'An Essay in Monism' contains a sentence initially disconcerting: 'There are circumstances—and I have had my fill of them—in which one becomes absolutely convinced of the contemptibility of the human race in general, and of the supreme importance of oneself in particular.' Yet this is not a confession of egotism, but a declaration that each man has to answer for himself, and maintain his own integrity. It may in part be good luck that preserves most of us from behaving badly, and he had paid for the moral bad luck of others. Though he later licensed the commonplaces of ordinary ethical thought within an 'intuitive' level of thinking, he could never trust them to remain undistorted and efficacious; as Plato had written, 'True opinions, as long as they remain, are a fine thing and all they do is good; but they are not willing to remain long, and they escape from a man's mind, so that they are not worth much until one ties them down by giving an account of the reason why.'[11] Philosophers are as subject to fashion as other men, and, when fashion turned against him with arguments that he thought confused, he stood firm as Hare *contra mundum*. His *anima* (if not *mens*) *naturaliter Christiana* gave him a sense, in philosophy as in life in general, of the symptomatic importance even of minor achievements and misdemeanours. This gave an intensity to his writing, as to his living, that was striking within the gentler ambit into which fate transported him. Within argument, syntax, conduct, and prosody mistakes mattered. It was equally Christian that he believed in putting them right.

II

After the war, Hare returned to Balliol to complete the four years of Greats. Even before he sat Finals, he was offered a lectureship at Balliol, which almost immediately became a fellowship. Philosophically, he had the good fortune to come under two influences that together led him to views that he could always retain. One was emotivism. He never adopted

---

[10] See, e.g., *Sorting Out Ethics* (Oxford, 1997), pp. 108–9. This book contains a complete list of Hare's publications up to that date.

[11] *Meno* 97e6–98a4, trans. Grube.

the verification principle of meaning dogmatically, and recoiled from any causal account of 'emotive meaning' that reduced moral discourse to emotional manipulation; yet he accepted a broadly empiricist view of facts that excluded moral facts in any unetiolated sense of 'fact'. The other influence was Kantian. From H. J. Paton's lectures on Kant, and articles by Reginald Jackson, he learnt that imperatives fall within the realm of reason. This led him into a study of imperative logic, a topic already being explored in Scandinavia (especially by Alf Ross), but unfamiliar in Britain. In his first published article, 'Imperative Sentences',[12] in his essay 'Practical Reason' entered for the T. H. Green Moral Philosophy prize in 1950, and in his first book, *The Language of Morals*,[13] he explored the possibilities of inferring imperative conclusions from imperative, or imperative and indicative, premises.

The Language of Morals introduced a distinction between prescriptive and descriptive meaning. Prescriptive meaning is defined in relation to imperatives: a statement is prescriptive if it entails, if necessary in conjunction with purely factual statements, at least one imperative; and to assent to an imperative is to prescribe action. Descriptive meaning is defined in relation to truth-conditions: a statement is descriptive to the extent that factual conditions for its correct application define its meaning. It is taken for granted, in the tradition of David Hume, that the factual is only contingently motivating: desire is no part of sincere assent to a purely factual statement. A moral statement has prescriptive meaning, but may also be partly descriptive. Thus 'A [a person] ought to φ' entails the imperative 'Let A φ', so that to assent to it sincerely is to have an overriding desire (which in application to oneself will amount, if its satisfaction appears practicable, to an intention) that A φ. If there are agreed reasons for φ-ing within a linguistic community, say that it is enjoyable, 'A ought to φ' may take on the descriptive implication of 'φ-ing is enjoyable'. 'X is a good F' prescribes choice within a certain range (e.g. for someone who is choosing an F); it takes on a descriptive connotation if there are agreed standards for assessing F's.

Hare never said that ethical statements *are* imperatives; however, it is striking that non-descriptive or evaluative meaning is defined in terms of imperatives. This at once gave a clear sense to his endorsement of Hume's denial that one can derive an 'ought' from an 'is'. It also coincided, at least in appearance, with Kant, and was to become essential for later

[12] *Mind*, 58 (1949).
[13] Oxford, 1952.

developments that brought results comparable to Kant's. However, a Humean who lacked Kant's belief in a purely rational will might prefer to make ethical statements more loosely expressive of wish or desire, or even aspiration; and this could avoid what is everyone's first objection to prescriptivism, that, intuitively, 'I ought to φ' does not entail 'I will φ' (expressing intention).[14] Hare took courage from the fact that Socrates and Aristotle incur much the same objection; as he liked to urge, Socrates wasn't simply making a mistake. His initial reply was that cases of failing to try to do what one admits one ought to do may involve psychological incapacity, or an off-colour use of 'ought' that sheds its full prescriptive meaning. He was to return more fully to the issue in a chapter of his second book, *Freedom and Reason*,[15] and again in a late encyclopedia article, 'Weakness of the Will'.[16] In this last piece he recognises, wisely, that different things go wrong in different cases. At times, the true story may even involve something like Plato's partition of the soul (which was designed to accommodate conscious self-contradiction).

The two features of prescriptivity and universalisability remained the twin pillars of Hare's theory ever afterwards. The term 'universalisability' was to become the title of a slightly later paper which also sorted out a confusion that causes real trouble in Aristotle and Kant.[17] 'General' *terms* (such as 'man' or 'Greek') contrast with 'singular' ones (such as 'Socrates'). However, in the case of *maxims*, one needs to keep two distinctions apart: a maxim may be 'universal', rather than 'singular' or (ambiguously) 'particular', in referring to no individuals (unless within the scope of a preposition such as 'like' which converts the name of an individual into the vague specification of a kind); a maxim may also be 'general', rather than 'specific', in identifying a *wide* class of agent or act—a difference that is one of degree (so that the universal rule 'Always give true evidence' is more specific than 'Always tell the truth', and more general than 'Always give true evidence on oath'). Any discussion of the

---

[14] It is characteristic of Hare's respect for linguistic intuitions (which he trusted more than moral ones) that the nearest the present author ever came to troubling him was by noting the evident and plausibly analogous failure of 'He ought to have got home by now' to entail 'He has got home by now.' 'He *must* have got home by now' is another matter; and one may wonder whether, in (effectively) equating 'ought' with 'must' in practical contexts, Hare was misled by his own conscientiousness.

[15] Oxford, 1963.

[16] This is reprinted in Hare's last collection, *Objective Prescriptions and other essays* (Oxford, 1999).

[17] 'Universalisability' (1955), reprinted in *Essays on the Moral Concepts* (London, Macmillan, 1972).

practicality and acceptability of 'general principles' needs to keep these distinctions apart. Hare's clarity on the matter is his most important non-disputable contribution to philosophy.

In his essay 'Practical Reason', he had already argued that many decisions are decisions of principle not in deriving from a principle, but in establishing one. As he remarked there, 'It is not easier, but more difficult, to decide to accept a very general command like "Never tell lies" than it is to decide not to tell this particular lie . . . If we cannot decide even whether to tell this lie, we cannot, *a fortiori*, decide whether to tell lies in innumerable circumstances whose details are totally unknown to us.' What, then, is to guide decision? In the second part of his essay, he attempted to find a secure basis for moral reasoning in such concepts as 'friend'; but he discarded that approach before trying it out in print. His paper 'Universalisability' (1955) stressed one's personal responsibility in making decisions that are also decisions of principle. The next important development came in a second book, *Freedom and Reason* (1963), in which the formal features of prescriptivity and universalisability generate a 'Golden Rule' form of argument. Hare offers a simple scenario: suppose that A owes money to B, who owes money to C, and that the law allows creditors to exact their debts by putting their debtors into prison.[18] If B simply decides 'I will put A into prison', there may be nothing to say to him. But can he say 'I ought to put A into prison'? If he does, he commits himself to a principle such as 'If this is the only way to exact the debt, the creditor should imprison the debtor.' B is unlikely to be willing to prescribe a likely implication of this, 'Let C put me into prison', since that would frustrate his own interests. Hare argues that the form of argument retains its force even if, in fact, B is not himself a debtor; for the judgement 'I ought to put A into prison', and the principle that it invokes, will still entail conditionals, such as 'Let me be put into prison if I am ever in A's situation', to which B is unlikely to be able honestly to subscribe.

In *Freedom and Reason*, Hare allows the argument to be evaded by the 'fanatic' who is so committed to some impersonal ideal (say that debtors deserve a hard time) that he is willing to disregard his own personal interests (including the interests that he has himself as a debtor, or would have if he were a debtor). A later tightening of the argument, first set out fully in 'Wrongness and Harm' (1972),[19] hoped to close off this possibility. In their practical force, ideals are equivalent to universal preferences that dif-

---

[18] *Freedom and Reason*, pp. 90–1.
[19] First printed in *Essays on the Moral Concepts*.

fer from personal preferences in their content, but owe their moral weight to the prevalence and intensity of whatever preferences their realisation would satisfy. That B would really rather go to prison himself than have debtors be treated leniently is possible, but improbable. A more likely fanatic is guilty of a kind of imprudence in failing to give due weight to his own interests, actual or counterfactual. The emergent ethical theory is a distinctive variety of utilitarianism, one that identifies the moral good with the maximisation not of some subjective state such as happiness, but of the satisfaction of preferences.

The argument excited much attention, and some scepticism. It seemed implausible that the very activity of prescribing universally should commit a speaker to a substantive ethical position, let alone one so distinctive. However, the logic of Hare's position became perspicuous in his third book, *Moral Thinking: Its Levels, Method, and Point*.[20] It is now set out as follows. In wondering whether he should assent to the statement '*A* ought to φ', the speaker has to reflect whether he can prescribe that everyone should act in the same way, whatever his own situation. 'I' connotes no essence (e.g., human): each of us *might* be anything, and so has, when prescribing for all situations, actual or possible, to be concerned on behalf of *everybody*. There is further a prescriptive aspect to the meaning of 'I': to take a role to be possibly *one's own* is to give weight to the preferences of the occupant of that role as if they were actually one's own. Hence, the speaker can rationally assent to a particular 'ought'-statement only if it is derivable from some universal principle that he will accept if he gives impartial and positive weight to all preferences whose satisfaction would be affected by its observance. Thus moral reflection generates a universalised prudence. Moral ideals register within this framework simply as universal preferences; to allow one's own ideals to override the stronger or more prevalent desires and ideals of others is a kind of egoism, and so excluded. Human decision remains free, however rational and informed, because anyone can avoid the constraints of morality by declining to moralise; for this reason, it remains true that no 'is' entails an 'ought'.

This is an extraordinary intellectual construction, and invites debate at many points. Zeno Vendler urged that we keep apart the semantic thesis (which may be true or nearly true) that 'I' is a pure indexical, from any metaphysical claim (which may baffle us) that it denotes a pure subject which can take on *any* state or role.[21] In his reply, Hare clearly shies away

---

[20] Oxford, 1981.
[21] 'Changing Places?', in *Hare and Critics*, p. 181.

from adopting a metaphysical position stranger than Vendler's own (which rejects Cartesian egos but does admit a transcendental ego). Yet he still supposes it to be true that 'I might be Napoleon', and that 'the world in which I was Napoleon would be a different world than this, though not in its universal properties'.[22] He even supposes that I can consider situations in which I am a stove, a mountain, or a tree—although, since I cannot care what happens to me if I become such a thing, the consideration is idle.[23] Hare seems here to have entered rather unexpected territory. It would have suited his usual common sense to permit me to imagine not *that I am* Napoleon, but *being* Napoleon, i.e. what it was like to be Napoleon; and that can suffice to incline one to ambivalence about the outcome of Waterloo. But he requires there to be a possible situation in which I am, at any rate, relevantly *just like* Napoleon if he is to maintain that prescribing, say, 'All men like Napoleon should receive their come-uppance' applies even *to oneself*, and so may be imprudent.

A danger remained of deriving a kind of imperative from an indicative. No doubt Napoleon very much wanted to win the battle. Does awareness of that fact commit me to prescribing, on the counterfactual supposition that I am Napoleon, that Napoleon be victorious? The answer came to Hare in a particular room in Stanford in the middle of the night (an hour that he usually thought unfitted for philosophy).[24] It was to suppose, further, that the meaning of 'I' is partly prescriptive; hence to hypothesise 'if I were Napoleon' is *already* to 'identify with his prescriptions', in the sense of prescribing that, other things being equal, they be satisfied within the scope of the hypothesis.[25] The solution is equally elegant and audacious. It may confirm doubts whether the situation of my being Napoleon is a *situation* at all. It also throws open questions about what identifying with Napoleon's prescriptions comes to. One might think that, if 'I' is *fully* prescriptive, I cannot prescribe that Napoleon be defeated in the situation in which I am Napoleon, since that is certainly not what he wanted or would ever have wanted; and, if so, I cannot honestly prescribe that all men like Napoleon be defeated, since, for one case (that in which I am Napoleon), I do *not* want that. What Hare requires is

---

[22] *Hare and Critics*, p. 285. This comes soon after a disclaimer that I have respected: 'I wish I had kept off the "possible worlds" terminology. It often sheds more darkness than light.' Yet, evidently, 'I might be Napoleon' is not a possibility realisable in the actual world (where that position is already occupied).

[23] Ibid., p. 283.

[24] 'A Philosophical Autobiography', 301.

[25] *Moral Thinking*, pp. 96–9.

a weaker identification: given that I am moralising, and hence prescribing for all situations of a given general kind, I must give *some* weight to the preferences that are mine in the situation in which I am Napoleon, but not *more* weight than I give to the preferences that are mine in any of the other situations; hence, in deciding what to prescribe universally, I must weigh all relevant preferences equally (relative to their prevalence and intensity). This is exactly where Hare intends to lead us; but he invites the question how he can prove that one is *taken* that way by the logic of 'ought' and 'I'.

A related query (which *Moral Thinking* leaves as 'unfinished business')[26] arises about the range of preferences that prescribing universally commits one to taking on board. If 'I' is fully prescriptive, it may further follow that to suppose that I am some person is to take on board *all* his preferences, including 'external' ones about matters (say his neighbours' sexual or dietary practices) that may never impinge upon his consciousness. Yet sometimes Hare only stipulates impartiality between interests, which is narrower. To accommodate precisely that, we might distinguish a sympathetic 'I': to suppose that I am some person might be to give full weight to his desires for his own happiness; this would still leave open whether I should take into account his prudential desires (now for then) for future happiness, or only his synchronic desires (now for now) for present happiness. Alternatively, we might admit an egocentric 'I': this would let us give weight to Cheops' desire that *he* receive a big funeral, but not to external desires that do not essentially refer to their possessor. Yet such options embarrass if the aim was to derive a precise ethical theory from the very logic of the concepts.

Outside *Moral Thinking* itself, a striking application of Hare's framework was to possible people, that is, to people who may exist, with preferences and interests to be satisfied, if we choose to bring them into existence. Ought we to do so, so long as this will increase the total satisfaction of preference? A positive answer has implications—though not, Hare argued, very radical ones—for population policy, and the morality of such practices as abortion and IVF. Hare reasons that, if I am glad that I exist, I tenselessly prescribe, *ceteris paribus*, that my parents bring me into existence; universalising the prescription, I must prescribe, *ceteris paribus*, the bringing into existence of others relevantly like me.[27] The

---

[26] Ibid., p. 105. Hare's final discussion is 'Preferences of Possible People', in *Objective Prescriptions*.

[27] See 'Abortion and the Golden Rule' (1975), and several later papers collected in *Essays on Bioethics* (Oxford, 1993).

argument is the most intriguing and ingenious of all Hare's contributions to practical ethics.

A different feature of his theory, first presented (in different terminology) in 'Ethical Theory and Utilitarianism' (1976),[28] and fully explored in *Moral Thinking*, is a distinction between a 'critical' level of thinking, conducted by 'archangels' with the use of 'Golden Rule' arguments, and an 'intuitive' level, conducted by 'proles' with the use of simple principles (often articulating emotional responses) whose acceptance can be justified at the critical level. These two levels define not two social castes, but two roles between which each of us learns to alternate as appropriate. The complication is actually inevitable within consequentialism, which has to separate the question *how one should act* from the question *how one should think* about how to act—for ways of thinking have consequences no less than ways of acting. A utilitarian assessment of practical principles has to consider not only their *observance utility* (OU), which is what good will come of enacting them, but also their *acceptance utility* (AU), which is (roughly) what good will come of intending to enact them. A broad generalisation that Hare favoured is that the highest OU is likely to attach to highly specific principles, though a higher AU may attach to some fairly general ones. This comes of human ignorance and self-deception. A principle, say, permitting adultery when a marriage is breaking up anyway might have a higher OU than one simply forbidding adultery; but, if there are potential Don Juan's around with a talent for false rationalisation, its AU may be much lower. This complication was both convenient, and problematic. Hare had long been wearied by familiar objections citing concrete cases where utilitarian theory appears to conflict with moral intuition, as when an American sheriff might judicially execute one suspect in order to prevent a mass lynching of others. He could now hope to accommodate these at the 'intuitive' level of thinking. An inability ever to countenance judicial murder may be recommendable *by* critical *to* intuitive thinking as a constraint upon practical reflection in an emergency. And given that the attitude is approved, if not reasserted, by critical thinking as Hare conceives it, how can it in itself tell against his conception of critical thinking? (It would be a case, so to speak, of biting the hand that fed one.)

---

[28] This is collected in *Essays in Ethical Theory* (Oxford, 1989).

However, there is a difficulty.[29] It is one thing to *make do* with intuitive ways of solving problems that are the best available within limits of time and information, while leaving them subject to correction at leisure or in retrospect; it is another to accept a theory that approves one's actually *assenting* to certain principles whose contents it cannot endorse. And yet a rule that is a mere 'rule of thumb' is a paper shield against temptation. All is well if the theory can be self-effacing, so that the agent discards it as and when he adopts an intuitive viewpoint; but, in Hare's scenario, in which he has internalised both critical and intuitive ways of thinking, how is he to keep out of mind, as he tests his practical commitment to some intuitive principle, that it is simply not of a form (being absolute, and yet evidently equivalent to no principle of utility) to be critically endorsable? Hare's way out requires a *tertium medium*: perhaps the agent may sincerely *accept* the guidance of a rule (with the effect that he can intentionally infringe it, if at all, only with compunction) to whose content he cannot strictly *assent*. It becomes a question, and a very interesting one, whether Hare's conception of prescriptions—and of moral judgements, no less than principles, as being prescriptive—can accommodate such a distinction.

Utilitarianism, of any variety, is not at present generally fashionable; yet one may be sure that it will never go away. Future reconsiderations of it may well return to these, and other, more commonsensical, aspects of Hare's intensely meditated elaboration and defence.

III

Hare always claimed to have learnt a lot from his pupils, and his early years at Balliol granted him outstanding ones—three of whom, Bernard Williams, Richard Wollheim, and John Lucas, were to join him both as professional philosophers, and as Fellows of the British Academy. Lucas gives a delightful account of how he and his contemporaries would plan a day's campaigning, with a succession of tutees concerting, through the day, objections to some settled opinion of Dick's, and replies to his replies—with Williams sent in last to deliver the *coup de grâce* that was never, in the event, fatal. Those who never experienced Hare's impromptu fielding of objections can really understand the resilience of even his less

---

[29] See Bernard Williams, 'The Structure of Hare's Theory', in *Hare and Critics*. Hare's reply is characteristically robust (ibid., pp. 287–93).

plausible convictions. And yet, despite some impressions, he was quite capable of admitting the force of fair counter-arguments. Neil Cooper, who warmly recalls Hare's personal kindness, also remembers an admission after an exchange at the Jowett Society about 'ought' and 'can': 'You thrashed me.' Hare had a faith that apparent disagreements can usually be resolved once confusions are removed;[30] this did go with a presumption that objections to his views rested on confusion. The style of his responses to essays can partly be gauged—except that he was kinder to pupils than to colleagues—from his 'Comments' within *Hare and Critics*, whose brusquely economical format he recognised might be taken amiss: 'In case anybody thinks that I have been discourteous to my critics in writing notes instead of essays, I must point out that this is what we commonly do to Plato and Aristotle (as in the Clarendon series of commentaries), taking their arguments one by one and treating them briskly but seriously.'[31] (What his critics did not occasion, as his students did, was equally precise and emphatic correction of vocabulary and syntax.) He was generous of his time but not a philosopher of the pub, deprecating discussions lasting more than an hour and a half on the sensible but sober ground that it is difficult to keep a clear head for much longer.

There could be a complaint that Hare was most interested in his own ideas. John Lucas had from Tom Braun a Balliol rhyme dating from soon after the publication of *The Language of Morals*:

> My pupils I have always taught
> You cannot get an 'is' from 'ought'.
> This is the burden of my song:
> 'It's in my book, or else it's wrong.'[32]

A contrasted experience is that of David Richards, who was never a pupil, but wrote a doctoral thesis that Hare examined: 'His comments on my dissertation were remarkably extended and detailed, always reasonable, and sometimes persuasive. I was struck in my correspondence with Hare by how seriously he took my discussion of his views and how much he was willing to enter into mine; indeed, he probably thought more of my dissertation than I (then) did, which is a bit amazing.' (The result was a book, *A Theory of Reasons for Action*,[33] that Hare recommended to his

---

[30] Whence the over-sanguine title of his last book, *Sorting Out Ethics*.

[31] *Hare and Critics*, p. 201. Hare was honestly disappointed that Oxford University Press refused him the title 'Hare and Hounds'.

[32] By mistake, *Balliol College Annual Record 2002* prints an earlier variant.

[33] Oxford, 1971.

pupils as the best defence he knew of the other side.) It is true that Hare was most appreciative of points helpful to his own reconsiderations; he could then be depended upon to be overgenerous. He always disparaged his own scholarship, though from a demanding point of view. (Few writers of long books on Plato can have first reread the whole of Plato in Greek, as Hare did before writing his very short one.)[34] Yet his interests were wider in range than his publications. I remember, in the years around 1970, classes focused on Frege, Wittgenstein, and more recent philosophy of mind and language. Though he was keen to claim ancestry (counting Socrates and Aristotle as, in part, the first prescriptivists),[35] his love of philosophy did not reduce at all to a love of his own philosophy.

His most amiable aspects were apparent to the undergraduates (by preference) whom, from early on, he invited to one of his reading-parties, first at Plas Rhoscolyn in Anglesey, and later also at Saffron House in Ewelme, beneath the Chilterns. It was there above all that he vividly communicated a sense of how worthwhile and enjoyable it is not just to read but to *do* philosophy. He was thus, however exacting his standards, a tremendously positive figure as a mentor. Some of his distinguished colleagues could be inhibited by a concern not to say anything that might not stand up to examination; Hare gave of himself in discussion in a manner that could be self-opinionated but was also self-forgetful. Though he was a man of his own generation in lacking the indiscretion that is now almost *de rigueur*, he could soon be enjoyably candid about other philosophers (though never about his pupils). If his tenor was then somewhat partisan, that increased the fun. His sense of humour was less distinctive than his sense of mission, but equally characteristic. Though I must keep back one *gaillardise* (not, indeed, an habitual vein), I can mention a long vacation, spent mostly on his back with a slipped disk, that was redeemed by Lady Longford's life of Wellington, from which he particularly cited the one lady of easy virtue able to make a comparison with Napoleon: 'Le duc était beaucoup le plus fort.' Hare was a Puritan of the traditional kind who shared Dr Johnson's approval of 'harmless pleasures'. His reaction to the relative austerity of Corpus after Balliol, in the 1960s, was of equal amusement and regret. He was concerned about the case against eating meat; but his eventual virtual vegetarianism was rather caused, he said, by gardening than by argument. Unusually for a philosopher, he had a strong practical bent, and rather

---

[34] *Plato* (Oxford, 1982), in the 'Past Masters' series.
[35] See his article 'Prescriptivism', in E. Craig (ed.) *The Routledge Encyclopedia of Philosophy* (London, 1998).

wished he had been an inventor; for Plas Rhoscolyn he created a bed on a design he had known in Burma. Some of his dislikes were distinctive: the music of Beethoven (which he came to find superficial), wearing socks (which he blamed on commercialism), drinking coffee (which he said affected his temper), travelling by train (which caused him anxiety), giving and receiving presents (when the recipient best knows what he wants). Ved Mehta recalls his working, for freedom from interruption, in a caravan on the front lawn of his house in Oxford. He had the courage, though not the extravagance, to be an eccentric.

It was initially at reading parties that his pupils encountered a part of his life equally important to him as philosophy: his wife and children. What he describes as 'a night of mostly bad dreams', starting with his mother's death in 1935, ended with his marriage in 1947 to Catherine Verney, which he calls 'the best thing I ever did, and a source of lasting happiness'.[36] Catherine connected him to a family with whose long distinction his egalitarianism had to come to terms. She also brought him a richly human affection and devotion, and a Christian heart and mind to which his home life owed a saving grace. They further shared a love of traditional Anglicanism (though her beliefs were more orthodox than his), and of music (especially choral and *a cappella*). A Hare reading party at Ewelme was always in part a music camp, with (for all those able to join in) a piano to play and madrigals to sing. Everything equally involved their four children, one son, John (who now unites parental influences by teaching ethics and religion at Yale), and three daughters, Bridget (who now works for the Bach Choir of Bethlehem, Pennsylvania), Louise (who took a doctorate in animal husbandry, but now practises speech therapy), and Ellie (who makes films). Without them, he would have felt incomplete even as a moral philosopher; for Aristotle's question 'What sort of person should I be?' gave way, for him, to the question 'What sort of person should I bring up my children to be?'

IV

John Hare's own words at the memorial service that took place in Oxford at the University Church of St Mary the Virgin in May 2002 expressed the judicious loyalty of a fully believing son to a quasi-believing father.[37]

---

[36] 'A Philosophical Autobiography', 272, 292.

[37] They too were published, as 'R. M. Hare: A Memorial Address', *Utilitas*, 14 (2002), 306–8.

Dick did not suppose that the modern thinking man could long remain what he called a 'simple believer'; so he welcomed attempts by R. B. Braithwaite and others to empty religion of dogmatic content. He called himself a 'Christian empiricist', but thought the question whether he was really a *Christian* terminological. What he retained for himself was what he once called a 'blik', an attitude to the world which somehow gave him confidence to live and think morally, trusting (as he put it) 'in my own continued well-being (in some sense of that world that I may not now fully understand) if I continue to do what is right according to my lights', as also 'in the general likelihood of people like Hitler coming to a bad end'.[38] John connects the inhibitions that held his father back from belief not just with modern scepticism, but with 'a philosophical doctrine about meaning which he inherited from Carnap and the logical positivists'; for 'he thought he could not make meaningful assertions about subjects, like God, which lay beyond the limits of possible sense experience'.[39] Thus he denied that the transcendental has anything to do with prayer, asking 'What is the difference between there being a transcendental God who listens to the prayer and directs events accordingly, and it just being the case that the events take place?', and answering 'None at all.' The upshot is fatal to the orthodoxies of belief as of unbelief: 'Where the transcendental is concerned, there is no difference between a true story and a myth; it is therefore wrong to speak of the person who prays having an *illusion* that there is somebody that he is praying to.'[40] Simple belief, it turns out, lacks even a content.

Also traceable to positivism was a recurrent tendency to doubt the substantiality of philosophical disagreement. Presumably Plato was making a mistake of a kind when, as Hare diagnosed it, he 'interpreted the experience which *we* call "having a particular mental image of a square" as "having, on a particular occasion, a mental look at the Square"'.[41] Within metaethics, however, Hare was inclined to suppose that such variations fail to be more than verbal. This suspicion was first expressed in an unpublished paper 'Moral Objectivity' (1949–50). Here Hare imagines a White (an objectivist) who calls 'a moral intuition' what a Black (a subjectivist) calls 'a feeling of approval', and wonders about the point at

---

[38] 'Theology and Falsification' (1950), collected in *Essays on Religion and Education* (Oxford, 1992), p. 38.
[39] 'A Memorial Address', 307.
[40] 'The Simple Believer', in *Essays on Religion and Education*, p. 27.
[41] 'A Question about Plato's Theory of Ideas' (1964), collected in *Essays on Philosophical Method* (London, Macmillan, 1971), p. 67.

issue: 'Now we may well ask, seeing that we are all agreed that there *is* this experience, no matter what you call it, what on earth is the point of having long philosophical arguments about what you do call it.' Take a case of disagreement about pacifism: 'The Whites describe this situation by saying that there is a difference of opinion between us as to whether fighting does or does not possess the quality right; the Blacks, on the other hand, describe it by saying that we have different feelings about fighting. But the situation which they are both trying to describe is precisely the same, and they know it . . . They are disagreeing merely about words.'[42] Hare pursued this scepticism in two published papers, 'Nothing Matters' (1957), and 'Ontology in Ethics' (1985).[43] Here he suspects of vacuity certain terms that get overworked: 'true', 'fact', 'world', 'objective', 'realist', 'cognitivist'; hence he thinks it much harder than many have done to define a position that is distinctively objectivist. (It is certainly not enough to reassert 'Murder is wrong' in a peculiar and, as it were, metaethical tone of voice, firm and yet unemotive.) What I have traced back to a verificationism that may now seem dated becomes well grounded when applied to abstractions that, as appropriated by philosophers, await a clear sense.[44] This is not the most familiar aspect of Hare's thinking, but it is one that retains a potential to be salutary.

V

Hare remained a tutor at Balliol for twenty years, and always felt attached to that institution above all others (whence the bequest of his *Nachlass*).

---

[42] Hare proceeds to confirm the connection drawn by John Lucas between his war experience and a vein of existentialism. He imagines being an interpreter in a Japanese prisoner-of-war camp who is trying to persuade the Japanese commander not to send sick people out to work on the railway: 'I ask him to visualise, not certain non-natural properties, but the very natural, real properties of the situations that the alternative courses of action will bring about . . . It is not by any appeal to intuition that I can conduct my argument; . . . it is by revealing to him the nature of his choice, and showing him what it involves, what in fact he is choosing. And when I have done all this, I can only leave him to choose; for it is after all his choice, not mine . . . At any rate I have myself chosen, so far as in me lies, my own way of life, my own standard of values, my own principle of choice. In the end we all have to choose for ourselves; and no one can do it for anyone else.' There is nothing comparable to this remarkable and poignant passage in anything that Hare put into print.

[43] The first is collected in *Applications of Moral Philosophy* (London, Macmillan, 1972), the second in *Essays in Ethical Theory*.

[44] One may compare the 'quasi-realism' of Simon Blackburn, which purports to ape the language of realism without incurring its ontology—but also, and perhaps better, the 'quietism' that Blackburn deprecates for reasons not altogether clear.

It was still during his time there, in 1964, that he was elected a Fellow of the British Academy. However, ineluctable promotion eventually removed him, in 1966, to the White's Chair of Moral Philosophy at Corpus Christi. There he took on a responsibility for the supervision of research students. (Balliol and Corpus Greats pupils still had the benefit of his reading parties, which for a time, while John was at Balliol, became biennial.) He also took his turn as chairman of the Philosophy Panel, which admits and oversees graduates, and chairman of the Faculty Board. His hopes of reforming the position of Philosophy within the framework of the University came to nothing, as such things do. He was more successful in raising the money to set up the Radcliffe Fellowships, which have benefited both the recipients (college tutors relieved of teaching for up to two years) and their replacements (temporary lecturers in need of teaching experience). Administration, it may be said, was a task with which he coped admirably, but, also admirably, refused to identify.

He recalls that most of his cousins on his mother's side were Americans; and two of his children emigrated to America and married Americans. Like all distinguished Oxford philosophers, he received many invitations there (of which the most welcome—to him as to others—was to the Center for Advanced Study in the Behavioral Sciences at Stanford, where he wrote both *Moral Thinking* and his little book on Plato). All this made less improbable his early retirement from Oxford in 1983, and his appointment as 'Graduate Research Professor of Philosophy' at the University of Florida at Gainesville. One desire was to escape from faculty politics at Oxford. A contributing factor was the publication of *Moral Thinking*, which left him immediately, he told me, nothing new to say in his staple lectures. Yet his main motive was the prospect of helping to set up a 'Center for Applied Philosophy'. Thumbnail sketches of philosophical change exist to mislead, and this is certainly true of a blinkered *aperçu* that recent moral philosophy, *post* but not *propter* Hare, has shaken off its dry dust and reconnected with the real world. The very phrase 'applied ethics', now so familiar (and yet, one may think, tendentious), presupposes a tradition of ethical theories, such as his, that invite practical applications. In fact, he published his first paper in practical ethics in 1955.[45] Better known is the last chapter of *Freedom and Reason*, which addressed the issue, then (it seemed) wholly recalcitrant, of

---

[45] 'Ethics and Politics', part of which is collected, under the title 'Can I Be Blamed for Obeying Orders?', in *Applications of Moral Philosophy* (London: Macmillan, 1972). There it is followed by three papers originally published in the 1950s, and more from the 1960s.

apartheid.[46] And much else followed, with a stream of papers, and memberships of various advisory bodies.[47] He was engaged especially by urban planning, where he favoured radial over ring roads, and biomedical ethics, in which he laboured to be logical and not just *bien pensant*. When a Society for Applied Philosophy was formed, he became its first President. So he looked forward to a profitable refocusing of his energies, and this, to an extent, occurred, even when the Center partly disappointed: as he notes, three out of four volumes of essays published between 1989 and 1993 fall within practical ethics.[48]

Dick and Catherine's translation from Oxfordshire to Florida had, to their friends, an appearance of paradox. Stephen Spender, who taught at Gainesville in 1976, describes in his *Journals* not only alligators whose snouts pointed just above the water-line like periscopes, but also 'brilliant green trees' that 'were white with ospreys, and looked like green hats dripping with ostrich feathers'; yet he calls Gainesville itself 'the most perfect non-place I have ever seen', a paradigm of American cities 'that have stopping places but no centres'.[49] The Hares, however, were well suited. They retained their house in Ewelme, and spent half the year (the warmer half) there, and half in Florida, where they acquired a spacious bungalow that cost less for its lack of shade. For an Englishman a visit was in part uncanny: as one saw a pile of copies of *The Times*, with shelves of English books and music, and heard the BBC World Service, one could wonder whether one was back in England.[50] And yet they were multiply social, joining *three* local choirs, including (as at Ewelme) that of their local Anglican church. Dick kept up a passion for walking, missing the hills of England, but savouring the natural novelties. An actual taste for tutoring marked him off from his un-Oxonian colleagues. Were his new pupils up to the standards of post-war Balliol? He did not complain. At least Floridan legislation made the timing of retirement a matter of choice.

---

[46] Yet candour lightens commitment on the very last page: 'When South African believers in white supremacy read this book, will they at once hasten to repeal the pass laws and make the blacks their political equals? This is highly unlikely; and in any case they will not read the book.'
[47] On this, see 'A Philosophical Autobiography', 294–5.
[48] Besides *Essays on Religion and Education* and *Essays on Bioethics*, already mentioned, there was *Essays on Political Morality* (Oxford, 1989).
[49] *Journals 1939–1983* (London: Faber & Faber, 1985), p. 318.
[50] Anyone who remembers Alan Bennett's play *The Old Country*, whose skill is to disguise until the end of the first act that the location is not the home counties but somewhere outside Moscow, will know just what I mean.

Their Indian summer was disturbed by the first, and slightest, of Dick's strokes. When they returned fully to Ewelme in 1994, further attacks cheated him of his hopes of continuing to combat 'the usual misunderstandings'.[51] He gave his last paper, appropriately, to an undergraduate audience at King's College London; its content was as lucid as ever, though his delivery was less fluent. He was still able to put together *Sorting Out Ethics* (1997), deriving from the Axel Hägerström Lectures that he had given at Uppsala University in 1991 (when he also received an honorary doctorate—his first doctorate—from the University of Lund). Their taxonomy of metaethical options rather reflected their origins in the 1960s than the state of play current in the 1990s (part of which blurred his boundaries). Yet as a final statement of Dick's own position, and a lucid mapping of the topography of ethics from his point of view, it enjoys a special status among his books.[52] His eightieth birthday was marked by the publication of a final collection of papers, *Objective Prescriptions and other essays* (1999).[53] As is common, his last months, up to his sudden but peaceful death on 29 January 2002, were not his happiest, for all Catherine's care. And yet we may be sure that he would still have testified, as he had written thirty years before, 'I do believe in divine providence (that, incidentally, is the main reason why I have such a firm conviction that the truth will prevail in philosophy, despite all the manœuvres that are available to falsehood).'[54]

A. W. PRICE
Birkbeck College, London

Note. I am grateful for the assistance of the librarians of Balliol College, Neil Cooper, Catherine and John Hare, John Lucas, and David Richards.

---

[51] A phrase applied, alas, to Philippa Foot; 'A Philosophical Autobiography', 304–5.

[52] The book also collects a paper intriguingly titled 'Could Kant Have Been a Utilitarian?' (1993).

[53] Perhaps the most ingenious and enjoyable of these is 'Some Subatomic Particles of Logic', first published in 1989 but drafted long before that. To it an anecdote attaches. Hare first offered it to a *Festschrift* for his old Corpus colleague J. O. Urmson. But when he was unable to prevail over the American publisher in the matter of punctuation, he preferred to have it printed (of course, with a gracious note of explanation) in *Mind*.

[54] 'A Simple Believer', in *Essays on Religion and Education*, p. 33.

GEOFFREY KIRK

Geoffrey Stephen Kirk
1921–2003

GEOFFREY STEPHEN KIRK was born at Nottingham on 3 December 1921, the son of F. T. Kirk, and his wife Edith (née Pentecost). His father's family came from northern Yorkshire and his mother's was of Cornish origin, but had long been established in Nottingham in the dyeing and bleaching trade. His father, a dashing and affectionate character whom his friends addressed as Ferdie, served in the First World War and won the Military Cross. His mother, however, was thought by people who knew her to have a somewhat difficult temperament.

Not long after Kirk's birth the family moved to Radlett in suburban Hertfordshire, where his father became chief administrative officer of the Northampton Polytechnic in London, now the City University. When he was eleven they moved back to the Midlands, his father having been persuaded by a relative to become manager of a factory at Stapleford, between Nottingham and Derby.

Kirk tells us something of his early life in his attractive small book *Towards the Aegean Sea: A Wartime Memoir* (1997). He writes that in general he was lucky in his schooldays, but that that did not prevent him from being 'self-conscious and withdrawn at times, and in his early teens, at least, fairly unhappy'. 'The development of a truly extroverted personality,' he writes, 'was something that took time to accomplish, and has never, to my regret and my friends' surprise, been entirely perfected.' This must indeed have come as a surprise to most people who knew him, especially those who knew him at the start of his career. He was strikingly

Proceedings of the British Academy, **124**, 141–148. © The British Academy 2004.

handsome, and had considerable charm of manner; he was not bad at games, as well as very good at work, and he did well at all his schools.

He got a good start in Latin at his kindergarten, Radlett House, and at the age of nine went on to a first-rate preparatory school called Shirley House, between Bushey and Watford, where he got excellent teaching. He thought of trying for a scholarship at Shrewsbury, but was persuaded to try at Rossall, mainly because the climate would be good for his hayfever, and he was successful.

Life in this school, some eight miles north of Blackpool, was, as he tells us, 'rather charmless'; Kirk, who was very sensitive to his environment, was glad when, after the outbreak of war in 1939, the school was evacuated to Naworth Castle, the seat of the Earls of Carlisle. But the teaching was of high quality. For a year he studied science, but then switched to classics, improved his Latin and learned Greek, and won a scholarship to Clare College, Cambridge.

Going up to Cambridge in August 1940, Kirk spent a year there before he joined the Navy. Cambridge at that time contained several classical scholars of high distinction. But some of these were austere and somewhat dry, and in general the teaching and lecturing was uninspiring. The classical don at Clare was N. G. L. Hammond, an ideal teacher for Kirk, as he showed after the war; but he was away, and Kirk was sent for supervision to R. M. Rattenbury of Trinity College, a sound scholar but by no means an inspiring teacher. When Kirk told him that he was leaving to join the Navy, Rattenbury exclaimed 'Good Heavens! Well, I don't suppose I shall be seeing *you* again!' However, Kirk made progress in his studies, and obtained a First Class in Part I of the Classical Tripos, though without getting a distinction in the composition papers. Despite having rooms in a very ordinary modern building in Clare College and working in the equally undistinguished Classics Library in Mill Lane, Kirk acquired a deep affection for Cambridge.

Having preferred to become a telegraphist rather than an ordinary seaman, Kirk was posted to HMS *Royal Arthur* at Skegness. But after a few weeks he was chosen to become a candidate for a commission, and after a ten-week course in HMS *Ganges* at Otley was posted to HMS *Hurricane*, in which he spent the severe winter of 1941–2 crossing and re-crossing the North Atlantic. Having been chosen by the Navigating Officer to be his 'Yeoman', he acquired valuable navigational experience, and since the *Hurricane* was commanded by Commander Howard-Johnstone, who had much in common with Captain Bligh, he became acquainted with some of the difficulties of naval life. After six months on that ship and a final course of intensive training at Lancing, he was commissioned in the late summer of 1942.

Wishing to have freedom and responsibility and to avoid regular naval officers trained at Dartmouth, Kirk opted for service with the Coastal Forces, that is to say, in motor torpedo-boats and motor launches. After a period of training he was chosen to be First Lieutenant of a new motor launch, which for some months was engaged in patrolling against E-boats in the western part of the English Channel and in landing agents in occupied France.

After his motor launch had been damaged and withdrawn from service, Kirk on the advice of a friend managed to call at the Admiralty, find the right office and indicate that he wished to serve in Greece. After a brief course in navigation and a fortnight spent in Oxford being taught some modern Greek, he was posted to the Levant Flotilla. This consisted of a dozen or so caiques (small Greek fishing-boats), based on Beirut, and operating among the Greek islands. Kirk made a hazardous journey to Castelorizo, an island off the Turkish coast located some forty miles east of Rhodes, which was the base of part of the Flotilla, and from there to the Turkish bay of Balisu, some forty miles north of Cos, where the headquarters of the Commander, Aegean Raiding Forces was located. This officer's command consisted of a dozen or so caiques fitted out with Army tank engines and a little concealed armament.

Early in 1944 Kirk became the Second Officer in one of these vessels, which were engaged in sailing around the Dodecanese and the Cyclades, surveying local conditions and dealing with German garrisons and with the difficult problems of navigation. After taking part in operations on Amorgos and on Santorin he made a trip to Mykonos under a First Officer who turned out to be a maniac. After taking over from him, he assisted in dealing with the German garrison on Symi and in a reconnaissance of Paros and Naxos and later in a general reconnaisance of the eastern Cyclades. He movingly records his delight at unexpectedly coming upon the ruins of the splendid temple of Apollo at Didyma, near Miletus, and later at visiting the sacred island of Delos. After about three months the Germans began reducing or even withdrawing their garrisons on the islands, though a cadre of 300 commandos was still moving around the islands and had to be avoided. Kirk now operated in the northern Cyclades and in Chios, and later took part in a trip to Symi, Piscopi and Nisyros.

By the end of 1944 the German presence in Greece and the islands was almost at an end. At that time Kirk was ordered to join the rest of the flotilla in Tourkolimano, a small-boat harbour on the edge of Phaleron Bay, where other caiques were waiting to hand themselves over to the Greek Navy. He had an agreeable stay in Athens and its neighbourhood, for part of the time acting as liaison officer to the Greek officer who was in charge of the group of boats, and enjoying the study of antiquities and delightful female company. In his own words, 'the trouble was that I liked, in one way or another, practically all girls'; Kirk was so handsome and had so much charm that the liking was usually reciprocated. He was now a full Lieutenant, and was offered the post of Flag-Lieutenant to the Admiral commanding in Greek waters. But he preferred to exercise his right to early demobilisation in order to return to Cambridge, and in September, 1945 left for home. Afterwards he was awarded the Distinguished Service Cross.

Returning to Clare College, he had an ideal director of studies in N. G. L. Hammond, who had now returned from Greece after his notably distinguished service in Epirus. But Hammond was an historian, and Kirk had decided to specialise in ancient philosophy in Part II of the Tripos. Again he was lucky, for he found a superviser who was both congenial and highly competent in F. H. Sandbach of Trinity College.[1] He got a First Class, and was elected to a Research Fellowship at Trinity Hall.

During his tenure of that post, Kirk spent the year 1947–8 at the British School in Athens, where he wrote a valuable article on the likenesses of ships on Geometric vases (*BSA*, 44, (1951), 93–153), and the year 1949–50 at Harvard as a Commonwealth Fund Fellow. His main concern was with his doctoral thesis, which dealt with Heraclitus.

In 1950 he was elected an Official Fellow of Trinity Hall. In the same year he married Barbara Traill; they had one daughter. Between 1949 and 1959 he published several valuable articles on Heraclitus and one on Anaximander; and in 1954 appeared his book *Heraclitus: the Cosmic Fragments*. By this title he indicated those fragments 'whose subject-matter is the world as a whole, as opposed to men', on which he supplied a learned and judicious commentary, which has stood the test of time. Gregory Vlastos wrote that 'a work as serious and thorough as this compels one to reconsider many things one has previously taken for granted'.[2] For so young a man, it was a remarkable performance.

---

[1] See *Proceedings of the British Academy*, 84 (1993), 485–503.
[2] *American Journal of Philology,* 76 (1955), 337 = *Studies in Greek Philosophy*, I (1995), 127.

In 1957 appeared the first edition of *The Presocratic Philosophers*, edited by Kirk in collaboration with J. E. Raven. This book is an invaluable substitute for the selection of texts from the almost complete collection of fragments and testimonies edited by H. Diels and W. Kranz that had been provided by H. Ritter and L. Preller (edn. 9, 1913), and it contains a commentary that for the most part is of high quality. Kirk dealt with the Ionian tradition and its forerunners, and also with the atomists and Diogenes, and Raven with the Italian tradition and also with Anaxagoras and Archelaus. In 1959 K. R. Popper tried to show that the study of the Presocratics supported his theory that scientific discovery begins not from observation or experiment but from theories or intuitions; Kirk replied to his argument, and had much the better of the controversy.[3] In 1959 Kirk, then aged thirty-eight, was elected a Fellow of the British Academy.

From about 1960 Kirk turned his attention to Homeric problems. Milman Parry had proved that the Homeric poems belonged to a tradition that had been oral, and for many years after that most English-speaking scholars assumed that they themselves must have been composed orally. In 1950 classical studies in Cambridge had been greatly stimulated by the appointment to the Regius Chair of Greek of Sir Denys Page, who in two sets of lectures given in America in the 1950s strongly advocated the view that Homer was an oral poet.[4]

In 1962 Kirk published the *Songs of Homer*, which is dedicated to Page and M. I. Finley; he by no means always agrees with Page, but Page's influence is never far away. Kirk believed that the epics were composed orally, but thought that two generations had elapsed between the composition of the poems and the time when they were written down. In 1965 *The Songs of Homer* was abbreviated and somewhat rearranged as *Homer and the Epic* (1965).

The articles relevant to this topic which Kirk published between 1960 and 1973, together with the J. H. Gray Lectures which he gave at Cambridge in 1974, are to be found in *Homer and the Oral Tradition* (1977). The book and these articles contain no reference to Wolfgang Schadewaldt, *Iliasstudien* (1938; 3rd edn., 1966) and *Von Homers Welt und Werk* (1944; 4th edn., 1965) or to Karl Reinhardt, *Die Ilias und ihr Dichter*

---

[3] See Popper, *Proceedings of the Aristotelian Society* (1958–9), 1. 24 and Kirk, *Mind*, 69 (1960), 318–39.

[4] On these works see H. Lloyd-Jones, *Proceedings of the British Academy*, 65 (1979) = *Blood for the Ghosts* (1982), pp. 300–1.

(1961) and *Tradition und Geist* (1960) who argue that the Homeric epics were composed with the aid of writing, and are coherent works of complex artistry.

But in 1966 Milman Parry's son Adam challenged this view.[5] Speaking of his father, he wrote 'It is up to us not to stop where he stopped' (*Yale Classical Studies*, 20 (1966), 212; *The Language of Achilles* (1989), pp. 135–6); and in 1971 he published a translation into English of the two famous theses which his father had written in French, with an excellent introduction in which he argued that, though his father had proved that Homer belonged to a tradition that had been oral, Homer himself must have used writing. Kirk replied to Adam Parry,[6] but not very effectively.

Between 1965 and 1970 Kirk, without ceasing to be a Fellow of Trinity Hall, held a professorship at Yale, and in 1969 he delivered the Sather Lectures at Berkeley, California. In 1970 he contributed to the series of translations published by Prentice-Hall a valuable rendering of Euripides' *Bacchae*. In 1971 he resigned from Trinity Hall and became Professor of Classics at Bristol, where he occupied an attractive house in Clifton. While he was at Bristol he was divorced from his wife, and married Kirsten (née Jensen), formerly wife of Professor Christopher Ricks.

In 1970 Kirk published his Sather Lectures under the title *Myth: its Meaning and Functions in Ancient and Other Cultures*. The book was the product of a large amount of learned labour. He had made a careful study of the Mesopotamian myths about which so much information had come to light during the preceding century, and treated the subject in a spirit of English empiricism. He examined critically the five major general theories that had been put forward, giving most attention to what was then the latest, the structuralism of Claude Lévi-Strauss, and showed how the proponents of each had made the mistake of insisting that their own particular theory explained all myths.

Curiously enough the part of this valuable book that seemed most open to attack was his treatment of Greek myth. He argued that a myth cannot be fully understood unless one understood its origins, and since he held that these origins sometimes went back not simply to the Mycenaean period but to a period earlier than the Bronze Age, they were not always easy to establish. Arnaldo Momigliano in a review argued that to under-

---

[5] *Yale Classical Studies*, 20 (1966), 177–216 = *The Language of Achilles and Other Papers* (1989), pp. 104–40.

[6] *Proceedings of the Cambridge Philological Society*, 196 (1970), 48–59 = *Homer and the Oral Tradition* (1976), pp. 129–45.

stand a myth it was not absolutely necessary to understand its origins, and that it was far more important to understand it in the light of its relation to its own period.[7] Kirk in his reply argued that many features of Greek myths can be understood only if we take into account oriental myths which may have influenced them, and that to discover instances of this kind of thing was more useful than to examine the enormous variations which myths can be seen to undergo in the period about which we have fullest information.[8]

Many readers were surprised by Kirk's complaint that Greek mythology lacked the fantasy and speculation that were found in other mythologies; 'so droht nun auch der klassischen Mythologie die edle Einfalt und stille Grösse zum Verhängnis zu werden' was Walter Burkert's comment,[9] and Brian Vickers delivered an excited but not entirely unjust criticism.[10] Kirk did better justice to Greek mythology in his small but very readable and useful book *The Nature of Greek Mythology* (1974).

In 1973 Sir Denys Page unexpectedly retired from the Regius Chair of Greek at Cambridge five years earlier than he need have done, and Kirk was elected to succeed him. Instead of returning to Trinity Hall, he exercised the claim of a Regius Professor to a Fellowship at Trinity College.

He did much good at Cambridge by instituting formal professorial seminars for graduate students. But he now occupied a fine house at Woodbridge in Suffolk, which was unfortunately far from Cambridge, with the result that after a time much of the work of running the seminar fell to others.

In 1979 he spent a semester as Andrew W. Mellon Professor in Tulane University at New Orleans. When he was asked to give the Gray Lectures for 1974 he had at first thought of speaking on *Vagaries of Athenian Taste, 450–350 BC*, and the only result of this that has come to my knowledge is an Andrew W. Mellon Lecture given at Tulane and published in 1979 by the Graduate School of Tulane University under the title of *Periclean Athens and the Decline of Taste*. In this Kirk considers the changes of taste to be seen in the literature and art of the period in question in a

---

[7] *Rivista Storica Italiana*, 83 (1971), 450–4 = *Quinto Contributo alla Storia degli Studi Classici e del Mondo Antico* (1975), pp. 908–11.

[8] *Rivista Storica Italiana*, 84 (1972), 565–83.

[9] *Gnomon*, 44 (1972), 128.

[10] *Towards Greek Tragedy: Drama, Myth, Society* (1973), pp. 197 f. and Appendix II (pp. 618–35); for other criticisms, see H. S. Versnel, *Transition and Reversal in Myth and Ritual* (1994), p. 46 n. 83.

stimulating and interesting way, and it seems a pity that he did not continue to pursue this line of enquiry. In 1980 Kirk made a solid and valuable contribution to the discussion of sacrifice at the Fondation Hardt,[11] repeating his warning against monolithic theories. In 1982, six years earlier than he need have done, Kirk resigned the chair, and moved to live at Bath.

In 1983 appeared a second edition of *The Presocratic Philosophers*. Raven, who had died in 1980, was replaced as an editor by M. Schofield, who rewrote the chapters on the Eleatics and Pythagoreans, the chapter on Empedocles and part of the chapter on the Atomists, and Kirk revised the earlier part of the book throughout, 'but with little complete rewriting'.

He now returned to Homeric studies, and began work as general editor of a commentary on the Iliad in six volumes, to be published by the Cambridge University Press. The commentary appeared between 1985 and 1993, Kirk himself being responsible for the first two volumes, dealing with the first eight books. Despite the effects of his adherence to the oralist theory, his part of the commentary is of considerable value, particularly in the treatment of the Catalogue of Ships in Book Two; and he gave much valuable assistance to the other contributors to the commentary.

His last years were sad, since he was plagued by sickness and manic depression. But there were periods when he was free from these troubles, and his friends found his company as delightful as it had always been. He moved to Sussex, and died in a nursing-home at Rove, in Hampshire, on 10 March 2003.

HUGH LLOYD-JONES
Fellow of the Academy

Note. Without wishing to suggest that he agrees with everything in this memoir, I would like to thank Dr Nicholas Richardson for his assistance.

---

[11] In *Le Sacrifice dans l'Antiquité* (Entretiens de la Fondation Hardt, vol. 27, 1981), 41–90.

VIVIEN LAW   *Dona Haycraft*

Vivien Anne Law
1954–2002

VIVIEN LAW was born in Canada, in Halifax, Nova Scotia, on 22 March 1954, the daughter of John Ernest and Anne Elizabeth Law. Both her parents were of English origin, her father being from London, her mother from Clavering (Essex). Her father worked in management for an international telecommunications company (her mother was happy to be described simply as a housewife), and it was a posting to Cable and Wireless in Halifax which had caused her parents to emigrate from London to Canada shortly before Vivien was born. A subsequent position in the Canadian equivalent of that company, Teleglobe (properly the Canadian Overseas Telecommunications Corporation, as it then was) caused the family, now comprising two children, Vivien and her younger brother Adam, to move to Longueuil, Québec (a suburb of Montreal on the south bank of the St Lawrence River), in 1959. In Longueuil Vivien completed junior high school at Lemoyne d'Iberville High School (to 1966), and then from 1967 onwards was able to attend high school at the Trafalgar School for Girls in Montreal, a private school of high academic distinction, where her natural gift for languages was carefully nurtured (she had mastered Greek and Latin, Spanish, French and German by the time she completed high school there in 1971). Throughout her life Vivien remained grateful for the excellent linguistic training which she had received at (what was affectionately called) 'Traf', and her first book is dedicated to Barbara Armbruster, the woman who taught her Latin and Greek (it was Barbara Armbruster who taught Vivien the quaint habit,

Proceedings of the British Academy, **124**, 151–162. © The British Academy 2004.

which she maintained throughout her life, of writing Greek without accents and breathing marks).

From the Trafalgar School Vivien went on to McGill University in Montreal (1971–4), where she took Double Honours in Classics and German, and where her inclination to medieval studies first became apparent (she took courses in Old English, Old Norse, Old High German, Church Slavonic, as well as Greek, Latin and Hebrew). The brilliance of her academic promise is already visible in her undergraduate essays (she was by nature a hoarder, and all the essays she ever wrote are carefully preserved among her papers), on such subjects as 'Ein kurzes Vergleich der angelsächsischen und althochdeutschen Sprachen' (she had spent the summer of 1973 at Freiburg as part of her honours degree, and spoke and wrote German fluently throughout her life), or 'The Impact of Byzantine Political Thought on Russia' or 'Henry I of Saxony', the latter accompanied by a dense apparatus of footnote references to texts printed in the MGH and to works in German by such scholars as Max Manitius and Carl Erdmann. But the bulk of her papers from these early years consist of vocabulary lists and tables illustrating (for example) the changes undergone by Latin vowels in the Romance languages, or the differences between Spanish and Portuguese. It was at McGill, too, that she compiled a substantial supplement (pp. 170–237) to *The McGill University Collection of Greek and Roman Coins. I. Roman Coins*, ed. D. H. E. Whitehead, which constitutes her earliest publication (1975). From her work at McGill, it was clear that her major intellectual orientation was linguistic, and that she had an extraordinary capacity for disciplined and concentrated research.

Upon graduating from McGill in 1974 (with a GPA of 4.0, the highest possible mark), having apparently won every prize that the University had to offer, including the Chapman Gold Medal in Latin, she won a Commonwealth Scholarship to Girton College, Cambridge. Her family recalls that she had conceived the desire to study in England, at Oxford or Cambridge, while she was still in high school; the award of the Commonwealth Scholarship enabled her to pursue this dream, and she crossed the Atlantic in September 1974 on the Polish liner *Stefan Batory*, in a high state of excitement, accompanied by few possessions except her flute, for which she had acquired an expensive carrying-case shortly before leaving Canada. (Her notebooks do not record that she pestered the crew members to be taught Polish; but the scenario is not improbable, given that she had good reading knowledge of Polish later in life.) She arrived at Girton in October 1974, intending to read for a second undergraduate degree as an affiliated student in the Department of Anglo-Saxon, Norse, and Celtic. Her Director of Studies at Girton was Jill Mann, who had treated the claims of Vivien's McGill transcripts with mild scepticism, on the grounds that it seemed improbable that a twenty-year old could have mastered so many languages to any serious level of competence. But it was immediately clear to those who taught her in Cambridge during her first term that such scepticism was misplaced, and that she did indeed possess an astonishing mastery of the languages registered on her McGill transcript, including a number of those taught in the department, such as (Insular) Latin, Old English, Old Norse and other Germanic languages. It was difficult to see what aim would be served by requiring her to spend two additional undergraduate years studying languages in which she already had formidable expertise. Accordingly, after a term's work, she was enrolled in January 1975 as a research student, and set to work preparing as her doctoral dissertation an edition and study of the *Ars grammatica* of Boniface (d. 754), under the supervision of Michael Lapidge. The topic was devised so as to draw on her expertise in Latin and her developing curiosity about the structure of languages; furthermore, at the time she started her research, there was no adequate edition of Boniface in print. The dissertation was completed in 1978, and examined by R. G. G. Coleman and Richard Hunt. Unfortunately her edition of Boniface was never published, possibly because an edition of the same work, done as a war-time doctoral dissertation at the University of Chicago by one G. J. Gebauer, was completed by B. Löfstedt and published in the Series Latina of Corpus Christianorum in 1980. The defects of the Gebauer–Löfstedt edition are clear from a masterly review which Vivien published (*Studi medievali*, 22 (1981), 752–64), but she never got around to preparing her own edition for publication. In any case, on the strength and promise of her dissertation, she was elected to a Research Fellowship at Jesus College, Cambridge, a post which she held from 1977–80.

The Research Fellowship gave her a stable base from which to pursue her study of late antique and early Medieval Latin grammar. From the outset her intention had been to situate Boniface's *Ars grammatica* within the wider context of late antique and early Medieval Latin grammar, not only in the British Isles but on the Continent as well. It should be remembered that, in 1975, although many of the most important late antique grammatical texts were available in collections such as Heinrich Keil's *Grammatici Latini* (1857–80), very few of the important Medieval Latin grammars—for example, those of Murethach, Smaragdus, Sedulius

Scottus, to say nothing of the large corpus of anonymous treatises—were then accessible in printed editions; and those grammatical works which had been edited, for example the writings of (the so-called) Virgilius Maro Grammaticus, were often represented by editions of an abysmally low scholarly standard. Accordingly, if Vivien was to acquire mastery of the field of late antique and early Medieval Latin grammar, her first task was to familiarise herself with the early medieval manuscripts in which grammatical texts were transmitted. This task necessitated constant travel to British and continental libraries (she was an indefatigable traveller) in order to provide herself with transcriptions of grammatical texts; it also necessitated the acquisition of a huge collection of microfilms of grammatical manuscripts. Her work on these manuscripts soon revealed a vast and uncharted sea of unedited and unstudied grammatical texts, for the most part anonymous. A major component of her life's work was the attempt to chart this sea.

Her earliest publications in the field already reveal a profound experience of grammatical manuscripts and a refusal simply to reiterate the opinions of earlier scholars. All these publications report new discoveries, such as previously unknown Old English glosses to the *Ars grammatica* of Tatwine, an early eighth-century Anglo-Saxon grammarian (*Anglo-Saxon England*, 6 (1977), 77–89), or unsuspected aspects of the relationship between Anglo-Saxon and continental learning as revealed in the transmission of the grammars of Boniface and Tatwine (*Revue d'histoire des textes*, 9 (1979), 281–8), or the true nature of the jumbled and misunderstood grammar attributed to the early Irish grammarian Malsachanus (*Cambridge Medieval Celtic Studies*, 1 (1981), 83–93). As she continued to investigate grammatical manuscripts, she inevitably uncovered more and more previously unknown texts, and it is a tragedy that her early death prevented her from publishing editions of many of them, such as the *Ars Sergilii*, an unconventional grammatical treatise arguably from the circle of the unconventional Virgilius Maro Grammaticus, or the (more conventional) late antique grammar of Scaurus, the discovery of which she announced in *Rheinisches Museum*, 130 (1987), 67–89, the publication of which was anticipated in the series Cambridge Classical Texts and Commentaries. Her unpublished notebooks contain hundreds and hundreds of pages of transcriptions of grammatical texts examined (not all of them previously unknown, of course) during her travels. In many ways the trajectory of her early career resembles that of the nineteenth-century German scholars who spent their summers touring libraries and their winters publishing their *Reisefrüchte*.

After delivering a set of lectures (by invitation) on early Insular grammarians to the Department of Anglo-Saxon, Norse, and Celtic in Lent Term, 1979, and at the urging of her colleagues, she felt confident enough to offer the preliminary survey of the terrain which is contained in her *Insular Latin Grammarians* (1982). This compact book of 131 pages provides the first systematic attempt to classify Late Latin grammars according to type, to identify the principal early medieval commentaries (nearly all of them anonymous) on standard texts such as Donatus and Priscian, and above all to establish the date and place of origin of such commentaries. How many such commentaries were produced in either Ireland or Anglo-Saxon England is a thorny question, as is that of distinguishing anonymous Irish from anonymous English authorship. Her incisive treatment of questions of attribution inevitably brought her into contact (and sometimes conflict) with a number of medievalists, especially in Ireland, and in particular with Louis Holtz of the Institut de recherche et d'histoire des textes in Paris, who had then recently published his monumental edition of Donatus (1981). Although Vivien and Louis Holtz frequently disagreed about attributions and origins of commentaries, the warmth and generosity with which they treated each other's work and shared their learning could well serve as a model for all medievalists.

Above all, *The Insular Latin Grammarians* illustrated the cultural context in which the achievements of scholars such as Boniface and Tatwine were to be understood. She showed, emphatically, that these Anglo-Saxons were the first grammarians who were faced with the problem of explaining the structure of Latin to students who were not themselves native speakers of the language. By contrast, the grammars of (say) Donatus and Priscian had been composed as reference works for Latin speakers, and therefore contain much material, especially etymologies and analogues in Greek, which were simply irrelevant to an audience of beginners. Anglo-Saxon grammarians were thus forced to devise more elementary texts of a nature radically different from those which were transmitted to the Middle Ages from late antiquity (as she showed, the layout of verbal paradigms which today is found in virtually every elementary grammar, no matter what language, was first devised by Boniface). Vivien (of necessity) began to elaborate a terminology to describe the various types of grammar which survive from late antiquity and the Middle Ages, and her terminology and the classificatory scheme which it entails—*regulae*-type grammars, *Schulgrammatik* grammars, elementary grammars, parsing grammars, and so on—is one of the most useful contributions that she made to medieval studies.

The huge amount of research underpinning *The Insular Latin Grammarians*, in combination with the ever-increasing flow of scholarly articles, all of them written with inimitable concision but displaying formidable erudition, led to her election as the David Thomson Senior Research Fellow of Sidney Sussex College, Cambridge, in 1980, a post which she held until 1984. By then, however, her work had naturally caught the attention of the Department of Linguistics, which, by the happiest of chances, not only needed someone who could teach the history of the subject but had a heaven-sent opportunity, under the 'New Blood' scheme devised by the then University Grants Committee, to establish a lectureship designed for her. When he saw advertisements for the post, the doyen of the history of linguistics, the late R. H. Robins, remarked that they might just as well have added: 'Only Vivien Law need apply'. The 'New Blood' scheme ran for only a few years in the 1980s, but many first-rate scholars were helped by it, in highly specialised fields; since then, regrettably, existing lectureships have increasingly been suppressed by faculties, and the thought of establishing a new one, even when there is a candidate so obviously brilliant as Vivien was, has now passed beyond a head of department's dreams.

A paper on 'The History of Linguistic Thought' was already an option in the Modern and Medieval Languages Tripos. Vivien therefore landed in the department running and, from the beginning, her course never lacked at least a handful of devoted students. Most papers, in most branches of the history of ideas, deal with a period of at best some centuries, in one perhaps quite small part of the world. Hers was very different. It was designed to cover two and a half millennia, from Ancient India and fifth-century Greece to American linguistics in the 1960s and beyond. Though centred in western Europe, it potentially included every other major civilisation, especially those from which ideas have fed into the European tradition. Nor could the history of linguistic thought be separated from the general intellectual and political history of successive periods, of which most undergraduates have been taught increasingly little. Only a scholar whose enthusiasm for learning knew no artificial bounds could have taken it on. In later years she was to remain, above all, a historian of grammar; the philosophy of language, and especially many of the theoretical preoccupations of the twentieth century, she was apt to regard with less sympathy. But the period on which her work was centred soon expanded, in line with her teaching, far beyond the early Middle Ages, to an extent that is hard to appreciate from the projects she was able to complete before she died. The most coherent group of publications are still in the field where she first gained her reputation. The rest are scattered glimpses of what should have been.

One never dared to speak to her of the 'Dark Ages'. Out of this period, however, in which we are nevertheless comparatively in the dark, the enigmatic figure of Virgilius Maro Grammaticus was one that continued to intrigue her. Of (arguably) Insular origin and seventh-century date, his grammatical treatises are so bizarre and unconventional that they have been regarded variously as nonsense or parody. For example, Virgilius refers throughout to grammatical authorities who are unknown outside the pages of his writings and whose very names invite derision: Balapsidus, Fassica, Galbirius, Galbungus, Glengus, Gurgilius, Sarbon, Terrentius, and others (including three authors named 'Vergil', none of them identical with the author of the *Aeneid*). He tells us that Galbungus and Terrentius debated for fourteen days and nights over whether the pronoun *ego* had a vocative case. He expounds twelve types of Latinity, of which the first, *usitata*, has the familiar word *ignis* to represent fire; but the eleven others, *inusitatae*, have words which are otherwise unrecorded (*quoquihabin*, which Virgilius declines in full, *ardon*, *calax*, *rusin*, and so on through all the remaining types). Because the structure of Virgilius's grammatical writings is evidently modelled on that of classical grammars such as the *Ars maior* of Donatus, earlier scholars have inclined to the notion that Virgilius was simply attempting to compose a parody grammar. But, as Vivien Law rightly pointed out, the excessive length of Virgilius's writings casts doubt on the parody hypothesis (a joke of this sort could have been made in a few pages, whereas Virgilius's grammatical writings occupy some 160 pages in the standard edition). While not denying the amusing nature of these writings, she sought a deeper, more satisfying explanation. Her *Wisdom, Authority and Grammar in the Seventh Century: Decoding Virgilius Maro Grammaticus* (1995), though characteristically brief (170 pp.), is a masterpiece of sustained and inspired analysis. By the meticulous elucidation of linguistic ambiguities embedded (one might say encoded) in his Latin, she was able to show how Virgilius enticed his readers towards a more profound and sophisticated understanding of the processes of perception and the acquisition, not merely of Latin grammar, but of knowledge divine and human. The study and analysis of Virgilius's treatises undertaken by any reader, reading with the *oculi mentis*, thus becomes the paradigm of human learning.

From her base, as it were, in the early Middle Ages one natural way to move was backwards, to the tradition of the Roman '*Ars grammatica*' and, behind it, its Greek sources. For many authorities the earliest Greek grammar is still the one ascribed to Dionysius Thrax, who died around 90 BC. Since antiquity, however, the authenticity of most of this text has been questioned: the doctrine of the parts of speech does not agree entirely with the views ascribed to Dionysius by ancient commentators, and suggests a date of composition, or at least reworking, some four centuries later. The controversy was revived at the end of the 1950s by Vincenzo di Benedetto, and Vivien's interest in it led, in particular, to a conference held in Sidney Sussex, whose proceedings she edited with Ineke Sluiter (*Dionysius Thrax and the* Technē Grammatikē (1995)). Her own approach was, characteristically, to look for detailed changes in the analysis of Latin in the late Imperial period, which the wording of Dionysius, or pseudo-Dionysius, might or might not parallel. In print, however, she made no more than, in her own words, 'a small beginning' (*History and Historiography of Linguistics*, eds. H. J. Niderehe and K. Koerner (1990), I. 89–96). Her projected edition of Scaurus, a grammarian earlier than Donatus and the others whose work has survived, would have shown her deep familiarity with the ancient tradition to which they belonged.

It was also natural that Vivien's interests should expand into the later Middle Ages, to include (for example) late medieval speculative grammar. The essay which resulted from her J. R. O'Donnell lecture (delivered in Toronto in 1998 and printed in *The Journal of Medieval Latin*, 9 (1999), 46–76), on late Medieval Latin verse grammars such as the *Doctrinale* of Alexander of Ville-Dieu, is a brilliant illustration of her intellectual range: in demonstrating why such poems were composed and how they were structured, she provides a fascinating glimpse of an otherwise neglected aspect of late medieval education. Few historians of linguistics have indeed been so consistently alert to the practical contexts in which grammars were written. Her early work had been informed by a rare understanding of the ways in which the teaching of Latin had to change, when beginners themselves spoke other languages, such as Old English, which had significantly different structures: a point that now seems obvious, but it was Vivien who showed how grammars were adapted to cope with the difficulty.

Many years later she was tempted away from Sidney Sussex, which she had served well as a teaching fellow and sometime Praelector since her appointment in the university, to a similar fellowship at Trinity College (1997). The conversation at the interview was largely about the tables of contents of grammars, in the Renaissance and later. Did they follow the pattern established since antiquity: first the noun, then the other parts of speech in their time-worn order? Or did the author ask which parts were easier or more difficult for someone trying to learn the language, and decide on both the order of topics, and the weight that should be given to each, accordingly? There seems little doubt that insights of this kind reflected her own practical experience as a learner, systematically acquiring language after language, by the method of working with pencil and paper through whatever materials were available.

One of these many languages (in total more than a hundred, it was believed) was Georgian, and a very different study which she did complete, as part of a collaborative project on 'Post-Soviet States in Transition', was of 'myths' of nationality and language among its speakers ('Language Myths and the Discourse of Nation-Building in Georgia', in G. Smith, V. Law *et al.*, *Nation-Building in the Post-Soviet Borderlands* (1998), pp. 167–96, 269–78). Among all her scholarly and other activities, she came to know both Georgia and Georgians very well (and tended to take their side in any discussion of Caucasian politics). By the end, however, she was concentrating above all on what was to be her last and posthumous book, on *The History of Linguistics in Europe from Plato to 1600* (2002). The original plan had been to end it at 1900, and Robins, who was by then a close friend, hoped very much that it would replace his own *Short History of Linguistics*, then over thirty years old. In the event she included only a 'brief overview', in less than thirty pages, of the period from 1600 to the present. But it became clear that an earlier cut-off made good sense. At heart, despite the breadth of her theme, she remained a medievalist, and had a western medievalist's appreciation of the ancient world especially. She gives far more space to Priscian, for example, than to Apollonius Dyscolus, although, as Priscian himself would certainly have told her, Apollonius, in second-century Alexandria, was the genius and he the follower. The Middle Ages are in effect presented at the heart of a continuous tradition, whose source lay ultimately in one great age of intellectual upheaval, in fifth-century Greece, and which was finally transcended in another, in the northern European Renaissance. It is not surprising, therefore, that the influence of religion is also central to her narrative. Her account of 'the early Middle Ages' is preceded by a separate chapter headed 'Christianity and Language', which lays weight on the theories of Augustine. The reason she gave for ending in 1600 is that, from then on, we are no longer dealing with a single homogeneous tradition, but with separate histories in separate nations that interact in much more complex ways. One cannot but feel, however, that the gradual secularisation of linguistics, as of other academic disciplines, might have proved an uncongenial topic.

The proposal for this book had originally been accepted by the editors of the 'Cambridge Textbooks in Linguistics', and it is written at that level, in a way designed quite brilliantly to inspire and guide students. At the end of the 1980s she had already published her scholarly manifesto as a historian of linguistics (in *An Encyclopaedia of Linguistics*, ed. N. E. Collinge (1990), pp. 784–842); but her last book, on *The History of Linguistics in Europe*, is a memorial to the way she had come to teach the subject: a simultaneous insistence both on the close study of texts and on the context, in the widest possible sense, in which they were composed. It is clear too that her ideal students would be those who were themselves preparing for research. The book is full of hints on how to become a historian of the subject, and of the basic information that researchers need. Both the medieval and renaissance chapters, for example, include indispensable charts of the types and dates of grammars, of Latin, of the European vernaculars and, by the end, of other languages, which will enable and encourage subsequent scholars to navigate previously uncharted seas.

A project like *The History of Linguistics in Europe*, covering 2000 years in a bare 300 pages and exhibiting a mastery of both detail and broad synthesis, could have been executed only by someone who had learned to write with perfect clarity and concision. Despite this enviable ability, however, Vivien was a very prolific scholar. In addition to the books already mentioned, she published some sixty-five articles, of which several of the most important, in her first field of research, were revised and reprinted in her *Grammar and Grammarians in the Early Middle Ages* (1997). This collection, used in conjunction with her bibliography of early medieval grammar published in a book which she edited (*History of Linguistic Thought in the Early Middle Ages* (1993), pp. 25–47), and with the wider coverage of the Middle Ages in her last book, provides an excellent introduction to the subject, and the complex problems of interpretation which it poses. It was on the strength of her work as a medievalist that she was elected to the British Academy in 1999, the letter from the Secretary coinciding, cruelly, with the diagnosis of her cancer and the knowledge that she would have to undergo what were, in the event, a series of operations. It was on the strength of this work too that she had been appointed, two years earlier, to a readership in the university. The title she chose, however, was Reader in the History of Linguistic Thought, without qualification as to period. It is the promise and resolve behind this choice that was to remain so sadly unfulfilled.

In spite of her commitment to study, Vivien was active in societies and remained easily accessible and deeply loyal to her many students, colleagues and friends. At her death she was still serving as the executive chairman of the Henry Sweet Society for the History of Linguistic Ideas, of whose publication series she had been a founding editor; she had only recently, in her final illness, resigned as chairman of the local regional society of the Institute of Linguists. She was also active in the Philological Society, and was the inspiration, amid all else, of a volume published posthumously in its series, of autobiographical essays by scholars in or near retirement, conceived as a primary source for later historians (*Linguistics in Britain: Personal Histories*, ed. Keith Brown and Vivien Law (2002)).

In 1978 she had married Nick (now Sir Nicholas) Shackleton, a distinguished quaternary geologist, with whom she shared a love of walking and playing chamber music. She herself played the flute and piccolo to professional standard, and they had met when she had asked if she could borrow a baroque bassoon from his (internationally renowned) woodwind collection. In the week before her memorial service in October 2002, at which he played a moving piece for solo clarinet, he received an e-mail from the last class of undergraduates, by then scattered across four continents, that Vivien had been able to teach for an entire year. Only a few words could be cited in the address delivered at the service. But it is a touching tribute to the kind of teacher of whom, as they put it, 'Cambridge legends are formed'. Being her student was 'an enormous privilege and a special joy'.

Before the end of that academic year, in 2000–1, her cancer had returned and was found to be inoperable. She received the news with an equanimity strengthened by her faith since childhood in anthroposophy, and began the following year determined to work normally, or as normally as possible, for as long as she could. She sent her last book to the press; she attended her last conference, of the Henry Sweet Society, at the end of September; and in October she started lecturing several hours a week to a final group of undergraduates, hoping to get through the whole field before Christmas. From then on candidates would do supervised projects. She simultaneously began work with her last research student. But, halfway through the Michaelmas term, even she could not continue. She was forced to abandon her teaching duties, and died a few months later, on 20 February 2002.

The tragic sense of loss at her premature death that is felt by all her students, colleagues and friends should not overshadow the very significant contributions which she made to our understanding of the fields of early medieval grammar and the history of linguistics. She trained a number of students who now have university posts and are in a position to carry on her work in these fields. And for those who did not know her and did not have the privilege of being trained by her, the substantial body of her publications will provide guidance in fields which before her were scarcely, or only dimly, known. Even scholars who have lived active lives through to decrepit old age have not always been able to achieve as much.

MICHAEL LAPIDGE
Fellow of the Academy

PETER MATTHEWS
Fellow of the Academy

Note. We should like to express our gratitude to Vivien's husband, Professor Sir Nicholas Shackleton, for generously allowing access to her papers and library, and to her brother, Dr Adam Law, for answering many queries about her early life and family. There is a bibliography of her publications by E. F. K. Koerner, 'Bibliography of Vivien A. Law, 1975–2002', in *Historiographia Linguistica*, 29. 1–2 (2002), 5–11. A number of personal recollections by her friends and pupils are gathered together in *The Henry Sweet Society Bulletin*, 38 (May 2002), 5–26. The text of the address delivered by Peter Matthews at her memorial service (19 October 2002) is printed in the *Trinity College Annual Record 2002*, 72–6. A volume of essays in her memory is being prepared by many of her former students.

JOHN LOUGH

John Lough
1913–2000

JOHN LOUGH was in very many ways an exemplary member of the British academic establishment. He was a punctilious scholar and industrious researcher, who shared the results of his inquiries with the intellectual community in a prolific series of books and articles. Although he was essentially a man of the written, rather than the spoken, word, he took his duties as teacher very seriously, and also played a prominent part in the governance of Durham University, where most of his career unfolded. There were, however, certain characteristic interests and commitments that distinguished John Lough from the typical academic figure of his generation, who was more likely to be found in the green pastures of the ancient universities in the south of England than in the more raw and bleak north east of the country.

In this urbane, self-protective man, with his quizzical gaze, dry humour and few words, it was difficult to discern the 'geordie', but John Lough was very much a man of his roots, and those roots were firmly in Newcastle-upon-Tyne and its hinterland. He was born in Newcastle on 19 February 1913, the third of five children. His father, Wilfrid Gordon Lough (1880–1962), had been taken into the family business, a butcher's shop in Jesmond, and he eventually became its proprietor. Through his mother, Mary Turnbull (née Millican) Lough (1885–1979), John Lough was descended from a long line of tenant farmers in north Northumberland. As a rather delicate child, John was sent away from the insalubrious city for longish periods, to be spent on his grandparents' farm and later in the nearby village where they retired. His deep attachment

Proceedings of the British Academy, **124**, 165–180. © The British Academy 2004.

to Northumberland was revealed only to those who had the good fortune to penetrate his basic shyness in his later years and hear about
those long ago visits to his rural relatives. Although such memories did
not lure this essentially bookish man to forsake his study for country
pursuits, it was undoubtedly his love of the North East that kept him so
contentedly in Durham for so many years. His very last book-length
publication was to be both a celebration and example of his fidelity to
his family. In it, he worked together with his sister, Elizabeth Merson, to
apply his professional expertise as an historian to writing a memoir of
his great-great-great-uncle, the Northumbrian sculptor, John Graham
Lough.[1]

John Lough's parents made considerable sacrifices to send all five of
their children to fee-paying schools. In Newcastle, for John, that could
only mean the Royal Grammar School, preceded by what he once
described as 'a kind of dame school', of a type that was still extant in
the region in the 1960s. The Royal Grammar School must have recognised quite early that they had gained an intellectually talented pupil, for
his fees were soon subject to a partial remission and were later waived
altogether. The school governors also awarded him a scholarship that
eased his financial situation throughout his undergraduate years at
Cambridge. Lough repaid this generosity by a no less generous recognition of what he owed the school in terms of his intellectual development. Apparently he was lucky in that a new headmaster, appointed
shortly after he joined the school, completely reinvigorated the teaching
by recruiting energetic new staff. Among them was the Anglo-Russian
modern language master, who must have influenced his star pupil's
choice of French and German in the sixth form. Modern languages was
not a high status academic discipline at that time. We possibly owe
Lough's career in the field, and the very considerable efforts he made
later to promote the study of French language and literature in the
school classroom, to the fact that he was educated at some distance from
the fashionable mainstream and its prejudices. Even so, his approach to
his studies must have been severely academic. He can have had no direct
contact with the peoples and cultures of Europe until he had the chance
of a school trip to Lübeck in 1929, a relatively rare opportunity for a lad
of sixteen from Newcastle. By then, he may well have internally constituted his view of France as that of the interested and intelligent

---

[1] (With Elizabeth Merson) *John Graham Lough (1789–1876), a Northumbrian Sculptor*
(Woodbridge, 1987).

observer, warily watchful but not immersed. His preferred mode of language learning was always translation, the one that emphasises difference. Much of his later investigation of seventeenth- and eighteenth-century French cultural practices adopted the point of view of eminent British travellers reporting home. Lough's own first journey to France was to Strasbourg in 1930, prior to taking up the major scholarship he had been awarded by St John's College in December of that year.

Lough arrived at Cambridge in the October of 1931, very conscious of his position as a first-generation student. He was shocked by the antics and conspicuous consumption of the gilded youth who played on the Cambridge scene, and not a little affronted by their disdain of the sort of serious academic work that had brought him there. The lean to the left in politics that one would expect from a young man's close experience of the North East, its decaying industries, unemployment, and bitter labour relations, was confirmed by this encounter. Moreover, Lough's student visits to pre-war France (as a graduate student he was in Paris for the Front Populaire's election victory in 1936) provided a wider context within which to establish informed political conviction. Despite this maturing of attitudes that were to be not without their bearing on the topics and methodology he was to choose for his more advanced work, Lough's time at Cambridge was almost exclusively devoted to his studies. Even in that respect he was shocked by practices that seemed to him to encourage mediocrity and shallow thinking. He was bored by the concentration on language studies in the first year, and came near to giving up modern languages altogether. He was surprised to have no contact at all with senior members of his college, which 'farmed out' all its modern language undergraduates to supervisors who did not have a university post. In his second year, he led a successful revolt against this system, largely because he wanted to be supervised in German by Roy Pascal, the only inspiring teacher he came across in three years. After Part I of the Tripos (in which he gained a First in French and German and an oral distinction in both languages), he chose to focus on France and Germany in the seventeenth, eighteenth and nineteenth centuries. These were studied from a very general perspective in which literature was by no means the privileged and ahistorical subject of inquiry it was shortly to become. It was viewed primarily as a rather inert product of the intellectual, social and political history of a period. For Lough, however, the historical content of the course whetted his curiosity as none of the rest of the syllabus had so far done. The possibility of examining how the ideas of important writers interact with their historical environment in its broadest sense provided him with the delighted discovery of where his intellectual gifts and energies might be profitably and pleasurably employed. He was awarded a First in Part II of the Modern and Medieval Languages Tripos in 1934. After realising that, without a guaranteed private income, he was disbarred from the diplomatic service, and having been reliably informed that his bad eyesight made him unfit for the consular service (the poor man's option, as he saw it), he decided to stay in Cambridge in order to gain the degree of Ph.D.

The subject of Lough's thesis was 'Some Aspects of the Life and Thought of Baron d'Holbach'. The title is very much of its time, both in its modest aspirations and in the 'life and works' approach. It was too original a subject for Cambridge, however, and no properly qualified expert was on hand to supervise it. Lough was advised by Harry Ashton, a scholar with a good general knowledge of the field, who proved extremely conscientious. Lough's account of his years as a research student focused on his constant need for financial support. This was obviously an anxiety for him, though an anxiety that was allayed before it became pressing, as he was awarded scholarships and grants year by year. The most important in terms of his intellectual development was the Esmond Scholarship, which he held at the British Institute in Paris for the whole of his second year. Thus began his intimate acquaintance with the holdings of French libraries and archive deposits. All his subsequent writings demonstrate his thorough mastery of this primary material, his scrupulous accuracy in transcribing it, and his deft judgement in selecting, managing and exploiting it. Lough also made the most of opportunities to meet French scholars of the Enlightenment, notably the most distinguished of their number at that time, Daniel Mornet, who encouraged the young Englishman by publishing his first review and with whom Lough was to remain on very amicable terms. More amicable still was his relationship with a female compatriot pursuing postgraduate research in Paris at the same time. Muriel Alice Barker (1913–98) had graduated from Nottingham, then under the aegis of the University of London, with a First in French. She and Lough were to marry in 1939, a partnership that was also a collaboration, for they were to publish several books as joint authors.

Lough submitted his thesis in 1937 and was awarded the degree of Ph.D., with some avuncular admonishment from one of the examiners about the dangers of excessive modesty. In fact, Lough had much to be proud of, because he was able to embark on his professional career much more speedily than was usual at the time. Even before the award of the degree he had been offered a post as Assistant Lecturer in French at the University of Aberdeen, solely on the recommendation of his supervisor. The department was very small and the system very hierarchical, but Lough was fortunate in having very congenial close colleagues who guided his beginner's steps. It was not long before this 'beginner', together with his wife, was to be the mainstay of the department. Lough's poor eyesight made him unfit for military service, so he remained at Aberdeen for the whole period of the war. His appointment, which was initially for five years, was renewed year by year. By the end of the war, he and his wife were virtually the only teachers of French at the university. Their students were mostly female. Lough was also commissioned to drill them in the exercise of putting out incendiary bombs (fortunately none fell in the vicinity). Typically, Lough was quick to exploit the eighteenth-century resources of Aberdeen's excellent library, and found much to support his work when travel to other libraries was difficult. He published some of the results of his researches in the *Aberdeen University Review*. This interest in promoting local material in a local context was to prove characteristic of Lough's loyalty to the place in which he functioned. After he moved to Durham, he would not infrequently publish papers connected with his ongoing research in the *Durham University Journal*.

In 1945, Lough was finally appointed to a full lectureship at Aberdeen, but he was ambitious to move on. In 1946, he returned to Cambridge as a lecturer, a very welcome move in terms of access to library provision, but not without its difficulties. Lough found himself the only lecturer without a college fellowship, and considerably hampered in this respect by his membership of a college that had no tradition of appointing fellows in modern languages. One senses that he must have felt socially somewhat isolated, for, although he was essentially a private and self-contained person, there is no doubt that he enjoyed the company and conversation of other men, especially dedicated scholars like himself, and could have flourished in a congenial high-table environment. His proximity to libraries, however, ensured that his research flourished. His rate of publication settled into a rhythm of one or, mostly, two articles each year, a pace that was to accelerate during the next forty years, but not decrease until well into the 1990s. It is in these Cambridge years that one notes his interests diversifying along the three routes that were to remain high on his agenda: the history of French Enlightenment thought; the social history of seventeenth-century

French theatre; and interactions between French and English thinkers in both these periods.[2] Nevertheless, Lough, still in many ways the 'provincial' outsider, was not any more enamoured of Cambridge than he had been as a student, and when the chance came to move to the vacant chair at Durham, he is unlikely to have hesitated. October 1952, therefore, saw him back in his beloved North East, and incidentally, in May of that year, the father of Judith, his only child.

Lough became Professor of French at Durham at the relatively early age of thirty-nine and remained so until his retirement in 1978. When he arrived there in 1952, the whole university comprised 1100 students. Lough oversaw the rapid expansion of his department, in terms both of students and staff, during the 1960s and he was much engaged in managing other changes, for example, the division of the old federal university into the two independent institutions of Durham and Newcastle, that occurred in 1963. He took very seriously his responsibilities as a senior member of the university for its good management. For twenty-five years almost without remission, he was a member of the University Senate. He was a relentlessly efficient Dean of the Faculty of Arts from 1965 to 1967, and at some time a member of almost every committee there was. His was a wise head, a moderate voice, injecting reasonableness and humour into debate, resisting extremism and helping the university to keep a steady course. This did not involve taking risks. In 1969, Lough resigned in the middle of his second term on the University Council in protest against the introduction of student members (Durham's modest response to *événements* that might have reminded Lough of the more violent aspects of French culture he had found very foreign in the years before the Second World War).

Lough did not belong to the democratic era of department administration. For almost all his tenure of the Chair of French at Durham he was automatically Head of Department. He managed his staff and students somewhat in the manner in which the benevolent despots of his

---

[2] Among articles published at this period of Lough's career were: 'The Earnings of Playwrights in Seventeenth-Century France', *Modern Language Review*, 42 (1947), 321–36; 'Condorcet et Richard Price', *Revue de littérature comparée*, 24 (1950), 87–93; 'The *Encyclopédie* in Eighteenth-Century England', *French Studies*, 6 (1952), 289–307. In the year after he left Cambridge, two important edited volumes appeared: *Locke's Travels in France, 1675–1679, as Related in his Journals, Correspondence and other Papers* (London, 1953); and Denis Diderot, *Selected Philosophical Writings* (London, 1953). Both were published by Cambridge University Press. Diderot was always central to Lough's preoccupation with Enlightenment thought. The Locke volume was to prove of perennial interest, and was reissued in facsimile by Garland (New York and London) in 1984.

beloved eighteenth century ran their domains (at least in popular conception). He kept himself a little aloof from the fray, but he always knew exactly what was going on, intervened to bring matters to a sensible conclusion at precisely the right moment and with an unerring knack of getting his own way without arousing overt antagonism. Colleagues deferred to him because they respected him as a man, as well as bowing to the authority of his standing in the world of scholarship. His qualities as an administrator and as a person were essentially those of the Enlightenment. He was rational, humane, tolerant, and very shrewd, with more than a touch of Voltairean irony about the follies and foibles of his fellows. All irrational and ill-founded convictions he regarded with a confident and benign suspicion. His younger colleagues were in considerable awe of him. He could seem disconcertingly distant, observing the world from behind the smoke-screen emanating from the pipe that was never out of his mouth, saying little, and apparently letting one flounder helplessly in unfinished sentences and inchoate opinions. Yet, once one had glimpsed the amused, but kindly glint in his eyes, once one realised that all the time one was being gently drawn towards paths that were sane, reasonable, and in everyone's best interests, one was delighted to find in him a supportive and utterly reliable mentor and friend. He was tolerant towards his female colleagues, if somewhat surprised to have them. His wife, whose intellectual gifts and achievements he respected, was doubtless a positive influence in this area, and they together were hospitable hosts at slightly formal sherry parties, at which his young colleagues vied in the consumption of cheese footballs. The abiding legend of Lough at Durham is one of the most admirable efficiency. Rumour has it that he polished off his teaching and administration in the mornings, and then betook himself to the library for the rest of the day to get on with what really mattered. It was said that he had a private key to the library and could be found hard at work on Christmas Day and Boxing Day, but that was unproven. Lough himself swore that this picture of effortless time-management was far from the truth, but the legend persists and speaks eloquently of the respect in which he was held and the reasons for it. His daughter's memory of her father is, happily, somewhat at variance with the legend. He did indeed leave the department at the end of the morning, when meetings allowed, but it was nearly always in order to come home, often to devote an hour or so to his well-tended, well-loved garden, and then to work in his study. Even she, however, allows that the only day in the year that her father took off was Christmas Day.

Lough's essential conservatism in the micro-politics of university administration arose primarily from a concern to preserve the highest professional standards in teaching and research. It did not denote any realignment of his political views with respect to the fabric of society in general. Lough had joined the Labour Party in 1937, and, despite his belief that a very broad all-party coalition government might have been best for the country in the immediate pre-war period, he resisted pressure by an academic colleague to join the Communists in 1938. His commitment to Labour was demonstrated by active campaigning on behalf of a friend contesting a County Durham seat at successive general elections. In his later years he let his party membership lapse, partly owing to the local party's failure to ask for his dues, but mainly because his opinions veered increasingly towards the cause of moderation in government. For this reason he voted for the SDP/Liberal Alliance in 1983 and 1987, hoping that no party would have a majority. His dearest wish, however, was 'to see the back of Mrs Thatcher'. He lived to see Labour's triumph and rejoiced in it. The lad from Newcastle, in politics, as in many things, remained true to his roots.

Despite his willing involvement in university management, it was clear to all at Durham that academic research and academic publishing were Lough's prime preoccupation and the centre of his life. His first and abiding love was for the thought and thinkers of the French Enlightenment. His left-leaning political opinions were not without their influence on his interest in the *philosophes*, those clever critics of establishment thinking and establishment *mores*. His scrupulously documented accounts of the broad historical context, political, social, and economic, in which they developed and functioned was essentially marxist, though Lough himself preferred to define his approach as a 'sceptical marxism, with a small "m"'. A particular facet of Enlightenment thought that Lough undoubtedly found sympathetic was its highly critical attitude to religious belief and practice. This exactly chimed with Lough's own views and confirmed them.

The single author from this period on whom Lough did most work was Denis Diderot. His careful collecting of documentary evidence on various aspects of Diderot's thought and career culminated in the volumes of Diderot's complete works that Lough edited in conjunction with a major French scholar, Jacques Proust, in 1976.[3] Many years prior to that, in 1953, Lough had also acted as Diderot's publicist in England with

---

[3] Denis Diderot, *Œuvres complètes*, eds. J. Lough and J. Proust, vols. V–VIII: *Encyclopédie* (Paris, 1976).

a volume of his selected philosophical writings published by Cambridge University Press (see above, n. 2). Lough was always intrigued by the ways in which ideas moved between France and Great Britain in the seventeenth and eighteenth centuries, and he did much by his own endeavours to ensure that the cross-channel flow continued. His promotion of Diderot, however, was part of a wider project. His object was to ensure that British scholars, as well as French, were in a position to have informed access to the whole of that vast compendium of eighteenth-century knowledge and Enlightenment opinion, the *Encyclopédie*, that Diderot had conceived, that he edited, and that he supplied with many of its more lively and controversial articles. In 1954, in parallel with his selections from Diderot's philosophical writings printed in the previous year, Lough edited some of Diderot's *Encyclopédie* articles for an English-speaking readership, along with others by Diderot's original co-editor, D'Alembert.[4]

On a broader front, and in less-well-travelled terrain, Lough applied himself to track down the identity of anonymous authors of articles in the *Encyclopédie*, disentangle its publishing history, and investigate its, often very hostile, reception in France and elsewhere. This invaluable detective work is documented in a series of pioneering articles written between 1952 and 1967.[5] It was finally embodied in book form in *Essays on the 'Encyclopédie' of Diderot and D'Alembert*, published in London by Oxford University Press in 1968, a collection of new essays on the history of editions of the *Encyclopédie*, on the articles written for it by D'Holbach and D'Alembert, and on the light thrown on its contents and history by contemporary books, pamphlets and periodicals. Meanwhile, Lough was also preparing a work of greater compass on the *Encyclopédie*. Perhaps only someone who has gazed with astonishment and awe at this huge, many-volumed work that constitutes a statement of

---

[4] *The 'Encyclopédie' of Diderot and D'Alembert: Selected Articles* (London, 1954).

[5] 'The *Encyclopédie* in Eighteenth-Century England', *French Studies*, 6 (1952), 289–307; 'Louis, Chevalier de Jaucourt (1704–1780): A Biographical Sketch', in E. T. Dubois *et al.* (eds.), *Essays Presented to C. M. Girdlestone* (Newcastle-upon-Tyne, 1960), pp. 195–217; 'Louis, Chevalier de Jaucourt: Some Further Notes', *French Studies*, 15 (1961), 350–7; 'The *Encyclopédie* and the Remonstrances of the Paris Parlement', *Modern Language Review*, 56 (1961), 393–5; 'The *Encyclopédie*: Two Unsolved Problems', *French Studies*, 17 (1963), 121–35; 'Mme Geoffrin and the *Encyclopédie*', *Modern Language Review*, 58 (1963), 219–22; 'Luneau de Boisjermain v. the Publishers of the *Encyclopédie*', *Studies on Voltaire and the Eighteenth Century*, 23 (1963), 1071–83; 'The Problem of the Unsigned Articles in the *Encyclopédie*', ibid., 32 (1965), 327–90; 'New Light on the *Encyclopédie*', *History Today*, 15 (1965), 169–75; 'The *Encyclopédie* in Voltaire's Correspondence', in W. H. Barber *et al.* (eds.), *The Age of Enlightenment: Studies Presented to Theodore Besterman* (Edinburgh, 1967), pp. 51–65.

the Enlightenment project and also a demonstration of that project applied to every form of knowledge conceivable in the eighteenth century can properly comprehend how ambitious Lough was. He was seeking to encapsulate its history, its content and its reception for students of the eighteenth century at all levels, the majority of whom would know it was crucial to their inquiries, but found it almost impossibly daunting. Lough's work of synthesis, *The 'Encyclopédie'*, published in London by Longman in 1971, was a very important landmark in eighteenth-century studies, and, indeed, in the general growth of interest in Enlightenment thought that is noticeable at that period. Its readers were provided with an account of the origins of the *Encyclopédie*, its difficult progress into print, a review of its contributors and subscribers, and an account of contemporary readers' recorded reactions to it. The nub of Lough's book seeks to answer questions about the intentions of its editors and authors: was it primarily a neutral work of reference or was it conceived as a vehicle to propagate the subversive views of the *philosophes* in the fields of philosophy, religion, politics, social structure and social practice? Chapters devoted to each of these subjects explore the way they are treated in the *Encyclopédie* by means of extended quotations from its articles and from contemporary critics. Lough was convinced that the 'true meaning' of many of the articles must be located in their eighteenth-century context and can often best be found in the way they were read at the time. This apparently slightly naïve justification of the method of exposition he decided to adopt conceals the expert judgement and acrobatic manoeuvres Lough displays in moving through the plethora of material collected in the *Encyclopédie* under apparently unrelated heads. The years in which Lough had been familiarising himself with the text and context of the *Encyclopédie* had equipped him to define the exact targets it was aiming for, and fully to comprehend its attacking stratagems and the extent of the damage it inflicted. This required a truly encyclopaedic knowledge of its contents, a fine response to the ironies deliberately employed in its allusive and digressive method, and a knowing selection of the most illuminating criticisms directed at it by its contemporaries. Lough's lucid exposition and explanations of the content of the work are extraordinarily efficient and informative, and it was probably as a source of information about this major, but rather inaccessible, monument of the Enlightenment that his book was most valued.[6] It was not, however,

---

[6] Its importance is attested by the fact that it was reprinted some time later: *The 'Encyclopédie'* (Geneva, 1989).

Lough's only contribution to knowledge of the *Encyclopédie* emanating
from this period of his career. In 1970, he had published a collection of
essays partially devoted to his favourite topic of the exchange of ideas
between France and England.[7] In 1973, in accord with the strong pedagogical bent to which we shall return later in this memoir, he published a
succinct account of the *Encyclopédie*'s contributors in a series intended
for undergraduates.[8]

The ways ideas travelled between France and Great Britain had been
part of Lough's research agenda since his youthful investigations of eighteenth-century French books that had been imported to Scotland and
had ended up in the University Library at Aberdeen. A predictable move
from voyaging books to voyaging authors had given him the topic of his
first book-length project in 1953, his edition of Locke's journals of his
travels in France in 1675–9 (see above, n. 2). This interest was to blossom
again in Lough's retirement with sporadic articles and the publication of
two books: *France Observed in the Seventeenth Century* (Stocksfield,
1985) and *France on the Eve of Revolution: British Travellers'
Observations 1763–1788* (London, 1987).[9] It might be said that these late
works mainly took the form of quotations connected by narrative, rather
than analysis, but, even so, it is remarkable that Lough's expertise in
selecting and transcribing this fascinating archival material, as well as his
choice of topic, coincided happily with the emphasis accorded to travel
literature by a new generation of scholars interested in the ways inhabitants of one culture regard the alien and in their angled reports of it. He
was rather pleased and amused to be consulted by his young historian
colleagues. His interest in the eighteenth-century *philosophes*, on the other
hand, apart from some retrospective articles and contributions to ency-
clopaedias, was to bear late fruit only in an attempt to chart their

---

[7] *The 'Encyclopédie' in Eighteenth-Century England and Other Studies* (Newcastle-upon-Tyne,
1970).

[8] *The Contributors to the 'Encyclopédie'* (London, 1973); it was considered valuable enough to
the scholarly community at large to be reprinted, with additions and corrections by the author,
in R. N. Schwab (ed.), *Inventory of Diderot's 'Encyclopédie'*, vol. VII, *Studies on Voltaire and the
Eighteenth Century*, 223 (1984), 485–568.

[9] Among the articles are: 'Two More British Travellers in the France of Louis XIV', *The
Seventeenth Century*, 1 (1986), 159–75; 'Encounters between British Travellers and Eighteenth-
Century French Writers', *Studies on Voltaire and the Eighteenth Century*, 245 (1986), 1–90;
'Regency France Seen by British Travellers', in *Enlightenment Essays in Memory of Robert
Shackleton* (Oxford, 1988), 145–61; 'France in the 1780s Seen by Joseph and Anna Francesca
Cradock', *Studies on Voltaire and the Eighteenth Century*, 267 (1989), 421–38.

after-life in *The 'Philosophes' and Post-Revolutionary France* (Oxford, 1982). It was a brave attempt to see how ideas propagated by eighteenth-century reforming thinkers were realised in reforming measures enacted by French political and legal authorities at the turn of the century and in the early part of the nineteenth century and subsequently. The topics covered are forms of government, social and economic questions, the law, and, perhaps closest to Lough's heart, the secularisation of society. Informative though the book is, it perhaps suffers, as Lough himself acknowledges in the conclusion, from having two distinct narratives: the ideas of the *philosophes* and the history of political, legal and cultural change. The direct influence of the first of these narratives on the second remains impossible to calibrate.

Eighteenth-century thought was not Lough's only enthusiasm, nor was it the only area in which his research made a substantial impact. It might even be said that the book for which he is best known is his very influential *Paris Theatre Audiences in the Seventeenth and Eighteenth Centuries*, published in London by Oxford University Press in 1957, some time before his magisterial work on the *Encyclopédie*. Here we see Lough the literary scholar. Yet, it is a very particular sort of literary scholar. His predilection was for theatre, of all literary activities the one most intimately connected to the social and economic fabric of the age by reason of its conditions of production and reception. It was precisely the material context of theatrical performance that interested Lough. The remark he makes in his introduction to the book defines its focus clearly in a way that is apparently defensive, but is in fact supremely confident:

> Such a book may repel and even shock people who prefer to study literary masterpieces in a complete vacuum and are content to register the impact which great plays make on their refined sensibility without ever wishing to know anything about the vulgar details of the conditions under which they were first produced.

Lough was essentially a historian, rather than a literary critic. He enjoyed working at the interface between the history of literature and social history, and as far as French theatrical history was concerned, his perspective and his methodology were unusual. Previous literary scholars had occasionally gestured in the direction of the importance of the audience in the history of dramatic production, but Lough pursued the topic much further. Delving into the archives of Paris theatres and companies of players, reconstructing the precise arrangements of auditoria and theatrical spaces, examining expense accounts for payments and receipts, he vividly recreated the experience of actors, theatre managers and theatregoers. Basing his conclusions about the social composition of the play-going public on a very accurate reading of documentary evidence, he provided a chapter of French social history that had not been written before. The enormously detailed information he assembled with admirable clarity has constituted a crucial point of reference in the field over many years.

In 1978, Lough returned to the social history of literary production with a very ambitious book that had been in gestation over many years. This was his *Writer and Public in France: From the Middle Ages to the Present Day*, published by Oxford University Press. The chronological scope, as the title indicates, is vast, perhaps a little too vast for someone whose expertise had been neither in the Middle Ages nor in the present day. The range of material is also vast. Lough includes all kinds of non-technical authorship, touching on newspapers and 'popular' literature, as well as poets, novelists and playwrights. It is a book about the material conditions of the production and consumption of books. Lough is most at home with statistics, account-books, legal material, the correspondence of writers, publishers and informed observers, with documentary evidence of all sorts. He uses it to investigate topics that have risen high on the scholarly agenda since he published this work and since the History of the Book became a burgeoning discipline. Issues of patronage, the relationship between authors and publishers, authorial rights, print-runs, sale of books, income from writing, literacy, censorship, and many more are recurrent themes. Yet, this book has not had the impact of Lough's previous work on Paris theatre audiences and the *Encyclopédie*. It could be that Lough's social history of authorship was ahead of its time in its subject matter, but when the academic community caught up with it, the narrative mode of Lough's 'marxist' history of writing gave the illusion that it was already dated.[10]

When Lough retired from the Chair of French at Durham in 1978, his standing in the world of scholarship, both in the United Kingdom and in France, had been ratified by the honours accorded him. He was elected a Fellow of the British Academy in 1975. Prior to that, he was awarded an honorary doctorate by the University of Clermont-Ferrand in 1967, followed by an honorary D.Litt. at the University of Newcastle in 1972, and he was made an Officier de l'Ordre National du Mérite in 1973. Those

---

[10] It did have a certain success in France, however, translated into French by A. Tadié and published at Paris as *L'Ecrivain et son public* in 1987.

honours were undoubtedly, and very properly, given him for the very substantial advances in knowledge he made by his research.

That was not, however, the whole story. Lough was a good teacher. His style was certainly not charismatic and one did not go to his lectures for histrionics or even for a display of rhetorical panache. But one of his more able students voiced the opinion of many when he said that 'one quickly learnt just how worthwhile it was to listen to what he had to say in lectures, and to be tutored by him was a joy'. Two of his research students counted themselves fortunate to work with him as departmental colleagues at Durham. What set Lough apart from the ordinary university teacher was his lifelong commitment to fostering the study of French language and literature in schools. Together with his wife, Muriel, he edited a collection of passages extracted from twentieth-century French authors for translation into English, and, with his former Head of Department at Aberdeen, he produced a companion volume of passages from modern British prose authors to be translated into French. The latter contains nearly one hundred pages of 'hints on translation into French', which is as good a synopsis of French grammar, syntax, and usage as one could hope to find.[11] The target audience was sixth-formers and undergraduates, and both books were very extensively used. The modern university teacher of French would regard them with amazement, both on account of the choice of extracts (severely limited to authors from within the intellectual élite), and because of Lough's total commitment to written translation as the ideal medium for foreign language acquisition. Since the 1960s, when these books were in current use, there has been a revolution in foreign language teaching that has ousted translation from the pre-eminent place it once had in the school and in the university curriculum. It is very doubtful whether the average undergraduate at Finals level could in these days make a passable attempt at rendering Trollope, Trevor-Roper, Iris Murdoch or Elizabeth Bowen into accurate and stylish French. Lough's students could, and most of them enjoyed doing it. Whether it was the most effective way of producing people who could think in contemporary French and use its whole range of discourse is another matter. The truly undoubted successes of Lough's pedagogical activity were the bridges he constructed whereby generations of sixth-formers made the crossing to a sophisticated comprehension of

---

[11] F. C. Roe and J. Lough (eds.), *French Prose Composition: Two Hundred English Passages Selected, with an Introduction* (London, 1963).

the historical study of literature in its political, economic and social context. These were his introductions to seventeenth-century France, to eighteenth-century France, standard reading for the pre-university student (and the undergraduate) for many years, and somewhat later, co-authored with his wife, a parallel introduction to nineteenth-century France.[12] They are extremely readable, packed with information, and accompanied by well chosen illustrations. The books were 'introductory', in that they assumed no prior knowledge, but they did not talk down to the young reader. For many, they were a first, exciting taste of social history and an initiation into the discipline of scholarly inquiry, its use of documentary evidence, and its style of exposition.

Lough's commitment to education was certainly motivated by his conviction that the study of cultural manifestations at any level of the curriculum should be historically grounded and by a concern to propagate his 'sceptical marxist' approach to students at a formative age. It is possible that it was also symptomatic of the left-leaning political stance of a man who had seen at first hand the educational disadvantage of the North East. The conditions of modern academic employment preclude such extramural endeavours. Lough's very real achievements here stand perhaps as a reminder of a duty we do not fulfil. Nevertheless, his introductions to the social, economic and cultural history of France belong to a period when foreign-language teaching in schools took history and literature seriously, and that period is no more. Lough himself, near the end of his life, concluded that the standpoint from which his most scholarly books were written was 'not exactly fashionable today', though these are the words of one who had little regard for fashion. It is true that they are devoid of theory, are oblivious to feminist concerns, and exhibit a concept of history that squares ill with the new historicism. Lough's history is a unilinear narrative, his instincts are always to impose synthesis, his witnesses are quoted with the unstated assumption that they are utterly transparent, and 'facts' are readily recognisable and unassailable. And yet, though the style and methodology are so different, the substance of Lough's work is at the heart of current interests in the social and material history of culture. Cultural materialism of any kind must start with

---

[12] *An Introduction to Seventeenth Century France* (London, 1954), reissued every second or third year for many years; *An Introduction to Eighteenth Century France* (London, 1960); (with Muriel Lough) *An Introduction to Nineteenth Century France* (London, 1978). A related book, *Seventeenth-Century French Drama: the Background*, was published by Oxford in 1979.

accumulated information. Lough's work stands as a depository of such information and it is a rich resource.

John Lough lived in retirement in Durham until his death on 13 July 2000. He continued his scholarly work almost until the end of his life. The memory of this elderly man making his daily trips to the library now constitutes a Durham legend.

ANN MOSS
Fellow of the Academy

Note. I am grateful to John Lough's daughter, Dr Judith Wale, for reading this memoir and contributing to it.

IAN MCFARLANE

Ian Joy

Ian Dalrymple McFarlane
1915–2002

IAN MCFARLANE belonged to the generation of scholars whose early careers were interrupted by the outbreak of the Second World War. Drawing on the sense of a new start and a radical break with past habits and prejudices that characterised the post-1945 era, that generation brought about a major renewal of modern languages as a university discipline, ensuring that it would henceforth be regarded as equal in status to other arts subjects. The importance of this task in post-war Europe could hardly be over-estimated, and Ian was certainly conscious of its magnitude.[1] He spent the thirty-eight years of his academic career training the modern linguists of the next generation, many of whom are now themselves leaders in the subject, and he set an example of meticulously thorough yet enlightened scholarship in each of the several distinct areas in which he worked.

I

The final paragraph of Ian's unpublished war memoir[2] emphasises how fortunate he and others like him felt to have survived five years of

---

[1] I have chosen to use Ian's first name only throughout this memoir because it reflects my own enduring memory of him as a teacher, colleague and friend. But it should be recorded here that his students, in my day at least, referred to him as 'Mac', and this may well be how he is still remembered by many.

[2] I am deeply grateful to Richard McFarlane, Ian's son, for sending me a copy of this important

Proceedings of the British Academy, **124**, 183–203. © The British Academy 2004.

captivity, given the fate of others at that time. 'What kept us alive', he says, was 'a feeling that somehow a future lay before us, in which hope and at least elements would survive from a world we had known, a widening of our human awareness, and most of all faith and personal emotions of which I have not felt it right or desirable that I should write here.' All those who knew Ian will recognise the refusal to complain, the optimism, and the sense of a common humanity. They will also recognise the reticence of the closing words. In the course of a life spent in many places and contexts, he built up an extraordinary network of friends and acquaintances; he enjoyed conversation and was never stiff or formal in manner; yet he rarely spoke about his own life or revealed his personal feelings. It has therefore not been possible to reconstruct anything other than a purely external account of his early years: there is no evidence, for example, of his relations with his parents.[3]

James Blair McFarlane, Ian's father, came from Glasgow, but his career as a naval engineer and shipyard manager took him to various other dockside cities, including Newcastle, where Ian was born on 7 November 1915. His first memory was of being frightened by 'the flapping of air-raid curtains in the darkened bathroom'.[4] His mother, Valérie Edith Liston Dalrymple, may have had French (or French-speaking) relatives, presumably on her mother's side;[5] at all events, records at Westminster School show that, in 1929, both parents were living in Marseilles, where Ian attended the Lycée Saint-Charles. If my memory serves me correctly, Ian also mentioned once in passing that he had stayed with his aunt in Marseilles, and in the war memoir he goes so far as to say that he was 'brought up in France'; his near-native command of French clearly dates from this period of his life.

However, at some point—perhaps in preparation for his Westminster scholarship examination—he also attended the Tormore School, a private preparatory school in Upper Deal, Kent, before going on to

---

document and allowing me to use it here. I very much regret that, for reasons of balance and length, I have only been able to draw on it for information about the earlier part of Ian's life and for some brief glimpses of his experiences as a prisoner of war.

[3] One small but perhaps significant exception: he once said to a colleague that he was distressed that his mother had died just too soon to see his edition of Scève's *Délie* appear in print in 1966.

[4] According to a note in the war memoir, his mother insisted against plausibility that this episode occurred when he was only seventeen months old. Dockyards were a prime target for attack by Zeppelins, and later by fixed-wing aircraft (the earliest of these occurred at Sheerness in June 1917), but Ian's memory could presumably refer to any period up to the end of the war.

[5] A passing reference in the war memoir indicates that he had an aunt who married a Belgian.

Westminster School as a King's Scholar. Like most brilliant schoolboys of that time, he was marked out to be a classicist, but he decided, somewhat belatedly and on his own initiative, that he wanted to become a modern linguist. His headmaster, it seems, was not pleased and tried to dissuade him; Ian persevered, however, and the headmaster reluctantly gave in: 'All right,' Ian reports him as saying, 'you can go over to languages, but you will come to no good.' He might perhaps have been mollified if he had known that Ian would later put his thorough grounding in Latin to excellent use.

In 1934, Ian won a Harkness Scholarship and went to St Andrews University. After his late start in modern languages at school, he needed to catch up in German, so he spent four successive summers in Germany during his time as a student. As a schoolboy, he had begun to form pacifist ideals; now, his first-hand experience of burgeoning Nazi propaganda—which he also encountered at St Andrews—and of the treatment of Jewish families with whom he came into contact led him to modify those views: some things were worse than war.

It was at St Andrews that he met and eventually became engaged to Marjory Nan Hamilton, the daughter of a Presbyterian minister, who was studying medicine at Dundee. Her version of the story was that she used regularly to see him cycling past her window on the way to play cricket, and decided that he was the man for her (how they actually met is not clear). There seems to have been some parental resistance to the match on one side or the other; at all events, after Ian graduated with a first class MA in 1938, he went off to Paris to begin research on the late nineteenth-century French novelist Paul Bourget while Marjory continued her medical course. By the summer of 1939, she was a year away from qualifying, and Ian had intended to return to Paris, but history soon overtook whatever plans they may have made for their personal life. The day after war broke out, Ian enlisted, not for reasons of patriotism but because he knew what Nazism meant; a few days later, on 12 September, he married Marjory. It was a quiet wedding, for more than one reason, and their honeymoon was to be deferred for a good deal longer than they expected.

After a short period of (apparently rather indifferent) training, Ian was sent to France as a Lieutenant with the First Battalion of the Black Watch. While awaiting its turn in the Dunkirk evacuation, his contingent became trapped near the coast by the rapidly advancing German troops under Rommel and on a cloudless day in June 1940 ('Hitler', said Ian, 'ruined the best cricketing summer in a decade'),[6] all 8,000 men were obliged to surrender. Ian spent the next five years in captivity. During the first few months he found himself in an officers' camp in the Archbishop's palace in Laufen, but he was then sent to a tuberculosis hospital for prisoners of war at Königswartha in Saxony. Because of his linguistic skills, he was put to use as an interpreter and mediator: the cosmopolitan world of the prison camps was also something of a Tower of Babel, and Ian took the opportunity to broaden his linguistic competence, acquiring, for example, a good speaking knowledge of Russian from an American whose father spoke only Ukrainian.[7] Reading between the lines of his memoir, it is clear that he did admirable work, giving encouragement to the sick and the dying, and defending victims of injustice wherever possible. As he puts it at one point, with consummate modesty, 'I was in nine different camps, having made myself in the politest fashion a nuisance to the Germans.' He also acquired a determined dislike of the bureaucratic mentality, and the liberal views that had already begun to form in his university years underwent a marked reinforcement:

> If liberalism is in its essentials the attempt to maintain the individual against the encroachment by the State, and by monolithic party rule, then Liberalism is my political creed. More than once I have wondered whether prisoner of war life with its rigid framework was not a training (in the wrong sense) for the postwar world and the welfare state.

It is characteristic that, in retrospect, he assessed in positive terms what for most of us would have seemed like a massive and even catastrophic disruption of our lives and careers: 'I believe that these years were not a break in my life, nor in the lives of those around me, but that they were just as valuable a part of my existence as others spent in freedom.'

II

After his liberation in 1945, Ian and Marjory had their deferred honeymoon. Having now been promoted to the rank of captain, he worked for

---

[6] This quotation and those that follow in this section are taken from an unpublished paper on Ian's wartime experiences written, I think, while he was at Caius (I heard him deliver such a paper at an essay-reading society in 1959 or 1960). The war memoir proper was written in its final form 'many decades later', according to Ian's own formula on the opening page.
[7] He had already acquired a basic knowledge of the language by attending voluntary classes at Westminster in 1931.

a few weeks in a British prisoner-of-war camp, again as an interpreter, but he also began to apply for academic posts. In August of that year, he was interviewed for a University Lectureship at Cambridge. The short list included several candidates who were destined to become leaders in their field. As Ian recounts in his war memoir, at least two of them 'were in resplendent uniforms and gave the impression of running the British army. One came out of the interview very shaken, saying "Christ, do you know what they are doing in there?—talking French!"' This was not a circumstance to alarm Ian, who was duly appointed and took up the post, after some delay in obtaining his demobilisation papers, in December 1945. Two years later, he was elected to a fellowship at Gonville and Caius College, thus becoming the first ever Fellow in French at the College.

In the post-war years, the prejudice illustrated by Ian's encounter with his headmaster in the 1930s was still widespread. College teaching for the Cambridge Modern and Medieval Languages Tripos, founded in its modern form as late as 1919, was given in the main not by fellows but by college lecturers; many were also polyglots and polymaths rather than specialist scholars. Caius, however, had made a valuable contribution to the subject in the first half of the twentieth century, and at the time Ian arrived, there were two Germanists among the fellows, both distinguished: Francis Bennett, who had entered the College in 1914, and the young Eric Blackall, who became a fellow in 1944 and a college lecturer in 1949.[8]

Ian was soon to discover that the College fellowship was deeply divided.[9] The 'Old Guard', who had held the fort during the war and were accustomed to govern the College, were largely (although not entirely) good teachers, but they took little interest in research. In the aftermath of the war, an insurgent group of younger fellows set up what in College legend is known as the 'Peasants' Revolt'. Ian was critical of current tutorial arrangements and admissions practices and sympathetic to the aims of the Peasants. On the other hand, his closest colleague in the fellowship was Francis Bennett, College lecturer in German, Senior Tutor since 1931, President from 1948, and a leading figure in the Old Guard.

---

[8] On the history of modern language teaching at Caius, see Michael Moriarty, 'Modern Languages in Caius', *The Caian* (Nov. 1988), 87–93.

[9] On this period in the history of the College, see Christopher Brooke, *A History of Gonville and Caius College* (Woodbridge, 1985; reprinted 1996), especially pp. 271–4. I am grateful to Professor Brooke for kindly providing me with further details of Ian's early years at Caius and his role in the renewal of the College; I have quoted some parts of his account verbatim.

Francis was greatly loved, but also much criticised: from this criticism Ian, an unflinching moderate, was able to stand somewhat aloof, and his relations with Francis remained genuinely cordial. In 1956, he himself became Senior Tutor, an office which it cannot have been entirely comfortable to hold given the continued tension between different factions. By that time, however, carefully targeted work in modern language admissions had enabled him, with the help of Eric Blackall, to build up a strong undergraduate cohort at the College: indeed, under his aegis Caius became one of the leading colleges for modern languages in Cambridge, a reputation it has maintained ever since.

Being convinced that a command of the spoken language was an essential aspect of an education in modern languages (a view not at all widely shared at that time), Ian also revived the lectorship in French which Caius had instituted as far back as 1904;[10] its most illustrious incumbent had been Henri Fluchère, an outstanding *angliciste*, later to become Director of the Maison Française in Oxford. For some reason, this post had been allowed to lapse after 1928, but from 1951 a new series of appointments began, and many Caius *lecteurs* have themselves become leaders in their generation.

One needs to bear in mind that, at the time of his first appointment, Ian had only had time for a single year of research, followed by a six-year break. Despite the demands of a new post, however, he took up the threads of his work on Paul Bourget in 1946 and completed a scholarly and well-documented thesis (written in French) on Bourget's relations with England and English literature under the direction of the distinguished comparatist Jean-Marie Carré;[11] he was awarded a doctorate of the University of Paris in 1950. The thesis remained unpublished, but a substantial two-part article on Bourget's critical writings appeared in the late 1950s,[12] and Ian's continued interest in the author is attested by another important article of 1969 on links between Bourget's writing and the aesthetics of symbolism.[13]

---

[10] See Moriarty, 'Modern Languages in Caius', 92.

[11] 'Paul Bourget et l'Angleterre', thesis for the *doctorat d'université* (Paris, 1950). A copy is held in the Library of the Taylor Institution, Oxford.

[12] 'La collaboration de Paul Bourget au *Parlement* et au *Journal des Débats* 1880–86', *Lettres Romanes*, 12 (1958), 413–35, and 13 (1959), 35–58.

[13] 'Paul Bourget: In Search of a Symbolist Aesthetic', *Australian Journal of French Studies*, 6 (1969), 376–409.

At Cambridge, Ian gave lectures and supervisions across a broad range, but those of us who were taught by him will remember him above all for his long-standing commitment to French Renaissance studies. This switch of intellectual focus seems to have taken place quite early, since a Caius colleague remembers him talking 'with real, personal enthusiasm' about sixteenth-century French poetry at High Table in the early 1950s. By the late 1950s, at all events, Ian's work on the Renaissance was already bearing fruit: what is virtually a short monograph on the Neo-Latin poet Salmon Macrin appeared in three parts in a leading French Renaissance journal in 1959–60;[14] it provides a meticulously scholarly appraisal of Macrin's life and works, together with a detailed bibliography, and remains a founding study and an essential point of reference for anyone working in this field.

At much the same time, Ian was gathering material for an edition of the dazzling and at times enigmatic cycle of love-poems known as the *Délie*, by the French vernacular poet Maurice Scève.[15] The preface begins thus: 'This edition owes its origin to my discovery, in the course of teaching, that Scève was a poet who appealed to succeeding generations of students.' Scève had certainly featured prominently in the supervisions he gave in the 1950s on sixteenth-century French literature, and one of his most brilliant doctoral students, the late Dorothy Coleman, was also working on Scève, no doubt at his instigation. It is characteristic of Ian that he saw teaching and research as complementary: if this ideal could hardly be achieved where his Neo-Latin interests were concerned, it was to be all the more evident, as we shall see, in his later publications. In fact, this edition is by no means merely a text for students. In addition to the 100-page introduction, it provides full variants, uses sixteenth-century orthography, copiously annotates Scève's idiosyncratic vocabulary and syntax, and reproduces extracts, in the original Italian, from one of Scève's major sources. It is also handsomely produced, and remains a monument to the revival of Scève studies that took place in the post-war years.

Meanwhile, the Buchanan chair of French at St Andrews had fallen vacant, and Ian applied, not only because it was his old university and a place of memories both for him and for Marjory, but also because the many duties of his Cambridge post were making it difficult for him to do

---

[14] 'Jean Salmon Macrin (1490–1557)', *Bibliothèque d'Humanisme et Renaissance*, 21 (1959), 55–84, 311–49, and 22 (1960), 73–89.
[15] Maurice Scève, *Délie*, ed. I. D. McFarlane (Cambridge, 1966).

as much research as he would have liked. He was, it seems, hesitant about his credentials for the job, but the electors thought otherwise, and Ian took up his post in 1961. Before we turn from Cambridge to St Andrews, however, one important episode needs to be recorded, in words inscribed on the plinth that stood on Ian's mantelpiece ever after, displaying a battle-scarred cricket ball:

> With this ball Ian McFarlane concluded his regular playing career with Camden Cricket Club by taking six wickets for thirteen runs at Fulbourn, Cambridge, on Sept. 9th 1961. In the course of doing so, he clean-bowled the Fulbourn nos 2, 3 and 4 with successive balls.

III

During almost a decade as head of the St Andrews French Department, Ian presided over a rapid increase in staff numbers (this was of course a time of expansion throughout the British university system) and the building of a new purpose-built home for the modern languages departments in Union Street: the building was appropriately named, like Ian's chair, after George Buchanan, the great sixteenth-century Scottish humanist, to whose life and works Ian was to devote much of his research time over the next two decades.

There is a certain irony in the fact that the arrival of new blood in the 1960s was soon to produce widespread changes in the running of university departments that threatened to turn Ian's own generation, despite its forward-looking ideals, into the 'Old Guard': the events of 1968 were only the culmination of a process that was already under way in the new universities and was soon to be echoed even in institutions conscious of their long traditions. Although Ian was by no means autocratic, he was thus one of the last representatives of an age when 'the Professor' was in charge of everything, assigning lecture schedules and administrative jobs to members of the department. In addition, his extraordinarily capacious memory became effectively the departmental filing system; this caused his successor some trouble when he found on his arrival in St Andrews that there were no departmental record cards. However, the French department prospered under his aegis: it benefited from his standing and example as a scholar, and it grew not only in size but also in range of interests and competence. Likewise, he was visibly devoted to St Andrews, as well as to French culture at the broadest level (he was known to play recordings of French music as a kind of intermission during his lectures to the

General Class), all of which made him a respected head of department and by and large a popular one.

Departmental politics aside, Ian's regime at St Andrews was characterised by his—and Marjory's—gift for easy, everyday relations with both staff and students. Hospitality at the house in Queen's Gardens, and later in North Street, was warm and open; there were some memorable trips to the Burn, the country house in the foothills of the Cairngorms which is used by the Scottish universities for reading parties; and inevitably there was cricket, including an impromptu game on the West Sands late on a midsummer evening, after an examiners' meeting.

It is clear from Ian's preface to his study of Buchanan that the origins of the book reach back to his earliest interest in Neo-Latin poetry.[16] The article on Salmon Macrin I have already referred to was apparently intended to be only the first instalment of a full-scale history of Neo-Latin poetry in Renaissance France, a project which Ian continued to work on throughout his career. But an intermittent preoccupation with Buchanan and his long and varied European career became an absorbing fascination when Ian discovered, on his return to St Andrews in 1961, the richness of the Buchanan material in the University Library. The study of the Scottish humanist took twenty years to complete, and the broader project was relegated to the sidelines, with consequences we shall return to later.

Written at the peak of Ian's career, and also at the peak of his intellectual and scholarly energies, *Buchanan* remains without any doubt his major contribution to Renaissance studies. It provides a comprehensive biography of a many-sided figure whose peripatetic life took him to England, France (chiefly Paris and Bordeaux), Coimbra, northern Italy, and home to Scotland, often crossing back and forth between countries. As Buchanan seems to have known, met or corresponded with almost everyone who was anyone in European humanist circles of the sixteenth century, together with an impressive list of statesmen and monarchs, the biography is complemented by a wide-ranging contextual study that attests to Ian's awesomely detailed knowledge of the field. Religious controversy is inevitably a central strand: inclined in his earlier career towards a non-schismatic Erasmian evangelism, Buchanan declared for Calvinism when compromise became impossible (but only when he had returned safely home to Scotland). Written in Ian's rugged, no-nonsense prose, the book thoroughly surveys Buchanan's writings—

---

[16] See *Buchanan* (London, 1981), p. ix.

psalm-paraphrases, secular Latin poetry, a cosmological treatise, a Biblical tragedy, a treatise on the limits of royal power, and a history of Scotland—and includes a wealth of bibliographical materials and other appendixes which remain an invaluable source for historians, intellectual historians and literary scholars. It is certainly an erudite work, but its aim, as the description of the book on the jacket puts it, 'is to go beyond the sphere of narrow scholarly research and to make [Buchanan's] life's work known to a wider public interested in the Renaissance and the development of Scottish culture'. It is, in effect, a major work of cultural history.

In the 1960s, however, the publication of *Buchanan* was still a long way off, although a number of trailers appeared over the years: the most substantial of these was published in *The Library* in 1969;[17] two were given at major conferences and subsequently published in the proceedings;[18] another featured in a special issue of *Forum for Modern Language Studies* jointly edited by Ian and later published in the United States as a separate volume.[19] The broad interdisciplinary scope of these publications, which range from what we would now call history of the book via intellectual history to literary analysis, shows the importance that Ian attached from the outset to the integration of Neo-Latin studies into the context not only of humanism as a historical phenomenon, but also of the national literatures of the Renaissance.

As with the *Délie*, Ian's own principal contribution to the understanding of French poetry during his years at St Andrews arose from his experience of teaching. Agrippa d'Aubigné's *Les Tragiques* is a huge poetic work of partisan inspiration, rhetorical fervour and abrasive energy which tends to exceed the limits of any teaching programme aiming to give an overview of sixteenth-century French literature. In order to secure a place for it in undergraduate courses, Ian compiled a generous selection from the seven books, omitting only the fourth (a Protestant martyrology) and provided it with notes, a glossary of historical refer-

---

[17] 'George Buchanan's Latin Poems from Script to Print: A Preliminary Survey', *The Library*, 5th ser., 24 (1969), 277–332.

[18] 'George Buchanan and French Humanism', in A. H. T. Levi (ed.), *Humanism in France at the End of the Middle Ages and in the Early Renaissance* (Manchester and New York, 1970), pp. 295–319; 'The History of George Buchanan's *Sphaera*', in Peter Sharratt (ed.), *French Renaissance Studies 1540–70: Humanism and the Encyclopedia* (Edinburgh, University Press, 1976), 194–212.

[19] 'Notes on the Composition and Reception of Buchanan's Psalm Paraphrases', in I. D. McFarlane, A. H. Ashe and D. D. R. Owen (eds.), *Renaissance Studies: Six Essays* (Towota, NJ, 1972) pp. 21–62; previously in *Forum for Modern Language Studies*, 8 (1971), 319–60.

ences, and an ample introduction.[20] Thirty years later, I was still using this selection regularly in my undergraduate teaching.

It was likewise during his tenure of the Buchanan chair that Ian did the groundwork for *Renaissance France 1470–1589*, one of the most outstanding contributions to the ambitious multi-volume *Literary History of France* published under the general editorship of P. E. Charvet. Well over a hundred pages longer than either of the two volumes that follow it, which deal with periods traditionally regarded as representing the peak of French literary culture, it tangibly seeks to revise perceptions of Renaissance literature as barely more than a preparatory phase for the grandeurs of French 'classicism'. The pages are also well filled, giving a densely packed account not only of the major figures and movements but also of innumerable *minores*, and Neo-Latin literature, predictably enough, is brought in from the margins: figures like Buchanan and Macrin, who wrote exclusively in Latin, are given a place alongside their vernacular colleagues, and the reader is reminded at frequent intervals that it was quite normal in that period to write in both languages. Because it is so thorough and so even-handed, *Renaissance France* is still enormously useful as a work of reference, but it is also much more than that. The historical and intellectual background is amply sketched in, and Pierre de La Ramée, Guillaume Postel, Jean Bodin, the Estienne family, Ambroise Paré, Bernard Palissy and many others who would not normally feature in a history of French literature are given more than a fleeting mention. In his preface, Ian suggests that the problems faced by Renaissance writers and thinkers are often analogous to those of our own times (there are perhaps echoes here of his wartime experiences): 'Tower of Babel or think-tank, the Renaissance raises in acute form all sorts of vital questions, not least the two cardinal ones of the relations between authority (tradition) and self-realisation, and of those between commitment and detachment.' Yet he is also aware, to an extent not shared by many of his contemporaries, of the otherness of Renaissance culture: 'there are [no] easy short-cuts to understanding the mental structures and categories within which the Renaissance mind tackled those problems'.[21] Written before the full impact of Foucault and his disciples became apparent, these remarks may in retrospect look cautious, and most of Ian's history is in fact written in a positivist vein, but one should not

---

[20] *Agrippa d'Aubigné*: Les Tragiques, ed. I. D. McFarlane (London, 1970).

[21] *Renaissance France 1470–1589* (London and Tonbridge/New York, 1974), pp. xv–xvi.

underestimate his desire to draw a new and more historically grounded map of French Renaissance culture.

Finally, it is important to mention the public service that Ian rendered during this busy period of his life. From 1966–7, he was a member of the Committee on Research and Development in Modern Languages set up by the Department of Education and Science and the Scottish Education Department. The chief concern of the Committee was with the practical teaching of modern languages at all levels, from primary school to university, and with the exploration of new pedagogical methods. Its report begins by affirming that 'the war showed the importance of practical skills in languages (and, in particular, oral skill)',[22] and by pointing to post-war developments that made this need still more urgent, such as the building of 'the Concorde Airliner' and Britain's current application to join the European Economic Community. One paragraph speaks of universities themselves being critical of 'the level of competency acquired by students in the use, in speech and in writing (and particularly the former), of the language they have studied';[23] Ian would certainly have concurred with such criticism. Since 1967, modern language courses at university level have indeed made oral proficiency a central element of the syllabus, although the ambition of the Committee to renew and expand modern language teaching throughout the educational system has regrettably fallen short of full realisation. Ian also served on the Scottish Certificate of Education Examination Board, and, from 1964–7, on the Academic Planning Board for the new University of Stirling. He was thus in the front rank of those who contributed to the transformation of the British university system in that decade; one might add that one of his former doctoral students, Donald Charlton, became the first Professor of French at the new University of Warwick in 1965.

IV

When a new chair of French Literature was created at Oxford in 1970, Ian applied for it, a decision his friends in Cambridge apparently found surprising; it was in fact typical of Ian to want to move on to new challenges. He was elected, and took up the chair, together with a professorial

---

[22] 'Committee on Research and Development in Modern Languages: First Report' (London: HMSO), 1968, p. 1.
[23] Ibid., p. 6.

fellowship at Wadham College, in January 1971. At that time, professorial posts at Oxford were regarded primarily as research positions. Professors were expected to give lectures, participate in examining, and supervise doctoral students, but they had no undergraduate tutorial duties. They were also entitled *ex officio* to a seat on the Faculty Board, although that did not imply any privileged position on the French sub-faculty—rather the reverse, since college tutors regarded professors as marginal creatures whose freedom from tutorial bondage disqualified them from any part in the running of the subject at the day-to-day level. For the same reason, some colleges were unwilling to provide a room for their professorial fellows, and this was the case at Wadham. Ian was taken aback, as other professors coming from outside Oxford have been, by this sudden and quite tangible loss of status and function, and I have the impression that a residue of disappointment remained even after his retirement (it hardly helped matters that the chair was then suspended *sine die*, only to be revived in 2002).

Ian none the less took such opportunities as he could to encourage good relations in the faculty. Many Oxford early modernists will remember with affection the informal lunch-time meetings he regularly held, not for political or administrative ends, but simply to give colleagues an opportunity to talk to one another about their work, to discuss French organ music or the latest cricketing news, or to enjoy some mild academic gossip. These meetings took place weekly during term in various public houses in central Oxford. One reason for this choice of venue was that Ian and Marjory had bought a house in Headington, just beyond the ringroad, which made it difficult for him to offer the personal hospitality for which they had both been renowned at St Andrews. Another was the lack of a college base. However, Ian's own preference was no doubt the predominant factor: he would have regarded the pub as fostering a more convivial, egalitarian dialogue (he was also known to meet his graduate students in pubs to discuss their work). Although these gatherings, as a manifestation of the faculty's 'research culture', would have earned few brownie points in today's Research Assessment Exercise regime, they were a positive innovation at a time when it was unusual for members of the French sub-faculty to meet informally except by private arrangement in their own colleges. Ian also used them from time to time to offer advice, which he did readily, sensitively and constructively; for example, it was his strong and consistently-held belief that colleagues should not spend their whole career in Oxford or Cambridge, but should move out and gain experience of other universities.

Ian was now at last able to devote himself full-time to his various projects with the ample resources of the Bodleian and Taylorian libraries at his disposal. *Renaissance France* was almost finished and would appear in 1974; *Buchanan* was already well advanced, and the comprehensive study of French Neo-Latin poetry he had conceived many years earlier now had a serious chance of being realised.[24]

Meanwhile, he had the opportunity to widen his contribution to French vernacular literature. He wrote a long essay for a volume of studies on Ronsard designed both as a marker for new developments in the understanding of French Renaissance poetry and as a broadly ranging introduction to the poet for the advanced student.[25] In focusing on Ronsard's *imaginaire*, he was responding in that essay to an important strand of Continental phenomenological criticism that reaches back to Bachelard but was arguably at its peak in the 1960s and 1970s.[26] However, the closing sentence of the essay gives this mode of critical reflection a characteristically human and indeed personal twist: '[Ronsard] reaches us because he is so close to the sources of fruitful consciousness and gives shape to attitudes and intuitions from which any proper response to life must start.' Ian, as we have seen, did not wear his heart on his sleeve, but it is clear that he had a profound sense of the importance of literature, and especially poetry, not only for the reader's inner life, but also for his moral experience of the world. In this respect, as he himself claimed, he was closer to William Empson, whom he greatly admired, and to the 'Cambridge school' of critics.

It is characteristic of Ian's determination to foster the pedagogical value of his research interests that he found time during this decade to compile an anthology of Renaissance Latin poetry.[27] Designed principally for students of English literature, it gives priority to poets widely read in Renaissance England. It is therefore not meant to be a representative selection of Neo-Latin poetry as a whole, nor does it (as Ian rather ruefully says in the introduction) 'express the anthologist's personal preferences'. However, the very fact that he was able to adapt his perspective

---

[24] His important article 'Pierre de Ronsard and the Neo-Latin Poetry of his Time', *Res Publica Litterarum*, 1 (1978), 178–205, is a sign of his continued activity in this field.

[25] 'Aspects of Ronsard's Poetic Vision', in Terence Cave (ed.), *Ronsard the Poet* (London, 1973), pp. 13–78.

[26] A later piece on Ronsard written for a Festschrift in honour of his old friend and colleague Alan Steele (Keith Aspley, David Bellos and Peter Sharratt (eds.), *Myth and Legend in French Literature. Essays in Honour of A. J. Steele* (London: Modern Humanities Research Association, 1982), 60–72) treats mythological themes in a similar way.

[27] *Renaissance Latin Poetry* (Manchester and New York, 1980).

in this way, trawling the vast field of European Latin poetry for the works that were popular and influential in England, shows that he remained faithful, in this domain also, to the comparatist ideal which is apparent in his work from his doctoral thesis onwards.

The final years of Ian's academic career were marked by a spate of publications. In addition to the Neo-Latin anthology, which appeared in 1980, and *Buchanan* (1981), two memorial volumes, jointly edited by Ian, were published in 1982: a Festschrift for the seventeenth-century scholar Harry Barnwell,[28] and an important collection of essays on Montaigne in memory of the distinguished Montaigne specialist Richard Sayce, whose premature death in 1977 had been a great loss not only to the sub-faculty of French at Oxford but also to the whole of the scholarly community.[29] Ian's prefatory *in memoriam* pays glowing tribute to Sayce's qualities as a scholar and a tutor, but it also includes a sentence which provides a characteristic glimpse of Ian himself as a young man: 'It may come as a surprise to some that Richard enjoyed games in his early days; I remember the last game of cricket we had before the War, when we played on a coconut matting at the Rugby Club de France in Paris against a team of anglophile Frenchmen.'[30] The subject Ian chose for his own essay in this volume was 'The Concept of Virtue in Montaigne'; drawing on his many years of familiarity with (and affection for) the *Essais*, he gives a detailed account of Montaigne's shifting ethical positions that owes less to the history of ideas and philosophical systems than to a close personal reading of the text.

Finally, in the same year, Ian contributed a volume to Margaret McGowan's new series 'Renaissance Triumphs and Magnificences'. This was a facsimile edition of the *livret* of Henri II's 1549 ceremonial entry into Paris,[31] for which Ian provided a long and thoroughly well-informed introduction. Such elaborately constructed cultural events have rightly attracted increasing attention in recent years as a point of access to a history which is once political, social and aesthetic—a small-scale cultural history, indeed. Ian handles this genre with a clarity and eye for

---

[28] William D. Howarth, Ian McFarlane and Margaret McGowan (eds.), *Form and Meaning: Aesthetic Coherence in Seventeenth-Century French Drama* (Amersham, 1982). In this volume, Ian's own paper was entitled 'Reflections on the Variants in Andromaque' (ibid., pp. 99–114).

[29] I. D. McFarlane and Ian Maclean (eds.), *Montaigne. Essays in Memory of Richard Sayce* (Oxford, 1982).

[30] Ibid., p. viii.

[31] *The Entry of Henri II into Paris 16 June 1549* (Binghamton, NY: Center for Medieval and Early Renaissance Studies, 1982).

significant detail born of many years of experience in reading Renaissance texts and investigating their contexts. One imagines that he would have enjoyed and appreciated the new historical turn taken by Renaissance studies since the 1990s, especially as he was visibly somewhat uncomfortable with the theoretical, anti-historical mode that had become increasingly influential during the middle years of his career and was still in full flow in the early 1980s.

Perhaps this was one among many reasons why the long-planned study of French Neo-Latin poetry never appeared in print. By the time Ian retired in 1983, or soon thereafter, he had completed a 1200-page typescript fully equipped with footnotes and manuscript corrections on points of detail. It could have been sent to a publisher in that form, but it was not.[32] When the typescript was discovered among his papers in the last weeks of his life and Ian was asked about it, he simply said that he hadn't thought it was good enough. It is hard to see what he meant by this: it is primarily a compilation, but an enormously useful one, drawing on years of primary research in areas of scholarship few are equipped to explore. The style and approach are not chic or 'innovative'; they belong to someone educated in the 1930s. Yet this is hardly a drawback given the relatively austere nature of the subject and the aim of meticulous coverage. Ian may none the less have felt that his erudition was no longer relevant to a younger generation many of whom (even if they chose to study the Renaissance) appeared to have deserted the old philological skills for the blandishments of theory.

V

Immediately after his retirement in 1983, Ian changed his horizons by spending a semester as Visiting Professor at the University of Virginia in Charlottesville, where he was lodged at the splendid Colonnade Club, designed by Thomas Jefferson. Reports suggest that both he and his hosts

---

[32] The typescript has since been deposited at the library of the Taylor Institution at the University of Oxford, where it is being catalogued and will thus become available to specialists. It is noteworthy that, in 1983, Ian published an article surveying the current state of studies in this field: 'La poésie néo-latine à l'époque de la Renaissance française—état présent des recherches', *Nouvelle revue du seizième siècle*, 1 (1983), 1–18. This retrospective view, in which his own work is barely mentioned, suggests that he had already renounced the idea of publishing his manuscript.

were delighted with this visit, which also included an excursion to give a lecture at Duke University.

Early in 1984, shortly after his return from the USA, he delivered the Zaharoff Lecture at Oxford, one of the most prestigious named lectures for French studies in Britain.[33] His choice of subject, the figure of the liar in the plays of Pierre Corneille, was perhaps surprising to some of his Oxford audience: was he not first and foremost a sixteenth-century scholar? Yet, while he was still at St Andrews, Ian had published *éditions scolaires* of two of Corneille's best-known plays,[34] and a central theme of the lecture, the relevance of Montaigne's *Essais* to Corneille's theatre, had equally interested him for many years. Behind Ian's deceptively good-natured critical style in this lecture lies an important revisionist argument: Corneille's plays are far more ambivalent about the ethics of heroism, and about the power-relations in which his heroes become engaged, than is often assumed. Equally, the connection with Montaigne is a fruitful one from which all the implications have by no means yet been drawn.

That same year, Ian received his own Festschrift, a volume honouring the major contribution he had made to Neo-Latin and French Renaissance studies.[35] It was presented to him at a dinner attended both by faculty colleagues and by most of the contributors, among whom were some distinguished European Neo-Latinists. However, in their foreword, the editors of this volume acknowledged that his versatility as a scholar could not be fully reflected in a collection devoted to a single topic and a single period of French culture, and in the following year, on the occasion of his seventieth birthday, a further volume was dedicated to him. This was a special issue of *Forum for Modern Language Studies*,[36] a journal of whose editorial board he had been a founding member while at St Andrews; the contributors were 'present members of the French Department who had the pleasure of working with him during his tenure of the Chair there'; it was also the twenty-first anniversary of the founding of the journal.

In these years, he himself edited (jointly with Pauline Smith) yet another Festschrift, this time for his old friend Klaus Mayer, on the attractively and appropriately conceived subject *Literature and the Arts in*

---

[33] Published as an occasional paper: 'The Liar and the Lieutenant in the Plays of Pierre Corneille' (Oxford, 1984).

[34] *Cinna ou la clémence d'Auguste* (Paris, 1965); *Horace* (Paris, 1971). His article on variants in *Andromaque* (see above, n. 28) was also written in the early 1980s.

[35] Grahame Castor and Terence Cave (eds.), *Neo-Latin and the Vernacular in Renaissance France* (Oxford, 1984).

[36] *Forum for Modern Language Studies*, 21:4 (1985).

the Reign of Francis I;[37] Ian's own paper returned to his Neo-Latin interests in relation to the poetry of Clément Marot. As early as 1971, Ian had
been one of the moving spirits in the founding of a new learned society
dedicated to Neo-Latin studies, the International Association of Neo-
Latin Studies, and in 1976 he had been elected as its first Vice-President.
He went on to hold the presidency of the Association from 1979–82; the
last year of his term of office coincided happily with the quatercentenary
of the death of George Buchanan, and the Fifth International Congress
of Neo-Latin Studies was held in St Andrews in that year. Ian edited the
Acta,[38] the first section of which is devoted to the Scottish humanist, a
tribute that implicitly embraces Ian also as the foremost Buchanan
scholar of modern times.

From the late 1980s, the number of his publications began to decline.
Some relatively brief Festschrift pieces and a few reviews continued to
appear into the early 1990s,[39] but some of these were probably written a
good deal earlier. One late piece deserves especial mention, however, since
it provides—poignantly enough—an echo of his early interest in nineteenth-century comparative literature. In an elegant and by no means
insubstantial article on the epigraph in the Romantic novel in France and
England,[40] he displays his old command of French and his virtuoso range
of literary reference. The opening sentence also offers what is no doubt a
fragment of autobiography that likewise evokes a beginning: 'De nom-
breux lecteurs de ma génération furent initiés à la littérature par les
romans de Walter Scott.'

For a few years, Ian continued to supervise the occasional graduate
student in his field and to enjoy his lunchtime meetings with faculty colleagues. He also maintained his connections with the scholarly community at a national level: in 1986, he became President of the Modern
Humanities Research Association, a position for which his exceptionally

---

[37] Lexington, Kentucky: French Forum, 1985.

[38] I. D. McFarlane (ed.), *Acta conventus neo-latini sanctandreani* (Binghamton, NY: Medieval
and Renaissance Texts and Studies, vol. 38, 1986).

[39] See for example 'Translation in the French Renaissance with Special Reference to Neo-Latin
Texts to and from the Vernacular', in Barbara C. Bowen and Jerry C. Nash (eds.), *Lapidary
Inscriptions: Renaissance Essays for Donald A. Stone, Jr.* (Lexington, Kentucky: French Forum,
1991), pp. 139–46; 'Langage et vérité dans *Les Tragiques* d'Agrippa d'Aubigné', in Jean Céard
(ed.), *Langage et vérité: études offertes à Jean-Claude Margolin* (Geneva, 1993), pp. 111–18.

[40] 'L'épigraphe dans le roman romantique en France et en Angleterre', in Georges Jacques and
José Lambert (eds.), *Itinéraires et plaisirs textuels. Mélanges offerts au Professeur Raymond
Pouillart* (Brussels, 1987; Université de Louvain: Recueil de travaux d'histoire et de philologie, 6e
Série, Fascicule 32), pp. 75–86.

broad range of literary interests and his knowledge of several European languages equipped him admirably. He was invited to edit the Renaissance volume in the Cambridge History of Literary Criticism and did some preliminary work on this, but his declining health sadly made it impossible for him to complete it.

Ian's public appearances also became progressively rarer from the late 1980s onwards. At an international conference on Montaigne in St Andrews in 1992 (the quatercentenary of Montaigne's death), he was invited to make the opening remarks; this he did, in French, but it was evident that he was no longer his old ebullient self. Marjory told me on that occasion that she thought he had had a very mild stroke, and this was consonant with his hesitant speech and slightly stiff walk. For the remaining ten years of his life, he lived quietly and privately, but he and Marjory received visits in their comfortable Headington house with their old warmth and hospitality. One sad event marred this period of tranquillity: their daughter Susan, who had suffered from recurrent health problems for many years, died suddenly in 1998 at the age of forty-nine, just at a time when she seemed to have found happiness in a late marriage.

Ian remained serene, clear-minded and communicative, albeit in a somewhat subdued mode, until the end. Marjory's sudden death, in December 2001, was a major and indeed a decisive blow. Unable to look after himself, Ian moved to St Andrews to be near his son Richard and his family. He was able to enjoy a few months of conversations and reminiscences with Richard, and to see something of his growing grandchildren, before his death on 17 August 2002.

VI

It seems appropriate to gather together here the honours Ian received during his long and distinguished career. He was awarded the MBE in 1946 for his services while a prisoner of war. In 1971, the French Government appointed him Officier des Palmes Académiques, a decoration reserved for outstanding academics. He was elected to a Fellowship of the British Academy in 1978. In 1982, he received an honorary doctorate of the University of Tours and was also awarded an honorary D.Litt. at the University of St Andrews. Gonville and Caius College elected him to an Honorary Fellowship in 1990, an honour of which he was especially proud.

Ian was a man of stocky build whose somewhat craggy exterior was tempered by a genial and always courteous manner. His facial expression and demeanour were mildly avuncular: a touch of diffidence, a ready smile and a sense of humour were likely to disarm any potentially awkward encounter (one is reminded of Montaigne's self-description in his essay *De la phisionomie*). He had what could be viewed either as a nervous tic or as a carefully calculated signal of self-irony: when he made a witticism or *bon mot* of some kind, he would insert a finger into his collar and pull on it while twisting his neck in the opposite direction, as if to relieve pressure; this mannerism was inevitably imitated in friendly caricature by his students and sometimes his colleagues, as was his tendency to repeat certain favourite words and phrases ('*Gleichschaltung*', '*vision du monde*', '*caisse de résonance*', 'a peg on which to hang . . .'). His manner was invariably low-key: he never sought to dominate or impress, although his students were sometimes liable to believe that he had a low opinion of their work because he was economical with expressions of approval, let alone praise. In his academic style as in his political and social views, he was an authentic liberal: those he taught were given plenty of encouragement but were allowed and expected to choose their own direction, and he supervised his graduates with genuine care but also with a light touch. Among his pastimes, cricket was his abiding favourite; he continued to play well into his retirement. But he also enjoyed music, especially French organ music of all periods from Couperin to the modern masters Messiaen and Dupré, whom he had heard playing at Trinité and Saint-Sulpice in Paris; he was also familiar with the brilliant younger generation of British organists in Cambridge and later in Oxford. In the last months of their life together, he and Marjory were enthusiastic about their recordings of French piano music, which they had recently discovered. He loved talking, especially about the astonishing number of people he knew and had known, but also of course about books and ideas: the bookshelves of his Headington home bore witness to an unusually broad range of reading and of intellectual interests. A historian who was at Caius in the later 1950s and who now holds an eminent academic position still recalls being interviewed by Ian for a place at the College: 'We talked about Croce's and Collingwood's theories of history, and I was entranced by his learning and his friendliness alike.' Above all, perhaps, Ian had a profound sense of the community of scholars and of the privilege of belonging to it. One of his former graduate students, now a distinguished Renaissance specialist and an Emeritus Professor, speaks of an occasion quite soon after she had embarked on her doctorate when, referring to a well-known scholar whom she greatly admired, Ian called him simply 'your colleague'. She felt as if he had taken her across a threshold, as indeed he had. He would have been glad to be remembered thus.

TERENCE CAVE
Fellow of the Academy

Note. I wish once more to express here my thanks to Richard McFarlane for generously supplying me with information about his father and for allowing me to make use of Ian's war memoir and other unpublished writings. I am grateful also to the following, without whose willing help it would have been impossible to write this memoir: Professor Peter Bayley, Professor Christopher Brooke and Mr Michael Prichard (Gonville and Caius College, Cambridge), Miss Julia Burrows (Westminster School), Professor Roger Green (University of Glasgow); Dr Anthony Hunt (St Peter's College, Oxford), Professor Mary B. McKinley (University of Virginia), Professor Ian Maclean (All Souls College, Oxford), Professor Michael Moriarty (Queen Mary, University of London), Professor Ann Moss (University of Durham), Professor John O'Brien (Royal Holloway, University of London), Professor Richard Parish (St Catherine's College, Oxford), Professor Quentin Skinner (Christ's College, Cambridge).

NEIL MACKENZIE *Inh. G. Schmuck*

David Neil MacKenzie
1926–2001

DAVID NEIL MACKENZIE passed away in Bangor on 13 October 2001, following multiple complications that resulted from a deteriorating heart disease from which he had suffered for some years. With him, Iranian Studies lost an outstanding representative, whose scholarly competence and interests spanned a broad range of ancient and modern Iranian languages: such comprehensiveness is becoming increasingly unusual in modern times. Several of MacKenzie's philological publications, especially those concerning (New Iranian) Kurdish and the two Middle Iranian languages, Middle Persian and Khwarezmian, are by now well established as standard works of reference and will surely remain so for a long time.

Neil (as he was known to his family and friends) was born in London on 8 April 1926, the first of the two children of the British colonial officer David MacKenzie (of Scottish extraction) and his wife Ada (known as Jerry), née Hopkins. His father served at various places in West Africa, but had to return to England in the early 1930s for health reasons. In the following years he worked as a civil servant, and the family changed their place of residence several times. His son Neil thus attended schools in Slough, Windsor and Cambridge. Shortly after the outbreak of the Second World War, Neil's mother left England for Canada, together with his younger sister. Neil chose not to go, but stayed in England with his father.

In 1943, after completing his secondary education in Cambridge, MacKenzie volunteered to join the British armed forces, to avoid being

Proceedings of the British Academy, **124**, 207–216. © The British Academy 2004.

drafted as a regular soldier. To what he would later consider his greatest luck, he was not sent to the European battlefields, but to India, where he gained a temporary commission at the Indian Military Academy at Dehra Dun (Uttar Pradesh). On board the ship that brought him to India, he stayed with a group of young Welshmen who often sang Welsh folk songs. MacKenzie could still remember some of them word by word fifty years later, after his retirement, when he moved to Llanfairpwll in Wales. After two years of service in Burma, MacKenzie was posted to the North West Frontier Province of India (now Pakistan), where he learned his first Iranian language, Pashto. His exceptional gift for picking up languages became clear at that time.

When the war was over, and following Partition in 1947, MacKenzie returned to England as a civilian, and enrolled at the School of Oriental and African Studies (SOAS) in London to study Persian. After passing his BA exams in Persian (1951, with Ann K. S. Lambton) he found his calling, and teacher, in Walter Bruno Henning, an emigré from Nazi Germany, under whom he obtained an MA in Old and Middle Iranian languages in 1953.

After graduation, MacKenzie married his first wife Gina (née Schaefer, together they had four children, born between 1952 and 1968), and started acquainting himself with Kurdish, which he chose (following Henning's suggestion) as the subject of his doctoral thesis. In autumn 1954, he left London with his family for a year, to do fieldwork on Kurdish in Iraqi Kurdistan. Since the Turkish authorities did not allow him to continue his work in Turkey, the survey of Kurdish dialects that resulted from of his fieldwork had to remain partly incomplete. The description of Kurdish dialects that he submitted in December 1957 as a doctoral thesis, however, was impressive enough, and the published version (*Kurdish dialect studies*, I, II (London, 1961, 1962)) established his fame as the world's leading expert in Kurdish linguistics.

The refusal of a permit to carry out research in Turkey did not help to make MacKenzie a close friend of that country. Neil once told me how in the train from Istanbul to Iraq, probably shortly before the Iraqi border, a Turkish policeman entered his compartment, asking for some documents that MacKenzie could not readily provide. The policeman pulled his hand-gun and shouted: 'Vouz êtes dans la Turquie!'—a sentence that would remain a deterrent for MacKenzie for the rest of his life.

MacKenzie had already been appointed 'Lecturer in Kurdish' at SOAS in 1955. During the late 1950s and the 1960s he gradually extended the range of Iranian languages on which he worked and which he could teach, adding Middle Iranian languages such as Middle Persian, Parthian, Sogdian and Khwarezmian to the modern Iranian languages, Pashto and Kurdish, which he had already made his own. The title of his position at SOAS was accordingly changed to 'Lecturer in Iranian languages' in 1961, and he was promoted to a University Readership in 1965. In 1967 and 1971, MacKenzie published two of his most important and influential works on Middle Persian, his article 'Notes on the Transcription of Pahlavi' and his *Concise Pahlavi Dictionary* (on both of which see below).

In 1975, when MacKenzie was acknowledged as one of the leading scholars in Middle and Modern Iranian languages world-wide, he was appointed Professor of Iranian Studies at the University of Göttingen, at the institute where his teacher Henning had studied under Carl Friedrich Andreas from 1926 to 1930. After some years in Göttingen, he got divorced from his first wife and married his second wife Gabi, but the marriage would last for only about three years.

In Göttingen, MacKenzie continued to work on a broad range of Iranian languages, but concentrated more and more on Middle Persian and Khwarezmian. After his retirement in 1994, he resolved to return not exactly to his home country, but to neighbouring Wales. In 1995, after a serious heart bypass operation, he moved to a small house in Llanfairpwll on the Isle of Anglesey, where he wanted to complete his major project, the Khwarezmian–English dictionary on which he had been working since the 1970s.

He never really felt at home in his new residence, often complaining (on frequent visits to Göttingen) that 'this is no longer the Britain that I knew'. He also increasingly felt isolated in Llanfairpwll, and cut off from scholarly libraries and other opportunities, and began to repent his move from Göttingen. In 2001, he resolved to move back to Göttingen, astounding everyone around him by the vitality and energy which he devoted to achieving this aim at the age of 75. Shortly before he could put this plan into practice, however, he was prevented from doing so by his deteriorating health, and the ensuing complications that took him from our midst.

From 1970 to 1996, he served as a treasurer of the Corpus Inscriptionum Iranicarum. He was a member of the Turfan Commission of the Berlin-Brandenburgische Akademie der Wissenschaften from 1994 to his death. In 1996 he was elected a Senior Fellow of the British Academy. In 1991 MacKenzie was honoured with a Festschrift (*Corolla Iranica. Papers in Honour of Prof. Dr. David Neil MacKenzie on the Occasion of his 65th Birthday on April 8th, 1991*, eds. R. E. Emmerick and D. Weber, Frankfurt

a. M. (u.a.), 1991), and in 1999 there appeared a collection of his major smaller works, containing also important corrigenda and addenda (*Iranica Diversa*. Vols. I, II, eds. C. G. Cereti and L. Paul, Rome, 1999). A memorial volume for him (edited by D. Weber) is under preparation, which will contain a full bibliography of his works.

The basis of MacKenzie's scholarly career was his amazing talent for learning languages and understanding their subtleties and grammatical structure(s). He did not, however, work on various languages, so to say, indiscriminately, but rather concentrated on a small set of New and Middle Iranian languages and their literatures. On the two modern Iranian languages 'of his youth', Pashto and Kurdish (in both of which he became a world authority) he would publish only occasionally after the mid-1960s. From then onwards, the three Middle Iranian languages Middle Persian, Sogdian and Khwarezmian absorbed most of his scholarly energy for the rest of his lifetime.

MacKenzie's command of the Middle Persian language and literature was proverbial. He was 'at home' in this dead language whose writing conventions and grammar abound in problems, and whose Zoroastrian and Manichaean texts are so important for the study of the history of religions. He could practically 'feel' if a Middle Persian construction was right or wrong, what a Middle Persian author wanted to say, or how a Middle Persian translator misunderstood his Avestan 'Vorlage'.

With his twenty-page article 'Notes on the Transcription of Pahlavi' (*Bulletin of the School of Oriental and African Studies*, 30 (1967), 17–29), MacKenzie laid the very foundation for a much improved understanding of the phonology and writing system of the language of the Middle Persian Zoroastrian books. Four years later, he supplemented this article with his *Concise Pahlavi Dictionary* (London, 1971), which soon became a standard work of reference for Iranologists. MacKenzie had prepared this dictionary on the basis of his intensive philological work on some of the most important Zoroastrian Middle Persian texts such as the *Bundahishn* and the *Wizidagiha-yi Zadspram*.

The editions of Manichaean and Inscriptional Middle Persian texts (*Shabuhragan*, inscriptions of Kartir) that MacKenzie prepared during his time in Göttingen are proofs of his philological mastery of Middle Persian. It is therefore regrettable that he never published a critical edition of any of the major Zoroastrian books that he had worked upon so intensively during the preparation of his *Concise Pahlavi Dictionary*. His reluctance to publish Zoroastrian Middle Persian texts was partly due to his perfectionism and scrupulousness. These texts had been so severely 'corrupted' by a long line of copyists that it seemed impossible to reconstruct a fully satisfying and reliable edition of any of them.

One of the most important of these texts, the *Bundahishn*, is particularly difficult to understand in its last sections. MacKenzie had already published the translation of its astrological chapter in 1964, and apparently had prepared for himself an edition of the greater part of the whole work by the end of the 1960s. In addition to the insoluble philological problems of the last chapters, there was a psychological factor that prevented him from publishing this text. The famous Iranologist Sir Harold Walter Bailey (1899–1996) had prepared (but not published) an edition of the *Bundahishn* already in the 1930s, which he allowed MacKenzie to use. MacKenzie feared that if he published the text, its good sides would be credited to Bailey, but its bad ones to himself. Later on, MacKenzie refrained from publishing the text, because in the meantime he had found so many errors in Bailey's edition that his own edition, with full references to Bailey's work, would necessarily compromise the latter (which MacKenzie wanted to avoid).

Sogdian, an East Middle Iranian language that was spoken in Central Asia approximately during the third to tenth centuries AD, was less important than Middle Persian for MacKenzie's scholarly work as a whole. Nevertheless, MacKenzie had a good knowledge and intuitive understanding of Sogdian, and published excellent editions of the Sogdian versions of several Chinese Buddhist texts (*The 'Sūtra of the Causes of Effects and Actions' in Sogdian*, London, 1970, and *The Buddhist Sogdian Texts of the British Library*, Leiden, 1976). These works showed that he had also familiarised himself with the Buddhist Chinese terminology whose understanding is a necessary prerequisite for a proper understanding of the Sogdian texts.

Khwarezmian, another East Middle Iranian language that continued to be used and written well into Islamic times (at least the thirteenth century AD), is known mainly from scattered sentences in Arabic law-books and glosses to Arabic dictionaries rather than continuous texts. Shortly after his teacher Henning's untimely death in 1967 at the age of 59, MacKenzie prepared the edition of a small part of the Khwarezmian–English dictionary that Henning had been working upon (W. B. Henning, *A Fragment of a Khwarezmian Dictionary*, ed. D. N. MacKenzie (London, 1971)). At the same time, he also wrote a series of comprehensive articles on Khwarezmian lexicology. He then left Khwarezmian for a while, but returned to it during the 1980s with the edition of an important part of the Khwarezmian glosses (*The Khwarezmian Element in the* Qunyat al-Munya (London, 1990)).

MacKenzie's long-awaited Khwarezmian magnum opus, a comprehensive Khwarezmian–English dictionary with full text references, was left unfinished. Shortly before his death, he completed the first third of it, covering the Khwarezmian entries up to the end of the letter βeta. I met Neil in summer 2000, when he was working intensively on Khwarezmian; he was freshening up his Arabic, to better understand the Arabic originals to the Khwarezmian glosses, and proudly said something like, 'my Arabic isn't that bad after all, is it?'

Altogether, MacKenzie's scholarly achievements and merits include an impressive range of New and Middle Iranian languages (Kurdish, Pashto; Middle Persian, Sogdian, Khwarezmian), in all of which—especially in Kurdish and Middle Persian—he produced philological standard works of reference that are unlikely to be replaced for a long time. In addition he occasionally published valuable works on other Iranian languages such as the Hawrami dialect of Gurani, a modern West Iranian language closely related to Kurdish (of which he wrote a short grammar, 1966), Early New Persian (especially Judaeo-Persian, see his important edition of a 'Judaeo-Persian Argument' of 1968), or Parthian (acting as editor of Diakonoff and Livshits' edition of the Nisa documents). MacKenzie did not publish on Old Iranian, but he knew both Avestan and Old Persian well. He also knew a number of non-Iranian languages like Arabic, Sanskrit or Armenian, whose knowledge is necessary for a proper understanding of various aspects and stages of Iranian linguistic history.

MacKenzie was—as he would jokingly say in his last years—one of the 'last dinosaurs' of 'traditional' Iranian philology. He was an excellent empirical linguist in the sense that he could grasp and explain the subtleties, and difficulties, of various Iranian languages, be it from listening to them (he had an excellent ear and pronunciation), or from written texts. He was not interested in linguistic theories; his approach to the description of languages was a mixture of traditional grammar and the Prague school of structuralism. In conversation, he sometimes made fun of 'modern' linguistic theories like the 'Chomsky-Momskian' one and their various ramifications. Without disparaging the sharpness of MacKenzie's linguistic insights, one might observe that he tended to analyse Iranological linguistic problems as phenomena *sui generis* (e.g., the 'indirect affectee' in Middle Persian, or the 'open compound construction' or the various forms of 'agential constructions' in Kurdish); one may sometimes miss at these instances a reference to non-Iranological, general linguistic (e.g., typological) terms or explanations. For example, he generally avoided the term 'ergative' in his description of Kurdish transitive past constructions, using 'agential' instead.

MacKenzie was interested in the Iranian languages as such, but he also regarded them as a means to an end. One of his major aims in studying the Zoroastrian and Manichaean texts of Iranian antiquity was to restore those which were fragmentary and to emend those which appeared to be corrupt, thus establishing their 'original' form as far as possible and laying the grounds for a proper understanding of their contents. He was a 'pure' philologist in the sense that his scholarly interest in Iranian history and religions was largely confined to the interpretation of the extant texts. I remember Neil saying once that everything that can be said about the early history of Zoroastrianism had already been said by Mary Boyce and that there was no point in writing any more books, or speculating about theories that cannot be proven or disproven, until new *texts* were found.

In more than one way, MacKenzie's scholarly work and approach can be seen as a continuation of those of his teacher Henning, whose philological genius and achievements he admired. While MacKenzie was at the beginning of his career, he followed Henning's advice to study modern Iranian languages (something which Henning himself seldom did), but during the 1960s, and especially after Henning had left London for Berkeley in 1961, he more and more followed in Henning's footsteps in focusing on Middle Persian (including Manichaean Middle Persian), Sogdian and Khwarezmian.

MacKenzie admired Henning's scholarly prose, by which his own style of writing certainly did not remain unaffected. Both Henning and MacKenzie were uncompromising in their publications: every letter and stroke had to be correct and verifiable (hence one of MacKenzie's favourite mottoes: 'always check your sources!'), there was no room left for 'prating', theorising, doubtful readings or dubious interpretations. Like Henning's, most of MacKenzie's articles are exemplary in their learning and philological scholarship. Both scholars' styles of writing are very precise, compact, 'dense' and artistic, using literary allusions or quotations, or word games, especially in the introductory parts or titles of their articles. For undergraduate students and those who are not native speakers of English, however, Henning's and MacKenzie's works are sometimes difficult to grasp and do not always provide easy access to the complicated subjects with which they are concerned.

MacKenzie was likewise uncompromising with respect to the works of others. He was a witty, keen and sharp reviewer who 'did not know friend or foe' if he found philological errors in an Iranological publication, or if the method by which a scholar approached a certain subject did not correspond to what he judged the 'right way'. Although his specific criticisms were often right, he was perhaps overcritical in some cases, where his irritation concerning errors of detail made him unduly overlook the real efforts or achievements of the author.

As a teacher, MacKenzie was at the same time demanding and unconventional. In his classes, he would not lose much time with preliminaries, but from the very beginning went straightway into the texts, and discussed, together with the students, their various philological and etymological aspects on a high scholarly level. He expected his students to acquire on their own the background knowledge in history, religions and so on which was necessary in order to be able to understand the texts fully.

He called his students by their first names and addressed each of them as 'Du', ignoring the normal usage in Germany. While attending one of his lessons, one could always expect, interspersed between two Middle Persian sentences, a joke or funny story about his military service in India, about one of his colleagues, or about a 'Knöllchen' (i.e. parking ticket; he loved the German word, which literally means 'small tuber') that he had just found on his car.

The number of students who took a degree under MacKenzie during his time in Göttingen was unfortunately lower than it should have been in view of his great scholarly expertise. On the other hand, MacKenzie's world-wide fame, especially in Kurdish and Middle Persian, often attracted advanced students from all over Germany and Europe, who came to Göttingen for a limited period to study a certain language with him, and then went on to other universities to obtain further degrees or a professorship there.

For those who were accepted by MacKenzie as serious students or scholars, his readiness to help and cooperate went far beyond what would be expected from a professor at a German university. For my doctorate, for instance, Neil not only familiarised himself with a modern Iranian language that he had not known before (Zazaki, which is closely related to Kurdish and Gurani), he also provided all the technical and computer assistance (i.e. software, fonts, concordances) that were necessary for work on a previously undescribed language, devoting an immense amount of time to all these tasks. Very ungrudgingly, he was also ready to share all his unpublished work, e.g. his preliminary edition of parts of the Middle Persian text *Bundahishn*, with any young scholar who he thought might be able to prepare an edition of it.

For MacKenzie, Iranology, like Zoroastrianism or Manichaeism, could be seen as a contest between competing personalities, usually 'the good' against 'the bad'. The 'good', represented by himself, his teacher Henning and a select list of other scholars, were almost always in the right but not always victorious; typically enough, he sometimes called this inner circle of Iranologists 'the family'. From the very beginning his students learned about, for instance, the conflict between Henning and the Swedish orientalist Henrik Samuel Nyberg, concerning the transcription of Middle Persian and various other matters. MacKenzie, who experienced the academic competition with Nyberg also as a personal rivalry, would later settle the whole matter with his famous 'Notes on the Transcription of Pahlavi' (1967) and his *Concise Pahlavi Dictionary* (1971). Right up to his last years, he would grow indignant when he remembered, for instance, how Nyberg, whom he met as a student, once disparaged his Swedish as a 'little tourist Swedish', though MacKenzie actually knew Swedish quite well.

To complete the picture of his personality, MacKenzie loved Franz Schubert and Isabelle Huppert, and was not a very good driver. Nevertheless, he liked to drive others and show them around in his BMW, which led to a number of fast prayers among his front-seat passengers.

In his last years, MacKenzie showed slightly increasing signs of bitterness, complaining that what he had done for Iranian studies would not last. He was certainly too pessimistic in this, as is shown by the continuing importance of his works, some of which have set a new scholarly standard in their area. But he must sometimes have felt like Don Quixote, tilting at the windmills of an enemy—human ignorance—that is impossible to overcome.

MacKenzie also had something in common with another hero of the Spanish chivalrous epic. MacKenzie loved and worshipped his mother tongue English, and its literature, and in his lessons (as in his writings) he loved to quote certain works, and speak 'in proverbs' and sayings drawn from them, as did Sancho Panza, Don Quixote's squire. To quote just two of his favourite sayings, MacKenzie used to characterise the philological incompetence of some of his adversaries with Humpty-Dumpty's words (from Alice in Wonderland): 'When I use a word, it means just what I want it to mean.' Whenever one of his adversaries, although MacKenzie had proven him to be wrong, remained obstinate, he would say: 'A man convinced against his will, is of the same opinion still.'

In his last years after his retirement, one of MacKenzie's favourite sayings was, sadly, 'Stop the world, I wanna get off!' Saying this, he also wanted to express his concern about the political situation especially in the Near and Middle East, which seemed to him to have deteriorated more and more during the last years. Indeed the world stopped on 11 September 2001, and shortly afterwards MacKenzie's body 'got off' and left the material world. Everyone who knew him and had seen him in summer 2001 would be convinced that this last saying was mere coquetry, and that MacKenzie's soul, spirit and wit did not at all want to 'get off'. Instead, he had many more things that he still wanted to write, to do, and to give to others.

LUDWIG PAUL
University of Hamburg

BARRY NICHOLAS

John Kieran Barry Moylan Nicholas
1919–2002

THE OXFORD LAW FACULTY flourished as never before in the second half of the twentieth century. Although his was not the most famous name, Barry Nicholas was the unobtrusive rock on which that success was largely founded. He also embodied the spirit in that time of Brasenose College, of which he became Principal. Even before the Second World War Brasenose could claim to be the strongest law college in the University. As tutor, professor, and ultimately Principal, he developed that strength and ensured that the College produced lawyers who took their study and their calling seriously.

The calendar of Oxbridge scholarship examinations in 1936–7 allowed Barry three attempts to get into one or other of the two universities.[1] His first two tries yielded only exhibitions. He was compelled to decline. He had to win a major scholarship. His mother, who to that point had battled to ensure that he got the education he deserved, could not otherwise bridge the funding gap. At his third try he won the top scholarship to Brasenose College. He need not have worried. His destiny could not have worked itself out if either of the first two attempts elsewhere had been

---

[1] For the period from the 1970s I have been able to rely to a certain extent on my own personal knowledge, but I am extremely grateful for very kind help from Barry's widow, Mrs Rosalind Nicholas. In particular she allowed me access to an autobiographical note which he wrote in his retirement for his son and daughter, without which my knowledge of the earlier years would have remained very sketchy. I have also been helped a great deal by Fellows and Emeritus Fellows of Brasenose, especially John Davies, Harry Judge, and Vernon Bogdanor. Arianna Pretto, one of the three Law Fellows, did invaluable research in the archives, with the help of the Archivist, Elizabeth Boardman, and the Librarian, Elizabeth Kay.

Proceedings of the British Academy, **124**, 219–239. © The British Academy 2004.

other than disappointing near-misses. After the war he competed for and won a place in the civil service and had to steel himself to decline it in order to accept election to a fellowship at Brasenose. And later still, when he had established an international reputation in the law as a Romanist and comparatist and had become Oxford's Professor of Comparative Law, that chair being attached to Brasenose, he was invited to accept election as President of Corpus Christi in succession to the legal historian Derek Hall. He trembled on the brink. More than one loyalty held him back. He managed to say no. Again that had to be. Just three years later he became Principal of Brasenose, in which office he succeeded another great lawyer, Herbert Hart. It is an extraordinary fact, although, as he himself said, not an important one, that he thus became the first Catholic Head of House since the Reformation. For Brasenose, which between the wars Principal Stallybrass had made the strongest law college in Oxford, and for the law faculty, and, more widely, for the academic study of law, it was immensely important that he was never distracted, not in 1937, not in 1946, and not in 1974.

By the time of his retirement as Principal of Brasenose in 1989 he had served the College and University for 42 years—or 52 if one counts from his first going up. He then reassumed the role of tutor. He taught the Brasenose undergraduates in Roman law into his eightieth year. Great scholar as he was, he would also want to be remembered as a teacher. These two aspects of an academic career were for him indissoluble. In the post-Nicholas world irresistible forces constantly drive scholars towards 'buy-outs' which relieve them from their distracting teaching duties. The separation of research and teaching is almost complete. He did not think that that was good for either, and he was right. The third strand of academic life is administration. He took that for granted and did far more than his share, brilliantly and invisibly. In a note written in 1988 Herbert Hart, his predecessor as Principal, spoke of his superb gifts in this respect and remarked that he had 'a kind of genius for cooperative work'.[2] One key was unfailing mastery of the brief and its background, another was his indifference to personal glory. He had no idea of a life that was not service to others. Rewards for self had no priority.

Among his pupils are numbered many who are now judges or professors. There is remarkable unanimity amongst them in their memories of their experience of Barry. All agree that he influenced them profoundly and, so to say, stayed with them through their lives. Three observations

---

[2] *Brazen Nose*, 23 (1988), 30–1.

recur. First, you were not told what to think. He never set out to push
the Nicholas line. He did not preach. His technique was to show you
where your railway lines where leading and to point to reading which
might throw doubt on the attractiveness of your destination. Secondly,
you learned not to hide an unsolved problem in imprecise or evasive
language and, which is part of the same turn of mind, not to expect
applause for inspired guesses for which you could offer no hard evidence.
Thirdly, and most important, and most difficult, you should not anyhow
be seeking to impress. Good work was good work. There was nothing to
gain by showing off, just a serious job to be done as well as possible. A
fourth report is of constant kindness and practical help to students in
difficulty or trouble.

I. Before the Second World War

Scholarships had been necessary all along, as well as help from kind
friends and relations. Barry was born on 6 July 1919 in Sydenham in
South East London. Soon afterwards the family moved to Folkestone,
but when he was about seven years old his parents' marriage broke up and
his father went to live in Liverpool, where he had obtained the post of
Chief Immigration Officer. There followed the legal separation and an
order for meagre financial provision. Although contact was not completely broken, the father played next to no role in Barry's life. His mother
was left to bring up the children. There were two sisters, Gwyneth older
and Rachel younger than Barry.

The father was Welsh. He went from grammar school in Aberavon to
Christ's College Cambridge and then began a career as a teacher. He
fought in the Great War, having been commissioned into the Royal Welsh
Fusiliers. Invalided home, he abandoned teaching for the immigration
service and in due course made his move to Liverpool. The mother came
from a vigorous, well-educated Irish family. Her paternal grandfather had
been Lord Mayor of Dublin. He married a sister of the Irish QC who
became the Law Lord, Lord Fitzgerald. Her father was educated at Trinity
College Dublin before joining the Colonial Legal Service. He married
into a family with sugar interests in the West Indies. She was the second
of the five children of that marriage who survived into adult life. In the
early days of university education for women she read modern languages
at Bedford College London and studied for a while in France before
becoming a teacher.

Barry's mother appears to have ceased teaching when she married. But in her reduced circumstances after the separation she remained resourceful and determined. With the help of a friend, a retired headmistress, she was able to keep Barry at a good preparatory school in Folkestone called Seabrook Lodge. Thence, the help continuing, he obtained scholarships to more than one public school and was sent to Downside.

Downside evidently suited him perfectly. For the rest of his life he reflected both the secure faith of the Benedictine monks and their clear-headed, tolerant rationality. His mother had taken care to bring him up able to speak French fluently. The monks of Downside kept up the French and took his Latin and Greek to a spectacular standard. On these foundations he won his Brasenose scholarship and went up in Michaelmas Term 1937 to read Classics. He took a First in Honour Mods in 1939 and then, starting in the Trinity Term, made the change to law.

Trips to the Continent played an important part at this time, usually cycling and youth-hostelling with friends or his sisters. The outbreak of war almost caught them on the wrong side of the North Sea. Cycling in Scandinavia they picked up a hint of the imminent invasion of Poland. In Copenhagen they waited for a ship for England and managed to get home only three or four days before Neville Chamberlain's grim announcement of the declaration of war on Germany on 3 September 1939.

II. The Second World War

A few days after the declaration he reported to the Oxford recruitment centre to join up but, having revealed a trivial knee injury suffered in the Downside gym, he was rejected as unfit. He then went to London to try again, this time making no mention of the knee. As a man whose head had been filled with Latin and Greek, and no science whatever, he was assigned to Signals and told to wait to be called for training. He fitted in one more term at Oxford, his second reading law. Brasenose had almost immediately been taken over as the place to which the Royal Courts would if necessary be evacuated. For Michaelmas Term 1939 the Brasenose men were accommodated in Christ Church.

At the end of the year the call came that he should report for training, first in Prestatyn and then at Catterick in North Yorkshire. A mixture of square-bashing and instruction in the mysteries of wireless and telephone brought him to his commission at the end of 1940. In January 1941 Second Lieutenant Nicholas sailed from the Clyde for what was to be an absence of four and a half years spent in every theatre of the war in the countries of the Eastern Mediterranean. As an officer in an Air Formation Signals Unit his job was to supervise the provision of communications facilities, chiefly telephone networks, usually for RAF bases. On account of U-boat activity, his outward journey to Suez followed a zig-zag route, from the Clyde to Canada, to Freetown in Sierra Leone, to Durban, and finally up the East Coast of Africa to the Red Sea. It took nine weeks. From Suez he was sent to Greece, but he arrived only shortly before the evacuation of British troops in the face of overwhelming German force. His ship was bombed—he was taking a much needed bath and did not bother to get out—but finally reached Crete safely, whence, as valuable technical personnel, he was withdrawn to Alexandria.

After a period in Egypt, he was sent to Palestine and thence to Beirut. He was in Lebanon for eight months, before being sent to Basra in Iraq. He had been promoted to Captain. His duties took him at times to Bahrein in the Persian Gulf, which he reached by Imperial Airways flying-boat. From Basra he was called back to Jerusalem and thence across the Sinai desert to Ismailia on the Suez Canal. At this time Rommel was threatening to break through at El Alamein. He was thrown into the preparations for what would be one of the decisive battles of the war. When the battle broke out on 23 October 1942 he heard the action but did not see it. His Signals unit was held back a mile behind the line. And for him and his men Montgomery's victorious advance went no further than Benghazi. They had to take care of the provision of communications for the big airbase there. After some months, now Major Nicholas, he and his commanding officer were moved to RAF HQ for the Eastern Mediterranean in Cairo, where in November 1943 he was involved in the security and communications aspect of the meeting between Roosevelt, Churchill, and Chiang Kai-Chek. He was now twenty-four years old.

In 1944 he was moved to Cyprus, then to Lebanon and finally to Palestine, where he was to prepare for an invasion of Greece which in the event never happened. When it became obvious that the war in Europe was coming to an end, he was sent on a mission to prepare to reinforce the troops still fighting in the East. Travelling once again by flying-boat he was to visit the usable airfields in East Africa and on islands in the Indian Ocean to assess the extent to which their communications systems would need upgrading for a major movement of troops by air. He completed his report and handed it in to the HQ in Cairo. In fact the war in the East was brought to its abrupt end before any troops from the West were relocated. After this mission he was assigned to the HQ staff at the Benghazi airbase. It was there that he heard of the surrender of Germany.

He found himself sent home to England with remarkable alacrity. His last posting was to Cheltenham, to the secret unit which later became known as GCHQ. A month or so later, when the war with Japan also ended, he was demobbed. He had the benefit of two priorities. Those whose university courses had been interrupted were to be allowed to resume them as soon as possible and, having signed up almost immediately after the declaration of war, he also had the benefit of what lawyers often refer to as the rule in *Clayton's Case*, 'first in, first out'. Coming back from the war unscathed, with the rank of Major and three medals, he later wrote that he had had too easy a time of it. He suffered the feelings of guilt which are said to affect the survivors of accidents in which many have died.

III. Post-war Oxford

By Trinity Term 1945 nearly six years had passed since he had signed up with the Signals. The habit of serious study was difficult to recapture. He was upset by the loneliness of studying in his Walton Street digs or in the library. He toyed with leaving. It was tempting to accept the degree which the special regulations allowed him to have without further examination. But he pulled himself together and decided instead to complete the full Final Honour School in Jurisprudence in four terms, taking advantage of the University's decision to increase its through-put by examining twice a year. He would take his final exams in Michaelmas 1946.

The real difficulty was to find tutors. Many Fellows had not yet returned. He found one, a Rhodes Scholar and later a Governor-General of Australia, who was little use to him. He talked all the way through the tutorials and only of his own opinions. In Roman Law he ended up with two, 'one of whom knew what the questions were but could not remember the "answers", while the other had forgotten the questions, but knew where to look for the answers'. The one was Stallybrass, the other De Zulueta, the Regius Professor of Civil Law at All Souls. In effect his first pupil was himself. He taught himself well. In Michaelmas Term 1946 his was the only First.

By this time his destiny had turned another page. In 1946 he had added to his burden the Civil Service examinations and the house-party assessments which followed for those who survived. He passed into the

Service. He would have been a great civil servant. It was not to be. The impression which he had made on Stallybrass contemporaneously resulted, even before his Finals, in his election as Official Fellow and Tutor in Law at Brasenose. He turned away the Civil Service. His duties as Fellow and Tutor would begin in the bitter weather of Hilary Term 1947.

Oxford was full to over-flowing, and Principal Stallybrass had made Brasenose the strongest law college in the university.[3] Barry's distinguished senior colleague, Humphrey Waldock, did not return from his war service to his Brasenose law fellowship. He accepted the Chichele Chair of Public International Law which was attached to All Souls. Ronald Maudsley was elected to succeed him but did not come at once. Barry therefore had eighty-four undergraduate lawyers to look after. Even after Maudsley arrived, he was teaching six hours every weekday, four in the morning and two, after games, before dinner, and four hours on Saturday mornings. He had some help from weekenders, but he himself covered all three undergraduate Roman Law courses, Contract, Legal History, Jurisprudence and sometimes International Law. To this has to be added the burden of regular University lectures. He was made All Souls Reader in Roman Law in 1948. The Readership was held concurrently with his Fellowship at Brasenose. Its effect was to raise his salary, at the cost of a considerably larger burden of lectures. If that were not enough, Stallybrass thought it not respectable to teach law without a professional qualification. Somehow Barry therefore found time to take the Bar exams and be called. He never practised, but later, in 1984, he was made an Honorary Bencher of his Inn, the Inner Temple.

To this picture of unremitting toil must be added the almost total absence of secretarial assistance and technology that did not go beyond typewriter and stencil. Moreover, colleges make demands which go far beyond teaching. They expect administrative and pastoral work to be done with no flaws and no fuss, and at this time they still insisted that Fellows dine in Hall and stay on to dessert. Nobody ever heard Barry complain of this load, even in retrospect. Nobody ever heard him complain of anything that concerned himself.

In the immediate post-war days a bachelor could just about cope with the burdens and reap some sense of satisfaction by way of reward. But

---

[3] Barry wrote a fascinating and typically balanced account of the Stallybrass days: *Brazen Nose*, 31 (1997), 22–9. At p. 24 he recalled that the residue of his estate was left for the advancement of the study of law in Brasenose and 'for the purpose of bringing to the College men who are likely to prove leaders in College life and to add to the prestige of the College'.

from 1948 Barry was not a bachelor. During the war he had met and fallen in love with a New Zealander, Margaret Heller, who was working as a nurse. Through postings and re-postings they had somehow managed maintain their relationship for several years. But that relationship came to an end; the return to normality caused them to drift apart. It was therefore as a bachelor that he re-entered Oxford and took up the duties of his Fellowship. But by the time he began to teach he had already met his future wife. In the winter of 1947 they began to see each other regularly, and in May 1948 they announced their engagement. They were married on 9 July that year in the Franciscan church in the Iffley Road. She was not a Catholic but moved one step nearer by becoming an Anglican. All her life she resented the rigour of the meanness of the Catholic hierarchy's attitude to mixed marriages and shared worship. In those days one forfeited one's Fellowship if one married without the Principal's consent. Stallybrass had given his consent but, as Barry recorded, not with a good grace. He thought the College was entitled to at least ten years' undistracted service.

His wife was Hildegart Cloos, the daughter of Germany's leading geologist, Hans Cloos, a professor at Bonn. Her family were strongly opposed to the Nazis. In 1939 Hildegart had come to England to see how Germany looked from the outside. She refused to go back. She was spared internment, and she managed to get a job with the Oxford City Architect. In Munich she had studied design and was sensitive to visual art. Later in life she was admired for her own mosaics. By the time of her marriage she had become a British citizen by naturalisation. Throughout his time at Brasenose Barry was able to rely on her support. She was fiercely loyal to him, and in later life anxious, as he was not, that his merits should be more publicly recognised. In 1951 their daughter Frances was born, and in 1955 their son Peter. In the unregenerate fifties colleges were not considerate of families. She was dutiful, as he was, and knew how to buckle under, but she never fully accepted that a college should have the lion's share of its Fellows' lives. 'Barry is married to the College', she said tartly to one Fellow, 'I am no more than his mistress.' Many marriages broke under that kind of strain. This one did not.

It must have been in the first years of his Fellowship that he got to know the emigré German jurists Schulz and Pringsheim.[4] It is clear that he was very fond of Schulz with whom he took tea quite frequently. He spoke of Schulz's copy of the *Digest* as 'used almost to destruction'. In

---

[4] On whom now see R. Zimmermann and J. Beatson, *Uprooted Jurists* (Cambridge, 2004), where Schulz's life is written by Ernst and Pringsheim's by Honoré, who was his pupil.

later years he had in his possession a copy of a letter written home by Schulz soon after the war in which he said, with a note of triumph, that the evil intentions of the Nazis had been thwarted since the harm they had hoped to do him had only brought it about that he had been the better able to write his *Classical Roman Law*.[5]

IV. The fifties and sixties

The inflated numbers subsided within a few years as the returning servicemen passed through. Nevertheless his teaching load in the fifties and sixties remained high by modern standards. He rarely taught less than fifteen hours a week in college, on top of his university lecturing stint. Ronald Maudsley, who was the other Law Fellow, had not quite the same dedication to teaching. By contrast John Davies, who succeeded Maudsley in 1966 when he resigned to take up a Chair at King's College London, was very much in Barry's own image and can claim a huge share of the credit for the continuing strength of Brasenose law all the way through to his retirement in 2000.[6]

Although Barry always stood out against publication for publication's sake, the burden of his teaching did not prevent his writing some superb articles even in his first decade as a Law Fellow. As early as 1953 he wrote what many people still accept as the definitive study of the Roman formal contract of stipulation.[7] And in 1958 he destroyed a heresy relating to liability for animals in Roman Law with surgical brevity.[8] There were other articles in the same period.[9] By the end of the fifties he had worked flat

---

[5] F. Schulz, *Classical Roman Law* (Oxford, 1951, reprinted Scientia Verlag Aalen, 1992, with a new preface by Wolfgang Ernst).

[6] J. W. Davies matriculated at Brasenose in 1954, already a graduate of Birmingham, and took a First in the BCL in 1956, winning the Vinerian scholarship. He then went to Chicago as a Bigelow Fellow, returning to an appointment as Lecturer in Law at Brasenose in October 1959 and Junior Research Fellow in April 1961. In 1963 he took up a lectureship in Birmingham University but returned in 1966 as Official Fellow and Tutor in Law. His lectures regularly, and uniquely, ended in prolonged applause. He was said to be one of the best tutors in Oxford and produced a long series of Brasenose Firsts. He retired in 2000.

[7] 'The Form of Stipulation in Roman Law', *Law Quarterly Review*, 69 (1953), 63–79 and 233–52.

[8] 'Liability for Animals in Roman Law', *Acta Juridica* [1958], 185–90.

[9] Notably *'Dicta Promissave'* in D. Daube (ed.), *Studies in the Roman Law of Sale in Memory of Francis De Zulueta* (Oxford, 1959), pp. 91–101, and with his lifelong friend Peter Fraser, 'The Funerary Garden of Mousa', *Journal of Roman Studies*, 48 (1958), 117–29, with further thoughts in *Journal of Roman Studies*, 52 (1962), 156–9; *'Videbimus'* in *Synteleia Vincenzo Arangio-Ruiz*, 1 (Naples, 1964), 150–4, followed later by *'Videbimus II'* in *Studi in Onore di Edoardo Volterra*, 2 (Milan, 1971), 577–604.

out for thirteen years without ever drawing on his sabbatical entitlement. He was entitled to leave every seventh term or seventh year, at his option. Harry Lawson, then still Professor of Comparative Law, and Hildegart seem to have worked on him to make him take a break. The sixties thus opened with a long trip to the United States and Canada.

Through Harry Lawson he had received an invitation to the law school of Tulane University in New Orleans for the Spring Semester of 1960. The whole family went, travelling by sea to save money and then by train. In New Orleans they bought an old Ford Mercury. At the end of the semester Barry drove it all the way to Vancouver, where the family settled again for three months before crossing Canada by rail to be home for the Michaelmas Term.

Tulane was an ideal place for a comparatist, Louisiana being the one civilian jurisdiction in the United States, albeit somewhat 'mixed' by reason of the overwhelming proximity of the common law. His principal duty in the law school was to teach a course in Unjust Enrichment. He also took a class on legal writing and was astonished to discover that the students, whom he liked very much and found bright and keen, lacked the vocabulary with which to discuss the structure of a sentence. The same is now true in England too.

It is no exaggeration to say that he found the domestic materials on unjust enrichment in total disarray. Nothing serious had been written to keep the cases in order, and nobody had kept an eye on the state of the French law, which would have provided suitable scaffolding. The history of Louisiana is more Spanish than French but its civil code belongs to its French period. This neglect made things difficult for him, but it also provided an opportunity. Almost all of Barry's published work was first hammered out and tested in his teaching. That partly explains its astonishing durability. In this case we can see that his course reordered the Louisiana cases with the aid of the French template. This appears from two very successful articles which later emerged in the *Tulane Law Review*.[10] Everyone who studies unjust enrichment seriously still reads

---

[10] 'Unjustified Enrichment in the Civil Law and the Louisiana Law', *Tulane Law Review*, 36 (1962), 605–46 and *Tulane Law Review*, 37, 39–66. In the same journal he later published 'Rules and Terms: Civil Law and Common Law', *Tulane Law Review*, 48 (1973–4), 946–72. It has been suggested that he constructed his articles on unjust enrichment with the deliberate intent of catching the eye of the courts: B. Markesinis, *Comparative Law in the Courtroom and Classroom* (Oxford, 2003), p. 98, discussed and doubted in the review by Sir Jack Beatson in *Law Quarterly Review*, 120 (2004), 175, 178. Beatson's doubts are more than justified, for nothing could be less like him, and in fact the memoir referred to in n. 1 above shows that his only immediate concern was

these pieces. In Louisiana they achieved a remarkable coup in that they were absorbed into the case law and are recurrently cited by the judges. 'More often cited than read' was the author's dry comment on this achievement.

During the summer months in Canada he worked on the book which many regard as his masterpiece, his *Introduction to Roman Law*, which came out two years later in the Clarendon Law Series.[11] Shortly before his death we were talking of bringing out a new edition. That discussion was commercially motivated. If truth be told, it needs no second edition. It is perfect as it stands. It does its job as well today as it did forty years ago. It has sold more than 50,000 copies, not counting sales in Spanish and in Mandarin. The author professed to be mystified by the book's success. He could not see where it found its market.

There is no single answer to his question. The book is first and foremost an elegant account of Roman law. Beyond that it is the best introduction to law that has ever been written. Lord Mansfield used to advise those toying with law to read Justinian's *Institutes*. The modern equivalent is 'Read Nicholas' *Introduction to Roman Law*.' Then again there is the unarguable fact that if you want to understand the modern law in any depth you do need to know the Roman story. In a world in which Latin has faded from the school curriculum, the self-serving fashion has been to deny this. But it cannot be denied. Even the young common lawyer has a real need for Justinian's *Institutes* if he is to understand the shape of his own law and the articulation of its parts. The *Introduction* satisfies that need. It is beautifully written and consequently easy to read, and it rewards the reader. There are lots of other introductory books on Roman law. By comparison they are all dogmatic, boring and locked in the ancient world. It is a great book. Nowadays it is becoming more difficult to persuade students that a book forty years old is still the best and most useful thing that they can read. For that reason alone it is a shame that he did not have time to touch it here and there, to allow it a 2002 date.

In 1964 Harry Lawson had to decline a visiting professorship in Rome and persuaded Professor Gino Gorla to invite Barry instead, and Barry to accept. His classical education and his catholicism called him. He went without the family, for just three months. He immersed himself in the city. In partnership with Gorla, and with Professor Giovanni Pugliese also

---

to give his students good value by providing them with as well-ordered as possible an understanding of the subject. The published articles were spin-offs from the pursuit of that primary goal.

[11] *Introduction to Roman Law* (Oxford, 1962).

choosing to attend, he gave a seminar at the Sapienza which even he
described with only slight hesitation as a success. The subject was sale,
studied comparatively on the basis of Italian, Roman and English law. He
had already taught and written on the Roman law. The Oxford course
required close comparison with the English law. He now 'got up' the
Italian law. Unknown to him this was important preparation for his later
work for UNCITRAL, to which we which we will return.[12]

It was at this time that he began to rise to positions of leadership outside the College. He did not seek power and influence, but he acquired
them. He was the master of the facts, present and past, of every issue,
and, although he was not given to long speeches, his judgement as to what
should be done invariably seemed right. Colleagues came to depend on
him, and he never let them down. In a period of exciting development his
hand was accordingly everywhere.

He first became a member of the Board of the Faculty of Law in 1958,
and he remained on the Board for thirty-three years, until he resigned
shortly after becoming Principal of Brasenose. During the sixties he was
also the Law Board's representative on the General Board of Faculties.
Although the decade ended in student revolution, this was a time, indeed
the very last time, when it could be said that universities were well-funded
and flourishing. The General Board was accordingly intensely busy but in
good spirits, and the Faculty of Law was in good heart, as never before.
Posts multiplied. There were no Research Assessment Exercises in those
days, no supposedly quantitative measures of success, but the sense of
strength and success crept up on the Faculty nonetheless. Rupert Cross,
Bill Wade, John Morris, David Daube, Herbert Hart, Humphrey Waldock
—these stars were all in one place, and others could easily be spotted
rising in the next generation.

One indication of the widespread optimism was the new St Cross
Building built largely but not exclusively for the Law Faculty, with the
Bodleian Law Library at its centre. Peter Carter of Wadham and Barry
were the law representatives on the building committee. The architect was
Leslie Martin. St Catherine's College, just down the road, was built by
Jacobson at the same time. Forty years later these two buildings have
some claim to be the best that modern architecture has been able to offer
Oxford. The good relationship between the lawyers and the architect
ensured that the law library would not only be aesthetically pleasing but
would work well. The one criticism on that front might be that the admin-

---

[12] See n. 18 below.

istration and information desk should have been sealed off from the reading area. The flat rooves have been recurrently troublesome, but by and large the building's sweeping horizontal lines have stood the test of time in a mostly vertical Oxford. Aesthetically it now discharges the further task of masking the inferior social science buildings which have sprung up against its eastern elevation, on the old territorial army site between it and St Catherine's.

As if his hands were not already full, he found a great deal of time to devote to the Catholic Chaplaincy, of which he was first trustee and then managing trustee. The story of his service there is long. It has to suffice here to say that as managing trustee he raised substantial funds for the Chaplaincy, restructured its operation, renewed its existing buildings and added new ones. His praise for Leslie Martin in relation to the new law library contrasts with his memories of battles fought with the architect chosen for the Chaplaincy, battles which he did not feel that he had won.

V. Professor of Comparative Law

He was elected to the Chair of Comparative Law in 1971, having served nearly twenty-five years as a tutorial fellow. The chair is attached to Brasenose. There was no need for him to move. He succeeded Sir Otto Kahn-Freund and, before him, Harry Lawson, whose memoir he wrote in these *Proceedings*.[13] Comparative law now occupies a strong and prominent position in Oxford and is at last beginning to slip into courses which do not formally bear the label. The Chair was founded to get that process started. Lawson was the first holder (1948–64), and by common consent it was the first four holders—the fourth was Bernard Rudden—who made its place secure. The teaching syllabus long committed the chair to an emphasis on French law. More recently it has broadened, to give the same priority to German law.

By publication date the first fruit of his tenure was work painstakingly done in his previous incarnation as a tutor, the third edition of Jolowicz's *Historical Introduction to the Study of Roman Law*, which very properly became 'Jolowicz & Nicholas'.[14] It means no disrespect to the original author to say that the third edition absolutely transformed the work. It

---

[13] *Proceedings of the British Academy*, 76 (1990), 473–85.
[14] H. F. Jolowicz and B. Nicholas, *Historical Introduction to the Study of Roman Law*, 3rd edn. (Cambridge, 1972).

was not merely updated but embedded more securely in the twentieth-century literature. It became a reference book which every Romanist has on his desk and every classicist uses when he wants to dip safely into Roman law. It also shows how seriously Barry took his teaching. It is manifest from every page that, for the sake of his lectures, he had been reading and reflecting on the new literature across the whole range of Roman law. It would have been impossible to achieve the success of 'Jolowicz & Nicholas' if that had not been his habit all along.

In much the same way his lectures as Professor of Comparative Law provided the foundations of another immensely successful book, namely his *French Law of Contract*, which did not actually come out until 1982, when he was already Principal of Brasenose.[15] Professor Sir Guenter Treitel's comment on the first edition cannot be improved upon:

> Perhaps the greatest difficulty facing a comparative lawyer is that of writing about one legal system in terms that will be intelligible to readers trained in another. Such a task requires not only legal bilingualism (which is relatively easy to attain) but a high degree of interpretative skill; or, in other words, the power to describe rules and institutions of one system with an eye on the categories of another, and to do so without distortion of either system. One of the merits of *French Law of Contract* is that it performs this task superbly. That it does so without apparent effort is another matter; it is good to see that even legal scholars are capable of the art that conceals art.[16]

The same high praise was paid to his work on the public law side of French law, especially his studies of French judicial review.[17] Although he was by nature sceptical of all forms of congratulation or public recognition, it must have pleased him that the French themselves recognised his learning in their law, in the form of an honorary doctorate awarded by the University of Paris, bestowed in 1987.

From 1972 Barry was the UK member on UNCITRAL (the United Nations Committee on International Trade Law). This met for two weeks every year, usually in New York but sometimes in Geneva or Vienna. The final text of the Convention on International Sales is known as the Vienna Convention, because it was signed in the Austrian capital (1980). He wrote important articles explaining the Convention.[18] Typically they

---

[15] Barry Nicholas, *French Law of Contract* (London, 1982).

[16] G. H. Treitel in P. Birks (eds.), *New Perspectives on the Law of Property: Essays for Barry Nicholas* (Oxford, 1989) p. 2.

[17] 'Fundamental Rights and Judicial Review in France', *Public Law* [1978], 82–101 and 155–77; cf. '*Loi, règlement* and Judicial Review in the Fifth Republic', *Public Law* [1970], 251–76.

[18] 'The Vienna Convention on International Sales Law', *Law Quarterly Review*, 105 (1989), 201–43; cf. *American Journal of Comparative Law*, 27 (1979), 231. There are a number of

fail to reveal his own pivotal role in the process. It is easy to see how he came to play such an important part. The text had to reconcile different legal traditions, different political perspectives, and different economic interests. He not only had the great comparative lawyer's capacity to see how different systems would perceive a problem but was also a uniquely subtle draftsman, ingenious in finding and expressing solutions acceptable to several points of view. Much more important in such a context, with national pride always near the surface, his indifference to personal glory made him the master of the art of giving others the impression that it was they who had hit upon his solution or had inspired the felicitous form of words to which all could assent. The fact that the Convention came very close to English law and had been largely made by their own delegate did not persuade the British Government to ratify it, preferring to maintain the position of English law itself as a rival vehicle of international trade. Opinions to this day are strongly divided as to whether ratification would or would not diminish the volume of legal business done in London.[19]

It was during his tenure of the chair that his reputation for wisdom, courage and moderation imposed on him a very heavy burden. The student revolution of the late sixties never reached the ferocity in Oxford that it mustered on the Continent. However, it flared up ominously in the early seventies in the outward form of a demand for a Central Students' Union. Students at Oxford had more and better social and leisure facilities than anywhere, but this one thing, a central union building, they did not have. In Hilary Term 1974 the campaign took an ugly turn when a hundred and fifty or so students occupied the university offices in the Indian Institute on the corner of Holywell and Catte Street. This incident led to charges against some sixteen students. The charges had to be tried by the University Disciplinary Court.

The University and the accused were legally represented. In very British style the University agreed to fund the defence. The chosen President of the Court was Barry. The proceedings were marked not exactly by violence

---

commentaries on the convention to two of which he was a contributor: *C. M. Bianca*/*M. J. Bonell* and *N. M. Galston*/*H. Smit*. The masterly *Law Quarterly Review* article stirred up debate and provoked a reply from Sir John Hobhouse (later Lord Hobhouse) *Law Quarterly Review*, 106 (1990), 530. See further, n. 13 above.

[19] The pros and cons of ratification were reviewed at a symposium held at All Souls on 1 May 1993, chaired by Barry himself. This was attended by practitioners, judges, and academics and engendered a vigorous debate. The lead papers (Steyn, Reynolds, Schlechtriem) were published in P. Birks (ed.), *The Frontiers of Liability*, Vol. 2 (Oxford, 1994), pp. 9–46.

but by the constant threat of violence and by violent language. There were raucous demonstrations outside and constant disruption and abuse inside, against which the President had no weapon other than repeated adjournment and a threat of last recourse to conduct the trial in private and in the absence of the defendants. The Court could not commit for contempt. The behaviour inside and outside the court was disgusting by any rational standard and extremely hurtful to dons who believed in a deep and unbreakable consensus that both teacher and taught were engaged in a single-minded search for truth through reason. The students were busy renouncing reason and anxious as it seemed to repudiate the notion that truth had some value.

The madhouse continued for one week, the President all along seemingly the unperturbed voice of tolerant rationality. The judgment, when it was delivered, was carefully devised to hurt but not to ruin the accused. They were all sent down, but with permission to come back a year later to complete their degrees if they gave certain undertakings. There was an appeal chaired by Sir Patrick Neill, QC. Since disruption could not help the appellants, they behaved more normally. All the same the appeals were dismissed, except in one case on medical grounds. The general judgement was that the University had come off well. Embodied for the duration in Barry Nicholas, it had shown that rationality, fairness and moderation could stand up to the voices of chaos and unfocused hatred. But for his habit of invariably suffering in silence we might have heard of the President's exhaustion and wounded disillusion. We heard nothing of that kind. But there is no doubt that the students' abnegation of reason was deeply wounding, made as it was of the same stuff as the Holocaust.

VII. Principal of Brasenose

Formally, he became Principal in 1978, after seven years as Professor of Comparative Law, and he held that office for eleven years. The underlying truth is rather different. His was already the guiding hand from the time of his return from Tulane in Michaelmas 1960. Sir Noel Hall was elected that year but could not immediately detach himself from his post as Head of the Administrative Staff College at Henley. The Vice-Principal, the philosopher McKie, then died and Barry was elected to that office for a three-year stint. For the year in which Sir Noel was disentangling himself from Henley, Barry thus did all the work of the Principal, and the truth was that for the remaining twelve years of Sir Noel's tenure all the work which required detailed organisation and administration continued to fall on him. And no decision of importance was taken against his advice. For example, it was at this time that Brasenose became the first men's college to decide to admit women.[20] That took some people by surprise, for the image of Brasenose culture was macho. It would have surprised nobody who knew whose hand was at the helm. The supposedly momentous change was carried through without a ripple. By the time of the implementation, in 1974, Sir Noel Hall had retired and had been succeeded by Herbert Hart. He was an enthusiastic supporter of the change. Indeed the fact that the decision had been taken was a factor which attracted him to Brasenose.

Herbert Hart was Principal for five years. He was his own man but nevertheless welcomed a species of dyarchy with Barry, who, unlike himself, knew everything that there was to know about the College and had no aversion to the minutiae of administration. Herbert Hart spoke openly of the pleasure he took in working with Barry. There was, he said, no better member of a team. He leaned heavily on him and on his loyalty and restraint.

The dyarchy achieved an enormously important coup. The College finances depended to a large extent on the Hulme Trust, a charity the income of which it shared with a number of schools in and around Manchester. Mismanagement and a certain degree of ill-will threatened to attenuate the income from the trust. At the cost of enormous expense of time and labour and long, patient negotiation, a complete restructuring of the trust was achieved which made the College's share safe for the foreseeable future. This achievement made possible other developments. The days of 'digs' were over. The College needed more accommodation. The Frewin site opposite St Peter's College was completely remade. Barry was in charge of that from the beginning. The architect was not someone who could be allowed free rein. Constant vigilance was required. Even so, some mistakes were made. One brand new building is to this day not pleasant to live in.

---

[20] The first moves were taken in the setting up of a committee in November 1966 (Vice-Principal's Register, 23, 30 Nov. 1966). The real difficulty came not from inside the College but from the opposition of the then women's colleges (Vice-Principal's Register, 23, 1 May 1968). However, after four other men's colleges made common cause with Brasenose on this issue further negotiations took place and it was with the agreement of the Principals of the women's colleges that the final steps were taken. In June 1971, by a vote of 24:8, Brasenose agreed 'to alter Statute I by the deletion of Clause 2 and the renumbering of Clauses 3 and 4 as Clauses 2 and 3. Clause 2 of Statute I reads: 'No woman may become a member of the College' (Vice-Principal's Register, 25, 16 June 1971). The approval of the Queen in Council was reported to the Governing Body in January 1973 (Vice-Principal's Register, 26, 24 Jan. 1973).

When he finally became Principal in name in 1978, his tenure was marked by humane modernisation, efficient administration, and a high degree of unity and confidence among the Fellows. The Principal knew every member of the community, the staff and students no less than the Fellows. He was quick to help anyone in trouble. But he was against inefficiency or time-wasting, and he knew that the times were changing and that the central purposes of the College would be impeded if care was not taken to improve its financial base. The time spent in meetings was cut dramatically. With the assistance of a strong bursar in the person of Robert Gasser he carried through a number of changes which were almost certainly unwelcome to him. New sources of income were sought, in conferences and films; new methods of staffing the College began to be used, as for instance contract cleaners. The sense of community had to give a bit, in the interest of economic reality.

Brasenose owned a large piece of inner south Oxford in the form of the crumbling Oxford City Football Club premises in Grandpont. Decayed as the old football ground was, it took an immense and sustained effort by Bursar and Principal to release the very considerable wealth locked up in it. A section of the local community was vigorously opposed. In the end both Grandpont and the College benefited from the development. Where once an immense growth of Russian vine did its best year after year to pull down the crumbling walls and buildings around the football ground, and neighbours winced at the thought that triffid-like it might turn on them, there now stands a large up-market retirement complex and, in the north-west corner, new social facilities have been built for St Matthew's Church.

On the intellectual front, the macho image of Brasenose culture receded and there was a strengthening insistence on intellectual endeavour, less tolerance for those who were not trying to do good work. The Principal kept Law strong, but attended no less vigorously to other fields. He encouraged growth on the science side. The Principal led by example. Many heads of house find it impossible to continue their research. He gave part of every day for his own work. He would not otherwise have produced his *French Law of Contract* (1982) which was discussed above because it was in large measure the fruit of his tenure of the chair of comparative law. It came out in a second edition three years into his retirement. It was in the Lodgings that he also wrote his important contribution to the seemingly endless debate on the nature of the *actus reus* in Roman theft, pointing out that the many scholars who had attempted to settle the question had failed to take account of the Byzantine materials and especially Theophilus' *Paraphrase*.[21] Most of his writing on the Vienna Convention was done as Principal.[22] Indeed his productivity seemed to increase with age, as he reaped the harvest of years of scholarship. We will come back to that in the final section.

After his much admired handling of the Disciplinary Court his stock rose further in central University circles, and in 1975 he was elected to the Hebdomadal Council. Among the tasks which fell to him as a member of Council was one which in his own words was the worst he ever had, worse even than being President of the Disciplinary Court. This was the chairmanship of the Staff Committee, which met every week for about three hours. At first, he said, he used to have to retire to bed to get over these meetings. The business of the committee was the relationship between the University and its non-academic employees, represented by three different trade unions. The stress derived from the unions' determination to turn every issue into a confrontation. They ruled out reasonable cooperation, even in relation to seemingly non-controversial issues such as safety in laboratories. Although he learned to cope, he thoroughly disliked his weekly encounter with institutionalised hostility within the university community.

VIII. The final chapter

The beautiful portrait in the Hall which was painted on his retirement as Principal in 1989 shows the same man as had lectured there in the sixties.[23] He had changed incredibly little. Nor did his work stop. He continued to cycle in from Charlbury Road in North Oxford to tutor Brasenose undergraduates in Roman law, and was daily to be seen doing his research in the libraries. In 1990, unforgivably late, the British Academy elected him FBA. A new edition of *The French Law of Contract* came out in 1992.[24] In 1993 he chaired a vigorous symposium in All Souls, on the subject of the Vienna Convention on International Sales Law, where the forces in favour of ratification were evenly matched by those against, who preferred to maintain the international role of English commercial law.[25] He

---

[21] 'Theophilus and *Contractatio*' in P. Stein and A. Lewis (eds.) *Studies in Justinian's Institutes in Memory of J. A. C. Thomas* (London, 1983), pp. 118–24.

[22] See n. 18 above.

[23] The artist was Mark Wickam.

[24] *The French Law of Contract*, 2nd edn. (Oxford, 1992).

[25] See n. 19, above.

did a great deal of work in the comparative law of unjust enrichment.[26] For the preparation of a comparative book of cases and other primary materials, which sadly did not appear until after his death, he assumed responsibility, not for the English law but for the French.[27]

He seemed completely undiminished. But a blow fell six years into his retirement. Hildegart died in 1995. She had been troubled for a long time by angina, from which her father had also suffered, and long before she had survived breast cancer after an operation in the sixties. Barry was desolate, and his friends anxiously supposed that he must decline in the long loneliness of a widower.

They were delighted to be proved completely wrong. When the period of mourning had passed he was able to find real happiness in a second marriage with Rosalind Williams, the widow of Professor Alan Williams FRS. If there had been one deficit in his long life it was not warmth or humour but fun. It was suddenly evident that he was hugely enjoying life with Rosalind. She is Australian. They went on an arduous holiday to visit her relatives and on shorter ones to explore parts of England familiar in childhood. They entertained friends, and he found that he was rather a good cook who enjoyed cooking. Since he looked so well we forgot even to wish that this happiness might be granted at least ten or so more years. Sadly it was not to be. Still apparently in perfect health when he went out, he became seriously ill at Mass on Sunday 24 February 2002. His aorta had ruptured. He was taken to hospital. The rupture was too close to his heart to allow an operation. He lived for one more week, in complete control of his senses. He died on 3 March, with Rosalind at his bedside.

In his contribution to the nineteenth-century volume of the history of Oxford University,[28] he recalls the meeting in 1884 at which the *Law Quarterly Review* was born. It took place in the rooms of Sir William

---

[26] His contribution to E. Schrage (ed.), *Unjust Enrichment: The Comparative Legal History of the Law of Restitution* (Berlin, 1995), which was a team-written book, went a good deal deeper than would be suggested by the co-authored initial chapter. He was the one who maintained intellectual contact between the members of the team, none of whom had his comparative experience. See also n. 27.

[27] J. Beatson and E. Schrage (eds.), *Cases, Materials and Texts on Unjustified Enrichment* (Oxford, 2003), in which each of six contributing jurisdictions had its own editor. Further evidence of his continuing mastery of the French law: 'Modern Developments in the French Law of Unjustified Enrichment' in P. W. L. Russell (ed.), *Unjustified Enrichment—A Comparative Study of the Law of Restitution* (Amsterdam, 1996), pp. 77–95.

[28] M. G. Brock and M. C. Curthoys (eds.), T*he History of the University of Oxford*, Volume VII(2) (Oxford, 2000), ch. 15. Here he time and again acknowledges his debt to F. H. Lawson, *The Oxford Law School 1850–1965* (Oxford, 1968).

Markby in All Souls and was attended by Anson, Bryce, Holland, Pollock, and Markby himself.[29] That meeting serves to mark a new beginning for the serious study of law in England and in Oxford. Two dreadful wars later, after the dust had settled, the Oxford law school entered on a golden age. Its new building was a symbol of something more important. Had the volume on the twentieth century not inexplicably decided to make no mention of jurisprudence at all, it would have had to applaud that achievement and meet the challenge of naming another five jurists who could claim to have made it happen. Nobody who knew the man and his work would have omitted Barry Nicholas. If he had gone into practice at the Bar he would have been a Law Lord. If he had accepted the post which he had won in the civil service, he would have been a Permanent Secretary. His contribution to the academic study of law, both through his writing and his teaching, was and remains immeasurable.

PETER BIRKS
Fellow of the Academy

Note.   Professor Peter Birks died before this memoir was published.

---

[29] Ibid., p. 394.

DIMITRI OBOLENSKY   *B. J. Harris*

Dimitri Dimitrievich Obolensky
1918–2001

BY THE TIME THAT HE completed his fiftieth year, Dimitri Obolensky had been Professor of Russian and Balkan History at the University of Oxford for nearly seven years and had achieved distinction in a number of fields. But it was a work then in progress that drew together his literary and historical talents to spectacular effect, offering a new vision of the development of East European history across a thousand-year span. A well-paced narrative and reliable work of reference within a clear conceptual framework, *The Byzantine Commonwealth* is likely to remain indispensable for anyone interested in exploring the pre-modern history of Europe east of Venice and the Vistula. The distinctive texture of the book not only derives from its blend of careful scholarship and bold advocacy of an idea. There is also a tension, well contained, between the scrupulous presentation of the facts and possible interpretations arising from them and passionate recall of the religious affiliations and values that once had underlain eastern Christendom.

In middle age, Obolensky liked to quote the response of one of his contemporaries to a questionnaire: 'Place of Birth: Petrograd; Place of Upbringing: Leningrad; Place of Residence: Paris; Preferred Place of Residence: St Petersburg'. Obolensky's life did not bear out this cycle precisely, but what had been a forlorn hope tinged with irony became, against all expectation, a fact of geography. While still an active scholar, Obolensky witnessed the collapse of the Soviet Union and his birthplace's recovery of its original name, St Petersburg. He was cautious about the prospects for peaceful change, having observed a succession of apparent 'thaws' that

Proceedings of the British Academy, **124**, 243–266. © The British Academy 2004.

reverted to frost. Obolensky records in his own memoir included in *Bread of Exile* that his father's younger brother, Peter, returned to the Soviet Union soon after Stalin's death, 'in the short-lived and mistaken hope that freedom was on the rise'.[1] Obolensky made his views clear in his address delivered upon receiving an Honorary D.Litt. from the University of Birmingham in July 1988; he referred to the prospect that 'evil' might now be overcome and expressed hope for the future of the peoples of the USSR and Eastern Europe. This forthrightness surprised some, given his usual public reticence. In private, certainly on first meeting, Dimitri Obolensky was apt to be equally reticent. Yet on closer acquaintance, a vein of wry humour would emerge from behind the courteous bearing.

Both the sentiments and the correct façade reflect Obolensky's origins and background. Devotion to his native land mingled with patrician disdain for nationalism and a certain reluctance to wear one's heart, or credo, on one's sleeve. He would remark, deadpan, on the 'Socialist Realist' features of the early Rus princes, which the celebrated Soviet archaeologist Gerasimov had 'reconstructed' from their skulls.

Birth and education

Prince Dimitri Dimitrievich Obolensky was born on 1 April 1918 in Petrograd. Both his parents were of ancient and distinguished lineage. Countess Maria Shuvalova was the daughter of the City Governor of Moscow at the time of his assassination in 1905. Her mother, Alexandra, had many years earlier received a proposal of marriage from the future Nicholas II, which she turned down with a presence of mind that would have served the Romanov throne well. Obolensky recalled from family tradition that when Nicholas asked 'Would you like us never to part?' she replied 'What a good idea! I will marry Paul Shuvalov, and you will appoint him your equerry: in this way, we won't part.'[2] The answer was worthy of one of Dimitri Obolensky's paternal ancestors, Princess Olga of Kiev, who likewise outwitted a marriage proposal from the Byzantine emperor Constantine VII Porphyrogenitus.[3] The Obolenskys could trace their ancestry back to Riurik, the first known head of the Rus princely

---

[1] D. Obolensky, *Bread of Exile. A Russian Family* (London, 1999), p. 215.

[2] Obolensky, *Bread of Exile*, p. 61.

[3] Olga reportedly pointed out that Constantine, as her god-father, was debarred by Church law from marrying her: *The Russian Primary Chronicle*, trans. and ed. S. H. Cross and O. P. Sherbowitz-Wetzor (Cambridge, Mass., 1953), p. 82.

dynasty and father of Olga's husband, Igor. Obolensky would occasionally refer, with a shy smile, to the eleventh-century Prince Oleg of Chernigov as 'my ancestor'. The name of Obolensky is threaded through the history of Muscovy and Imperial Russia. While individual members of the family had scholarly inclinations, the family's outstanding characteristic was unstinting service to the tsar balanced by a sense of decency and the common weal.

Obolensky's father, Prince Dimitri Alexandrovich Obolensky, evinced these qualities, and his memoir of life in Imperial Russia is that of an observant, nature-loving landlord who took his public duties seriously.[4] The humour and stoicism running through the memoir remained with him through the vicissitudes that followed the October Revolution. Such, at least, is the impression given by his son's affectionate reminiscences, which recount, *inter alia*, his misapplied zeal as a night-watchman in Paris.[5]

Bread of Exile, Obolensky's last publication, is a series of family portraits from memoirs, notes and diaries. The book conveys in dreamlike contrast the rhythms of pre-Revolutionary life and the pillar-to-post existence of the émigré world in which Obolensky himself grew up. Obolensky's own memoir gives a fairly detailed picture of his childhood and education. His mother and grandmother travelled with him from Petrograd to the Crimea; then, as the Bolshevik armies approached early in 1919, they were evacuated on a British warship. The 'brief, unhappy marriage' of Obolensky's parents ended, Maria re-married Count Andrey Tolstoy, and from 1923 they lived in Nice. These years Obolensky described as 'the happiest years of my life'.[6] In 1929 financial pressures obliged Count Tolstoy to transfer the *ménage*—which included an English nanny—to Paris, where a larger Russian community resided and where prospects of employment looked brighter.

Dimitri Obolensky's life underwent another abrupt transition when he was sent to Lynchmere, an English preparatory school run by the former tutor of Count Tolstoy in Russia, one Harry Upfield Gilbert. Obolensky was soon immersed in the genial brutality of English private education, literally so in the case of the ritual 'plunge'. Before breakfast, each one of the small, naked boys had to swim two lengths of an often icy swimming pool and anyone who tried to heave himself out prematurely would have

---

[4] Obolensky, *Bread of Exile*, pp. 22–30.
[5] Obolensky, *Bread of Exile*, pp. 214–15.
[6] Obolensky, *Bread of Exile*, p. 202.

his fingers stamped on by the ever-watchful Gilbert, to the roar of 'Get back, you rotter, get back!'[7] Nevertheless, Obolensky remained grateful for Gilbert's teaching of classical Latin and years later, he would present his fiancée, Elisabeth Lopukhina, with the collected adventures of Bulldog Drummond as an introduction to the more extrovert sides of English life.

Obolensky received his secondary education principally at the Lycée Pasteur and grew conscious of the kaleidoscopic quality of the Russian émigré communities in Paris. Avant-garde artists, writers, civil war veterans and ancient bloodlines were forced together in the common and unremitting quest for daily bread. Count Tolstoy, a capable man of the world, found employment in a film factory, but budgeting was tight and luxuries came fitfully: invitations to lunches with the smart set gave the young Obolensky an opportunity to ignore parental frowns and gorge. One fixed point in this flux was Obolensky's redoubtable mother, whom he adored. Another was his membership of the Russian Orthodox Church, and Obolensky served as an altar boy in Russian churches in Nice and Paris. Obolensky was not one to speak readily about his religious convictions, but his faith was profound and abiding and he would receive the sacraments regularly until the time of his death.

Obolensky's secondary education in pre-war Paris nurtured his interest in moral philosophy and also made him alert to subsequent trends in French thought. He would often acknowledge the value of Fernand Braudel's work in drawing his attention to historical geography and the unfolding of *la longue durée*, and in *Bread of Exile* he records his post-war friendship with the great historian of the seventeenth-century Russian Church Schism, Pierre Pascal.[8] One of Obolensky's first international accolades was the bestowal of an Honorary Doctorate of the University by the Sorbonne in 1980.

Obolensky won a scholarship to Trinity College, Cambridge and went up in Michaelmas Term 1937 with the intention of reading Moral Sciences, but switched to Modern and Medieval Languages and proceeded to take Firsts in both Russian and French. He enjoyed the social life of Cambridge, making lasting friendships and gaining in self-confidence. He also excelled at tennis, for which he was awarded a Blue while an undergraduate.

Upon graduation in 1940, Obolensky was willing to enlist in the armed forces, but was handicapped through being a 'stateless person',

---

[7] This vignette, which Obolensky was fond of relating in later years, is recorded in *Bread of Exile*, pp. 207–8.

[8] Obolensky, *Bread of Exile*, pp. 226–7.

possessor of several possible identities or none. In the event, he embarked on research into the history of the Balkan Dualists known as the Bogomils. Obolensky himself acknowledged that the choice of topic was determined by his supervisor, Elizabeth Hill, then Lecturer in Slavonic Studies. It was an inspired choice, drawing upon Obolensky's knowledge of Slavonic languages, fascination with the Orthodox Church and its past, and concern for the basic questions about Good and Evil that the Bogomils themselves had purported to answer. Later Cambridge gossip had it that Obolensky and Steven Runciman were working on the same subject in Trinity at the same time. This is untrue. Runciman left Cambridge at the end of Obolensky's first undergraduate year, and had virtually completed his book on Dualism by the outbreak of war, but this was only published in 1947 as *The Medieval Manichee*. The undeniable overlap in their research work did not prevent Obolensky and Runciman from later becoming friends, and Obolensky would serve as his honorary assistant at the ceremonial for renaming a street in Mistra after Runciman in 1976.

Obolensky completed his dissertation with remarkable speed and on the strength of it was elected to a Prize Fellowship in Trinity in 1942. The Fellows made him welcome, and he looked back with gratitude and affection to friends such as Patrick Duff, Denys Winstanley and George Kitson Clark. But the young scholar did not lose touch with the wider world or with his religious community. For two years he held the post of Temporary Assistant Keeper in the Department of Printed Books in the British Museum, and so spent much of his time in London. It was probably during this period that he was ordained Sub-Deacon in the Russian Orthodox Church. He would periodically exercise his ministry in the Russian cathedral in Ennismore Gardens for some time after the war, reading the Epistle and other parts of the Services. One of those present would recall, long afterwards, how 'his fine, resonant voice—with his beautiful articulation of the Slavonic texts which he loved so much—filled every corner of the large church'.

While working in the British Museum, Obolensky also received a powerful intellectual stimulus relating to his field of study from the Czech-born scholar, Francis Dvornik. Dvornik was doing research in the library, but he was also a Catholic priest and Obolensky fondly recalled the comfort and 'little kindnesses' he brought to those working in the library 'while the German bombs were falling on London'.[9] Dvornik had

---

[9] D. Obolensky, 'Father Francis Dvornik', *Harvard Slavic Studies*, 2 (1954), 1–9 at 9.

already rescued the missionaries Cyril and Methodius from relative neglect by historians and was then writing important studies on East–West relations, showing how much the different branches of Christendom still held in common in the earlier Middle Ages. His ecumenical outlook appealed to Obolensky, as did his meticulous scholarship. Obolensky would sometimes say that he learnt from Dvornik the technique of organising complex subject-matter and providing 'signposts' for the general reader. Obolensky's mastery of this technique is already manifest in the work which emerged from his Prize Dissertation as *The Bogomils*.[10] The formidable problems concerning their beliefs, the origins of those beliefs and the reliability of the (mostly hostile) sources about the heretics are handled with great clarity and insight. Later reprinted, this is still the fundamental survey of the subject in a Western language.

Obolensky's command of the history of eastern orthodox religious history and culture in the Middle Ages was at once recognised as magisterial. In 1946 he had been made Lecturer in Slavonic Studies in the University of Cambridge, and in January 1949 he took up the newly created post of Reader in Russian and Balkan Medieval History at the University of Oxford. Moving to Oxford with his wife Elisabeth, Obolensky was elected to a Studentship at Christ Church, Trinity's sister college, in 1950.

Life and work in post-war Oxford, 1949–71

Obolensky's post in Oxford gave him scope to pursue his historical interests and future lines of research were set out in 'Russia's Byzantine heritage'.[11] In this wide-ranging paper, Obolensky surveyed the nature of Russia's debt to Byzantium and addressed the question of whether the regions and peoples of the Balkans and Russia had enough in common to be viewed as a cultural unit. He took issue with A. J. Toynbee over the 'totalitarian' nature of Byzantium and whether such totalitarianism, as institution or *mentalité*, might have passed on to Kievan and eventually Soviet Russia. His remarks about the dynamics of the interplay between the Byzantine Church and holy men, on the one hand, and the imperial Establishment on the other have not lost their force. Nor has his point that Peter the Great looked to the West for models when he determined

[10] D. Obolensky, *The Bogomils: A Study in Balkan Neo-Manichaeism* (Cambridge, 1948) (repr. Twickenham, 1972; New York, 1978).
[11] D. Obolensky, 'Russia's Byzantine heritage', *Oxford Slavonic Papers*, 1 (1950), 37–63.

to subsume the Russian Church within his newly-fashioned State. This study had been reprinted four times by the end of the twentieth century[12] and the issues raised in it would recur in Obolensky's later publications and, in direct form, one evening in the Kremlin (see below, p. 262).

Obolensky's early years in Oxford saw him teaching Russian literature as well as the history of Russia and the Balkans. His lectures, in particular, were much admired: standing straight and poised, he would deliver them in mellifluous tones without notes, aiming, as he once put it, 'to talk to' his audience. Students were encouraged to make the imaginative leap to the worlds of the early Slavs, epic poems, migrating nomads and displaced Byzantine missionaries.

The principal fruit of these years was *The Penguin Book of Russian Verse*. Ranging from the *Lay of Igor's Campaign*—of whose authenticity Obolensky was a staunch champion—to a poem by Aleksandr Tvardovsky,[13] Obolensky's prose translations and introduction were a labour of love, tracing with insight the development of Russian poetry from the *byliny* of early Rus. Obolensky felt deep affinity for the poems of Pasternak, particularly his evocations of the Russian land. Anna Akhmatova he described as 'the greatest living Russian poet'[14] and noted her rare ability to interweave private emotions with the march of historical events. Obolensky's respect for Akhmatova took an active form and he was instrumental in arranging for her visit to Oxford in 1965, when she was awarded an Honorary D.Litt. A cherished ambition which ill-health prevented him from achieving in the 1990s was to revise *The Penguin Book of Russian Verse* and include a new generation of Russian poets whose voices had yet to be heard in the West.

Obolensky derived great pleasure from his membership of Christ Church, making presentations to visiting groups of school-teachers and attending College meetings. He would tell stories (against himself) of the effect of his occasional interventions in them. Obolensky formed many lasting friendships in the college, among them Charles Stuart (a fellow-sufferer at Lynchmere), Henry Chadwick and Ronald Truman. Obolensky also made his mark after dinner, where his skills at card games were renowned and sometimes yielded modest financial winnings. The junior,

---

[12] Details may be found in the bibliography of Obolensky's works compiled by D. L. L. Howells (see below, n. 64).

[13] The celebrated editor of *Novy Mir*.

[14] *The Penguin Book of Russian Verse* (Harmondsworth, 1962), p. xxiv. See also Obolensky's obituary of Akhmatova, where he terms her 'Russia's greatest woman poet', *The Times*, 7 Mar. 1966.

card-playing members would occasionally tease the older, more staid members of the House by leaving their wager slips—with several noughts added—lying around the Senior Common Room. Obolensky also played his part in university administration, whose more arcane features afforded him quiet amusement. A member of the Modern History Faculty Board for much of the 1960s, and serving as Chairman in 1971–2, Obolensky was thought to exercise a calming influence; he later commented, however, that he had 'too thin a skin' to feel entirely comfortable in the post.

In the 1960s, Obolensky's long-standing interest in the interrelationship between Russian history and the Greek-speaking world and the Orthodox Church began to bear fruit. His understanding of Byzantium owed something to Father Gervase Mathew, Lecturer in Byzantine History, as he readily acknowledged.[15] But it was also advanced through contacts with America. Obolensky retained close ties with his mother and stepfather, who lived in New York, as did his second cousin, John Meyendorff, the theologian and church historian. Meyendorff's studies on the later Byzantine spiritual movement known as Hesychasm were inspired by, and themselves affected, Obolensky's later works. Another friend and scion of the Russian *émigré* communities in Paris between the wars was Fr. Alexander Schmemann, an authority on the Orthodox Church liturgy, who had moved to New York in 1951.

Obolensky had a lasting and creative association with the Dumbarton Oaks Center for Byzantine Studies in Washington, DC. During his first Fellowship, in 1952–3, he encountered A. A. Vasiliev, the venerable but jovial Russian Byzantinist. Vasiliev would reminisce about his own master, the founder of Byzantine studies in Russia, V. G. Vasilievsky, whose advice to the young Vasiliev, upon completing his doctoral thesis, had been to 'take a couple of girls, travel widely, and learn Arabic'.[16] Another prominent figure in Dumbarton Oaks was Obolensky's mentor, Francis Dvornik, while one of the warmest and most enduring friendships forged with near-contemporaries there was with Ihor Ševčenko; Obolensky was ever appreciative of Ševčenko's critical acumen and fertility of ideas.

Through the 1960s the lines of Obolensky's historical thought began to unfold. His contribution to the commentary on Constantine VII's treatise, the *De administrando imperio*, concerns the celebrated chapter 9,

---

[15] See, for example, Obolensky's 'Russia's Byzantine heritage', 58 and Note K on 63.
[16] This advice from Vasilievsky was relayed by Obolensky, with due qualifications, to the present writer upon completion of his own thesis.

describing the Rus' journey each spring to trade their wares in Byzantium. Lucid and erudite, it remains the surest guide to a chapter which has fuelled many and acrimonious debates, including the 'Normannist question' about the origins of the Rus.[17] Obolensky also turned his attention to Byzantium's diplomatic dealings with the peoples to its north, offering a wide-ranging yet coherent survey in 'The Empire and its Northern Neighbours, 565–1018'.[18] His admiration for the missionary enterprises of Cyril and Methodius, and keen interest in the literary language and translated texts which they and their students furnished to the Slavs, were reflected in conference papers.[19]

These publications displayed Obolensky's strengths as a rigorous source critic and as a cultural and diplomatic historian capable of synthesis. They did not, however, allow much outlet for his literary impulses, or amount to a vision of the overall pattern of development of Eastern Europe. These various sources, well-springs and streams would at last merge together and turn into a mighty river, worthy of Russia itself, in the work that is virtually synonymous with his name.

The Byzantine Commonwealth

The title of Obolensky's masterwork[20] encapsulated his thesis that much of 'Eastern Europe' in the broadest sense (including European Russia) belonged at one time or another to an overarching politico-religious order. Obolensky expressly drew on the works of earlier scholars such as Franz Dölger, Georg Ostrogorsky and André Grabar, who had suggested that a 'family of princes' had been an important element in Byzantine political thought and diplomacy. Other Christian rulers were supposed to have a quasi-familiar relationship with the Byzantine emperor, as 'brothers' or 'sons'. Over those rulers who had accepted baptism from him or his predecessors, such as the Bulgars, the emperor claimed spiritual parenthood. Obolensky linked this concept with the broader Byzantine claim

[17] See R. J. H. Jenkins (ed.), *De administrando imperio. II Commentary* (London, 1962), pp. 16–61, repr. in Obolensky's *Byzantium and the Slavs: Collected Studies* (London, 1971), no. 5.

[18] J. M. Hussey (ed.), *Cambridge Medieval History*, IV.1, 2nd edn. (Cambridge, 1966), pp. 473–518; repr. in *Byzantium and the Slavs*, no. 2.

[19] D. Obolensky, 'The heritage of Cyril and Methodius in Russia', *Dumbarton Oaks Papers*, 19 (1965), 47–65, repr. in *Byzantium and the Slavs*, no. 10; 'Cyrille et Méthode et la christianisation des Slaves', *Settimane di studi del Centro italiano di studio sull'alto medioevo*, 14 (1967), 587–609, repr. in *Byzantium and the Slavs*, no. 11.

[20] D. Obolensky, *The Byzantine Commonwealth. Eastern Europe, 500–1453* (London, 1971).

that all Christians owed the *basileus* deference, and argued that the sphere of influence created by those polities which adopted Christianity from Byzantium constituted a kind of 'Commonwealth'. Acknowledging that the circumstances and nature of conversion varied greatly between peoples, and that their adherence to Byzantine institutions and behavioural and cultural norms was labile, Obolensky investigated the uses to which the leaders of the most prominent and enduring structures put the texts, techniques and ideas which they took from Byzantium. He paid particular attention to the literary language that Cyril and Methodius created for the Slavs. Although account is taken of other peoples who partially or wholly came within the Byzantine Orthodox fold, for example the Hungarians and the Alans, the spotlight is on the Slavonic-speaking peoples, notably the Serbs, Bulgarians and Rus. A narrative of relations between these peoples' leaders and Byzantium is provided for the period up to the eleventh century. Thereafter, cultural ties and the circulation of ideas and spiritual values between the various components of the Commonwealth come to the fore. This is not inappropriate, seeing that the territorial empire collapsed in 1204 and was only partially restored from 1261, while a Byzantine Commonwealth was emerging 'as a recognisable cultural and political entity'.[21] The alteration in the book's treatment of the later Middle Ages corresponds with one of its main themes: the interest shown by external political and spiritual leaders in Byzantium's rich stock of religious texts, examples of piety and visual media, notably art and architecture. The attempts of rulers such as Stefan Dušan to appropriate these and, arguably, to take over the 'God-protected city' of Constantinople itself provide a narrative thread for these later centuries. The birth-pangs and convolutions of new political formations and their various adaptations of Byzantine law and art are made more comprehensible by a scene-setting chapter at the beginning of the book. There, the landscape and the communications network of Eastern Europe is presented, with due emphasis on the tortuous nature of the river-valleys and passes running through the Balkan massif. The reader is left to wonder that, in such broken and, to the north of the steppes, infertile terrain, a series of complex structures should have arisen at all.

Initial reactions to the publication of *The Byzantine Commonwealth* in the United Kingdom were favourable, if somewhat muted. Reviewers recognised its value as an introductory survey: an 'outstanding' feat of synthesis which would 'long remain the standard work' on the history of

---

[21] Obolensky, *Byzantine Commonwealth*, p. 203.

Eastern Europe.[22] Perspectives and circumstances in Eastern Europe were rather different. The new publication was itself the talk of the Fourteenth International Congress of Byzantine Studies convened in Bucharest in September 1971, where Obolensky's paper on 'Byzantine Frontier Zones and Cultural Exchanges'[23] received enthusiastic applause. Set against the background of the Cold War and occurring shortly after the 'Prague Spring', the Congress amounted to a declaration of Romania's own close affinity with East Rome, in ostensible defiance of Moscow: indeed, Nicolai Ceauçescu's use of Byzantium's aura for self-legitimisation gave a new edge to concepts such as the Byzantine Commonwealth.

The most forthright recognition of the book's importance, and the more substantive critiques, came from scholars outside the United Kingdom or from adherents to political creeds which still seemed set to redraw the intellectual map. North American reviewers recognised that this was the first major survey of Byzantium's relations with the rest of Eastern Europe and the first careful assessment and comparison of the receiving cultures.[24] The then-Soviet Byzantinist, Alexander Kazhdan, accepted Obolensky's basic concept of a Commonwealth whose ideological core was orthodoxy,[25] but two other scholars, G. G. Litavrin and Robert Browning, raised objections to the very concept of a Commonwealth that was some sort of functioning political entity.[26]

Obolensky's book cannot be said to have rapidly engendered works by other scholars, following up or supplementing its main theses. A noteworthy exception is John Meyendorff's *Byzantium and the Rise of Russia*, which acknowledges Obolensky's inspiration and provides important evidence of the waves of exchanges between far-flung communities in the orthodox world in the fourteenth century.[27] More than twenty years passed, however, before the appearance of a work applying Obolensky's thesis to other aspects of Byzantium: Garth Fowden's *From Empire to*

---

[22] Review in the *Times Literary Supplement*, 12 Nov. 1971, p. 1423 [David Talbot Rice].

[23] D. Obolensky, 'Byzantine Frontier Zones and Cultural Exchanges', *Actes du XIV Congrès International des Etudes Byzantines, Bucharest 1971*, I (Bucharest, 1974), pp. 303–13; repr. in his *The Byzantine Inheritance of Eastern Europe* (London, 1982), no. 1.

[24] See, for example, P. Charanis, *Speculum*, 48 (1973), 394–6; A. E. Alexander, *Slavic and East European Journal*, 16 (1972), 270–2; D. Abrahamse, *Slavic Review*, 31 (1973), 657–8; J. V. A. Fine, Jr., 'The Byzantine political and cultural structure', *Byzantine Studies/Etudes Byzantines*, 1 (1974), 78–84.

[25] A. Kazhdan in *Vizantiiskii Vremennik*, 35 (1973), 261–2.

[26] G. G. Litavrin in *Voprosy Istorii* (1972), no. 5, 180–5, esp. 182–3; R. Browning in *English Historical Review*, 87 (1972), 812–15.

[27] J. Meyendorff, *Byzantium and the Rise of Russia. A Study of Byzantino-Russian Relations in the Fourteenth Century* (Cambridge, 1981), especially pp. 2–3.

Commonwealth. The title was deliberately evocative of what Fowden termed the 'Second Byzantine Commonwealth', in succession to the 'First' eastern Roman empire of late Antiquity. Fowden differs from Obolensky in making no claim that the emperor functioned as an active law-maker or sovereign. He emphasises instead the value of a monotheistic creed as the binding constituent of a commonwealth, while acknowledging that the memory of former military might supplied a certain edge. But in the voluntary aspects of membership of commonwealths lay their advantage, 'provid[ing] most people with a practical frame of reference wider than the state to which they were immediately subject'.[28] Such traits in the western Christian 'empire' were also attracting attention from medievalists, and the importance of consensus based on shared religious beliefs, rites and values as well as material interests was gaining recognition.[29]

Material findings and new methodologies have also made a contribution towards re-appraisal of Obolensky's thesis. Archaeological excavations have shown that an economic nexus spanned the territories associated with the Byzantine Commonwealth and although the trading pattern is certainly not coterminous with them, there is (as Browning had suggested)[30] a connection. Thus the countless finds in the land of Rus of amphorae and cross-medallions originating in Byzantine regions register the pulse of demand for oil and wine used in religious rites after the adoption of Christianity by the Rus ruling élite.[31] Research is underway into the properties attaching to particular substances in Byzantine eyes, and the forces which they could supposedly conjure up. Byzantinists now appreciate the fineness of the line between invocation of legitimate saints, relics and wonder-working icons on the one hand, and recourse to other, unauthorised, incantations and powers on the other.[32] These extraordinary forces could be represented as at the emperor's command, as befitted his unique and God-given status, endowing his diplomatic gifts of

---

[28] G. Fowden, *From Empire to Commonwealth. Consequences of Monotheism in Late Antiquity* (Princeton, 1993), p. 169.

[29] See e.g. J. L. Nelson, 'The Lord's Anointed and the People's Choice. Carolingian Royal Ritual', repr. in her *The Frankish World 750–900* (London, 1996), pp. 99–131.

[30] Browning, *EHR*, 87. 814.

[31] See T. S. Noonan and R. K. Kovalev, 'Prayer, illumination and good times: the export of Byzantine wine and oil to the North of Russia in Pre-Mongol times', *Byzantium and the North. Acta Byzantina Fennica*, 8 (1995–6) (1997), 73–96; id. 'Wine and oil for all the Rus! The importation of Byzantine wine and olive oil to Kievan Rus', ibid., 9 (1997–8) (1999), 118–52.

[32] The lurking presence of 'magic' in Byzantine society was demonstrated by the contributions to H. Maguire (ed.), *Byzantine Magic* (Washington, DC, 1995). See especially Maguire's introduction, pp. 1–7.

gold and other valuables with an unearthly charge. Such products of the sacred palace were 'not only a sign of the emperor's overlordship, but also a conduit of his protection'.[33] Conversely, those who crossed the emperor or injured his subjects might fall foul of the hidden forces at his disposal. A Byzantine chronicle tells of a statue deemed to be an 'image' (*stoicheion*) of Symeon of Bulgaria which stood in Constantinople; at the very moment when the statue was deliberately shattered, Symeon dropped dead.[34] Whether true or false, the story is likely to have been propagated by Byzantine diplomats, and belief in the occult powers of the monuments and statuary of Constantinople—prophetic, prophylactic and obnoxious—was still widespread and intense on the eve of the Fourth Crusade.[35]

Mentalités of this sort are not likely to have been confined to the Byzantines, even if they were seldom articulated or even admitted in the written word. Strong support for the concept and, at some level, reality of the Byzantine Commonwealth is provided by social anthropology, a discipline which Obolensky himself utilised, when he applied the concepts of 'cultural diffusion' and 'acculturation' to set out the workings of Byzantium's sphere of influence. Byzantium had a wealth of credentials to act as an 'exemplary' or 'superordinate centre', with 'acquisitional societies' seeking material gifts, marks of respect, regalia and participation in its religion.[36] These societies, mostly lacking in organised priesthoods, literacy and advanced technical skills, more or less correspond with those adjudged by Obolensky to belong to the Byzantine Commonwealth. Southern Italy, Venice and Georgia did not, in this sense, constitute 'acquiring societies': although their elites shared cultural values, common strategic interests and, sometimes, even a language with the Byzantines, they did not need to acquire fundamentals such as the Christian religion or advanced technical skills from them. Obolensky's exclusion of them from the scope of his Commonwealth thus gains some vindication and his vision of the Commonwealth was, in more than one respect, ahead of its time.

---

[33] H. Maguire, 'Magic and money', *Speculum*, 72 (1997), 1037–54 at 1039.

[34] Theophanes Continuatus, ed. I. Bekker (Bonn, 1838), pp. 411–12; L. Simeonova, 'Constantinopolitan attitudes towards aliens and minorities, 860s–1020s. Part One', *Etudes balkaniques* (2000), no. 3: 91–112 at 106–7.

[35] R. Macrides, 'Constantinople: the crusaders' gaze' in R. Macrides (ed.), *Travel in the Byzantine World* (Aldershot, 2002), pp. 193–212 at pp. 205–7.

[36] M. W. Helms, *Craft and the Kingly Ideal. Art, Trade and Power* (Austin, TX, 1993), pp. 173–209. See also C. Geertz, *Negara. The Theatre State in Nineteenth-Century Bali* (Princeton, 1980).

Characteristically, Obolensky did not enter into polemics with the early critics of *The Byzantine Commonwealth*. Apart from a paper on 'Nationalism in Eastern Europe in the Middle Ages' delivered before the Royal Historical Society on 15 January 1971,[37] he wrote little further about the theoretical underpinnings of the Commonwealth. Obolensky did not lose sight of earlier interests, contributing the chapter on early Russian literature to the *Cambridge Companion to Russian Studies*, a three-volume project which he planned and saw through the press with his co-editor Robert Auty.[38] Obolensky's interest in historical geography and 'the unchanging land'[39] is shown in studies on the Crimea and the key Byzantine stronghold on its coast, Cherson.[40] The changing doctrines of the Bogomils also received their due.[41] However, some of Obolensky's most important studies were those filling in parts of the framework of his principal thesis.[42]

After completing *The Byzantine Commonwealth*, Obolensky conceived of the idea of writing a set of biographies; this eventually took the form of his book, *Six Byzantine Portraits*.[43] The book is devoted to six person-alities of the eastern orthodox world, ranging from the Balkan-born Slavonic-speaker Clement, archbishop of Ochrid, to Maximos the Greek. These individuals belonged to disparate milieus and can hardly be said to have held a common political agenda. It is, for example, questionable whether Clement, the loyal collaborator with Symeon of Bulgaria, can be considered 'Roman-thinking' in quite the same vein as Theophylact of Ochrid. And while Vladimir Monomakh had a Byzantine mother and used her illustrious family name—Monomachus—on his earliest seals, it was during his political ascendancy that the Greek language was replaced

---

[37] D. Obolensky, 'Nationalism in Eastern Europe in the Middle Ages', *Transactions of the Royal Historical Society*, 5th Series, 22 (1972), 1–16 at 11, repr. in Obolensky's *The Byzantine Inheritance of Eastern Europe* (London, 1982), no. 15.

[38] D. Obolensky, 'Early Russian Literature' in R. Auty and D. Obolensky (eds.), *Cambridge Companion to Russian Studies*, II (Cambridge 1977), pp. 56–89, repr. in *The Byzantine Inheritance*, no. 8.

[39] The phrase is Hugh Trevor-Roper's, writing of *The Byzantine Commonwealth* in *The Sunday Times*, 5 Dec. 1971, p. 39.

[40] 'The Crimea and the North before 1204', *Archeion Pontou*, 35 (1979), 123–33, repr. in *The Byzantine Inheritance*, no. 21; 'Byzantium, Kiev and Cherson in the tenth century', *Byzantium and its Neighbours*, V. Vavřínek (ed.) (= *Byzantinoslavica*, 54 (1993)), 108–13.

[41] D. Obolensky, 'Papas Nicetas: a Byzantine Dualist in the Land of the Cathars', C. Mango and O. Pritsak (eds.), *Okeanos. Essays presented to Ihor Ševčenko on his Sixtieth Birthday* (= *Harvard Ukrainian Studies*, 7 (1983)), 489–500.

[42] See, for example, 'Some notes concerning a Byzantine portrait of John Palaeologus', *Eastern Churches Review*, 4 (1972), 141–6 and figs. 1–3, repr. in *The Byzantine Inheritance*, no. 10.

[43] D. Obolensky, *Six Byzantine Portraits* (Oxford, 1988).

by Slavonic on princely seals. Nonetheless, the aggregate of individuals who make up what might be called the 'thinking quotient' of the Commonwealth held a number of beliefs and fundamental values in common, albeit without subscribing to a single, clear-cut, code of earthly conduct. Participation was essentially voluntary, as might be expected in respect of the exemplary centre that Constantinople constituted. And while a case can be made for Athos as being the true centre of the Commonwealth from the thirteenth and fourteenth centuries onwards, this did not entail dissolution of the ideal of a Christian order under 'Roman' imperial tutelage. So long as an unimpeachably orthodox emperor reigned in Constantinople, no other orthodox potentate could afford overtly to disengage from or wholly to ignore that ideal, even if the *basileus* had no direct impact on their own regime. With his gallery of portraits, Obolensky provided a rejoinder to those who objected to the lack of evidence of active imperial law-making in his Commonwealth. Ragtag as these and other lesser-known members of the 'international society' were, they were engaged in a polyphonous yet not incoherent 'discourse' extending beyond conventional definitions of 'religion' or 'culture'. It was Obolensky's signal achievement to have discerned this phenomenon and to have attempted to portray its dynamics.

Life after the Commonwealth

The Byzantine Commonwealth was conceived—and much of it was actually written—in Katounia near Limni, on the island of Euboea. Philip Sherrard of King's College London, the authority on Eastern Christian spirituality and Mount Athos, had bought a group of cottages there, and these were let out to his friends. Obolensky belonged to this circle and he and his wife spent weeks, sometimes months, of summer vacations at Katounia before and after publication of the *Commonwealth*. Their cottage was small and almost spartan, but Elisabeth, helped by her Parisian upbringing, could transform modest materials into *haute cuisine* and evenings were enlivened by dinner with the Sherrards, among others. Obolensky is still remembered in Katounia for his throbbing bath-time bass and reciting Pushkin in the sea.

Friendships nurtured in Katounia, and which remained firm for the rest of his life, included those with John Campbell, the historian of modern Greece and Fellow of St Antony's College, Oxford, and with Patrick Leigh Fermor. He would often stay at the latter's house at Mani, in the southern

Peloponnese, and Leigh Fermor wrote movingly, upon Obolensky's death, of 'his kind, youthful, scholarly and spectacled glance'.[44] Not far from Limni was the residence of Francis Noel-Baker, whom Obolensky had known since their undergraduate days together in Trinity, and sometimes there would be long Sunday lunches at the 'Noel-Bakery'.

Obolensky's friendships stretched far beyond the English-speaking colonies of Euboea and Athens. He spoke Modern Greek fluently and had many contacts and friendships with Greek and Greek-born scholars,[45] especially in the universities of Athens and Thessaloniki, where he presented papers that were later published.[46] He was a Corresponding Member of the Academy of Athens, and among his friends was the distinguished historian and politician, Andreas Stratos. Obolensky contributed a study to one of the volumes commemorating Stratos, and in this he demonstrated conclusively that there is no good reason to doubt Theophylact of Ohrid's authorship of the *Life* of his distant predecessor Clement.[47] Theophylact might describe himself as an exile from Constantinople, in whose court circles he had flourished, but this did not hold him back from care for the souls and material welfare of his Bulgarian flock, or from writing approvingly of Clement's use of Slavonic in his pastoral work. Theophylact is, in fact, a prime example of the binary—or multiple—identity of many members of the Byzantine Commonwealth, and perhaps Obolensky sensed in him a fellow-spirit.

Obolensky's affection for Greece encompassed its landscape, people and poetry. He would sometimes say that he went there 'in order to live', in the full sense of that word. It is no accident that he continued to travel to Greece in old age, when few other long-distance journeys appealed, and sojourns there seemed to reinvigorate him. He spent happy, sun-lit, weeks staying with his cousin-by-marriage, Chloe Obolensky, on the island of Spetsai, over the Easter and in the autumn of 2001. Obolensky appreciated the intricacies and imagery of modern Greek poetry, and could quote extensively from it, albeit not as readily as from Russian verse. Citations from Kavafy and Seferis prefaced the first edition of *The*

---

[44] *Daily Telegraph*, 7 Jan. 2002.

[45] Among these were Dionysios Zakythinos and, of younger generations, Hélène Glykatzi-Ahrweiler, Anthony-Emil Tachiaos and Angeliki Laiou.

[46] Respectively 'The Byzantine impact on Eastern Europe', *Praktika tes Akademias Athenon*, no. 55 (Athens, 1980), 148–68, repr. in his *The Byzantine Inheritance*, no. 3 and 'The cult of St Demetrius of Thessaloniki in the history of Byzantine–Slav relations', *Balkan Studies*, 15 (1974), 3–20, repr. in *The Byzantine Inheritance*, no. 4.

[47] D. Obolensky, 'Theophylaktos of Ohrid and the Authorship of the *Vita Clementis*', in *Byzantium: Tribute to Andreas N. Stratos, II, Theology and Philology* (Athens, 1986), pp. 601–18.

Byzantine Commonwealth. A sense of the Greeks' role in upholding eternal values against the odds may have contributed to Obolensky's reverence for Mount Athos. He visited the 'Holy Mountain' several times and was, in Hugh Trevor-Roper's words, 'transformed' by his experience there. The majesty of the mountain and the cells for contemplation exerted a powerful hold on Obolensky. He wrote of 'walking from monastery to monastery' and noted with satisfaction the resurgence of many of the monasteries in the closing decades of the twentieth century.[48] It must be conceded that Trevor-Roper's reaction upon his one and only visit was characteristically Gibbonian. Years later he remembered Athos as peopled with 'dirty old monks', although he had found the (Russian) house of St Panteleimon more congenial.

Differences in outlook did not stand in the way of a firm friendship from the time of Obolensky's arrival at Christ Church, when Trevor-Roper was the Junior Censor. On several occasions they travelled in the Balkans together and they served as British Co-Chairmen of Anglo-Bulgarian and Anglo-Romanian Conferences of Historians (in 1973 and 1975 respectively). As well as allowing for the presentation of serious historical papers,[49] these affairs paraded the national pride and Party loyalty of the hosts. Obolensky would later claim greater success in keeping a straight face than Trevor-Roper through the unrelenting speeches, a faculty that had also been to his advantage during the games of after-dinner poker in Christ Church, and the surrealia of life in the Communist Balkans did not escape their eyes. In Romania, they discovered that no one under the age of forty was permitted to attend their lectures, for fear that they might corrupt the young. On another occasion, they were greeted at the railway station in Bucharest by a deputation of *apparatchiki*, who warned them of the serious risk that their train might catch fire. The local committee of the Party had determined that the train should proceed on the basis that going uphill was acceptable, but downhill would be unwise. As their carriage began to lurch on its way, the two travellers' gaze rested on the bottles of Veuve Cliquot which they had brought with them. It would, they decided, be a pity to waste such very fine champagne if the train did catch fire during one of its unavoidable descents.

---

[48] Obolensky, *Bread of Exile*, p. 238.
[49] The proceedings of the conferences received coverage from M. Nikolaeva, 'Anglo-Bulgarian scientific conference of historians', *Etudes balkaniques* (1974), no. 1, 141–2; A. Pantev, 'Scientific meeting between Bulgarian and British historians', *Bulgarian Historical Review* (1974), no. 1, 95–9; A. Pippidi, 'Colloque anglo-roumain', *Revue des études sud-est européennes*, 14 (1976), no. 1, 168–70.

Happily—Trevor-Roper would later recall—they arrived in Cluj unscathed and with the Veuve Cliquot well accounted for.

Obolensky was elected a Fellow of the British Academy in 1974 and gave the Raleigh lecture on History in 1981.[50] He was not averse to taking on major administrative duties, having borne the burden of being General Secretary of the Thirteenth International Congress of Byzantine Studies in Oxford in 1966 and of seeing the proceedings to press.[51] Obolensky, who was knighted in 1984, served as Vice-President of the British Academy from 1983 to 1985. His administrative talents were put to good effect, and from 1985 until 1993 he was Chairman of the British National Committee of the Association Internationale d'Etudes du Sud-Est Européen.

Ties with the United States of America, where he was a Foreign Member of the American Philosophical Society, were not forgotten. He paid several visits to Dumbarton Oaks and—together with, among others, Robert Browning—he conducted lecture tours to colleges on behalf of Dumbarton Oaks with the aim of alerting students to the existence and opportunities of Byzantine Studies. He had also, at various stages, been a Visiting Professor at Yale, the University of California at Berkeley, Wellesley College Massachusetts, and Princeton. Obolensky carried on with these activities after retiring from his Oxford Professorship in 1985. The dinner held one summer's evening in Christ Church to mark his retirement was convivial, while redolent with memories. To Obolensky's right, frequently chortling, sat a dear friend, Isaiah Berlin, 'the guest from the Future' whom Anna Akhmatova had encountered in Leningrad in early January 1946.[52] Lines from her poem form the final words of Obolensky's *Bread of Exile*. As well as becoming an Emeritus Student of the House, Obolensky was in 1993 elected a Senior Associate Member of St Antony's, where he became a familiar figure.

Obolensky's personal life, however, was not unclouded. His marriage to Elisabeth had included long periods of apparent companionship and, as the foreword of *The Byzantine Commonwealth* acknowledges, she

---

[50] D. Obolensky, 'Italy, Mount Athos and Muscovy: the three worlds of Maximos the Greek', *Proceedings of the British Academy*, 67 (1981), 143–61.

[51] J. M. Hussey, D. Obolensky and S. Runciman (eds.), *Proceedings of the XIII International Congress of Byzantine Studies, Oxford, September 1966* (London, 1967).

[52] Their extraordinary meeting which, in her words, managed 'to confuse the twentieth century' features in Akhmatova's *Poem Without a Hero*; one of its dedicatees is Isaiah Berlin. For an edition of the poem, see A. Haight, 'Anna Akhmatova's *poema bez geroya*', *Slavonic and East European Review*, 45 (1967), 474–96 at 477 and n. 4, 479–80; A. Haight, *Anna Akhmatova. A Poetic Pilgrimage* (Oxford, 1976), pp. 140–3, 146–50.

typed the manuscript of the work twice. Having in common a background in the pre-war White Russian community in Paris, they also shared devotion to the Orthodox Church. The Obolenskys would attend services in the House of St Gregory and St Macrina in Oxford and they played an active part in the project to build the church of the Holy Trinity and the Annunciation in the grounds. Nonetheless irreconcilable differences led to their separation and eventually, in 1989, the marriage ended in divorce.

By the late 1980s, great changes were afoot in the wider world and these would bring Obolensky satisfaction, relief and even joy. The changes were concurrent with an anniversary that was foreseeable and long planned: the Millennium of the conversion of Russia to Christianity in (most probably) 988 or 989. Obolensky published an important paper relating to the event[53] and participated in a number of commemorative conferences. He relished an invitation to attend the great council of the Russian Orthodox Church and its celebration of the thousandth anniversary of the baptism of Prince Vladimir. His status was that of an official lay delegate, but he was welcomed as if to a homecoming. The Church was enjoying new freedoms and, as Obolensky put it, 'listening to laughter'. His election in the same year, 1988, to the Serbian Academy of Sciences and Arts was another straw in the wind. But no one could have foreseen the sequence of events following the fall of the Berlin Wall, a drama which Obolensky himself followed keenly, sometimes from the stage itself. Travel restrictions with Eastern Europe eased rapidly and conferences planned as a means of mitigating the mutual isolation of eastern- and western-bloc scholars turned out to be celebrations. A notable example was the symposium held in Bechyně, Czechoslovakia, in September 1990.[54] Russian scholars were able to converse freely with westerners in a manner unthinkable only a few years before. Several commented on Obolensky's spoken Russian: elegant, clear and in some ways a voice from the past, yet also a reminder of what their language could achieve.

Another subject of informal discussion at Bechyně was whether the Eighteenth International Congress of Byzantine Studies, scheduled to take place in Moscow in the following August, would actually convene, in view of the difficulties with funding and organisation. Obolensky, as the Vice-President of the International Association of Byzantine Studies, was

---

[53] D. Obolensky, 'Cherson and the conversion of Rus: an anti-revisionist view', *Byzantine and Modern Greek Studies*, 13 (1989), 244–56.

[54] The 'amazing atmosphere' was remarked upon by the symposium's director, Professor Vladimír Vavřínek, in his preface to the Proceedings: *Byzantium and its Neighbours*, pp. 3–4 at 4.

involved in the sometimes anxious run-up to the Congress. The Congress' plenary sessions were held in the Great Auditorium of Moscow State University and Lenin's exhortations remained emblazoned on the walls on either side of the platform: 'Study, Study, Study!'. The proceedings were, however, opened by Patriarch Alexei, the head of the Russian Orthodox Church, and the colloquia sessions devoted to hagiography, Church history and theology were notably well-attended. To one seasoned western journalist, it seemed as if these constituted an alternative Congress, where 'young Russians, some of them in the black robes of priesthood . . . pressed into the seminar rooms determined to find nothing less than their souls, their roots, their own Russian path to revelation and holiness'.[55] The address which Obolensky delivered at the close of proceedings was rather more feet-on-the-ground, picking out the main scholarly findings and themes that had emerged in the course of the Congress. His avowedly 'more personal' introduction and conclusion were expressed in Russian.[56]

The tenor of the Congress was a far cry from the Bucharest Congress of twenty years earlier, although both provided examples of the invocation of the Byzantine phenomenon for purposes of legitimising local initiatives. Obolensky was among a handful of scholars summoned to the Kremlin one evening to meet the Vice-President of the USSR, Gennadi Ianaev. In his paper-strewn office—complete with camp bed—Ianaev complained that Mr Gorbachev was sunning himself at his villa on the Crimea, leaving him to do all the work. According to Obolensky, who enjoyed recounting the anecdote, Ihor Ševčenko provided the most compelling response to Ianaev's question 'Was there totalitarianism in Byzantium?': Byzantine imperial ideology and aspirations amounted to totalitarianism, but the means to implement them had been lacking.[57] How far Byzantine precedents and a presumed Russian inheritance from Byzantium would have been invoked had Ianaev's own plans succeeded will never be known. What is certain is that a few days after this soirée, Gorbachev was placed under arrest in his villa at Foros (near the Vorontsov summer palace at Alupka, whence Obolensky had 'wisely fled

---

[55] N. Ascherson, *The Black Sea. The Birthplace of Civilization and Barbarism* (London, 1996), p. 46.

[56] D. Obolensky, 'Le discours de clôture prononcé par le Vice-Président de l'Association Internationale des études byzantines', *Bulletin d'information et de coordination de l'Association internationale des études byzantines*, 17 (1992), 51–6.

[57] The story is recounted in Obolensky, *Bread of Exile*, p. 244.

at the age of one' in 1919)[58] and a Committee of National Salvation was proclaimed.

Ianaev had been taking his history lesson from Obolensky and his fellow-Byzantinists on the eve of a bid to put a stop to the ultimate 'thaw'. The failure of the putsch and the dissolution four months afterwards of the USSR opened the way to more overt acceptance of Obolensky's ideas and scholarship in the former Communist countries. His election to the Russian Academy of Sciences in 1994 brought him particular pride, and in the same year a Russian translation of his paper on the conversion of Rus was published.[59] Preparations began for further Slavonic translations of *The Byzantine Commonwealth*, which had already been rendered into Greek and Serbo-Croat. Conditions in Russia and Eastern Europe delayed their publication. News of the Bulgarian translation's recent appearance—nearly ten years after being submitted to the publishers—brought Obolensky a wry smile as he lay on his final sick-bed.[60] He had been able to write a brief foreword to the Russian translation of the *Commonwealth*, which was combined with a translation of *Six Byzantine Portraits*. Obolensky acknowledged the shortcomings of 'influence' as a term and concept in cultural history and signalled his preference for Lotman's idea of 'asymmetrical partnership' between an ancient centre and the periphery. He also endorsed the propositions concerning cultural transfer and transplanting of D. S. Likhachev, a scholar whose work on Russian literature and culture he had long admired.[61] Obolensky had been instrumental in bringing Likhachev to Oxford for the bestowal of a D.Litt. in 1967, as he had been for Akhmatova's visit a couple of years earlier.

---

[58] Rose Macaulay's *bon mot* is cited in Obolensky, *Bread of Exile*, p. 186.

[59] D. Obolensky, 'Kherson i kreshchenie Rusia: protiv peresmotra traditsionnoi tochki zreniia' appeared in the flagship Russian journal of Byzantine studies, *Vizantiiskii Vremennik*, 55 (1994), 53–61.

[60] D. Obolensky, *Vizantiiskata obshchnost. Iztochna Evropa 500–1453*, tr. L. Simeonova (Sofia, 2001). Postscripts were provided by the translator and by the pre-eminent Bulgarian Byzantinist, Professor Vasilka Tapkova-Zaimova. Dr Simeonova's postscript includes part of an interview which she conducted with Obolensky in September 1989. This was to have been published in a dissident newspaper but was crowded out by the rush of events that autumn. For the text of the interview, see Obolensky, *Vizantiiskata obshchnost*, pp. 491–501 at pp. 491–4. The volume also contains a useful bibliography of the reviews of *The Byzantine Commonwealth*, based on material supplied by Jelisaveta Allen of Dumbarton Oaks: *Vizantiiskata obshchnost*, p. 511.

[61] The Russian translation was begun after Obolensky had given his consent at the Moscow Congress, and G. G. Litavrin wrote a foreword. For Obolensky's own foreword, dated 7 July 1996, see *Vizantiiskoe sodruzhestvo natsii. Shest' vizantiiskikh portretov*, tr. S. A. Ivanov, N. V. Malykhina *et al.* (Moscow, 1998), pp. 11–12.

Thanks to the new atmosphere, Obolensky was able to travel to Russia without hindrance and to converse with colleagues such as Likhachev, whom he had previously seen only at long intervals. It is probably no coincidence that in these years, Obolensky became more explicit about his Russian roots, for all his caveats against exaggeration of the differences between 'Russian' and 'Western' ways of thinking. Such is the clear implication of the title and the closing pages of his book, *Bread of Exile*. This had been a long-cherished project and the book was dedicated to James Howard-Johnston, whose selfless support and guidance steered it to final publication. Its title alludes to Dante's verses: 'Thou shalt prove how salt is the taste of another man's bread'.[62]

Fixed points, family and old friends remained important as Obolensky passed his mid-seventies and he became increasingly frail. He kept in close contact with his two brothers born to his mother and her second husband: Ivan Tolstoy, based in Scotland and Paul Tolstoy in Montreal. He continued to travel and—as ever—took pleasure in return visits to Cambridge. His old college, Trinity, had elected him to an Honorary Fellowship in 1991, and a dining companion at Feasts would sometimes be Steven Runciman, also an Honorary Fellow of the College. Obolensky savoured Cambridge as a place, and walking down the avenue across the Backs to Trinity in springtime he was apt to quote Housman's lines:

> Loveliest of trees, the cherry now
> Is hung with bloom along the bough.

The stark outlines of the Fen country in winter also appealed greatly. His sister-in-law Margie Tolstoy was able to offer him hospitality just outside Cambridge and he took an interest in new generations of students of eastern Christendom in Cambridge. It was to the Institute for Orthodox Christian Studies there that he donated his library in 2000. Among the numerous items are notebooks and personal papers as well as his library of books, periodicals and offprints. The archive has much to offer students of twentieth-century cultural history, as well as Byzantinists and Slavists.[63] Obolensky attended his last International Congress of Byzantine

---

[62] Dante, *Divine Comedy, Paradise*, Canto XVII, trans. J. D. Sinclair (Oxford, 1971), p. 245; Obolensky, *Bread of Exile*, pp. vii, 246.

[63] At the time of writing, only a fraction of the holding has been catalogued, and its materials have not been utilised in composing this memoir. Enquiries may be directed to The Principal, The Institute for Orthodox Christian Studies, Wesley House, Jesus Lane, Cambridge CB5 8BJ; tel: 01223 741350; fax: 01223 741370; e-mail: principal@iocs.cam.ac.uk.

Studies in Copenhagen in 1996, serving as an Honorary President of the International Association.

Obolensky's eightieth birthday was signalled in volume 31 of the *Oxford Slavonic Papers* with the editors' greetings and a portrait of Obolensky on its frontispiece. Beside articles by pupils, the volume contains an invaluable scholarly bibliography of his publications compiled by D. L. L. Howells, Librarian in charge of Slavonic and Modern Greek Books in the Taylor Institution Library.[64] As well as a festive family dinner, attended by both his brothers and their families, a group of former pupils and colleagues held a dinner for him on his birthday in New College, Oxford. There he spoke briefly but from the heart of the value he placed upon their friendship.[65] Ihor Ševčenko observed of his relations with his pupils, in an address delivered at Obolensky's Memorial Service, that 'he loved them all', and 'they tried to repay their debt to him'.

More vital than any of these ties, however, was that formed and long maintained with Chloe Obolensky, the theatre and opera designer. They shared a love of Russia and all things Russian, and Chloe's artistic vision found expression in her book, *The Russian Empire: a portrait in photographs*. Published in 1979, this has a foreword by Max Hayward, a friend of them both. The book offers striking *aperçus* of a vanished world, reminiscent of *Six Byzantine Portraits* (which Dimitri dedicated to Chloe) and in some ways it foreshadows Dimitri's collection of his own family's 'portraits'. Chloe did all that could be done to enrich Dimitri's life and bring him happiness in his later years, making him at home in her residences in France and Greece. In the words of Ševčenko in his memorial address, she 'loved him . . . and remained with him to the end'.[66]

Dimitri Obolensky died in The Cotswold Home, near Burford, on 23 December 2001. Among the condolences came those from the Pushkinskii Dom in St Petersburg, which had itself lost D. S. Likhachev two years earlier. A minute's silence in memory of Obolensky was observed at the Institute of Slav and Balkan Studies in Moscow, and an obituary planned for *Vizantiiskii Vremennik*. The funeral was held in the Orthodox Church of the Holy Trinity and the Annunciation, and the Memorial Service in the Cathedral of Christ Church, on 18 May 2002. In the latter church,

---

[64] D. L. L. Howells, 'The publications of Sir Dimitri Obolensky', *Oxford Slavonic Papers*, NS 31 (1998), 1–10.

[65] Those present were Professor A. A. M. Bryer, Dr S. Franklin, Professor S. Hackel, Professor R. Milner-Gulland, Professor G. Smith and Dr J. Shepard.

[66] The text of Professor Ševčenko's address was printed 'instead of an obituary' in *Byzantinische Zeitschrift*, 95 (2002), 399–401, here at 401.

Bunyan's 'To be a pilgrim' rang out and there was a reading from *Six Byzantine Portraits*—on Maximos the Greek's old age and death amid the narrowing cultural horizons of sixteenth-century Muscovy. It is tempting, but misleading, to fasten the labels of 'Russian', 'Greek', 'English' or 'French' onto this man of many worlds. His sympathies were too broad and his sense of justice too profound. His Orthodox loyalties did not contain his revulsion at the bombardment of Sarajevo by the Bosnian Serbs, and he wrote with feeling about Milošević's manipulation of Serbian national traditions to further his own political ends.[67] Perhaps his cosmopolitan upbringing among a high aristocracy fallen on hard times contributed to this outlook, but it is not the whole story. Obolensky's vision of the Byzantine Commonwealth as an international society of personal ties and basic Christian values was one by which he sought to live out his own life, with no small success.

JONATHAN SHEPARD
Formerly University of Cambridge

Note. I am most grateful to all those who have helped me in a variety of ways towards the completion of this Memoir. They include Simon Bailey, Anthony Bryer, Richard Clogg, Jacqueline Cox, Judith Curthoys, Garth and Elizabeth Fowden, Nicholas Hearn, James Howard-Johnston, Sergei Ivanov, Jacqui Julier, Dimitri Korobeinikov, Chloe Obolensky, Marcus Plested, Richard Ramage, Alexandr Rukavishnikov, Liliana Simeonova, Margie Tolstoy, the late Hugh Trevor-Roper, Evgenij Vodolazkin and Kallistos Ware.

---

[67] D. Obolensky, review of N. Malcolm, *Bosnia. A Short History* (London, 1994) in *Times Literary Supplement*, 8 April 1994, 15–16 at 15.

JOHN PLUMB

John Harold Plumb
1911–2001

SIR JOHN PLUMB, who died on 21 October 2001, having celebrated his ninetieth birthday two months before, had been in ill health for some time —but in rude health for a great deal longer. To his friends, and also to his enemies, he was always known as 'Jack', and he invariably published over the uncharacteristically tight-lipped by-line of J. H. Plumb. On both sides of the Atlantic, the many obituaries and appreciations rightly drew attention to his memorable character and ample wealth, to his irrepressible vitality and unabashed delight in the good things of life, to the light and the dark of his complex and conflicted nature, and to the ups and downs of his professional career. They also stressed his equivocal relationship with Cambridge University (where he failed to gain an undergraduate scholarship, but was Professor of Modern British History from 1966 to 1974), his nearly seventy-year-long connection with Christ's College (where he was a Fellow from 1946 to 1978, Master from 1978 to 1982, and then again a Fellow until his death), and his latter-day conversion (if such it was) from impassioned radical to militant Thatcherite. And they noted the human insight and sparkling style that were the hallmarks of his best work, his lifelong conviction that history must reach a broad audience and inform our understanding of present-day affairs, and his unrivalled skills in nurturing (and often terrifying) youthful promise and scholarly talent.[1]

---

[1] Throughout these notes, I have abbreviated Sir John Plumb to JHP, and C. P. [Lord] Snow to CPS. For JHP's obituaries, see: *The Guardian*, 22 Oct. 2001; *Daily Telegraph*, 23 Oct. 2001; *The Times*, 23 Oct. 2001; *Washington Post*, 23 Oct. 2001; *New York Times*, 23 Oct. 2001; *The Independent*, 27 Oct. 2001. For an earlier, and vivid evocation, see N. McKendrick, 'J. H. Plumb: A Valedictory Tribute', in id. (ed.), *Historical Perspectives: Studies in English Thought and Society*

Proceedings of the British Academy, **124**, 269–309. © The British Academy 2004.

At the height of his powers and the zenith of his fame, Plumb was indeed a commanding figure, both within academe and also far beyond. He was as much read in the United States as in the United Kingdom; he was a great enabler, patron, fixer and entrepreneur; he belonged to the smart social set both in Mayfair and Manhattan; a race horse was named after him in England and the stars and the stripes were once flown above the US Capitol in his honour; and he appeared, thinly disguised but inadequately depicted, in the fiction of Angus Wilson, William Cooper and C. P. Snow. For Plumb was never easy to pin down: he was a complicated, cross-grained and contradictory character, who was both a vivid presence yet also an elusive personality. At his Balzacian best, he radiated warmth, buoyancy, optimism and hope; but in his more Dostoyevskian mode, he was consumed by doubt, loneliness, envy and disappointment. And his often searing self-knowledge was matched by an ignorant unconcern about the effect of his own personality on others that would have been almost endearing in someone less difficult than he so often was. 'It may not be apparent to many of you', he observed at one of the dinners arranged to honour his eightieth birthday, in a remark that exemplifies both these traits, 'but I have never been a happy man.' Of course he hadn't been; but how could he have believed that this was news to other people?

Yet in all the column inches of celebration and censure, evocation and exasperation, one important aspect of Plumb's career was repeatedly ignored and overlooked: for while his life was an unusually long one, his productive period as a significant historian was surprisingly, almost indecently, brief. He was born in Leicester on 20 August 1911, but did not publish his first major work, *England in the Eighteenth Century* (Harmondsworth, 1950), until he was already thirty-nine. There followed two decades of extraordinary activity, as books, articles, essays and reviews cascaded from his pen in torrential abundance. But when he published *The Death of the Past* (London, 1969), it turned out to be a more aptly named book than anyone could ever have guessed, for it also signalled that his serious, lasting scholarly activity was almost over. He would live for nearly another third of a century, becoming more wealthy, more famous, more disappointed and more bad-tempered; he would dabble in other subjects, and continue to exhort and inspire the gifted young; but (to borrow his own later words of censure on the Cambridge History Faculty, which applied

in Honour of J. H. Plumb (London, 1974), pp. 1–18. For a later, more astringent appraisal, see J. Black, 'A Plumb with an acerbic aftertaste', *The Times Higher Education Supplement*, 16 Aug. 2002. For a more positive analysis see T. Hunt, 'Professor Plumb and the victory of reason', *The Times*, 17 Jan. 2004.

more plausibly to himself), 'nothing exciting, nothing original, nothing creative' appeared in print with his name attached to it.[2]

I

The slow beginning is perhaps easier to explain than the later, lengthening, lingering diminuendo. For Plumb was an outsider who came up the hard way, it took him a long time to get his career launched and to gain the necessary academic momentum, and the belligerence and the combativeness (to say nothing of the bruises and the scars) to which this gave rise remained with him all his life. Not for him the comfortable circumstances, the family connections, the metropolitan sophistication, the public-school education, the Oxbridge scholarships, and the immediate college fellowships that were enjoyed by those confident, privileged members of the upper middle class, who would form the backbone (but not always provide the spine) of the inter-war generation of intellectuals to which Noel Annan would later give the name *Our Age*.[3] Plumb's background, by contrast, was provincial and proletarian: Arnold Bennett rather than Bloomsbury. His father worked on the shop floor of a local shoemaking factory, and he himself remembered the lines of Cannock Chase miners queuing up for bowls of soup during the General Strike in 1926, when he was journeying to Wales to look at the castles.

But for all his humble origins, he managed to obtain a place at Alderman Newton's, the local Leicester grammar school, where he was taught by an inspired history master, H. E. Howard, who was a considerable (and controversial) figure in the town, and was Plumb's first mentor and patron. Howard was radical in his politics, uninhibited in his sexual appetites, and full of hope for the young people who gathered round him. Part of Howard's inspirational teaching method consisted in the seemingly unpredictable bestowal of excessive praise alternating with devastating censure, a technique which Plumb would later use to such good —and often disconcerting—effect with his own pupils in Cambridge. But it was clearly a tough apprenticeship. At the end of one lengthy disagreement, lasting until three o'clock in the morning, and ending outside the gates of the town gaol, Howard dismissed Plumb thus: 'Sir, you've

---

[2] JHP, *Collected Essays*, vol. i (London, 1988) (hereafter *E*i), p. 370.
[3] N. Annan, *Our Age: English Intellectuals Between the Wars: A Group Portrait* (New York, 1990), pp. 3–18.

misunderstood your facts, you've misread your psychology, you've got a third-rate mind, and you're probably impotent. Good night.'[4] But Howard also discerned in Plumb unusual gifts of curiosity and creativity, insight and imagination, which initially inclined him to be a writer of fiction (he was especially enamoured of Proust), and which would eventually become the outstanding features of his history. Plumb remained loyal and grateful to Howard all his life; he dedicated the second volume of *Walpole* to him; and when Howard was forced to flee the country in the early 1960s to avoid prosecution for molesting and seducing young boys, Plumb and his Leicester friends rallied round to look after him.[5]

In an appropriately love–hate sort of way, Leicester was very important to Plumb—as a powerful formative influence, but also as the place from which, urged on by Howard, he very much wanted to escape. (He was briefly engaged at this time, but his fiancée dumped him for a local policeman.) And it was at Leicester that Plumb made friends with C. P. Snow, who would later immortalise Howard as George Passant in his *Strangers and Brothers* sequence of novels. For the young Jack Plumb, eager, ardent and ambitious, Snow was an influential and an exemplary figure, and they became lifelong allies. Both were determined to get out of the provinces and make their way in the great world beyond; both saw themselves as far-left radicals, struggling against established opinion and entrenched elites; both disliked metropolitan condescension, and 'the stuffed, envious and self-righteous'; both were fascinated by the human condition and by the impact of personality on power and of power on personality; and both were inclined to use such similar (and revealing) phrases as 'time of hope' and 'we've had a victory'.[6] In their years of achievement and fame, Plumb matured into a much better writer than Snow: his prose was more buoyant and colourful, he could capture a character in a phrase or a sentence, and he was unrivalled in his capacity to set a scene and evoke an atmosphere. But in the early days of their friendship, Snow was very much the older, dominant, senior figure (he had been born in 1905), blazing the trail, pointing the way, making his career.

Snow left Leicester for Cambridge in 1928, to pursue scientific research, and Plumb was determined to join him as soon as he could. But although he won an undergraduate place to read history in the following year (no mean achievement in those days for a provincial grammar school

---

[4] McKendrick, 'Valedictory Tribute', p. 5.
[5] M. Drabble, *Angus Wilson: A Biography* (London, 1995), pp. 108–9, 183, 379; Snow MSS, 166.8: JHP to CPS, 14 June 1961; 166.10: JHP to CPS, 20 Jan. 1963.
[6] Plumb MSS, Snow file: CPS to JHP, 26 Jan. 1955.

boy), he was not given the college award to which he felt himself entitled, and which was essential if he was to make ends meet. He was, in short, a scholarship boy—but without a scholarship. So ended in defeat his first attempt to get to Cambridge, and he did no better the following year. It was a rebuff that went so deep that Plumb's relations with the university would never be easy, and although he later became settled and famous there, he would never feel fully comfortable or accepted. (Perhaps this was also because he never quite got over his first visit, to sit the scholarship exam, when he had shown up in a bowler hat, only to discover that it was the headgear of college porters, but not of would-be undergraduates.) Meanwhile, he was compelled to remain becalmed in the provinces and he took an external London degree at the fledgling University College, Leicester. This was scarcely a stimulating or nurturing environment, and the first-class honours Plumb eventually secured (an event unprecedented in the history of the place: no wonder the college, when it became a university, gave him an honorary degree) was a tribute to his determination no less than to his talent. Only then, in 1934, was he finally able to get out of Leicester and into Cambridge.

Thanks to his friendship with Snow, who had been elected a Fellow in 1930, Plumb secured admission to Christ's College, where he began research into the social structure of the House of Commons in the late seventeenth century. His supervisor was George Macaulay Trevelyan, then Regius Professor of Modern History and (after Howard) the most influential academic figure in his life. At that time, Trevelyan was completing his great trilogy on *England Under Queen Anne* (London, 1930–4), in which parliament and party politics featured prominently, and this made him the ideal mentor for Plumb, although it is not true, as is sometimes alleged, that he was Trevelyan's only research student.[7] Their personal relations were not close: Plumb was understandably unsure of himself, Trevelyan responded with his inimitably intimidating amalgam of 'barking shyness', and they met infrequently. But Plumb greatly admired Trevelyan's national histories and sympathetic biographies, he imbibed his view that historians should write with style and grace for a broad public audience, and (no doubt urged on by Snow) he dared to hope that he might one day succeed him as Regius Professor. Although Plumb was for a time attracted by other approaches to the past, he remained convinced that Trevelyan was the greatest historian (and the greatest man) he had known.

---

[7] Plumb MSS, Snow File: CPS to JHP, 2, 10 July 1934; D. Cannadine, *G. M. Trevelyan: A Life in History* (London, 1992), pp. 114–19, 217.

After the Second World War, he wrote an appreciative account of his work (*G. M. Trevelyan*, London, 1951), and he also edited a Festschrift, *Studies in Social History* (London, 1955), for Trevelyan's eightieth birthday.[8]

Soon after he began his research, Plumb encountered the second historian who was to be a powerful, but more equivocal, influence on him, Lewis Namier, who had recently published two path-breaking books, *The Structure of Politics at the Accession of George III* (London, 1929), and *England in the Age of the American Revolution* (London, 1930). By careful, painstaking study of the parliamentary constituencies and of ministerial manoeuverings, Namier had undermined some of the key props to the Whig interpretation of the past, so beloved of Trevelyan and his great uncle, Lord Macaulay. In particular, he insisted that George III was no tyrant or unconstitutional monarch, and that the party labels 'Whig' and 'Tory' were largely meaningless at a time when faction was the dominant mode of political organisation, and when men were motivated by naked ambition rather than ideology.[9] Plumb could scarcely ignore this powerfully articulated interpretation, and in his dissertation he vainly struggled to reconcile Trevelyan's belief in the two-party system with Namier's scornful dismissal of it. For the next twenty years, Plumb was much in thrall to Namier's view of the eighteenth century, but it was not an easy accommodation. For while both of them were outsiders, who were additionally disadvantaged by difficult and troubled temperaments, Namier was deeply conservative in his politics, whereas Plumb, like many of his contemporaries, who were appalled by what was happening in Nazi Germany and despaired of the domestic political scene, was actively embracing Communism.[10]

The third figure he encountered early in his time as a Cambridge research student was Herbert Butterfield of Peterhouse. He was ten years older than Plumb, had been elected a Fellow of his College on graduation, had never needed to take a Ph.D., and was the coming man in the Cambridge History Faculty. In the thirties, he also made his name by attacking the Whig interpretation of history, but during the 1950s, he would become Namier's most severe and sustained critic.[11] Inevitably, this meant Plumb and Butterfield were drawn to each other, as much to argue

---

[8] Plumb MSS, Trevelyan file: Trevelyan to JHP, 3 Dec. 1934, 9 July 1955.

[9] L. Colley, *Namier* (London, 1989), pp. 50–68.

[10] Plumb MSS, H. S. Hoff file: JHP to Hoff [undated, *c.*1937].

[11] H. Butterfield, *The Whig Interpretation of History* (London, 1931); id., *George III, Lord North and the People, 1779–80* (London, 1949); id., *George III and the Historians* (London, 1957).

as to agree, and for over half a century, they enjoyed a love–hate relationship, each simultaneously appalled and bewitched by the other. Plumb was baffled by Butterfield's religious commitment, repelled by his right-wing politics, captivated by his delight in paradox and peverseness, intimidated by his cleverness, and envious of his professional standing. Butterfield came to admire Plumb's literary gifts ('he could pile up a beautiful paragraph, add colour to a scene, provide thumbnail sketches of individuals'), but never felt he wrote history at the highest level of intellectual distinction, conceptual sophistication or scholarly accomplishment.[12] During the 1960s, when Plumb achieved his greatest professional successes in the Cambridge History Faculty, and also suffered his greatest professional reverses there, it seems likely that Butterfield was even handed in both promoting him and in thwarting him.

Thus stimulated, intimidated and not-a-little confused, Plumb duly completed his Ph.D. in 1936, when it was examined by Sir Keith Feiling and Harold Temperley. As he himself later admitted, it was an immature piece of work, lacking confidence and authority: the analysis of parliament was entirely derived from Namier, and took up the majority of the dissertation; the shorter second part gave an account of the Convention Parliament, and contradicted itself on every other page about the existence of party; there was no introduction, no conclusion, and (literally) no thesis; and there was little sign of the great and famous historian he would later become.[13] Nevertheless, with Trevelyan's help and encouragement, Plumb worked up some of the material into an article on the elections to the Convention Parliament of 1689, which was accepted for publication by Temperley in the *Cambridge Historical Journal*; but then Butterfield took over as editor, and his response was far from encouraging: 'I'm personally disappointed', he wrote, urging that Plumb should 'take much more trouble' with any future work he did. The article was eventually published, but Plumb's self-confidence was severely damaged, he made no effort to revise the dissertation for publication, and he found it hard to continue with his researches. Indeed, his only other published work at this time was a history of his father's firm, which he completed in 1936, and which was strongly on the side of the downtrodden workers

---

[12] Butterfield MSS, 241/3: draft *Times* obituary of Plumb, eventually published with modifications.

[13] JHP, 'Elections to the House of Commons in the Reign of William III' (University of Cambridge, Ph.D. Dissertation, 1936), esp. pp. 238–50.

against the exploitative bosses.[14] Beyond that, he was more interested in fiction and, encouraged by Snow, he wrote several novels, but they failed to find publishers.

'As soon as possible', Plumb told Snow in 1937, 'I shall get out of academic history into writing, journalism, etc.—life on my own terms.' Yet this was not to be. He applied for university jobs in a desultory sort of way, indulged in love affairs with members of both sexes, and was generally depressed and dispirited.[15] But, until he was elected to the Ehrman Fellowship at King's College in the summer of 1939, Plumb lived a hand to mouth existence from undergraduate teaching—not for Christ's (he was not considered distinguished or senior enough for that: in those days a Ph.D. was a badge of inferiority rather than a passport to preferment), but primarily for Girton and Newnham. For someone who was eager to catch up, both personally and professionally, and who knew there was a great deal of it to do, this was a fretful and frustrating period on the margins of Cambridge life. 'I seem to have wasted a lot of my time', he admitted to Snow at this time.[16] He was a member of one of the less smart colleges, his mentor was little esteemed by the rising generation of historians, and he never made it socially with such fashionable figures as Dadie Rylands. For Plumb was short of stature and unprepossessing of appearance, he was made to feel his provincial inferiority (boots and shoes and co-operatives, indeed!), and although well qualified as both a bisexual and a Communist, he was disappointed not to be elected to the Apostles, the University's most exclusive (and secret) society.

These slights, too, Plumb never forgot—or forgave. Hence the wounding tongue he had initially cultivated in self-defence against public-school arrogance and high-table condescension. Hence (in part) his life-long dislike of Anthony Blunt, who had once invited Plumb to his exquisite rooms in Trinity, but ('I don't know if I didn't smell right, or what') had never asked him again. And hence his subsequent, determined pursuit of social acceptance, public fame and worldly success, far beyond the poisoned-ivory tower. But hence, too (and this remained, to the end of his days, one of his most winning qualities) his later determination to promote the careers of talented young historians, who might thereby enjoy the early opportunities he felt he himself had been unjustly denied. For

---

[14] JHP, *Fifty Years of 'Equity Shoemaking': A History of the Leicester Co-Operative Boot and Shoe Manufacturing Society Ltd* (Leicester, 1936); *Ei*, pp. 29–44; Plumb MSS, Historians file: Butterfield to JHP, 10 July 1937; Trevelyan file: Trevelyan to JHP, 22 May, 22 Oct. 1937.
[15] Plumb MSS, Snow file: JHP to CPS, 30 March 1937.
[16] Plumb MSS, Snow file: JHP to CPS, 25 March 1937.

the Second World War meant his own career was held up again, as he was plucked from King's, having scarcely taken up his Fellowship, to join the code breakers at Bletchley Park. Unlike the much younger Harry Hinsley, Plumb did not cut a glamorous figure, and he consolidated his reputation for being as good at making enemies as friends among his academic contemporaries. But despite his radical politics, he was also beginning to appreciate the good things of life, having been introduced to claret by his college tutor, Sydney Grose, and during his time at Bletchley, his taste for fine wine was further developed when he lodged with Anthony Rothschild.

II

By 1945, Plumb had, as he saw it, 'wasted' nearly ten years of his life, and this was something he never ceased to regret and resent, especially as younger people started catching him up. By now, he had learned how to charm and to captivate, to bully and manipulate: 'my effect on people', he admitted to Snow, in an earlier display of self-ignorant self-knowledge, 'is very odd'. But he was still not fully convinced that history was his 'true *métier*': 'I envy you your purpose', he wrote to Snow in August 1945, 'I still search for mine.'[17] At the end of the war, he returned to King's, where he hoped his position might be made permanent. But with Keynes's support, Noel Annan had already been elected a fellow (and also an Apostle), and Plumb spent several anxious months before he was welcomed back to Christ's as a fellow in May 1946, at the not-exactly tender age of thirty five. As a bachelor don (he had again been engaged at Bletchley, but the relationship petered out when the code-breakers went home), he resided in what would become increasingly splendid rooms above the chapel in first court, and though he would much preferred to have stayed at King's, he became a loyal and lifelong college man. During the next twenty years, Plumb was Director of Studies in History, Tutor, Steward, Vice-Master and Wine Steward; he once came within a single vote of becoming Bursar (a strange ambition for someone whose self-image was always that of a creative writer rather than a bureaucrat); and he was a long-serving member of the College Council.

But while Plumb was abidingly grateful to Christ's for providing him with 'the rope ladder which leads from the suburbs to the stars', his temperament was ill-suited to its consensual and claustrophobic

---

[17] Snow MSS, 166.1: JHP to CPS, 24, 29 Aug. 1945.

collegiality. 'Back in this hellish hole', he ruefully told Snow in 1952, 'I hate it.'[18] Indeed, his acerbic tongue (especially at Governing Body meetings and postprandial combinations) and his scornful agnosticism (he deliberately ran his bath water to coincide with chapel evensong), made him many enemies. One such was Canon Charles Raven, who was Master from 1938 to 1950, and whom Plumb despised as a 'cheap and vulgar character': 'I'll get him and hurt him sooner or later.' A second was Lucan Pratt, the Senior Tutor, against whom Plumb waged a ferocious campaign, forcing him to resign from overseeing college admissions in 1961.[19] Most importantly, there was Professor Alex Todd, who had been elected a fellow in 1944, and for half a century, Plumb and he were bitter college rivals. This was partly academic: the arts versus the sciences. It was partly political: Plumb, though no longer a Communist, remained a radical, whereas Todd was a Scots Tory. It was partly personal: for unlike Plumb, Todd was dour, apparently untroubled by doubt—*and also very tall*. And it was partly professional, as Todd garnered with seemingly effortless and inexorable ease all the glittering prizes that he himself aspired to win: a knighthood and a peerage (would he, Plumb wondered, take the title 'Lord Christ?'), the Nobel Prize and the Order of Merit, the Mastership of the College, the Presidency of the Royal Society, and the chancellorship of a provincial university.[20]

While Todd spent most of his time in his university laboratory and on committees in London, Plumb became an outstanding teacher of undergraduates, and among his earliest college pupils were Rupert Hall, Eric Stokes, Neil McKendrick, John Thompson and John Burrow. By the mid 1950s, he was also supervising a succession of gifted research students, including John Kenyon, Brian Hayes, Ester Moir and Brian Hill. No historian of Plumb's generation spotted talent so unerringly, or helped launch so many brilliant and varied careers; but being mentored by Plumb was not for the squeamish, the second-rate or the faint-hearted (they were soon ruthlessly cast aside). Having learned his lessons from Howard, Plumb got under their skin, found and probed their weaknesses, tore their work to shreds, and then lavished them with fulsome praise, wrote them dazzling references, and exerted himself mightily on their

---

[18] Snow MSS, 166.5: JHP to CPS, 11 Jan. 1952.

[19] Snow MSS, 166.2: JHP to CPS, 15 Jan. 1948; 166.8, JHP to CPS [undated, *c*.1961].

[20] Snow MSS, 166.9: JHP to CPS, 10 April 1962. I have discussed the relations between JHP and Todd (and also CPS) in D. Cannadine, 'The Age of Todd, Plumb and Snow: Christ's, the "Two Cultures" and the "Corridors of Power"', in D. Reynolds (ed.), *Christ's: A Cambridge College over Five Centuries* (forthcoming, 2005).

behalf. Thus chastened, intimidated, alarmed, unsettled, stimulated, exhorted and supported, many of his protégés eventually went on to write bigger, better books than Plumb himself—something which caused him satisfaction but also, and increasingly, consternation. He liked his pupils to do well, and took real delight in their successes; but in later life, he was visibly disconcerted when some of them started doing better than he himself had done.

Plumb's election to a Christ's fellowship was accompanied by his appointment as a University Assistant Lecturer in History, and for the next twenty years he was a star performer at the podium—theatrical, witty, irreverent, iconoclastic, and drawing a large and appreciative audience—even though he endured agonies of apprehension beforehand. But he was out of sympathy with the right-wing religiosity of many of his colleagues, and in 1949 he was joined by Geoffrey Elton, who soon became as much his rival in the faculty as Todd was in the college.[21] Both were outsiders, both were small men, both were fundamentally unhappy and insecure, and both were often abominably rude—especially to (and about) each other. For they were very different historians, who were intent on practising, preaching and promoting very different kinds of history. As a pupil of Trevelyan's, Plumb intended to write for a broad public audience, and urged his protégés to follow their own interests in whichever directions they lead. But Elton despised what he regarded as Trevelyan's patrician amateurishness, he concentrated on narrow, technical issues concerning the Tudor government and constitution, and he expected his graduate students to work on limited topics in sixteenth-century history, which would only be of interest to fellow scholars. Throughout the 1950s and 1960s, Plumb and Elton were constantly in competition for promotion and preferment, they clashed on appointments committees as they pushed their respective protégés hard for the same jobs, and their animosity was further intensified by the fact that Plumb bought claret, whereas Elton drank whisky.

A College Fellowship, a University Lectureship, a string of outstanding pupils: these were the foundations of Plumb's late-starting but soon to be vividly flowering academic career. 'The years are getting shorter', he had told Snow in 1948, 'and yet there is everything to be done.'[22] In particular, he needed to write, though he hated waiting for the reviews to come in, and he never forgave or forgot hostile notices. Much more than

---

[21] *E*i, p. 165.
[22] Snow MSS, 166.1: JHP to CPS, 1 Jan. 1948.

in the 1930s, eighteenth-century history was dominated by Namier, who was now at the height of his fame and influence in academic and government circles (Harold Macmillan was both his publisher and patron). In Cambridge, Butterfield was confident enough to criticise Namier for his lack of interest in ideology and in popular politics, for his misunderstanding of party, and for his mistaken interpretation of George III's kingly conduct.[23] But Plumb had still to make his reputation as a Hanoverian historian, in which endeavour Namier's imprimatur was by now essential, and during the early 1950s, he worked hard to obtain it. Urged on by the Master, he considered revising his thesis for publication. He undertook to edit the volumes covering the period 1688–1714 in the recently revived *History of Parliament*, Namier's grand project in his final years. He produced two technical, scholarly pieces on quintessentially Namierite subjects: the cabinet in the reign of Queen Anne and the county politics of Leicestershire. And he took every opportunity to praise Namier for the brilliance of his scholarship and for the originality of his interpretations.[24]

Yet in 1956, he told Snow that 'I stand for something quite different to the Namier school'; and so, in a sense, he did.[25] The true Namierite believers imitated the great man by writing detailed accounts of short periods of political history, which paid no attention to party, ideology, or to the broader world beyond Westminster, and which made no impact on the general reading public. However much he deferred to Namier, Plumb had no intention of joining them: he decided against publishing his thesis, he withdrew from the *History of Parliament*, and in two measured but critical reviews, of books by J. B. Owen and R. W. Walcott, he expressed serious reservations about the Namierite methodology in the hands of lesser scholars.[26] More positively, Plumb's main concern was to write history of a high academic standard, and fully informed by recent research, which would also reach a broad general readership. His first book, part of the new *Pelican History of England*, did precisely that, surveying the century from 1714 to 1815 in twenty-four brief but arresting chapters,

[23] See the works cited above in note 11.

[24] Plumb MSS, History of Parliament file: JHP to Namier, 15 Nov. 1951; Namier to JHP, 9 May 1952; JHP to Namier, 5 June 1952; *Ei*, pp. 45–96; JHP, *England in the Eighteenth Century* (Harmondsworth, 1950), p. 216; id., *Men and Places* (London, 1963), pp. 43–66.

[25] Snow MSS, 166.6: JHP to CPS, 28 April 1956.

[26] R. W. Walcott, *English Politics in the Early Eighteenth Century* (Oxford, 1956); J. B. Owen, *The Rise of the Pelhams* (London, 1957); J. Brooke, *The Chatham Administration, 1766–68* (London, 1956); I. R. Christie, *The End of Lord North's Ministry, 1780–82* (London, 1958); *Ei*, pp. 100–8; Plumb MSS, History of Parliament file: JHP to Namier, 13 Feb. 1956.

which clearly owed much to his Cambridge undergraduate lectures. It was followed by his short life of *Chatham* (London, 1953), which vividly evoked his manic-depressive temperament and the triumphs and setbacks of his political career, and which provided the most compelling account of this flawed yet mesmeric figure since Macaulay's famous essay. Then came his Hogarthian group portrait of *The First Four Georges* (London, 1956): it insisted that 'the monarchy was the mainspring of political life' in the eighteenth century, and it depicted the Hanoverian sovereigns as rather commonplace men who were caught up in extraordinary circumstances.[27]

All these books were written with a verve, brio, zest and élan that were unusual among university lecturers and professional historians, they abounded in broad panoramas and memorable vignettes, they showed real insight into people and places, they brought the past vividly alive, and they sold in considerable quantities throughout the English-speaking world and also in foreign translations. They were, in short, the very antithesis of Namierite 'technical' history, and owed much more to the Trevelyan templates of national narrative histories and sympathetic biographies. But the insight into character was all Plumb's own, and so was the scintillating style. Here he is on Walpole's ineffectual efforts to muzzle the young William Pitt: 'as well might he attempt to stop a hurricane with a hairnet'. And here he is on George III in his mad and sad old age: 'a pathetic figure in his purple dressing-gown, with his wild white beard and hair, totally blind, totally deaf, playing to himself on his harpsichord and talking, talking, of men and women long since dead'.[28] (Attentive readers might also have noticed the extraordinary fury of much of Plumb's language: *Chatham* is preoccupied with anger, hatred, revenge and above all *rage*, while *The First Four Georges* depicts Hanoverian England as a nation characterised throughout by violence and aggression.) At the same time, Plumb was writing essays for *History Today* and other periodicals, on subjects ranging from Chatsworth to Cecil Rhodes, Sir Robert Walpole's wine to Georgian Bath, and he was also beginning to review in the weeklies and the quality newspapers.[29]

But his chief literary preoccupation during these years was his full-dress biography of Walpole (*Sir Robert Walpole*, vol. i, *The Making of a Statesman* (London, 1956); vol. ii, *The King's Minister* (London,

---

[27] *Ei*, p. 45; JHP, *The First Four Georges* (London, 1956), p. 10.
[28] JHP, *Chatham* (London, 1965 edn.), p. 13; id., *First Four Georges*, p. 146.
[29] Many of these essays were collected in JHP, *Men and Places*.

1960)).[30] The enterprise was conceived on a lavish scale, its planned three volumes owing something to Trevelyan's Garibaldi trilogy, with each of them prefaced by a panoramic survey ('Walpole's England', 'Walpole's Europe', 'Walpole's Empire') which was clearly indebted to Macaulay's *History of England*.[31] Drawing heavily on the Cholmondeley papers at Houghton and on Archdeacon Coxe's earlier life, it was Plumb's only major work of sustained scholarly research, and he was much assisted by R. W. Ketton-Cremer (on the Norfolk background) and by Snow (on structure and organisation).[32] The first volume brought Walpole to the threshold of power in 1722, and offered a major re-interpretation of his part in the South Sea Bubble, and the second traced his personal rule down to the Excise crisis of 1733, and provided new information on his building and collecting. Much of the conviction of the books derived from Plumb's close identity with his subject—the conquest of provincial obscurity, a delight in politics, patronage and manipulation, a pleasure in food and wine, pictures and porcelain, and a certain parvenu vulgarity. 'The more that I have come to know this great man', he observed, 'the stronger has my admiration grown. His imperfections were many and glaring. He loved money; he loved power; he enjoyed adulation and hated criticism. But in everything that he did, he was richly varied and intensely human.'[33]

In general, the books were well received, and they attracted widespread attention. A. L. Rowse and C. V. Wedgwood praised them highly. John Owen and Richard Pares were enthused. Trevelyan (and, up to a point, Butterfield) thought they proclaimed Plumb's emergence as an historian of the first rank. Snow was ecstatic: 'it makes so many of our early hopes come true'. And Plumb himself finally felt that he had 'begun to make a bit of a reputation'.[34] But not eveyone was impressed, and least of all those for whom it signalled an end to Plumb's involvement with tech-

---

[30] See also JHP's preliminary writings: 'Sir Robert Walpole and Christ's College', *Christ's College Magazine* (1951), pp. 4–6; 'Sir Robert Walpole and Norfolk Husbandry', *Economic History Review*, 2nd ser., 5 (1952–53), 86–9; 'The Walpoles: Father and Son', in id. (ed.), *Studies in Social History: A Tribute to G. M. Trevelyan* (London, 1955), pp. 179–207.

[31] J. P. Kenyon, *The History Men: The Historical Profession in England since the Renaissance* (London, 1983), p. 232.

[32] W. Coxe, *Memoirs of the Life and Administration of Sir Robert Walpole*, 3 vols. (London, 1798); JHP, 'Robert Wyndham Ketton-Cremer', *Christ's College Magazine* (1970), pp. 172–3; Plumb MSS, Snow file: CPS to JHP, 27 March 1956, 2, 8 April 1956, 26 Jan. 1959.

[33] JHP, *Sir Robert Walpole*, vol. i, *The Making of a Statesman* (London, 1956), p. xiii.

[34] J. B. Owen, *English Historical Review*, 72 (1957), 318–31; R. Pares, *Cambridge Historical Journal*, 13 (1957), 88–91; G. M. Trevelyan, *The Sunday Times*, 30 Dec. 1956; H. Butterfield, *Time and Tide*, 7 April 1956; Plumb MSS, Snow file: CPS to JHP, 1 Jan. 1956; Snow MSS, 166.6: JHP to CPS, 10 July 1957.

nical, scholarly history. Namier's lengthy review was more précis than praise, and thereafter relations between them cooled considerably, as the acolyte turned apostate.[35] Romney Sedgwick thought the volumes highly derivative: *Coxe et praeterea nihil*; John Brooke summarised them as 'Macaulay with a dash of Freud'; and A. J. P. Taylor wondered why Plumb found Walpole an admirable man.[36] There were also more specific criticisms. Plumb provided little serious analysis of how Walpole dominated parliament or ran the Treasury, and phrases such as this were no substitute: 'his instinct directed him with the sureness of an arrow to its target—to power absolute and undivided'.[37] The handling of Walpole's foreign policy, and his discussion of the exceptional complexities of European diplomacy, did not commend itself to the experts. And as in much of Plumb's work, the volumes were stronger on evocation than analysis, the prose was often more scintillating than the (often torpid and monotonous) events being described, while the paragraphing and punctuation were (as in almost all his writings) idiosyncratic and erratic.[38]

Nevertheless, the publication of these two volumes established Plumb as the leading authority on English history for the years 1660–1730, and in 1957 Cambridge awarded him a Litt.D. in recognition of his by now substantial oeuvre. Yet as Trevelyan appreciated, but Namier regretted, Plumb was in many ways, and by conscious choice, not a conventional academic historian at all. He had written only occasional learned articles for what are now termed 'refereed journals', he had refrained from publishing his pre-war Ph.D. dissertation, and he never attempted a scholarly monograph. He had little time for history's professional organisations, or for academic conferences or postgraduate seminars, or for the arcane output of university presses. He considered many of his colleagues to be dull, petty, myopic and untravelled, with limited social horizons, and with no interest in (or capacity to afford) the finer things of life—and he did not hesitate to tell them so. And although his own work concentrated in the late seventeenth and early eighteenth centuries, he was unusually widely read in other periods, cultures and civilisations, and he deplored the

---

[35] L. B. Namier, *The Spectator*, 6 April 1956; Butterfield MSS, 531: JHP to Butterfeld, 6 May 1956. Namier had told Plumb 'I mean to give you all the praise you deserve'. He gave scarcely any. See Plumb MSS, History of Parliament file: Namier to JHP, 9 March 1956, 6 April 1956.

[36] R. Sedgwick, *The Listener*, 19 Jan. 1961; J. Brooke, *New Statesman*, 13 Jan. 1961; A. J. P. Taylor, *New Statesman*, 21 April 1956; *The Observer*, 15 Jan. 1961.

[37] JHP, *Sir Robert Walpole*, vol. ii, *The King's Minister* (London, 1960), p. 3; G. R. Elton, *Political History: Principles and Practice* (London, 1970), p. 35.

[38] H. Pitt, *Time and Tide*, 20 Jan. 1961; P. G. M. Dickson, *Oxford Magazine*, 15 June 1961; E. Hughes, *History*, 47 (1962), 76–7.

increasingly rigid demarcation lines that were growing up between political, social and economic history. He was undoubtedly (and often intimidatingly) *clever*, but as befitted a novelist manqué, it was an *intuitive* rather than an *intellectual* form of cleverness. The historian's purpose, he would later write, was 'to produce answers, in the form of concepts and generalisations, to the fundamental problems of historical change in the social activities of men'. But in his own rattling narratives and vivid evocations of character, this was something he himself rarely attempted—except once, and very successfully, and then again, but with much less happy or complete results.[39]

As a 'literary' rather than a 'scientific' historian, Plumb scorned the Eltonian pieties which clothed mundane scholarly activity and academic hack work in the sacerdotal, pretentious and exclusive garb of truth and righteousness and virtue—and humbug. Like Trevelyan, he believed passionately in history's broader public function and deeper social purpose, and more than any writer of his generation, this gave him a powerful sense of mission and a vivid sense of *audience*. History should be written, he believed, not just (and not primarily) for fellow academics, but to educate, to enlighten, to entertain those whom Hugh Trevor-Roper once called 'the laity': in short to be an integral part of the broader national culture of the day.[40] And he further believed that history had a message which it was the historian's duty to proclaim: namely that for the majority of people living in the 'affluent society', things were getting better and better and better. History, for Plumb, spelt *progress*: material improvement, economic modernisation, social advancement, political reform, secular gain, enhanced freedom.[41] Hence, in his own work, a lack of sympathy with losers, religion, tradition, nostalgia and for the practitioners of conservative politics. And hence, in a covertly aspirational and auto-biographical way, his absorbing interest in the rich, the powerful and the successful—and if they had difficult temperaments (Chatham, George III), or lived well (Walpole, George IV), then so much the better.

Thus Plumb on the past; but thus, also, in many ways, Plumb on Plumb. His researches in the great Whig houses brought him into closer contact with the rich and titled whose company he relished and whose acceptance he increasingly craved. *Chatham* had been dedicated to the Rothschilds, and the first volume of *Walpole* to Lord and Lady Cholmondeley, and Plumb soon became a frequent visitor to Houghton, their stately pile in

---

[39] JHP, *The Death of the Past* (London, 1969), p. 106.
[40] H. R. Trevor-Roper, *History, Professional and Lay* (Oxford, 1957).
[41] *Ei*, p. 171.

Norfolk, and to other country houses. And as his royalties increased, he bought pictures, collected silver, amassed porcelain, drove fast cars, and clad himself in stylish garb. He built up the finest private wine cellar in Cambridge, was a founder member of the Bordeaux Society, and was elected to the Saintsbury Club. And he was a fiercely competitive sailor, presiding over regular gatherings of his Cambridge protégés and Leicester friends on the Norfolk Broads. Despite his still-radical politics, he had no interest in the studied unostentation of the quiet rich. His college rooms were magnificent, he acquired an interest in a mill in the south of France, and he bought an old rectory at Westhorpe in Suffolk, where he entertained lavishly and did most of his writing. Like Snow, Plumb had come a long way from Leicester, and as his career gathered momentum, his earning power increased, and his public reputation consolidated, he became admired and envied, and an object of anecdote, gossip and speculation, in ways that few other historians were important or interesting enough to be.

Plumb first appeared in fiction in a short story by Angus Wilson entitled 'Realpolitik', and published as part of *The Wrong Set* (London, 1949). The two of them had become friends at Bletchley during the war, and Wilson depicted Plumb as John Hobday, a sparkling (and bullying) young museum director, ruthlessly weeding out the dead wood among the (increasingly worried) staff. In the following year, he was portrayed by William Cooper (who had read Natural Sciences at Christ's, became a schoolmaster at Alderman Newton's, and whose real name was Harry Hoff), in *Scenes from Provincial Life* (London, 1950). Tom (surname witheld) is a young, red-haired, Jewish accountant, who is intelligent, high-spirited, and with a formidable personality. He sees himself as 'a great understander of human nature, a great writer, a great connoisseur of the good things of life, and a great lover'—of both men and women.[42] (Plumb himself by now seems to have settled down to intense liaisons only with men: but he was ferociously secretive—and unhappy?—about his private life.) Soon after, Cooper rendered his friend again, as the eponymous character in *The Struggles of Albert Woods* (London, 1952). Woods is humbly born in the provinces, but overcomes these obstacles to make a brilliant career as a scientist. He is also socially ambitious, in thrall to the aristocracy, and craves honours. His singular characteristics are energy, enthusiasm—and rage. And he spends his life struggling with his own temperament—and also with other people's. It was a shrewd,

---

[42] W. Cooper, *Scenes from Provincial Life* (London, 1950), esp. pt. i, chs. 1 and 5; pt. iv, chs. 4 and 5.

perceptive and prescient portrait, which may explain why Plumb and Hoff subsequently fell out.[43]

<h1 style="text-align:center">III</h1>

The 1960s were Plumb's golden decade, and in more senses than one. 'Your time is coming', Snow told him towards the beginning, 'one can smell it in the air.' 'I have a strong suspicion', Plumb agreed, 'that the tide is with us.'[44] So, indeed, it was, as the sixties seemed to offer the prospect of a brave new world, and not just in Britain, but in America too, where a revived and rejuvenated history might play a central part. The death of Namier in 1960 lifted a great weight from Plumb's shoulders, gave him the freedom and the confidence to think more imaginatively and creatively about the past, and thereafter he became much more critical of Namier in print, scorning his myopic methodolgy, his political conservatism, his love of tradition, and what he believed to be his veneration for Edmund Burke. Plumb had no time for what he now dismissed as this 'rubbish', and he had even less time for the Master's rigidly imitative protégés, dismissing John Brooke as a 'rat-like, poor, depressed, Ultra-Tory Namierite hack'.[45] As these remarks suggest, and notwithstanding his increasing financial and social success, Plumb's radicalism remained unabated during these years, when it was as easy for him to dislike Namier's scholarly conservatism as to deplore Macmillan's political conservatism. Indeed, when a suitable opportunity presented itself, he was happy to do both at the same time, as in one review in *The Spectator*, where he scorned both the old, faded, elite history (as practised by Namier or Elton), and its audience: 'those who had nannies, prepschools, dorms, possess colonels and bishops for cousins, and now take tea once a year on the dead and lonely lawns of the palace'.[46]

The 1960s were also the decade when Plumb's friendship with Snow reached its apogee. When Snow delivered his 'Two Cultures' lecture, dividing the world into reactionary humanists and progressive scientists, Plumb was willing to accept such a characterisation, but also encouraged his friend to consider a possible third culture, peopled by demographers,

---

[43] W. Cooper, *The Struggles of Albert Woods* (London, 1952), pt. i, chs. 1 and 2; pt. iv, ch. 5.

[44] Snow MSS, 166.7: CPS to JHP, 11 May 1960; 166.10, JHP to CPS, 11 Sept. 1963.

[45] *Ei*, pp. 10–19, 24–8, 108–12; Snow MSS, 166.7: JHP to CPS [undated, *c.*1961–2].

[46] JHP, *The Spectator*, 16 March 1962.

sociologists, economists, political scientists and social historians, who took a broader view of the past than Namier, and embraced a much more optimistic interpretation of the Industrial Revolution than the Marxist-pessimists.[47] When Leavis attacked Snow, in his famously vitriolic denunciation of the 'Two Cultures', Plumb rushed to his friend's defence, berating Leavis in the correspondence columns of *The Spectator* for his 'senseless diatribe', full of 'folly', 'arrogance', and 'sheer blind ignorance'. 'We must smash the influence of this man as remorselessly as we can', Plumb told Snow.[48] And when Labour won the 1964 general election, Plumb's elation knew no bounds. 'I admired Wilson throughout the campaign', he told Snow, 'and now admiration borders on idolatory.' 'The whole government', he continued, 'is moving with a pace and certainty that I never expected.' It was 1906 or 1945 all over again: a time of hope when the final defeat of the forces of tradition and obscurantism seemed at hand. Snow duly became Parliamentary Secretary to the Minister of Technology, and this brought Plumb for the first (and only?) time close to the corridors of power. Plumb was delighted, and urged Snow to come down to the next feast at Christ's, so he could 'rub Todd's nose in it'.[49]

Throughout the sixties, Plumb enjoyed unprecedented success in the college and the faculty. He taught his most dazzling undergraduates yet, among them John Vincent, David Blackbourn, Geoffrey Parker, Roy Porter, and Simon Schama; he attracted rising stars from other colleges, including Quentin Skinner, Norman Stone and Jonathan Steinberg; and the research students continued to flock in, such as John Beattie, John Money, Paul Fritz and Clive Holmes. In the faculty, he was made a Reader in 1962, given an *ad hominem* Professorship four years later, and he was a noticeably brisk chairman of the faculty board from 1966–8. (Even Elton, it was claimed, by some admiringly, by others disapprovingly, did not have time to say much.) And recognition was extended from beyond Cambridge. He delivered the Ford Lectures in Oxford in 1965, he was elected a Fellow of the British Academy three years later, and he became an Honorary Member of the American Academy of Arts and Sciences in 1970. In addition, he was appointed a Syndic of the Fitzwilliam Museum in Cambridge, and a Trustee of the National Portrait Gallery, appropriately following in the footsteps of Macaulay

---

[47] Snow MSS, 166.9: CPS to JHP, 24 May 1962; JHP to CPS, 1 July 1962, 7 Dec. 1962; 166.10: CPS to JHP, 3 Sept. 1963.

[48] JHP, *The Spectator*, 30 March 1962; Plumb MSS, Snow file: CPS to JHP, 7 March 1962; Snow MSS, 166.10, JHP to CPS [undated, *c.*1962].

[49] Snow MSS, 166.11: JHP to CPS, 19 Oct. 1964, 11 Nov. 1964; *Ei*, p. 190.

and Trevelyan. By now, Plumb was well on his way to becoming a minor member of Britain's 'great and the good'. But it was also in these years that he discovered America, reached a bigger audience on both sides of the Atlantic, and made his most distinctive and original contribution to writing history.

In 1960, with the encouragement of Richard Hofstadter (whom he had met in Cambridge in 1958–9), Plumb went to Columbia University in New York as a visiting professor, and he was so captivated by the place that he vainly tried to arrange to divide his time between Cambridge and Columbia thereafter. He discovered that he was better known in the USA than he had realised, he delighted that 'the commited active intellectual is a figure of respect', and he was taken up by such Kennedy supporters as Arthur M. Schlesinger, Jr.[50] For the rest of his life, America brought out the best in Plumb, and five of his seven honorary degrees would be awarded there. Freed from the social slights and professional rivalries of Cambridge, he became more relaxed, more buoyant, more confident, more hopeful; he admired a country which was a product of the eighteenth-century Enlightenment, which rewarded self-improvement and celebrated self-help, and which felt neither guilt nor resentment at fame and success; and he fell in love with New York, where he made many grand friends (eventually including Pat Moynihan, Brooke Astor and Ben Sonnenberg), and where he later had the use of an apartment high up in the Carlyle Hotel. During the next twenty years, he visited the USA at every possible opportunity, he lectured in virtually every American state, and he was much in demand as a writer. Indeed, his work was as likely to appear in the *New York Times*, the *New York Review of Books* or the *Saturday Review* on one side of the Atlantic as in *The Times Literary Supplement*, *The Spectator*, or *The Observer* on the other.

Plumb's jaunty, accessible style was ideally suited to the requirements of the higher journalism, and he prided himself on writing to length and meeting deadlines. He reviewed an astonishing range and number of books—in British, European and American history—and he also wrote extensively on current affairs providing (to borrow a title from the regular column he published in the *Saturday Review*) 'historical perspectives' on contemporary events. To re-read these essays nearly forty years on is to be reminded just how unsettling the sixties were, how vividly Plumb caught the contradictions of the time, how broad were the historical

---

[50] Snow MSS, 166.10: JHP to CPS, 19 March 1963; JHP, *Collected Essays*, vol. ii (London, 1988) (hereafter *E*ii), pp. 180–9.

insights he brought to bear on them, and how liberal were his social and political attitudes. He deplored the assassinations of John and Robert Kennedy, he admired Lyndon Johnson's 'Great Society' programme but feared the worst in Vietnam, and he was dismayed at Richard Nixon's triumph in 1968. He thought New York 'the most remarkable city built by man', 'a city to love and a city of which to be proud', and he relished its daring, its bold experimentation, and its inexhaustible capacity for self-criticism; but he also regretted its crime (he was once mugged on Brooklyn Bridge, but made more money from selling the story than he had lost at knife-point), its poverty and its violence.[51] Yet he remained convinced that liberalism was triumphing on both sides of the Atlantic, that (his notion of) history had an important part to play in this advance, and that there was a greater concern with social justice, with the poor, the sick and the deprived, than ever before.

Plumb's talents were also now much sought after by publishing houses, which hoped to benefit from his unique blend of academic expertise, professional contacts, social connections and public renown. He became historical adviser to Penguin Books, European editor for Horizon, editor of the *Fontana History of Europe*, and general editor of the Hutchinson *History of Human Society*—a dazzling portfolio of appointments, which also gave him considerable powers of patronage. At Penguin, he steered a host of books into paperback by such leftish authors (shades of his own Communist past?) as Christopher Hill, Eric Hobsbawm, E. H. Carr and E. P. Thompson.[52] At Fontana, he gave commissions to upcoming grandees such as John Hale, J. H. Elliott and Olwen Hufton, to protégés such as Geoffrey Parker and Norman Stone, and also, slightly oddly, to Geoffrey Elton, whose *Reformation Europe, 1517–1559* (London, 1963) was the most successful book in the series. And at Hutchinson, he brought a large variety of wide-ranging projects to fruition, which treated the past in a much more imaginative and inclusive way than narrow-minded Namierite or Eltonian history, among them C. R. Boxer on *The Dutch Seaborne Empire* (London, 1965) and *The Portuguese Seaborne Empire* (London, 1969), J. H. Parry on *The Spanish Seaborne Empire* (London, 1966), Donald Dudley on *The Romans* (London, 1970) and Raymond Dawson on *Imperial China* (London, 1972). Together, these series raised Plumb's profile (and his income) still further, and in the heady days of the sixties, they were avidly read, both by the general public

---

[51] *E*ii, pp. 229–35.
[52] E. J. Hobsbawm, *Interesting Times: A Twentieth-Century Life* (London, 2002), p. 306.

and by the unprecedented number of history undergraduates on the new and expanding university campuses on both sides of the Atlantic.

But Plumb was also busy with his own writing and publishing projects. His creative energy and intellectual curiosity were at their peak, and in a post-Namier, post-Macmillan world, he eagerly turned his attention to what seemed the much more vital and relevant issues of the sixties. What purpose could the past serve in the brave new, secular, radical, scientific, modernising world that was now coming into being on both sides of the Atlantic? And what sort of history should historians now be writing? These were pertinent questions, and Plumb had many reasons for wishing to answer them convincingly. As a student of Trevelyan's, he believed that history must be an integral component of the national culture, and thus must be sensitive to the changing national mood. As a friend of Snow's, he was anxious to make the case for history having more in common with the progressive sciences than the reactionary arts. As a supporter of Harold Wilson, he was eager to show that the study of the past could be mobilised to underwrite and validate a modernising political enterprise. And as someone who aspired to follow Trevelyan as Regius Professor of Modern History at Cambridge, he was determined to establish his position as the most publicly (and politically) engaged historian of his day.

'I've produced a lot', he told Snow in 1960, 'but I've still got, I think, another five to six years of really hard work before I break through.'[53] He set about realising these objectives in a clutch of influential and inter-connected works. The immediate result of his involvement with American publishing was the *Horizon Book of the Renaissance* (New York, 1961), in which he brought together a remarkable array of talent (including Kenneth Clark, Jacob Bronowski, Garrett Mattingly and Hugh Trevor-Roper) to write about one of history's most remarkable eras, and himself con-tributed a series of linking essays on Milan, Rome, Venice and Florence. The book was his first venture outside his own area of expertise; it sold better than anything he had previously published, and made a great deal of money.[54] Two years later, he published *Men and Places* (London, 1963), the first of several volumes of collected essays, which brought together many of his most sparkling occasional pieces and reviews, on subjects as diverse as the American Revolution and Brighton Pavilion. And in 1969 he wrote a major study of Winston Churchill as an historian, which was one of the earliest and most influential reassessments of the

---

[53] Snow MSS, 166.7: JHP to CPS [undated, 1960].
[54] Plumb MSS, Trevor-Roper file: Trevor-Roper to JHP, 3 Dec. 1961.

great man which began to appear soon after his death. It opened with a *fortissimo* evocation of Blenheim Palace, it explored Churchill's passionate belief in the Whig interpretation of the English past, it stressed how he always saw himself as an historical personality and heroic figure, and it examined both his family biographies and his personal histories with a critical insight and an imaginative sympathy which remain unsurpassed.[55]

By then, Plumb had already published *Crisis in the Humanities* (Harmondsworth, 1964), which he edited and introduced, and which addressed head on the question of how arts subjects might (and must) 'adjust to the educational and social needs of the modern world'. In his opening manifesto, Plumb took off from Snow's hostile characterisation (in 'The Two Cultures') of literary intellectuals as reactionary, irresponsible and self-absorbed. Dominated as they were by such people, Plumb insisted, it was small wonder the humanities were in crisis. 'They must', he urged, 'either change the image they present, adapt themselves to the needs of a society dominated by science and technology, or retreat into social triviality.' 'Old, complex, tradition-haunted societies', he went on, in a characteristically vivid and arresting turn of phrase, 'find change as difficult to make as rheumatoid arthritics to move.' 'What is needed', he concluded, in words that Snow himself could have written, 'is less reverence for tradition, and more humility towards the educational systems of those two great countries—America and Russia—which have tried to adjust their teaching to the urban industrial world of the twentieth century.'[56]

As for history itself, on which Plumb also wrote the substantive chapter, the challenge was clear. For many academics (and this was clearly a hit at Namier and Elton), it was merely a self-enclosed world, an intellectual pastime, obsessed with scholarly technique and nothing else. Yet the real justification of history was its broader public purpose: to record, explain and celebrate progress, both material and intellectual, especially with reference to 'industry, technology, science'. If historians accepted their obligation to describe and explain the past in this way, and if they broadened their range of interests beyond mere narrow politics, they would give their contemporaries a greater understanding of the present, and also an increased control over the future, and their rejuvenated discipline would thus fulfill its prime social function 'in government, in administration, in all the manifold affairs of men'.[57] Here Plumb was flinging down the gauntlet, and making

---

[55] *Ei*, pp. 226–52.

[56] JHP, 'Introduction', in id. (ed.), *Crisis in the Humanities* (Harmondsworth, 1964), pp. 7–10.

[57] JHP, 'The Historian's Dilemma', in id., *Crisis in the Humanities*, pp. 24–44.

a case very similar to that which E. H. Carr had recently advanced, namely that the purpose of studying history was to 'enable man to understand the society of the past, and to increase his mastery over society in the present'. It was, of course, anathema to those on the right, and to Geoffrey Elton in particular. Indeed, his *Practice of History* was as much a reply to Plumb as to Carr, denouncing his belief in history as progress, and also a guide to our own time.[58]

Having sketched out a revived and relevant future for the humanities in general and for history in particular during the sixties era of white-hot Wilsonian technology, Plumb provided a specific example of how this could be done in *The Growth of Political Stability in England, 1675–1725* (London, 1967), derived from the Ford Lectures which he had given in Oxford, at the invitation of Hugh Trevor-Roper.[59] From one perspective, this was his best and most infuential work of history, where he successfully sought for the only time in his career to address, define and solve a big and serious problem: how did the revolutionary England of the seventeenth century become the stable England of the eighteenth century? He had been brooding on this question ever since his days as a research student, and at one level the book represented his mature efforts to reconcile the world of party rage and strife that Trevelyan had evoked in *England Under Queen Anne* with the non-party world that Namier had found in the late 1750s.[60] In depicting pre-1714 England as a nation locked in bitter political disputes between Whigs and Tories over foreign policy, religion and the succession, he advanced a much more trenchant critique of Walcott than he had felt able to do a decade before, accusing him of 'mistaking genealogy for history'. In giving attention to the size of the electorate, and to popular protest, he cast his eye much more widely over the political scene than Namier ever did. And in stressing the success with which Walpole managed to calm and close things down, and move England towards becoming a one party (and eventually a no-party) state, he provided a more convincing historical context for situating and understanding his hero than he had been able to do in the two volumes of biography.

[58] E. H. Carr, *What is History?* (Harmondsworth, 1964), p. 55; G. R. Elton, *The Practice of History* (Sydney, 1967), pp. 41–50.

[59] Plumb MSS, Trevor-Roper file: Trevor-Roper to JHP, 5 Nov. 1963. For a fuller discussion of this work, see D. Cannadine, 'Historians in the "Liberal Hour": Lawrence Stone and J. H. Plumb Re-Visited', *Historical Research*, 75 (2002), 316–54.

[60] JHP, *The Growth of Political Stability in England, 1675–1725* (London, 1967), ch. 5, is called 'The Rage of Party'.

But in addition to offering a major re-interpretation of seventeenth- and eighteenth-century English history, *The Growth of Political Stability* was also a tract for the times, for its broader concern was to explore the complex relations between inertia and change in the past, and to tease out some contemporary implications. Like many sixties historians, Plumb explained change with reference to long-term social and economic forces, topped off by political action—usually leading to revolution, but just occasionally, as in this case, leading to stability. As Plumb saw it, stability did not just happen: it was not, as Namier and his friends believed, the inevitable, Burkeian result of tradition, custom, and slow evolutionary development. On the contrary, it was the outcome of deeply rooted economic and social forces, which were realised and made actual by specific political decisions, taken and implemented by particular political actors. As Plumb presented it, the achievement of stability was thus a relatively rare thing in human history (as in 1930s Mexico, 1950s Russia and 1960s France), which ought to be of interest to contemporary governments and policy makers around the world. Indeed, by globalising and universalising his case-study in this way, he was making the strongest claim for the 'relevance' of the past to the problems of the present.

But there was also a more explicit domestic agenda, which was simultaneously (and predictably) anti-Tory and pro-Labour. The true villains of the book were Bolingbroke's post-1714 Tories, whom Plumb dismissed as culturally xenophobic, religiously bigoted, economically backward and politically maladroit, and as taking flight from the challenges of the present in the comforts and delusions of the past. In an oft-quoted passage, which owed more to rhetoric than detail, Plumb exulted in the demise and defeat of the forces of conservatism:

> The Tory Party was destroyed, destroyed by its incompetent leadership, by the cupidity of many of its supporters, by its own internal contradictions; weakened by its virtues and lashed by events, it proved no match for Walpole; feeble, divided, lost, it failed . . . to provide an effective barrier to Walpole's steady progress towards a single-party State. By 1727, Tories were outcasts, living on the frontiers of the political establishment; denigrated as political traitors, they were permitted little more than minor local office. By 1733, . . . Toryism as far as power politics at the centre was concerned, had become quite irrelevant.[61]

---

[61] JHP, *Stability*, p. 172.

Thus the Tories in the 1720s and 1730s: perhaps also (the inference was plain) the Conservatives in the 1960s and 1970s. But while the Whigs had successfully overwhelmed the Tories, and thereby established political stability, this was far from being a happy ending. For they had thereby created what soon became an inert political culture, based on patronage and place, rather than merit and worth, which for the next two centuries, 'failed to adjust its institutions and its social system to the needs of an industrial society'. Hence, too, the nation's current difficulties. Once again, the implication could scarcely have been clearer: it was high time that these long-overdue reforms and adjustments were made, and Wilson was the man to make them.[62]

The Growth of Political Stability was an audacious way to link Queen Anne's England with Harold Wilson's England, by solving a specific and substantive historical problem, but which also insisted that what happened in the English past was of contemporary global interest, and which simultaneously validated and reinforced a modernising domestic political agenda. Plumb regarded it as 'my best work, better than Walpole, more original and more profound', and this was the general verdict.[63] Among reviewers, the book was praised for introducing a new concept into historical inquiry; for specifying and solving a particular problem which, once he had defined it, seemed both obvious and crucial; for bringing clarity and recognition to a period of English history which in recent decades had been both confused and neglected; for combining an awareness of long run change with an appreciation of the importance of politics and personalities; and for making the politicians, the planners and the policy makers more aware of what a complex, problematic and unusual thing 'stability' actually was. But there were also critics, who came mostly from the right and from Oxford. Did this 'modish new look' significantly advance things beyond the 'traditional interpretation' of Trevelyan's era? Was stability suddenly brought about as a self-conscious and deliberate political act? Did patronage have the marked effect of subduing the opposition that Plumb claimed? Was it right to inflate the peaceful change of dynasty and government into a world-historical scenario about the creation of stability? And what, exactly, did 'stability' mean, how did it 'grow', and how valid was the concept?[64]

---

[62] See *Ei*, pp. 113–49, for further extensions (and contemporary implications) of this argument, esp. p. 149: 'Conservative forces continued to dominate English life in spite of universal suffrage. Not until 1945 did Britain have a really radical government.'

[63] Snow MSS, 166.12: JHP to CPS, 31 Jan. 1967.

[64] Cannadine, 'Historians in the "Liberal Hour"', 340.

These were good questions, and as such, they were also a measure of the book's stature and significance, but they would not be seriously addressed until the political and intellectual climate fundamentally changed. Meanwhile, and having demonstrated the renewed relevance of imaginatively conceived history to Wilson's white-hot world, Plumb offered some more general reflections on this subject in *The Death of the Past*, based on the Saposnekow Lectures he delivered in New York, early in 1968.[65] His aim was to outline the place and purpose of history in a society where tradition and obscurantism were (thankfully) in retreat, where secular progress was in the ascendant, and where historians must engage with 'the new scientists and technologists, the men who man or run the power stations and computer services'. For Plumb, 'the past' had been misused in earlier centuries—by religion, by genealogy, by kingly cults, by ancestor worship, by myth and legend—to sanctify elite dominance and authoritarian regimes. Such 'doom-laden', 'ghost-haunted', 'backward-looking' attitudes had resulted in 'bigotry, national vanity and class domination'. But the growth of scholarly, scientific history, combined with the transforming impact of the industrial and technological revolutions, meant a new and better society had recently come into being: urban, democratic and meritocratic, which rejected the old 'past' of custom, precedent, faith and unreason. Accordingly, the purpose of history was to speed this discredited 'past' on its way to oblivion, and to give humanity confidence in its progress and possibilities: in short, to give people 'social hope' in a 'forward-looking, scientifically-orientated' world. The past had been for the few, and was dead; but history was alive, and for the many.[66]

The Death of the Past was Plumb's last systematic statement of his belief in history as progress and progress as history, and it was also an impassioned reaffirmation of his view that the subject must serve a broad public purpose and reach a broad public audience. His arguments were also buttressed by a formidable range of learning, from the ancient Middle East to imperial China, which must have owed much to his editorial work for the *History of Human Society*. But even more than with *The Growth of Political Stability*, not everyone was convinced. Those on the right (among them Herbert Butterfield and Maurice Cowling) did not share his view that the use of 'the past' to justify hierarchy, religion and inequality was necessarily bad. And there was a more general anxiety that

---

[65] For other sketches and elaborations of the same argument, see *Ei*, pp. 288–90, 358–62.
[66] JHP, *Death of the Past*, esp. pp. 14–17, 24–5, 42, 56–7, 65, 104–7, 142–5.

Plumb was seeking to hijack historical scholarship to underwrite a radical, democratic, secular, technological, urban, modernising agenda which not everyone shared.[67] And so, although it was widely reviewed and translated, the book was less successful than Plumb had wished. This was partly because of the limitations of the argument; but it was also because the book's quintessentially sixties brand of secular, liberal hope, for which it offered uncompromising historical validation, was already becoming out of date by the time it appeared. In Britain, there was devaluation, the end of Wilsonian optimism, and the election of Edward Heath; in the United States there were protests against the Vietnam War, the humbling of Lyndon Johnson, and the triumph of Richard Nixon; and in this changed and darker climate, *The Death of the Past* resonated much less effectively than it would earlier have done.

For Plumb, as for many on the left, the sixties had begun with unprecedented optimism, but ended much more somberly, and in his case, these political disappointments were reinforced by professional rebuffs. For his great ambition during the 1960s was to be elected to an established chair in Cambridge, and in this aspiration he was twice thwarted. In the History Faculty, no less than in his college, Plumb had offended many people, and when the opportunities presented themselves, they did not hesitate to take their revenge. He was passed over for the chair of Modern History in 1965 (which went to Charles Wilson), but this was as nothing compared to his disappointment about the Regius chair. He had hoped to get it in 1963, when on the retirement of David Knowles it had gone to Herbert Butterfield.[68] This was never a realistic expectation, but his chances were much better four years later: he was the most highly profiled historian in Cambridge; he was as well-known in America as in Britain; there was (he believed) a sympathetic government; he did everything he could to promote his case; and he enlisted Snow in his support. But in the end, it went to Owen Chadwick, who was a decade younger than Plumb (those ten 'wasted years' once again!) and his rage and disappointment knew no bounds. 'I am very sorry to see the news of the Regius', Snow wrote consolingly. 'But does it really matter much? Your books will be read for a long time, and you've made a name. What more do you really want?' For the rest of his

---

[67] Butterfield MSS, 241/3: draft review of *Death of the Past*; G. Leff, *History*, 56 (1971), 326–7; M. Cowling, *Religion and Public Doctrine in Modern England* (Cambridge, 1980), pp. 394–9.
[68] Plumb MSS, Snow file: CPS to JHP, 6 March 1963, 30 April 1963, 23 Oct. 1963; Snow MSS, 166.10: JHP to CPS, 12 April 1963.

life, both personal and professional, Plumb would vainly attempt to answer that question.[69]

IV

Like many sixties liberals, Plumb found the seventies an unhappy and uneasy decade, as right-wing reaction, in the shape of Heath and Nixon, was then replaced by left-wing incompetence, in the form of Wilson–Callaghan and Carter. 'About this country', he wrote to Snow in 1972, 'I despair. For me, the Labour Party is in near ruins. Heath gives me goose-flesh. At times, I doubt whether I shall be able to vote at all next time.' And his beloved America seemed no better, where campus riots, urban terrorism, soaring inflation, drug abuse and political corruption presented unprecedented 'threats to social order and stability'.[70] Increasingly repelled by the contemporary world, Plumb sought consolation in the bosom of the very establishment he had previously taken such delight in denouncing. He was elected to Brooks's in 1972, he was a member of the Wine Standards Board from 1973–5, and he mobilised his friends, especially Snow, in the hope of obtaining a title.[71] But although his name originally appeared on Harold Wilson's infamous 'Lavender list' of resignation honours in 1976, it was subsequently removed, along with that of Asa Briggs, on the grounds that they were both distinguished enough to be recognised by other prime ministers, whereas for Wilson's (sometimes suspect) cronies, this was their last opportunity.[72]

Instead of getting Plumb the peerage he so ardently craved, Snow bestowed on him a fictional ennoblement as Lord Ryle in his novel *In Their Wisdom* (London, 1974)—an uncharacteristic piece of Snowvian wit, this, for if there was one thing Plumb certainly knew how well to do, it was indeed to rile. Like Plumb, Ryle was a product of the provinces, and a wholly self-made man, who has travelled upwards through many layers

---

[69] Plumb MSS, Snow file: JHP to CPS, 8 Dec. 1967; Snow MSS, 166.16: CPS to JHP, 8 Dec. 1967.

[70] *E*i, pp. 309–47; *E*ii, pp. 169–254; Snow MSS, 166.14: JHP to CPS [undated, *c*.1972]

[71] JHP, 'The World of Brooks's', in P. Ziegler and D. Seward (eds.), *Brooks's: A Social History* (London, 1991), pp. 13–24; Plumb MSS, Snow file: JHP to CPS, 7 Feb. 1975, 7 June 1976; Snow MSS, 166.15: CPS to JHP, 7 Feb. 1975; JHP to CPS, 8 Feb. 1975; 166.16: JHP to CPS, 8 Jan. 1976, 13 Jan. 1977.

[72] B. Pimlott, *Harold Wilson* (London, 1992), pp. 686–90; P. Ziegler, *Wilson: the Authorized Life of Lord Wilson of Rievaulx* (London, 1993), pp. 494–8.

of society. Like Plumb, he is an 'historian by trade, inquisitive by nature'. And, like Plumb again, he was also very well-off:

> Comfortable professional jobs over a lifetime, but that didn't explain it all, or nearly all. Histories which had sold well, especially in America, and used as text books. Consultancies with publishers. Investments which had started early, for a poor young man.[73]

Ryle's temperament was more equitable and less conflicted than Plumb's: but both of them, during the 1970s, were brooding on old age and worrying about national decline. Such a mood of pessimistic bitterness may also explain why, when Anthony Blunt was unmasked as a Communist and a traitor, Plumb launched a sustained and ferocious attack to expel him from the British Academy. But there was clearly more to it than that. How far did those social rebuffs of the thirties still rankle, and how far did he want to cover his own Communist (and homosexual) tracks? Even admirers of Plumb like Isaiah Berlin were appalled: 'This wasn't *odium academicum*: it was *odium personali.*'[74] But in the end, Blunt was obliged to resign, and Plumb felt vindicated.

Although he had largely given up supervising undergraduates when he became a professor, Plumb continued to lecture in the Cambridge History Faculty during the early 1970s, and to supervise graduate students. Indeed, this last generation was a vintage one, including as it did John Miller, Derek Hirst, John Brewer (who produced the most cogent critique yet of Namier's treatment of the 1760s), and Linda Colley (who exposed the severe limitations of Plumb's largely rhetorical dismissal of the post-1714 Tory Party and appreciated his 'generosity and historical verve' in supporting iconoclasm directed against himself). But he was increasingly bored with what he had earlier described as the 'time-consuming hackwork of academic life—the endless supervisions and lectures and examinations', and with no prospect of further promotion, and with many of his most gifted protégés kept out of junior appointments by Geoffrey Elton, he resigned his professorship early in 1974.[75] The faculty gave him an appropriately splendid farewell dinner, and he was not unmoved by the 'very nostalgic evening'. But he was also 'glad . . . to see the back of them', and he spent much of the remainder of the decade as a visiting

---

[73] CPS, *In Their Wisdom* (London, 1974), esp. ch. 4.

[74] M. Carter, *Anthony Blunt: His Lives* (London, 2001), pp. 491–3; K. Dover, *Marginal Comment: A Memoir* (London, 1994), pp. 212–20.

[75] *Ei*, p. 187. L. J. Colley, *In Defiance of Oligarchy: The Tory Party, 1714–60* (Cambridge, 1982), p. 8.

professor in Texas and New York, and even toyed with the idea of moving permanently to America. Meanwhile, some of his students gathered together to produce a Festschrift: *Historical Perspectives: Studies in English Thought and Society in Honour of J. H. Plumb* (London, 1974). It was a dazzling line up of Christ's based historians (including Hall, Kenyon, Skinner, Burrow, Supple and Stokes), and if its remit had been extended beyond the college and beyond Britain, it could easily have been three times as big.[76]

As for Plumb himself, his original intention, on reaching his sixtieth year, was to write 'two or three decent-sized books', and in this endeavour he was much encouraged by Snow.[77] But the Regius rebuff was such a blow that his creative career was ended almost as prematurely as it had been belatedly begun. The titans of his generation (Southern, Hobsbawm, and Chadwick in England, Van Woodward, Bailyn and Gay in America) were scholars (to borrow one of his own phrases) of 'elephantine stamina', who kept working and kept writing well into their seventies and eighties.[78] But having got so near the top, and having been tripped at the final hurdle, Plumb's reaction was to quit the race, leave the stadium, and give up the serious writing of history almost completely. To be sure, there was another book of essays, *In The Light of History* (London, 1972), which ranged from 'The Royal Porcelain Craze' of the eighteenth century, via historical reflections on riots, clothes and the family, to evocations of the Victorians and Edwardians.[79] But despite his claims that he was actively working on it, the third volume of *Walpole* never appeared: he did not wish to kill off his hero, and he had become increasingly aware of the shortcomings of the first two instalments. He had also intended to write a study of *The British Seaborne Empire, 1600–1800*, to accompany those by Parry (Spain) and Boxer (the Netherlands and Portugal) in his *History of Human Society*, but it was never even begun, and the whole series soon fizzled out.

Instead, he flirted for a time with a new project, the spread of leisure in eighteenth-century England: thereby putting forward a social-history concept to match the political-history concept he had propounded in

---

[76] Snow MSS, 166.13: JHP to CPS, 25 Aug. 1970, 6 Dec. 1973.

[77] Snow MSS, 166.13: JHP to CPS, 20 Aug. 1970.

[78] *Ei*, p. 233.

[79] Butterfield urged that it showed JHP's 'thought can lack a certain resonance ... he is so satisfied to be in tune with prevailing trends': Butterfield MSS, 251: Draft review of *In the Light of History*, published in the *Times Literary Supplement*, 24 Nov. 1972. In fact, by then, JHP no longer was.

The Growth of Political Stability. Social history, he had opined in his introduction to the Trevelyan Festschrift, was the field 'in which the greatest discoveries will be made in this generation', and he now seemed determined to deliver on this promise.[80] It was also, in some ways, a natural extension of his earlier work and opinions: on his discussion of prosperity and spending as long-term forces making for early-eighteenth-century political stability; on his essentially opimistic view (contra Leavis) that the Industrial Revolution had improved material life for the majority of the people; and on Walpole and the four Georges as builders and collectors. But now, he planned to face the subject head on, and produced preliminary lectures and exploratory essays on children (changing attitudes, better schooling, more books, games and toys), on the commercialisation of leisure (newspapers, libraries, novels, music, concerts, assembly rooms, shopping and theatre), and modernity (horse-breeding, dog shows, auricula cultivation, carnation growing, scientific societies and public lectures).[81]

Like the opening survey chapters in *Walpole* and *The First Four Georges*, these articles were vividly panoramic, and also contained much new material. But thereafter the enterprise stalled. To be sure, Plumb had always been good at setting a scene and evoking an atmosphere; but by the 1970s, social history could no longer be written on the basis of anec-dote and example alone. It needed to be more rigorous, more interdis-ciplinary, more in touch with the burgeoning social sciences. But while he had advocated these new subjects in the sixties, Plumb had never truly mastered them. As a result, he was far from happy in dealing with long-term social and economic change; he lacked the necessary quantitative and economic skills to demonstrate why, how and when domestic demand had grown; he often confused demand with taste and fashion, and did not relate them convincingly to supply; the idea of 'social emulation' as an impulse driving demand was not properly developed; he never explained where the increased money necessary to power this process had come from; and unlike 'stability', the concepts of 'leisure', 'commercialisation' and 'modernity' were too vague to sustain the enterprise. Nor was it altogether clear how great or how irreversible were the changes he was

---

[80] JHP, 'Introduction', in id., *Studies in Social History*, p. xiv.

[81] JHP, 'The Public, Literature and the Arts in the Eighteenth Century', in P. Fritz and D. Williams (eds.), *The Triumph of Culture: Eighteenth-Century Perspectives* (Toronto, 1972), pp. 27–48; id, *The Pursuit of Happiness: A View of Life in Georgian England* (New Haven, 1977); id, *Georgian Delights* (London, 1980); N. McKendrick, J. Brewer and J. H. Plumb, *The Birth of a Consumer Society: The Commercialization of Eighteenth-Century England* (London, 1982), pp. 265–334.

postulating. 'The gates to happiness', he concluded one of his essays, in words which well conveyed these uncertainties, 'had been opened, but only narrowly; they were not wide open for all and sundry, yet they could not, in Britain, be closed again.'[82]

Put more positively, this meant that Plumb had sketched out a subject which was only taken up in earnest, and dealt with in a manner appropriate to its many complexities, by a later generation of scholars.[83] But this was not the only sense in which the enterprise was ahead of its time. At one level, Plumb's interest in horse-breeding and flower-growing might be seen as expressing his revulsion with and escape from a dismal decade characterised by Heath's three day week, and Callaghan's 'winter of discontent'. But in stressing the importance of individual consumers rather than collective producers, in emphasising 'trickle down' economics as an agent of generally enhanced prosperity, in approving of the less well off aspiring to the lifestyles of their betters, and in drawing attention to the importance of the free market, Plumb was also sketching out arguments which anticipated many of the things that Margaret Thatcher would say about Britain in the 1980s. Indeed, if Plumb had seen this project through, he would not only have completed a major lifetime scholarly oeuvre: he would also have provided significant historical validation for Thatcher, and 'Georgian go-getters', though less immediately resonant than 'Victorian values', might have become one of the slogans of her time; and his latter-day incarnation as a card-carrying Thatcherite would have been all the more credible (and all the better recognised?) as a result.

But instead of completing his leisure–commercialisation–modernity project, Plumb moved his attention higher up the social scale, from the bourgeoisie to the monarchy, and wrote the scripts for *Royal Heritage: The Story of Britain's Royal Builders and Collectors* (London, 1977), a sumptuous, seven-part television series, from medieval sovereigns to the present day, which was presented by Huw Weldon and appeared in 1977, the year of Queen Elizabeth II's Silver Jubilee. At one level, this was *The First Four Georges* writ large: with character-sketches of kings and queens, descriptions of their castles and houses, and glimpses of their pictures, furniture, books and stamps. At another, it urged that 'each society,

---

[82] JHP, *Pursuit of Happiness*, p. 28. For a powerful critique of this approach, see B. Fine and E. Leopold, 'Consumerism and the Industrial Revolution', *Social History*, 15 (1990), 151–79.

[83] See, especially: J. Brewer and R. Porter (eds.), *Consumption and the World of Goods* (London, 1993); A. Bermingham and J. Brewer (eds.), *The Consumption of Culture, 1600–1800: Image, Object, Text* (London, 1995); J. Brewer and S. Staves (eds.), *Early Modern Conceptions of Property* (London, 1995); J. Brewer, *The Pleasures of the Imagination: English Culture in the Eighteenth Century* (London, 1997).

from the middle ages to the present time, has created an image of monarchy which has given a sense of coherence and often of purpose to the nation at large'—not quite the view of things that he had taken in his earlier, radical days.[84] At yet a third, it provided Plumb with unprecedented opportunities to socialise with the royal family and he took full advantage of them. The programmes, and the book derived from them, were highly lucrative, and they also made him better known with the general public than he had ever been before. But the division between writer and presenter meant that they lacked the unifying individual vision of Kenneth Clark's *Civilisation* or Alistair Cooke's *America*, and although it had some interesting things to say about the culture of royalty over a millennium (and, sometimes, the lack of it), the series earned him little scholarly respect, and a great deal of academic envy.

By now, Plumb's days as a serious historian were over, but he had not entirely abandoned his academic interests and ambitions. He became a Trustee of the Wolfson Foundation, established the Wolfson History Prize, and ensured that a disproportionate number of his friends and protégés were awarded it. He was chairman of the Centre for East Anglian Studies at UEA from 1979 to 1982, and a member of the Council of the British Academy during the same period. He was greatly disappointed not to become its President (as with the Regius chair, the position went to Owen Chadwick), but his belligerent intransigence over the Blunt affair can hardly have helped. And so, once again, his hopes were turned back to Christ's College, where he had long since become a Life Fellow. He retained his rooms and kept his cellar, he remained on the College Council, and he continued to take an interest in the brightest history undergraduates. And he still cherished the ambition that he might become Master, even though he was only slightly younger than Lord Todd, who had been elected unopposed in 1963, and who was determined that Plumb should not succeed him. But Todd was obliged to retire in 1978, and Plumb eventually won a controversial election, fully worthy of the college in which Snow had set *The Masters*. Todd was against, doing 'everything that he decently, indeed, almost indecently, could' to stop it, the Bursar was opposed, and so was the Senior Tutor. But Plumb got there in the end. 'I don't believe', Snow told him, with a rare combination of tactfulness and

---

[84] J. H. Plumb, *Royal Heritage: The Story of Britain's Royal Builders and Collectors* (London, 1977), p. 10.

truthfulness, 'anyone else who had expressed his temperament so freely could have made it.'[85]

As with his Professorship, the Mastership of Christ's was something Plumb had very badly wanted. But it came too late, his term of office was of short duration, he had cold feet about taking it on ('too much pettiness in a place like this'), he was often unwell, and he did not always seem to enjoy it.[86] But he threw himself wholeheartedly into what he knew must be his last appointment, chairing all the college committees, insisting on high academic standards, and raising substantial sums of money. And although it was brief, his Mastership was undeniably brilliant: the 'treasure-stuffed' Lodge, known as 'Jack's Palace', was splendidly decorated, his lavish parties delighted the undergraduates, his superb food and wine attracted his smart friends from London and New York, and he took particular pleasure in entertaining Princess Margaret ('time for another of my Cambridge jollies').[87] But he was too authoritarian for some Fellows' tastes, and once again, he aroused (and relished?) admiration and disapproval in equal proportions. As he had earlier written of Walpole, whose painting by Charles Jervas dominated the reception rooms of the lodge: 'He gloried in his power, spoke roughly if not ungenerously of others, and let the whole world know that he was master.'[88] On his retirement in 1982, Plumb was knighted, and thereafter became publicly known as 'Sir John' rather than 'Sir Jack', because, as he portentously explained, 'the royal family do not like diminutives'. But while he was glad to have been recognised at last, it was not the peerage he craved.

V

The last twenty years of Plumb's life were increasingly lonely and unhappy. By this time, with the Labour Party internecinely (and almost suicidally) unelectable, he had long since abandoned his earlier left-wing beliefs, and had become an ardent admirer of Margaret Thatcher. 'There

---

[85] Snow MSS, 166.16: JHP to CPS, 31 Oct. 1979; Plumb MSS, Snow file: CPS to JHP, 17 Oct. 1979. Gorley Putt, the Senior Tutor, feared (Diary, 14 June 1977), 'a reign of venomous and vengeful partiality, which could make Christ's an uncomfortable home for any but his [i.e. JHP's] cronies and creatures'.

[86] Snow MSS, 166.16: JHP to CPS, 22 June 1978.

[87] Gorley Putt Diary, 11 Oct. 1978.

[88] JHP, *Walpole*, vol. ii, *The King's Minister*, p. 331.

is', he opined, when confronted by his apostasy, 'no rage [that word again!] like the rage of a convert.'[89] As a self-made provincial, who hated metropolitan condescension, who believed in hard work, self-help and wealth creation, who adored the freedom and opportunities of America, and whose work on leisure had anticipated some of her own views of the economy and society, this was not a wholly implausible re-invention. But as befitted the biographer of Walpole, Plumb also had his eye to the main chance: perhaps the hoped-for peerage might yet materialise? And so, in two volumes of collected essays, linked by an autobiographical commentary, he claimed that he had been a Thatcherite before Thatcher.[90] (He also paid off many scores against his Cambridge enemies, especially Elton and Chadwick, and reaffirmed his faith and delight in America.) But the sincerity and completeness of his convictions were widely questioned by the true-blue-rinse brigade, the books were not well received by academics, they did not appeal to the general public, they were uncharacteristically un-sure-footed in their tone and pitch, and this project, like the peerage, got no further.[91]

By this time, Plumb was putting most of his (still considerable) energy, and much of his (still expanding) fortune into his social life, where he hoped he might become the 'Chips' Channon of his day. (As a result, his diaries and some of his correspondence will remain closed for many a decade.) To his unconcealed delight, he had been invited to the wedding of the Prince of Wales and Lady Diana Spencer (he was a regular visitor to Althorp during the days of Raine), and even after ceasing to be Master, he still entertained Princess Margaret and her entourage in lavish style. As a single, available man, and as someone who kept a good table and now had time on his hands, Plumb was well placed to play a supporting part in the matriarchal soap opera of the House of Windsor. But it was hard and sometimes humiliating work. Sitting up into the small hours on Mustique with Princess Margaret was not an obvious way for anyone else to enjoy themselves, and he was never as fully accepted in these exalted circles as he liked to claim. 'Funny little man, Plumb', the late Lord Spencer once remarked. But he was far more in thrall to this world than anyone of his once-sceptical and radical intelligence should ever have been. Indeed, by the mid 1980s, the scion of the suburbs had trans-

[89] *New York Times*, 23 Oct. 2001.
[90] *Ei*, p. 156.
[91] M. Cowling, 'The Sources of the New Right', *Encounter*, Nov. 1989, p. 8. See also two reviews of *Ei–ii*: J. P. Kenyon, *Times Literary Supplement*, 23–9 June 1989; J. C. D. Clark, *English Historical Review*, 105 (1990), 989–91.

formed himself into an almost parodic version of a crusty clubland member: deaf, purple, snobbish, choleric and reactionary—more Evelyn Waugh than Arnold Bennett. 'Most people in old age', one colleague correctly observed, 'become caricatures of themselves. With predictable unpredictability, Jack has become a caricature of someone else.'

One sign of this was that the darker side of his temperament became ever more in evidence. This was partly a matter of age and ill health: minor strokes, prostate trouble, and a broken back—indignities and discomforts which he bore with stoical courage and often unappreciated fortitude. But he also came increasingly to feel that his career (to borrow one of Snow's more ponderously knowing phrases) had never quite 'come off'. His resentment at those 'wasted years' before 1945 intensified as he grew older; and he railed ever more against those in the faculty and the University who he felt had kept him down and out. He had ample justification for such views, having held real power only for two years as chairman of his Faculty Board, and for four years as Master of his college. Yet like Snow, and as his own writings on Walpole had shown, Plumb had never really understood power, or known how to get it, or quite how to wield it. He once observed that Todd hungered 'for the trappings of power like a sex-starved adolescent for girls'.[92] But this was a serious misjudgement: Todd, like Butterfield and Chadwick, knew exactly where it lay—in the colleges and departments of the university, and in the corridors of power in London—and he grasped it and wielded it with assurance and determination for many decades. Plumb, by contrast, thought he might achieve the same ends by entertaining Princess Margaret. 'The way to the "Headmistress"', he told a baffled and sceptical Roy Strong, after a right royal dinner at Brooks's, 'is through her sister.' 'Whatever is he after?', Strong wondered. 'Endless lunches and dinners and Princess Margaret for the weekend won't get him anywhere.' It was a damning, but also a very shrewd, remark.[93]

Just occasionally, Plumb could still give reminders of his earlier buoyancy and warmth, as in *In Search of China* (Cambridge, 1986) (on porcelain: 'Master the scholarship; never begrudge a dealer his profit'), and in *Vintage Memories* (Cambridge, 1988) (on claret: 'Petrus is a Gothic wine, Lafite pure Palladian'), but these were no more than autobiographical vignettes.[94] His many protégés, who by now occupied senior positions in

---

[92] Plumb MSS, Snow file: CPS to JHP, 26 Jan. 1955; Snow MSS, 166.9: JHP to CPS, 7 Dec. 1962.
[93] R. Strong, *The Roy Strong Diaries, 1967–1987* (London, 1997), p. 283. I am grateful to Sir Roy Strong for permission to quote from an unpublished entry in his diary.
[94] JHP, *In Search of China* (Cambridge, 1986), p. 13; id., *Vintage Memories* (Cambridge, 1988), p. 10.

the great universities of England and America, dedicated their books to him and rendered thanks and homage; but all too often, he seemed incapable of returning their affections. He might (like Isaiah Berlin in Oxford) have become the doyen of his faculty and his university, but the appointment of Geoffrey Elton to the Regius Chair in 1983 in succession to Owen Chadwick only increased his feelings of alienation and disappointment, to which he gave full and ill-judged vent in the first volume of his collected essays. And while he was one of the grand old men of his college, a generous benefactor to it, and a great fund-raiser for it, his implaccable hostility to Lord Todd, and also to his own successor in the Mastership (whom he much disliked, and lost no opportunity to criticise), meant he was too bitter to play the part of elder statesman. 'The true creators', Plumb had opined, in his introduction to the Trevelyan Festschrift, wrote history 'to ease the ache within'; perhaps, at a deeper level, he had given up on the past because for him, the therapy had never actually worked. And how often, in these later years, did he recall the closing words of the second volume of *Walpole*: 'The future would bring the death of friends, the decline of powers, age, sickness and defeat'?[95]

Plumb's sunset years were further darkened because his earlier writing on the eighteenth century became the object of intemperate attack by members of the new Thatcherite right, who questioned the sincerity of his latter-day conversion to their cause, and who never forgave him his fashionable sixties opinions. Urged on by Geoffrey Elton, and claiming to be donning the mantles of both Namier and Butterfield, the young J. C. D. Clark assailed Plumb with a ferocity that had not been seen in academe since the 'storm over the gentry' and the 'standard of living' controversies of the 1950s: for being too teleological, too whiggish, too secular; for giving insufficient attention to the church, the aristocracy and the monarchy; for over-stating the contrast between the revolutionary seventeenth and the stable eighteenth century; for failing to explain how patronage and place were the essentials of Walpolean power; and for being himself at the centre of a web of academic patronage from which others had been ruthlessly excluded.[96] There was some, though not much, truth in these charges, especially insofar as they concerned Plumb's delight in progress, disdain for religion, and his unsatisfactory treatment of Walpolean power. But even in his radical days, he had hardly been a figure to neglect

---

[95] JHP, 'Introduction' to *Studies in Social History*, p. xiii; id., *Walpole*, vol. ii, p. 333.

[96] J. C. D. Clark, *English Society, 1688–1832: Ideology, Social Sructure and Political Practice During the Ancien Regime* (Cambridge, 1985); id., *Revolution and Rebellion: State and Society in England in the Seventeenth and Eighteenth Centuries* (Cambridge, 1986).

aristocracy and monarchy (vide *The First Four Georges*), it could scarcely be denied that Stuart England was more turbulent than Hanoverian England, and Plumb had never been as invincible a patron as some imagined, least of all in Cambridge itself.[97] But like many bullies when paid back in their own coinage (Geoffrey Elton was another, when berated by David Starkey), he was visibly disconcerted by the savagery of these assaults, and was at a loss how to reply.[98]

Yet at the same time that Plumb was subjected to these late-in-life attacks, and in a manner that was both indirect and ironic, his own career was now reaching its supreme culmination—not so much because of anything he himself was still doing, but rather through the endeavours and accomplishments of his most outstanding and illustrious protégés: among them Roy Porter, who was writing even more prolifically than Plumb had during the 1950s and 1960s; Simon Schama, whose best selling books, television series and New York fame eclipsed anything Plumb had ever achieved; Quentin Skinner, who was appointed to the Regius Professorship of Modern History that Plumb had vainly coveted; and Neil McKendrick, whose long tenure of the Mastership at Gonville and Caius made him a college proconsul in ways that Plumb at Christ's had never quite been. At one level, this gave Plumb enormous pleasure, triumphing over his enemies at one remove, and ensuring that his influence would live on. But he also became deeply resentful of his most successful students, who had once been his clients, but who had subsequently gone on to achieve more than he had. One protégé who fared less well was J. P. Kenyon, who in later life transferred his scholarly allegiance from Plumb to Elton, reviewed the collected essays critically, and wrote appreciatively of Jonathan Clark. Kenyon died too young in 1996, and Plumb wrote a devastating obituary in the *College Magazine*: 'a deep sense of despair . . . a journey to nowhere . . . he deserved the highest honours but he failed to reach them'.[99]

As old age and infirmity took their toll, Plumb ceased to be able to travel—to his beloved New York, to France, or even to London. He sold his rectory and most of his cellar, and resigned spectacularly from the Bordeaux Society on the occasion of its fiftieth anniversary dinner. Confined to the college, and ever more enraged and frustrated, he became

---

[97] JHP's last work on monarchy was *New Light on the Tyrant George III* (Washington, DC, 1978).

[98] Cannadine, 'Historians in the "Liberal Hour"', pp. 343–50.

[99] JHP, 'John Philip [*sic*] Kenyon', *Christ's College Magazine* (1996), p. 71; J. S. Morrill, 'John Philipps Kenyon, 1927–96', *Proceedings of the British Academy*, 101 (1999), 441–61; Plumb MSS, USA Letters File F–K, Kenyon to JHP, 1 Oct. 1988.

a high-table hazard, whom Fellows took pains to avoid, and guests encountered at their peril. But during the 1990s, he finally realised what had become his two most deeply cherished ambitions, outliving his great rivals in the college (Todd died in 1997), and in the faculty (Elton died in 1995) with ample time to spare. But these were pyrrhic victories: like so much in his life, they had come too late to give him real pleasure or satisfaction, and they carried with them inevitable intimations of his own mortality. By turns colourful and controversial, complex and conflicted, Plumb was a wholly unique and genuinely original character, sometimes splendid, generous, and irresistible, sometimes maddening, outrageous and impossible—a small man who in every other way was larger than life, and who (as he had written of Chatham, and as William Cooper had written of Albert Woods) was locked in a titanic struggle with his own temperament, in which everyone who got near him was eventually caught up, and which was never resolved, but only ended, with his death.[100]

VI

As befitted someone so familiar with the darker side of life, who had spent many insomniac hours confronting the long and lonely reaches of the night, Plumb had brooded extensively on what he regarded as the comic-cum-cruel finality of death, and his will had been through many iterations. True to his lifelong unbelief, and to his fundamental unease with himself, he was buried at a private, secular funeral at Westhorpe in Suffolk, having expressly forbidden the presence of any guests or mourners, or the holding of a social gathering or a memorial service in the college chapel. He had no wish to give the dwindling band of his enemies an opportunity for public gloating at his demise, and he had no confidence that his remaining friends would want to mourn and mark his passing. This latter feeling was wholly genuine—and also utterly mistaken. He had made many enemies, and his greatest days were long since over: but it *had* been an extraordinary career, he had often (though not invariably) been a force for good, he had done interesting and original and important work, he had changed many people's lives for the better, and his admirers and protégés would have wished to render thanks and pay a final tribute—perhaps best expressed in these lines from

---

[100] JHP, *Chatham*, p. 157; Cooper, *Struggles of Albert Woods*, pt. iv, ch. 5.

Walpole, which bear repetition as Plumb's own epitaph: 'in everything that he did, he was richly varied and intensely human'.[101]

The true extent of Plumb's wealth, and the details of his benefactions, were awaited with the same mixture of enthusiasm, interest, expectation, anxiety, trepidation and distaste that he had so often aroused and provoked in the heady days of his power and fame. The furniture, the books, the pictures, the silver and the porcelain from his college rooms were sold at a remarkable auction held in Cambridge in May 2002. His total estate amounted to £1.4 million, which was slightly less than Lord Todd's, and substanially less than many people had expected.[102] After a limited number of bequests (to friends, to his driver, and to the College staff), the residue was applied to a charitable trust, of which Christ's was to be the principal beneficiary. Plumb's darker side died with him: the rages, the rudeness, the resentment, the regrets; the life so often lived (as he had written of Namier) at odds with his own nature—and with other people's, too.[103] But his happier, sunnier, warmer, more creative, more exuberant, more expansive side lives on: in his books, which still captivate with their high-spirited prose and unexpected insights; in his students and protégés, ensconced in high positions on both sides of the Atlantic, who will never forget his unique brand of inspirational (and often intimidating) magic; in his considerable and carefully nurtured archive, which will not reveal its innermost secrets for many years to come; and most lastingly in Christ's College, which is both a poorer and a richer place without him.

DAVID CANNADINE
Fellow of the Academy

Note. In preparing this memoir, I have been greatly assisted by Alan Bell, Linda Colley, Rupert Hall, Eric Hobsbawm, Peter Linehan, Neil McKendrick, Simon May, William Noblett, David Reynolds, Quentin Skinner, Sir Keith Thomas and George Watson. Since this is not only a formal memoir, but also a personal appreciation, I am particularly anxious to stress that the opinions and judgements expressed herein are mine alone. Among Plumb's own works, I am especially indebted to his *Collected Essays*, 2 vols. (London, 1988). I have consulted the Butterfield MSS (Cambridge University Library), the Plumb MSS (Cambridge University Library), and the Snow MSS (Harry Ransom Research Center, University of Texas at Austin) and I have also seen extracts from the diary of S. Gorley Putt, in the possession of Simon May.

[101] JHP, *Walpole*, vol. i, *The Making of a Statesman*, p. xiii.
[102] Cheffins, Sale Catalogue, *The Sir John Plumb Collection* (Cambridge, 2002).
[103] *Ei*, p. 100.

NICOLAI RUBINSTEIN   *The Warburg Institute*

Nicolai Rubinstein
1911–2002

NICOLAI RUBINSTEIN was born in Berlin on 11 July 1911. His father was a publisher and his parents were Hungarian (i.e. initially Austro-Hungarian) subjects, though his father had come to Berlin from Riga and had taken Hungarian citizenship on the insistence of his future parents-in-law. Both parents were Jewish by descent. In Berlin he attended the Französische Gymnasium, but left at fourteen on account of health problems and spent two and a half years first in Switzerland and then in the Black Forest. He began his university studies in Berlin in 1930, his subjects (after a false start with political economy) being history and philosophy. An influential teacher whose seminar he attended was Erich Kaspar, historian of the early medieval papacy, but he also went to lectures by Friedrich Meinecke—an impressive link with the past!

At the end of 1933 Nicolai and his family emigrated when the Nazi regime came to power, his parents and sister to France, he to Italy. He registered as a student at the University of Florence, where he proceeded to the *laurea* in 1935, his principal teacher being Nicola Ottokar, Professor of Medieval History and of Russian. Ottokar, author of *Il comune di Firenze alla fine del Dugento*, was a big influence on the historical technique and outlook of Rubinstein, who became his *assistente*. At this stage he knew Robert Davidsohn, the great historian of medieval Florence, but gained the impression that in Davidsohn's view there was no room for further treatment of that field. In 1938 racial laws came to Italy, but Nicolai stayed on, courageously—and illegally, since Jewish refugees were now banned from Italy. It was around this time that he made a friendship

Proceedings of the British Academy, **124**, 313–330. © The British Academy 2004.

which proved fateful for his survival and career. William Buchan (second son of John Buchan, first Lord Tweedsmuir, and now third baron) was staying at Casa Brewster on the slopes of Bellosguardo on Florence's southern outskirts. Buchan became friendly with a circle of German expatriates, mostly art history students, many of them Jewish. Among these was Nicolai, then living in an apartment in the village of Bellosguardo. He remembered Nicolai in the spring of 1938 for his warm welcome and his verses in German and French which 'had a special quality of freshness, economy and immediacy'.[1] When Buchan returned to England in 1938 he had invited Nicolai to come to stay with him as his guest for as long as he liked. He was probably unsurprised to receive a letter the following spring in which Nicolai (alleging the 'disagreeable weather' in Italy) asked whether he might accept the invitation. He reached London safely that summer and stayed with Buchan in Kensington, where 'it was a great pleasure to see Nicolai applying a formidable intelligence, a lively, amused interest in people and in social life in all its aspects, to comprehending the new world in which he was now to make his life'. Some of the shopping habits of the British aristocracy were to remain with him as a relic of that period.

Soon he moved to Oxford. By then he was in receipt of a grant from the Society for the Protection of Science and Learning. It was a condition of the grant that he had to teach and he was able to undertake some teaching (including teaching of Italian to pupils of Cecilia Ady's 'special subject' on the Renaissance) and lecturing for the Faculty of Modern History. In January 1942 this rather hand-to-mouth existence came to an end with his appointment to a temporary Lectureship at the University College of Southampton. From 1943 to 1945 the history staff at Southampton numbered two; his solitary colleague Alwyn Ruddock taught all English history and he European history from 476 to 1914! He was able to keep ahead of his pupils—so he claimed later—because he was able to read books in German. These must have been dark years for him. Both his parents were taken from Paris and perished in concentration camps, but his sister evaded capture and survived to have a successful career in films; at the time of writing she still lives in Paris. Nicolai himself had vivid memories of June 1944 in Southampton. Military convoys preparing to embark for the Normandy landing filled the streets around his lodgings.

---

[1] William Buchan, *The Rags of Time. A Fragment of Autobiography* (Southampton, 1990), pp. 248–9, 269–70.

In 1945 he was appointed to a Lectureship at Westfield College (University of London), which was to be his academic home up to the time of his retirement in 1978 (he was promoted to Reader in 1962 and to Professor in 1965). At Westfield he taught European history 400–1500 AD, the History of Political Thought from the classical to the early modern period, and a 'special subject' (studied in Italian texts) 'Florence and the Renaissance, 1464–1532'. He also, from 1949, conducted a weekly seminar at the London University Institute of Historical Research and came to have close links with the Warburg Institute (also part of the University). That Institute for many years provided him with a room which was the central office of the edition of Lorenzo de' Medici's letters. Both the Institute and Westfield made him an Honorary Fellow.

I am most grateful to Professor Olive Anderson for the following sketch of how Nicolai Rubinstein appeared to a young colleague, who became a close friend, when she joined the Westfield staff in 1949:

> When I arrived, male members of staff were a rarity—'your two men' said the ladies of the other Departments, rather satirically, of the History Department's two male lecturers, Francis Carsten and Nicolai Rubinstein. Both had been born in Berlin in 1911 (within three weeks of each other) and had reached England as part of the great diaspora resulting from Nazi policies; both were living in separate flats within the same Frognal house; and both were plainly serious scholars and conscientious teachers. Between them they taught whatever was not covered by the four-strong Department's then Head, Eveline Martin, and its medievalist, Rosalind Hill. But they were deeply unlike, and a continual source of instructive contrasts to a young colleague fresh from a very traditional Oxford women's college. Mary Stocks' combative talk gave some worldly bite to the High Table and Senior Common Room of this small, all but enclosed female Hampstead community; but Nicolai's ready friendship offered an alluring whiff of cosmopolitan scholarly glamour. Here was an academic man-about-town, a scholar party-goer, unfailingly companionable and at ease. His network of multi-national connoisseurs, Sotheby's experts, and art historians was far from unworldly; and any mutual Oxford friends we proved to have in London were always social if not academic high-fliers. To be invited to accompany him to some special lecture seemed an enormously stimulating compliment—and one that called for careful judgment in such matters as hats and gloves. In the summer of 1954 we each married, and took to repairing after our high table lunch to a certain secluded sunny bench sheltered by a high brick wall, where we talked indiscreetly; and thirty years later we still laughed over our chagrin when we hurried off to our 2 o'clock teaching after some particularly uninhibited exchanges and found one of the gardeners working behind that high brick wall.

In his Westfield years Rubinstein supervised a considerable number of doctoral candidates and many of these pupils are now familiar names in the world of Renaissance studies. The thesis, when presented, was always thorough, well organised and well written (as fellow-examiner I can bear witness to this). Rubinstein was a very frequent participant in Italian *convegni* and in the late days of his eminence his attendance was sought with such enthusiasm that his mere presence was subsidised, whether or not he was to read a paper. A very significant contribution to the study of Florentine history was the volume he planned and edited, *Florentine Studies* (1968). The quality of the fifteen essays was notably high and the influence of this collection has often been remarked upon in Italy. At the risk of being invidious, one may mention two contributions in very different fields, Charles Davis's on 'Il buon tempo antico' and Philip Jones's 'From manor to *mezzadria*'. If one may venture a contribution to 'gender studies', it should perhaps be noted (as indeed it has already been by others) that all the contributors were male. This would surely not have been the case if the volume had been planned a few years later.

Retirement from his chair meant the end of undergraduate teaching and of college committees and university boards, but otherwise academic existence continued as before. He was for many years a member of the council (*Kuratorium*) of the German Kunsthistorisches Institut in Florence —this was another important connection, as were the Harvard foundation (Center for Renaissance Studies) at I Tatti and the Istituto Nazionale di Studi sul Rinascimento. He benefited from spells at the Princeton Institute for Advanced Study where scholars are cocooned in order that their notes may turn into books. He gave a course of lectures at the University of Florence (1983) and held seminars at the Pisan Scuola Normale (1985). By now he was laden with honours, a Fellow of the British Academy (1971) and then recipient of the Serena medal (1974), holder of the Premio Internazionale Galileo Galilei (1985), Honorary Citizen of Florence (1991) and much more. The concept 'retirement' was absent from his vocabulary. A few weeks before his death he discussed with me the next book that he projected. This was to have been an essay illustrating the history of Florence through a number of buildings chosen to typify various stages in the city's development.

* * *

Rubinstein's first published work, based on his *tesi di laurea*, was 'La lotta contro i magnati', but only the first section appeared (1935) in the *Archivio Storico Italiano*. The main part, on 'Le origini della legge sul sodamento' was printed as a separate publication by the Florentine firm of Olschki through the good offices of Niccolò Rodolico, editor of the *Archivio Storico Italiano*, since writings by Jews were now banned from Italian journals. The striking achievement of 'Le origini' was to affirm the place of Florence's anti-magnate legislation in an older medieval European tradition: 'possiamo mettere la legge in stretta relazione colle leggi di Pace pubblica'. This European approach to the topic, a new and most important contribution, was set out with precocious erudition. 'La legge sul sodamento', he proceeds to explain, was 'diretta contro la parte cavalleresca della popolazione cittadina, perchè in essa si vedeva il principale focolaio delle guerre interne'; 'la vendetta si è radicata nel sistema di vita della nobiltà cavalleresca'. One effect of the anti-magnate legislation (not insisted on in the article) was to create a new class, the magnates. Nicolai once told me how the realisation of this came to him one day when he was taking a walk up to Pian dei Giullari. It occurred to him that this effect was analogous to the consequences of the Nazi anti-Jewish legislation in Germany. Some people hitherto not given to thinking of themselves primarily as Jews had now been penned within a new legal category and the same must have been true of *magnati* some 650 years earlier.

Owing to his second forced emigration, several years passed before Rubinstein was able to complete his next important Florentine article. In June 1939 he wrote (in German) from a London address to Edgar Wind, then an editor of the Warburg Institute's *Journal*, asking if he might discuss with him an article on which he was working, which might interest the Institute. Nearly three years passed before he could offer for publication an article (clearly the one mentioned in 1939) on 'The Beginnings of Political Thought in Florence. A Study in Medieval Historiography'. In this piece Rubinstein began by pointing out that 'historiography as a primary source for the history of political thought is all too often neglected'. His main topic was the *Chronica de origine civitatis*, written *c*.1200, whose author had alleged an ancient antagonism between Florence and Fiesole in the light of the situation in his own time. The *Chronica* (influential on Dante and Villani, among others) also illustrated how 'throughout the Middle Ages, memories of ancient Rome had maintained their hold on mind and imagination'. No less original and convincing than 'La lotta contro i magnati', this constituted a debut so brilliant that it is impossible not to regret that its author returned only once to the thirteenth century for his principal themes. At the meeting which commemorated Nicolai and his wife Ruth (24 January 2003) one of the speakers, Professor Bill Kent, singled out the article on 'The Beginnings of Political Thought in

Florence' as the inspiration which led him to come from Australia to be a Rubinstein pupil.

The serious return to the thirteenth century was 'Dante and Nobility', the Barlow Lectures delivered at University College London, in May 1973 and now published for the first time in the first volume of the three-volume collection of selected articles by Rubinstein (Edizioni di Storia e Letteratura, Rome). The postponement in publication was probably due initially to the need to undertake wider reading than had proved possible in 1973 and in fact quite a few subsequent publications are cited in the footnotes of the published version. The lectures returned to the old topic of the vendetta and wrestled with this and other institutions connected with the concept of nobility. Much light is cast. Nobility defies precise definition, but many people said interesting things about it.

The next publication after 'The Beginnings of Political Thought' was 'Florence and the Despots', a paper read to the Royal Historical Society (1952) which dealt with some aspects of Florentine diplomacy in the fourteenth century and presented the pro-republican, anti-Signoria propaganda of Florence in the period of the wars against Visconti Milan. In a way it reads now as a tribute to Hans Baron, who had taught Rubinstein in Berlin and who took this subject as the main theme of his influential but surely unconvincing *The Crisis of the Early Italian Renaissance* (1955). Rubinstein seems to have felt that the theme was rather a dead end as far as he was concerned (the status and influence of political propaganda are not defined with much conviction) and he did not return to this field, except obliquely in the 1981 lecture on '*Florentina Libertas*'. The suggestion that he was still feeling his way and not yet firmly committed to a field of study seems to be confirmed by his agreement, around this time, to undertake an edition of Paul the Deacon's History of the Lombards for the Nelson series of Medieval Classics. This edition of a fascinating historical source was not destined to materialise.

The next dozen years (1953–66) were an immensely productive, versatile and innovative period in Rubinstein's career. It is difficult to know to what extent his new interests were the product of the Special Subject he was now teaching on 'Florence and the Renaissance', but the influence seems quite clear. The subject itself was to no degree his own invention, but was already being taught at Bedford College by Miss Marian Tooley at the time of his coming to Westfield and was similar to one which had long been taught at Oxford by Edward Armstrong and later by Cecilia Ady. Among the texts set were Francesco Guicciardini's *Storie fiorentine* and *Dialogo sul reggimento di Firenze*, both works of absorbing interest which had been little studied (though Guicciardini had been the subject of a recent book by Vittorio de Caprariis, whose view of the *Storie fiorentine* Rubinstein found unconvincing). In 'The *Storie fiorentine* and the *Memorie di famiglia* by Guicciardini' (1953) he was already into his stride, impressively familiar with the sources in the Florentine Archivio di Stato and benefiting from access to the Guicciardini family archive, and was able to pinpoint the sources used by the writer. This most satisfying and convincing article reveals a strong interest in the Medicean regime, and he was to return to Guicciardini in his Introduction to the *Maxims* and two later articles.

This was the period also of the first article of many on Machiavelli, 'The beginning of Niccolò Machiavelli's career in the Florentine chancery' (1956), but more obviously deriving from the Special Subject was a debut in the field of fifteenth-century Florentine political history, 'I primi anni del Consiglio Maggiore di Firenze (1494–9)' (1954). This quite lengthy article analysed the complicated constitutional tinkering of the first years after the flight of Piero de' Medici. Its detailed treatment made clear how the Florentine archival and unpublished chronicle sources could be used to illuminate the realities of *accoppiatori*, *tratte*, *abili*, *beneficiati* and the rest of this crucial field, up to then virtually untilled. He was to return to this period, with a rather broader approach, in his piece for the Cecilia Ady memorial *Italian Renaissance Studies*, 'Politics and Constitution in Florence' (1960). By then he had an ally and friend in rewriting the political history of Renaissance Florence. This was Felix Gilbert, once German and now American, who had embarked in this realm even before the Second World War. Gilbert's 'Florentine Political Assumptions in the period of Savonarola' (*Journal of the Warburg and Courtauld Institutes* (1957)) was a pioneering and fruitful piece.

The article on the Consiglio Maggiore was accompanied chronologically by two on the 'problem of the Empire' in Florentine policy (in *Archivio Storico Italiano* (1954) and *Bulletin of the Institute of Historical Research* (1957)). The potential threat from the Emperor Maximilian and the Florentines' difficulty in assessing its seriousness would have been encountered in reading for the Consiglio Maggiore articles, and the 1957 piece (originally a communication to the 1955 International Congress of Historical Sciences) portrayed the background to the 'imperial problem' of Maximilian's time. Both were careful, conscientious pieces, but one senses that Rubinstein came to feel that 'straight' diplomatic history was not his forte.

Something more original and exciting was to follow. This was 'Political Ideas in Sienese Art: the Frescoes of Ambrogio Lorenzetti and Taddeo di Bartolo in the Palazzo Pubblico' (1958). The crucial theme here was the derivation of Lorenzetti's political notions, conveyed in one of Europe's most fascinating masterpieces, which had been curiously neglected by previous writers (not by subsequent ones, not all of them as clever and learned as Nicolai Rubinstein!). The main contention of the article was that the background to Lorenzetti was Aristotle as interpreted by Aquinas. The mysterious regal figure represented 'the Common Good'. This article was to be productive in controversy as well as in enlightenment. In 1986 the imposing figure of Professor Quentin Skinner entered the lists (*Proceedings of the British Academy*, 72 (1986): 'Ambrogio Lorenzetti: the Artist as Political Philosopher'). He widened the question to the general one of Roman as opposed to Aristotelian influences in medieval European political writings. Ciceronian and Senecan virtues were more evident than Aristotelian qualities, he claimed, and Brunetto Latini was more enlightening than Aristotle. The regal figure was not the Common Good but a 'symbolic representation of the type of magistracy by which a body of citizens can alone hope to create or attain an ideal of the common good'. In his response of 1997 Rubinstein accepted in part the consequences of Skinner's contention that 'the political theory of the Renaissance . . . owes a far deeper debt to Rome than to Greece'. For him, the haunting regal figure was now the city of Siena, but 'rappresenta anche il Bene Comune'. Skinner was to return to the fray in 1999 (*Journal of the Warburg and Courtauld Institutes*, 62, 1–28) with a new definition of the regal figure and a fresh emphasis on the significance of the festive dance of the young men in the well-governed city. A fertile article indeed, then, that of 1958. Much more will no doubt follow from it, though it is in the nature of the topic that no final resolution can possibly emerge that will satisfy all.

Some of the earlier contributions on Renaissance historiography also date from this period (the pieces on Poliziano, Poggio and Scala, 1954–65), but the star offering, original and authoritative, was the article on 'Marsilius of Padua and the Political Thought of his Time' (1965). Marsilio was presented, at last, in his setting; 'it is difficult to evaluate Marsilius' political theory adequately without taking into consideration contemporary political thinking in his native country and the political developments in the city in which he was born and educated, and in which he spent his formative years'. The *Defensor Pacis* was 'the fullest and most coherent defence of Italian republicanism that had yet been made'. Like

'Political Ideas in Sienese Art', this was a convincing and influential sortie into a new realm, one into which its author had probably been attracted by the inclusion of the *Defensor Pacis* in the accepted canon of texts studied in the university syllabus, within the paper on 'The History of Political Thought'.

This particularly fertile period was followed by the publication of Rubinstein's *magnum opus*. Only the piece on Guicciardini's early writings had been concerned with the political history of the Medicean period, so the book was also yet another debut. In the Preface to *The Government of Florence under the Medici, 1434–1494* (Oxford Warburg Studies, 1966) Rubinstein emphasised that 'the rich archive materials preserved at Florence have hardly been tapped by modern historians for a study of Medicean government'. 'The political regime which was founded by Cosimo de' Medici and perfected by his grandson Lorenzo differed from the despotic states of fifteenth-century Italy in the preservation of republican institutions.' 'Italian princes, not unlike later historians, tended to see the Medici as rulers of Florence.' But the situation was much more complicated than this. 'Control of elections was one of the chief instruments of Medici policy. The way in which it was established, developed, and handled is therefore the central subject of our study.' The achievement of the book was to depict the Medicean regime as an exemplar of family-led authority, not of 'tyrannical' rule. The interplay between the Medici and Florence's political class was set out with magisterial subtlety, and the reader learned how Medicean authority was developed through the piecemeal constitutional changes which secured its hold. Sortition (choice by lot) was diluted and evaded through elections by smaller numbers (*a mano*), previous constitutional institutions were replaced by less formal gatherings (*balie*) and later control was channelled through new Councils of one hundred and seventy. It was not always easy to maintain authority, hence the complaint of a Medicean that 'scrutinium omnia perturbavit' (the 'scrutiny' for the choice of councillors and office-holders had thrown everything out). The nature of the governing class was illustrated by the list of those declared eligible for the leading post of Gonfaloniere di Giustizia (1466); forty of these came from five families (ten Pitti, nine Medici, seven each from the Ridolfi, Acciaiuoli and Bartoli). What went wrong for the Medici in 1494 was not merely a disastrous foreign policy, but also Piero's handling of the *cittadini principali*. The chapter on the period 1469–92 was entitled 'The Medici at the Height of their Power', revealing the author's lack of interest in Tuscan history after 1532, but a totally new picture had emerged from his great book.

There was a second edition (1997), with small adjustments throughout taking account of the publications of the intervening thirty years, and three new Appendixes. Both editions, naturally, appeared in Italian translations. This book is far from easy reading and assumes much background knowledge and linguistic equipment of its readers. It is certainly not fare for undergraduates, although undergraduates taking the Florentine special subject were expected to familiarise themselves with it. Yet, filtered through adequately equipped readers, it has revolutionised the accepted picture of Medicean Florence.

At around the same time Rubinstein became closely involved in the relaunching of the edition of the letters of Lorenzo de' Medici. The project had been conceived in 1938 and a beginning made, but nothing had been published when it became a victim of the Second World War, and it was not revived till the 1950s. Rubinstein, who became the General Editor, and Professor Pier Giorgio Ricci were those principally involved. The Letters became a major preoccupation and Rubinstein himself edited the third and fourth volumes (1977, 1981: covering the years 1478–80). An early decision was that 'l'edizione dovesse essere accompagnata da un commento storico soprattutto su fonti archivistiche inedite'. This decision Rubinstein was later to ascribe to the 'ottimismo di un periodo giovanile della mia vita',[2] and he came to have doubts about the dimensions implied by it, but the *Lettere* have reached Volume IX and the year 1486 and have gained a new General Editor in the person of Professor F. W. Kent (himself a former pupil of Rubinstein). Professor Michael Mallett has explained (personal communication) that Rubinstein 'was a very active and hugely influential general editor, and insisted on seeing and commenting on every word written by his *curatori*. With the resources of the Warburg at his disposal he would check all the references that he could, and make frequent suggestions for the improvement of the drafts.' *The Government of Florence* had entailed the use of sources far from Tuscany (London and Paris as well as Modena and Milan); the *Lettere* involved Venice and the Vatican also—not to mention visits which proved unproductive.

Work for the *Lettere* is not reflected to any very considerable extent in Rubinstein's later publications, though this is not true of the essay in *Renaissance Venice* on 'Italian Reactions to Terraferma Expansion in the 15th Century' (1973) nor of the much later 'Das politische System Italiens in der zweiten Hälfte des 15. Jahrhunderts' (1988), a most useful synthesis which certainly merited—but did not achieve—translation.

---

[2] Acceptance speech, Fondazione Premio Internazionale Galileo Galilei (Pisa, 1985), pp. 10–11.

The Government of Florence led on to many articles on the politics of Medicean Florence, often brought about by the requests of organisers of *convegni* and Festschriften. A particularly important one, linked with both internal politics and diplomacy, was the British Academy lecture entitled 'Lorenzo de' Medici: the Formation of his Statecraft' (1977), which covered much new ground in depicting Lorenzo's apprenticeship. Another article, an intellectual voyage clearly giving pleasure to its author as well as to readers, was 'Lorenzo's Image in Europe' (1996), with a fascinating glance at the treatment of Lorenzo by Jacob Burckhardt, for whom Lorenzo was 'l'uomo universale', although his political role was ignored and there was no mention of him in the famous chapter on 'The State as a Work of Art'! But the most important of the articles carrying on from *The Government of Florence* is the paper on 'Oligarchy and Democracy in 15th-century Florence' (1979), a contribution to a conference on *Florence and Venice: Comparisons and Relations*. This was a masterly treatment of a crucial theme. Proceeding from the question of the representation of the Lesser Guilds to Benedetto Dei's list of two hundred ruling families (*c.*1472), he then moved on to wealth and ancient lineage, to the 'principali dello stato e del ghoverno' and 'secondary' and 'tertiary' collaborators. 'Sortition was gradually replaced by election for nearly all the most sensitive posts', a principal finding of *The Government of Florence*. Finally, 'the acceptance by the reformers of 1494 of the *veduti* of the Medicean period as the basis of the new ruling class seems to me a remarkable affirmation of continuity in the social structure of Florentine politics during the 15th century'.

After the *magnum opus* Rubinstein's publications are so versatile in the topics covered that chronological treatment seems unsatisfactory. Consequently writings on political thought will be touched on first, then those concerned with art and architecture, and finally the later pieces on historiography and humanists. The allocation is not always an easy task and this itself is an interesting observation.

Two of the articles which I treat under the heading 'political thought' bear witness to Rubinstein's fruitful insistence on the development of political vocabulary. The 'Notes on the word *stato*' (1971) analyses the earlier uses which lie behind the various senses in which Machiavelli employs the word. An ingenious element is the quotation of the text of a 1450 treaty to illustrate the use of these senses in an official document. Much later (1987) Rubinstein turned to 'The History of the word *politicus*'. This piece, which makes very good reading, is a learned and amusing pursuit which follows a word the whole way from the twelfth century to

Shakespeare. 'Le dottrine politiche nel Rinascimento' (1979) and 'Problems of Evidence in the History of Political Ideas' (1989) are syntheses, yet interesting new points emerge such as that Villani was fifteen years out in the date of death he attributed to Marsilius of Padua and that the *Principe* shocked contemporaries not because its doctrines were amoral but because they might teach the young Lorenzo de' Medici how to seize absolute power in Florence.

Rubinstein also returned a number of times in his later years to Machiavelli. The most weighty of these contributions is 'Machiavelli storico' (1987), a definitive treatment of an aspect which has received too little attention. The article deals with the classical and humanistic models followed, the sources (none of them archival, but some primary ones already in print) and the tact and omissions involved in dealing with Medicean aspects. Notable in the late piece on 'An unknown Version of Machiavelli's *Ritratto delle cose della Magna*' (1998) is the magisterial identification of the anonymous owner of the notebook containing the text analysed and published: he was (of course!) Antonio Maria Bonanni of San Gimignano—of whom a *curriculum vitae* is provided.

The later pieces on Francesco Guicciardini also include a major contribution, the 'Guicciardini politico' of 1984. One of the merits of that author was his ability to put in a nutshell the *credo* of so many Florentine *ottimati*: 'È interesse della città che in qualunque tempo gli uomini da bene abbino autorità' and in his ideal city 'tutto 'l pondo del governo si riduce alla fine in sulle spalle di molto pochi'.[3]

Rubinstein's last article, on 'Le origini medievali del pensiero repubblicano' was an appropriate finale. Republican notions were detectable in the vocabulary of twelfth-century communes. The crucial episode was Moerbeke's translation of Aristotle. Yet Remigio de' Girolami and the *Oculus Pastoralis* are also relevant. Here we return to the battle over the sources of Ambrogio Lorenzetti.

As Professor Caroline Elam (to whom this paragraph is much indebted) has explained, Rubinstein's art-historical contributions 'concentrated largely on political iconography and on the intersection of architecture and politics'. 'His seminal work on the Government of Florence under the Medici made Nicolai increasingly curious about how the architecture and interior decoration of the Palazzo della Signoria reflected the complex evolution of government in the city, as power

---

[3] Quoted by Rubinstein in 'Francesco Guicciardini' from the *Ricordi* and in 'Guicciardini politico' from the *Storie fiorentine*.

shifted from large public councils in huge halls to smaller committees in back rooms.' His first published piece on the Palazzo Vecchio was 'Vasari's Painting of the Foundation of Florence' (1967); this was related to the article of the same year on 'Machiavelli e le origini di Firenze' and took him into a later period than any of his other Florentine articles. It is a reminder of its author's versatility, since it was based not only on manuscript sources but on secondary literature on coins and much that had been published in Germany. He was certainly helped by his links with the Kunsthistorisches Institut in Florence. Understandably reluctant for some years to return to Germany, he accepted an invitation in 1981 to read a paper in Berlin and thereafter he went back several times. The next article on the Palazzo Vecchio (1987) was on classical themes in the decoration of the Palazzo, much of it subsequently destroyed. Based on a lecture given fifteen years before, it may be taken as an early hint of the eventual book. This was *The Palazzo Vecchio, 1298–1532. Government, Architecture and Imagery in the Civic Palace of the Florentine Republic* (Oxford Warburg Studies, 1995; Italian translation forthcoming). No other author would have possessed the extraordinary command of the archival sources which meant that architectural and artistic developments were linked to the political background. 'While extremely sensitive to the beauty of works of art, in his writings on them he was primarily concerned to understand their meanings or functions, conscious without immodesty that he could bring to these problems an unparalleled knowledge of political documents and texts.'[4] He also investigated every nook and cranny of the Palazzo Vecchio. As Professor Kate Lowe remembers, 'he would stand outside and we would discuss the placement/displacement of the windows on each floor'.

There were other writings which had architectural implications, such as the paper on 'Palazzi pubblici e palazzi privati al tempo di Brunelleschi' (1980), informed by interests in taxation and the question of the 'extended family', and that in the Hale Festschrift (1995) on 'Fortified Enclosures in Italian Cities under Signori'. The latter concludes with the rueful but forthright reflection (too late to offer to Hans Baron) that 'the Florentines . . . applied different criteria to liberty at home and in their dominions'. Another late article was 'Youth and Spring in Botticelli's *Primavera*' (1997) which links the Roman poets and Poliziano—and a good deal else—to insist that the figure next to Venus is 'Juventus as well

---

[4] Caroline Elam, 'Nicolai Rubinstein', *The Burlington Magazine*, Jan. 2003, 40–1.

as Ver'. This was (as Caroline Elam has pointed out) doubtless a product of his bedtime perusal of Horace.

Last of the themes (the allocation is somewhat arbitrary) in the later writings are 'humanism' and 'historiography'. There had been many earlier articles in these fields and very often the topic was humanist historiography. This applies to 'Bartolomeo Scala's *Historia Florentinorum*' (1964), 'Poggio Bracciolini. Cancelliere e storico di Firenze' (1965) and 'Il Bruni a Firenze. Retorica e politica' (1990). In these papers Rubinstein explained the classicising attitude of the humanists to historical writing, as exemplified in particular by the fictitious speeches attributed to leading participants. This was sometimes—oddly, as it now seems to us—compatible with some dependence on primary archival sources. Standing rather apart from these papers was 'Die Vermögenslage Florentiner Humanisten im 15. Jahrhundert' (1983) which used fiscal and other sources (including material in the Prato Archivio di Stato) to amplify the treatment of this topic in Lauro Martines' *The Social World of the Florentine Humanists*.

If it should appear that this Memoir has concentrated on the shorter pieces at the expense of the two books, it should be noted that Rubinstein once defined himself as 'one of those scholars who write articles rather than books'.[5] Among his greatest strengths as a historian was his patient determination combined with his highly organised approach to the Florentine archival and other manuscript sources. He had a fine memory, yet he must also have depended on a superb body of notes. He 'asked the right questions', but his answers depended on his methods to carry conviction in the way they did. Mining in the Archivio di Stato and the Biblioteca Nazionale, he dug out the fuel which illuminated the working of the Medicean regime over several decades. And his extraordinary knowledge of these repositories was put to the use of dozens of fellow researchers, as well as his own.

He benefited also from his broad, cosmopolitan approach, which itself was in part the product of his upbringing (he never ceased to marvel at the intellectual barrenness of that of many of his pupils). His own advantages show clearly in his very first published piece, which treats an Italian theme in the light of European precedents and parallels, an approach which has been lacking all too often in Italian historiography. Nor were his researches as solely Florentinocentric as they might at first appear.

---

[5] P. Alter (ed.), *Out of the Third Reich. Refugee Historians in Post-War Britain* (London/New York, 1998), p. 243.

Marsilius was a Paduan (and Nicolai himself had hesitated before choosing Florence rather than Padua as the university in which to continue his studies). Work for *The Government of Florence* and the *Lettere* involved research in archives outside Tuscany and a number of his articles are concerned with wider Italian and even European themes.

Despite his original intention of specialising in political economy at Berlin University, 'after the first year I decided that statistics and business managament were not for me'.[6] Economic history was then in its infancy as a discipline and that fact, combined with Rubinstein's own temperament, accounts for the most noticeable lacuna in his armoury. Though well equipped to detect the wiles of politicians, he was not very down to earth when it came to economic and social realities. I once quite failed to convince him that there were fifteenth-century Italians who could move their domiciles easily because their hovels had no foundations. He was puzzled when I quoted to him a passage in a fourteenth-century writer which advocated that merchants should always give a misleading version of their intended itineraries, for he had failed to link this with robbery on the roads. And he once explained to me that a publisher had (quite justly) increased the proportion of royalties which were to accrue to him as general editor of a projected volume, but was horrified when I mentioned that therefore the other contributors would receive less! His readers should bear in mind that his social *point de vue* tended to be a somewhat lofty one. To him Luca Landucci, that invaluable pharmacist, was 'humble' —which of course he was in the eyes of a Florentine ottimato. When Piero Guicciardini writes of *artefici* (craftsmen), this is rendered, surprisingly, as 'lower classes' (*The Government of Florence*, pp. 216, 319). In fact 'the people' are virtual absentees from his writings, to appear only, rather like a Shakespearian army, in rare Florentine *parlamenti*—but they are not his theme. John Najemy has justly remarked, of both Ottokar and Rubinstein, that 'the politics studied with these methods has been the politics of elites'.[7] In a sense, judgement on Rubinstein as an historian is misplaced. He himself felt strongly that writing about the past had taken a wrong turning when antiquarians were superseded by historians. His view was that things were better before causality came into the question and he would have been happy to be counted among the great *eruditi*.

---

[6] Ibid., p. 239.
[7] John M. Najemy, in A. J. Grieco, M. Rocke, F. Gioffredi Superbi (eds.), 'Politics: Class and Patronage in Twentieth-century Italian Renaissance Historiography', *The Italian Renaissance in the 20th Century* (Florence, 2002), pp. 119–36 (quotation is from p. 126).

Charm can be observed rather than defined, but many could testify to Nicolai Rubinstein's. It was certainly felt by his pupils. One Westfield student enquired of him whether the 'desperate' rumour of his engagement was well-founded! Children felt it strongly. Among his close friends were the Sienese Giovanni and Anne Grottanelli de' Santi. He was staying with them at a stage when their daughter Miriam was struggling with the meanings of adjectives and they were delighted when she pronounced that 'Nicolai è molto perfetto'. Not only was he a most affectionate friend, but he was never heard to speak ill of anyone, an extremely uncommon quality. He should be remembered also as a reader. Favourites were Horace (bedside reading), Herodotus and Thucydides (these in the interleaved Loeb editions), also Montaigne, Henry James and Proust. He quoted Montaigne, on duelling, to good effect in the first of all his articles ('Le origini della legge sul "sodamento"', 36, n. 89; the quotation is from *Essais*, Bk. I, ch. 23, 'Divers evenements de mesme conseil') and he was reading Montaigne in hospital in the days before his death on 19 August 2002.

Nicolai's wife Ruth (née Olitsky) was an American art historian, for many years a central figure at the Warburg Institute. In the Institute's Photographic Collection she had special responsibility for the Census of Antique Art known to Renaissance artists and she was the author, with Phyllis Bober, of *Renaissance Artists and Antique Sculpture* (1986). Her interests did much to stimulate and encourage his own forays into art history. Their hospitality in their Hampstead flat was warm and generous and her enthusiasm and unselfish support were crucial to his achievements. She survived him by ten days only, dying after a long illness on 29 August 2002. As mentioned above, they were commemorated jointly at a meeting organised by the Warburg Institute on 24 January 2003.

DANIEL WALEY
Fellow of the Academy

Note. My thanks are due to Professor Olive Anderson, Professor Alison Brown, Professor Giovanni Ciappelli, Mr William Collier, Dr Peter Denley, Mrs Jean Floud, Professor George Holmes, Professor Kate Lowe, Dr Dorothea McEwan, Professor Michael Mallett, Dr Jenny Stratford, Professor Neil Stratford, Professor Joe Trapp.

Publications

Rubinstein's publications up to 1988 are listed in his Festschrift *Florence and Italy*, pp. 515–23 and the list is continued up to 1991 in *Bulletin of the Society for Renaissance Studies*, 8,2 (May 1991), 8.

Books and articles published since 1991 (and forthcoming):

Books:

The Government of Florence under the Medici (2nd edn., 1997, Oxford Warburg Studies: also Italian translation of 2nd edn., 1999).

The Palazzo Vecchio, 1298–1532. Government, Architecture and Imagery in the Civic Palace of the Florentine Republic (1995: Oxford Warburg Studies. Italian translation forthcoming).

Studies in Italian History in the Middle Ages and the Renaissance, ed. G. Ciappelli, 3 vols., Rome (Edizioni di Storia e Letteratura): Vol. I, *Political Thought and the Language of Politics. Art and Politics*, 2004: Vol. II, *Politics, Diplomacy and Constitution in Florence and Italy*, 2005: Vol. III, *Humanists, Machiavelli and Guicciardini*, 2005.

Articles:

'Machiavelli and the mural decoration of the hall of the Great Council of Florence', *Musagetes. Festschrift für W. Prinz* (Berlin, 1991), pp. 275–85.

'Cosimo *optimus civis*', *Cosimo il Vecchio de' Medici, 1389–1464* (Oxford, 1992), pp. 5–20.

'Lorenzo de' Medici. The formation of his Statecraft', in G. C. Garfagnini (ed), *Lorenzo de' Medici. Studi* (Florence, 1992), pp. 41–66.

'Fortified enclosures in Italian Cities under Signori', *War, Culture and Society in Renaissance Venice* (London, 1995), pp. 1–8.

'Piero de' Medici, *Gonfaloniere di Giustizia*', in *Piero de' Medici "il Gottoso" (1416–1469)* (Berlin, 1993), pp. 1–8.

'Lorenzo's Image in Europe', in M. Mallett and N. Mann (eds.), *Lorenzo the Magnificent. Culture and Politics* (London, 1996), pp. 297–312.

'Le allegorie di Ambrogio Lorenzetti nella Sala di Pace e il pensiero politico del suo tempo', *Rivista Storica Italiana*, 109 (1997), 781–802.

'Youth and Spring in Botticelli's *Primavera*', *Journal of the Warburg and Courtauld Institutes*, 60 (1997), 248–51.

'An unknown version of Machiavelli's *Ritratto delle Cose della Magna*', *Rinascimento*, 2nd ser., 38 (1998), 227–46.

(with M. M. Bullard) 'Lorenzo de' Medici's acquisition of the *Sigillo di Nerone*', *Journal of the Warburg and Courtauld Institutes*, 62 (1999), 283–6.

'Savonarola on the Government of Florence', in S. Fletcher and C. Shaw (eds.), *The World of Savonarola. Italian élites and perceptions of crisis* (Aldershot, 2000), pp. 42–54.

'Le origini medievali del pensiero repubblicano del secolo XV', in *Politica e Cultura nelle repubbliche italiane dal medioevo all'età moderna* (Rome, 2001), pp. 1–20.

Volume I of *Studies in Italian History in the Middle Ages and the Renaissance* (see above) includes 'Dante and Nobility', hitherto unpublished (pp. 165–209).

Bibliography

N. Rubinstein, Acceptance speech, Pisa, 1985 (cited above, footnote 2).

'Nicolai Rubinstein' in P. Denley and C. Elam (eds.), *Florence and Italy. Renaissance Studies in Honour of Nicolai Rubinstein* (London, 1988), pp. xi–xiv (unsigned: by D. Waley).

P. Denley, 'The Craft of Nicolai Rubinstein', *Bulletin of the Society for Renaissance Studies*, 8, 2 (May 1991), 2–8.

P. Alter (ed.), *Out of the Third Reich* (cited above, footnotes 5 & 6), pp. 239–45 (essay based on an interview given by Nicolai Rubinstein to the editor, 1996).

Studies in Italian History in the Middle Ages and the Renaissance (see above), I, includes an Introduction by D. Waley (pp. vii–xix) and a 'Nota del curatore' by G. Ciappelli (pp. xxi–xxxiv).

MICHAEL WALLACE-HADRILL

John Michael Wallace-Hadrill
1916–1985

JOHN MICHAEL WALLACE-HADRILL was born in Bromsgrove, Worcester-shire, on 29 September, Michaelmas Day, 1916: he was usually known by the second of his given names. His father, Frederic, for long second master at Bromsgrove School, was a deeply formative influence on his life. Frederic, despite his double-barrelled name (which he assumed) and his insistence on 'gentlemanly' behaviour, was a self-made man, the son of a junior clerk working in the naval yards at Chatham, Edward Hadrill, who died young leaving his widow, Louise, and young son penniless. Louise remarried Frederick Clayton, a technician who installed science laboratories in public schools. Frederic Hadrill (to his lifelong resentment) did not receive enough education to take him to university, but was able to take an external degree in science by correspondence at London University. Such family history fascinated Michael, who even wrote it up for his own interest. Frederic was determined that none of his three sons should suffer his disadvantages: all three were sent to Cheltenham School, and won places at Oxford. David Sutherland (born 1920) and Francis Gordon (born 1924) became, like their father, second masters of public schools (Aldenham and Cheltenham respectively). Like Michael, both had marked scholarly inclinations, and David, who after ordination into the Church of England took a doctorate in theology at Manchester, became a notable patristic scholar, working on Eusebius of Caesarea.

Michael always remembered his father with devotion: a strict disciplin-arian and a mordant wit, he lavished affection on his sons and was deter-mined to see them do well. But Michael also felt himself to be born with

Proceedings of the British Academy, **124**, 333–355. © The British Academy 2004.

a number of disadvantages, which included a hare lip (rather clumsily sutured), poor sight, and above all left-handedness, to which he attributed his hatred of the mechanical world. In addition he felt an educational disadvantage deriving from his schooling: he attended a small preparatory school, where no Greek was taught, which was run by a friend of his father's, a brutal man whom he later recalled with loathing. As a result, when he moved to Cheltenham School, he was not placed in the classical stream, and a feeling of inferiority to classicists was made stronger by his winning a scholarship to the classics-dominated Corpus Christi College, Oxford (1935). It is significant that he ensured that his two sons should be classically trained. His own (perceived) sense of not belonging to the classical world is a key to his ambivalent reading of the Early Middle Ages as both admiring and not belonging to the Ancient World, and also to his careful avoidance of the eastern Mediterranean.

At Corpus his proudest achievement as an undergraduate was winning the Lothian Prize in 1938 for an essay on 'The Abbey of St Denis in the Twelfth and Thirteenth Century'. The energy which he expended on this first piece of research, which included a trip to the Bibliothèque Nationale, was a factor in his failure to achieve a First, though he also felt badly neglected by his tutor, Denis Brogan, and indebted for last-minute coaching to Max Beloff. The Second was a bitter blow, and it was something he kept hidden, even from members of his family. Nevertheless he immediately embarked on the study of the legendary history and posthumous reputation of Charlemagne, under the supervision of F. M. Powicke. Sir Maurice, by no means a specialist in the period that Michael was to make his own, was to remain a major influence. Shortly before death, in a conversation vividly recalled by one of his students, Michael talked of his fascination with an episode which occurred at Peatling Magna in 1265: Sir Maurice's influence can surely be seen in this interest in a minor episode in the days following the death of Simon de Montfort. Research on Charlemagne's *Nachleben* was soon curtailed by the outbreak of war, and it was never taken up again as a single topic of research, although the subject was to surface in numerous later publications: *The Frankish Church* of 1983, for instance, has several illuminating paragraphs on the matter, not least on the *Lives* of Charlemagne written by Einhard and Notker the Stammerer, while the historical traditions of the monastery of St Denis are considered in numerous of Michael's publications, from all periods of his scholarly life.

Corpus had elected him to a junior research fellowship in 1939, but in the event he joined up on day one of the war. Initially he served in the intelligence corps. After Dunkirk he was transferred to the Foreign Office (MI6), where he rose to be a major. He was engaged in matters of some secrecy, working at one point under Kim Philby; he would never discuss in detail his war service, and was angered by others who subsequently ignored the Official Secrets Act. What is clear is that his fluency in both French and German served him well in interrogation. The brutality of the war distressed him deeply (interrogators were required to attend the executions of enemy agents they had questioned). Then in 1946 Michael returned to Corpus, this time as a Fellow of the College, before moving on after a year to neighbouring Merton, where he was Fellow and Tutor from 1947 to 1955. He was to retain a great attachment for his colleges, Corpus, Merton, and in later years All Souls, although he was never a college man in the sense of enjoying High Table (he disliked rich food, and would often ask for an omelette), and indeed could be critical of Senior Common Room extravagance. But the wit of his conversation ensured that his colleagues sought out his company. To Corpus and Merton he showed his affection in the dedication of two of his books, *Early Germanic Kingship in England and on the Continent*, and *The Frankish Church*.

Michael's career would be marked by a series of distinctions, notably an Oxford D.Litt. in 1967, his election to the British Academy in 1969, and his CBE in 1982. He would also hold two prestigious chairs, in Manchester and Oxford. It is, however, through his publications that he is best seen. The first of these appeared during his first years at Merton. The earliest article was a piece for the *Manchester Guardian*, on 'Alfred the Great, 849–899, his European setting'. Although a slight piece, it already announced concerns that would recur throughout his work: Alfred would receive attention in *Early Germanic Kingship*. More important was the insistence on seeing English history in a Continental context.

Almost as notable as articles in Michael's output were the book reviews that started appearing in 1947. There were to be over seventy of them, not including the equally numerous short notices. Here, more even than in his books and articles, one can see Michael responding directly to the work of other scholars, at times—as for instance in the review of the Krusch–Levison edition of the *Histories* of Gregory of Tours—offering profound comments on the nature of texts and editions: on other occasions—as in the review of A. H. M. Jones's *The Later Roman Empire*—making crucially important deductions on points of detail. Reviewing for Michael was an activity to be taken very seriously: as Editor of the *English Historical Review* from 1965 to 1974 he was particularly well placed to show how valuable a task it could be. He was also much concerned about the tone of reviews. He would recount to first-time reviewers his own salutary experience, when having reviewed two books of Francis Oppenheimer somewhat critically, he received a letter from the author, a clergyman and amateur scholar, lamenting that the reviews had destroyed his life's work. Thereafter, however much he disagreed with a scholar, or thought the work under par, he chose his words carefully. There is criticism of others in his writings, but it is usually of his peers, and it is expressed in such phrases as 'I can see no reason for', 'I cannot accept that', or 'It is difficult to believe, as some do, that'. Alternatively he will quote a whole sentence, agree with half, and disagree with the remainder. Academic courtesy was something he valued highly.

Michael's first substantial article, 'The Franks and the English in the ninth century: some common historical interests', appeared in 1950. It was a version of a paper delivered at the Anglo-French Historical Conference that had been held in Oxford the previous year. At this stage in his career Michael's Continental contacts were, perhaps understandably, Francophone rather than Germanophone—in later years it would be the reverse. As with the nearly contemporary *Manchester Guardian* article this early piece signalled several later interests. Again England is linked emphatically to the Continent. Equally important is the sense of what matters in a source: 'It does not seem to me to matter very much whether Charlemagne in fact lived as Einhard says he did.' This sense of almost Irenaeic adiaphora was to become a hallmark of Michael's writing. In many a subsequent piece one can find a comment indicating that certain lines of enquiry are a waste of time. Michael was concerned to understand the world as a ninth-century man would have understood it, and here most of all perhaps one can see the influence of Sir Maurice Powicke. If anything, Michael's earlier writings are more sceptical of twentieth-century readings than his later books were to be. Even two years later, in *The Barbarian West*, he was more inclined to accept the notion of epic tradition than he had been in 1950. It is still possible to think that the earlier scepticism was justified.

The matter of how to read a source was yet more central to Michael's subsequent piece on 'The Work of Gregory of Tours in the light of modern research'. The article, the first of two papers he gave to the Royal Historical Society, marks his earliest foray into the sixth century, and more specifically into the writings of Gregory—material which from now on he would make his own. For a while, indeed, he would become first and foremost a scholar of the Merovingian period: only towards the end of his career did his Carolingian interests come to predominate, before being overshadowed by his growing attachment to Bede. This first essay on Gregory showed, once again, just how concerned he was to understand an author on his own terms, and not as a quarry for facts.

The Royal Historical Society lecture was followed up by his first book, *The Barbarian West*. Published in 1952, it was suggested by Sir Maurice Powicke, whose influence is readily acknowledged in the preface. In many respects it is an essay—as Michael himself was happy to acknowledge. It is most certainly not a text-book. Powicke thought of the readership as being 'the man in the train'. It begins with a crucial statement about the Late Roman Empire. This introduction is followed by discussions of the earliest of the barbarian incomers, and then by a chapter on the Lombards and several on the Franks. As a tour of the barbarian world it left much out: whole peoples are omitted: for instance the Burgundians, and more curiously the Anglo-Saxons. In the first two editions Visigothic Spain was ignored, although it was to be the subject of a chapter added in the third edition of 1967. Despite the oddities of the coverage, the emphases of the book were carefully chosen. As in his later writings, Michael deliberately spent time on the Late Roman Empire, for, despite or because of his schooling, he had an acute sense of the extent to which Rome under-pinned what followed: 'The Roman West had become barbarized, and yet it looked back. It remembered Rome.' Just as important as the late Empire itself were some of its leading thinkers: in particular Michael drew attention to Augustine, whose influence on the early Middle Ages he never underestimated. He would teach the Augustine Special Subject in Oxford for much of the 1960s until he felt that it was better left to Peter Brown. As in his previous articles, there is the same emphasis on what the sources say, as opposed to any narrative the historian might want to reconstruct: 'We can never be certain what was happening. But we can often guess what contemporaries thought was happening.' It is an approach that prompts sharp comments on such authors as Cassiodorus and Paul the Deacon.

Yet for all the emphasis on authors, the book shows a concern about social underpinnings, which is an issue that resurfaces regularly through-out Michael's writings, and provides another of the pegs on which his imaginative understanding of the past was pinned. Thus Gregory the Great's concern for the poor attracts surprising emphasis. Equally impor-tant for Michael's own developing interests, *The Barbarian West* contains his first comments on feud, and its relation to written law, Roman or Germanic. The sense that a historian had to understand both the struc-ture of society and the thoughts of its leading writers was one that was central to Michael's approach. It was a sense that would be picked up deliberately in 1983 when a group of his students offered him a Festschrift in which the articles were dedicated to the theme of *Ideal and Reality in Frankish and Anglo-Saxon Society*—a title chosen astutely by Patrick Wormald.

Perhaps not surprisingly, given the chronological scale of the work, other of the themes that would occupy Michael for much of the rest of his career were also signalled in *The Barbarian West*. The issue of kingship among the Franks inevitably attracts attention. The approach is, as ever cautious, indeed more sceptical than it would later be. The notion of sacrality is questioned to a greater extent than in subsequent writings—and justifiably so. More prosaically, the interpretation of the seventh century, or at least the first half, in terms of the rise of the Arnulfings or Carolingians is questioned. With regard to the Carolingian period itself, the notion of a Renaissance, a topic that would come to the fore in work of the late 1970s, is examined and carefully interpreted in its barbarian context. Typical of the approach and the tone is a comment on Charlemagne: 'What a recent scholar has termed his personality as a statesman does not and probably never did exist.'

Alongside his acknowledgement of his debt to Sir Maurice Powicke, in the Preface to *The Barbarian West* Michael also thanked his mother and his wife. The former meticulously typed and retyped his early works. The latter would type later works, as, in time, would his daughter-in-law. There had been a first marriage, to Ethel ('Tibby') Irving, contracted during the war, which ended bitterly after six years, in 1949, following his return to Oxford. His second marriage, to Anne Wakefield, in 1950, was the start of a new and lasting happiness: by the time of the publication of *The Barbarian West* in 1952 they already had one son, Andrew (born 1951), and a second, James, was soon to follow (1953). Both would follow in his footsteps to Corpus: the former as a classicist, the latter as a physicist. Michael's marriage to Anne was of immense importance. He would express his gratitude to her in his books on a number of occasions, and his 1975 collection, *Early Medieval History*, would be a very real present for their silver wedding anniversary.

Meanwhile, in 1952, Michael brought together his interests in the Merovingian and Carolingian periods in a piece on Hincmar and the *Lex Salica*. Published in the *Revue du Droit*, it is unusual, although not unique in Michael's oeuvre, in devoting considerable space to rebutting a single author, Simon Stein. Hincmar's use of history was to be a topic to which Michael returned on numerous occasions throughout his life. Michael's own sense of the importance of manuscripts, which forms the other pole in this 1952 article, also recurs in later work, though with declining frequency. It is, perhaps, more noticeable in his reviews than in his other writings. Michael's sensitivity to manuscripts was something that Donald Bullough singled out in his appreciation, which prefaces *Ideal and Reality*. In time he came to look at manuscripts less often, rarely spending time in Continental libraries, although he talked with wonder at being served coffee in the library of St Gallen, while he still had a ninth-century manuscript open in front of him.

The second half of the 1950s saw a temporary interruption in Michael's otherwise unbroken Oxford career. In 1955 he moved to a chair at Manchester, where he remained until 1961. He felt obliged by the precedent of Tout and Powicke to accept the Manchester chair, but was never fully at his ease there, though there were attractions like the eventual new home in Higher Disley, on the edge of the Peak District, and the academic environment was stimulating. The university library was well stocked: some of its volumes of the Monumenta Germaniae Historica bear annotations which suggest that a scholar of a previous generation, perhaps Tout, had already been pondering Gregory of Tours. There was also the John Rylands Library, in those days not yet taken over by the university. The first fruits of this period, however, bear no mark of the new environment, but rather pick up on concerns that had already been signalled. 'Frankish Gaul' was Michael's own contribution to a volume, *France, Government and Society*, which he edited jointly with John McManners. It returns to the combination of Roman and Germanic, to *Lex Salica*, and also to the issue of feud. Again, Michael saw no mystique in barbarian kingship, stressing that Clovis's genealogy only extended back four generations. This particular scepticism would fade in subsequent work. There are, however, some new emphases in 'Frankish Gaul': Childeric's grave is briefly given prominence, and is read in the same hardheaded way as is Clovis's genealogy, suggesting 'the successful business man as much as the ruthless warrior'. The grave itself would feature again in Michael's works, and would also be presented in a different light. Another issue to make its first appearance was that of migration caused by the Vikings. Overall, however, the emphasis was one that appears nowhere else in Michael's writings in the same terms: 'The vital strand running through Gallo-Frankish society from the fifth to the tenth centuries is seigneurie, lordship.' Exactly what that meant he tried to pin down by envisaging a number of precise relationships.

If 'Frankish Gaul' was still a piece associated with Oxford, the next works were more clearly attached to Manchester. Two were delivered as public lectures at the John Rylands Library, while a third, which had been given at the Anglo-American Conference in London in 1955 was published in the library's *Bulletin*. The London lecture concerned Fredegar, or rather the earliest Fredegar compilation, as preserved in a Paris manuscript of around the year 700. It is a remarkable musing on the author's sources, and on his view of his contemporaries. Looking at the factional fighting which closes the chronicle, Michael saw not Burgundian and Frankish regionalism, but rather a more complex interplay of local interests. This unquestionably marked a deepening understanding of the seventh century.

At the start of the Anglo-American paper Michael announced that the Paris manuscript of Fredegar should be the basis 'of any future edition worth the name'. When it came to editing Fredegar, however, this was not the version that he himself chose to concentrate on. Rather, he edited the fourth book of the eighth-century recension of Fredegar, with its Carolingian additions. Much of the work was done during family holidays in the Scilly Isles, as were many of the book reviews. One may lament the decision not to edit and translate the Paris manuscript: even now historians have to struggle either with the manuscript itself, or with a less than ideal edition prepared by Gabriel Monod in 1885. On the other hand, in terms of the value for the historian, and especially for the student historian there can be no doubt that the choice that Michael made was the right one. And, after all, students constituted the intended audience of the Nelson's Medieval Texts series, in which the volume was published. Essentially he put into the hands of generations of students and scholars a text full of extremely important information, which is by no means easy to understand without the help of a translation. One might even say that the translation is too good: it is sometimes necessary to go back to the Latin to be sure of the implications of Michael's elegant prose. Not everything in the introduction has stood the test of time: the matter of the authorship of the Fredegar chronicle has continued to be debated, and the brave discussion of the language of text has been overtaken by more recent work on Late Latin. But there can be no question that the edition as a whole opened up the seventh-century in Francia in a way that nothing had done before or has done since.

The next piece from this Manchester period was on 'The Bloodfeud of the Franks'. Published in the *Bulletin of the John Rylands Library*, it originated in a lecture given there. The feud was an issue that had already attracted Michael's attention in *The Barbarian West*. In many ways it was central to his imaginative understanding of early medieval society, and Manchester proved an ideal place to develop that understanding. Crucial was the influence of a colleague, Max Gluckman, Professor of Anthropology at the university, whose *Custom and Conflict in Africa* underpinned the approach adopted. It became possible to understand how an early medieval feuding society avoided falling into anarchy: even to understand how the feud and royal legislation were compatible. Michael was not the first historian to approach a social problem from an anthropological point of view. On the other hand 'The Bloodfeud of the Franks' predates the vogue for the use of anthropology by historians, and indeed helped create that vogue. Since 1959 feud itself has come to be more tightly defined: nevertheless, in its depiction of feuding society Michael's article remains the central text.

Between 'The Bloodfeud of the Franks' and the second of his lectures delivered at the Rylands Michael made his only visit to the major Italian gathering of medievalists, the Settimane di Studio at Spoleto. In Donald Bullough's words, 1960 was, 'the last year when both Paul Lehmann and F.-L. Ganshof were there to bring much-needed rigour to the notorious *interventi*'. Ganshof was already a friend, whose help had been acknowledged in footnotes. Michael's contribution, 'Rome and the Early English Church: some questions of transmission', once again set English history firmly in a Continental context. Central to the argument was the role played by the Gaulish Church and the Franks in relations between England and the Papacy. The word 'transmission' in the title is no minor addition. The article also pointed forward to the future development of Michael's work in one crucial respect. For the first time a spotlight was shone on Bede.

Concern with Anglo-Saxon England is again apparent in another piece of the same period also to find an Italian home, in *Studi Medievali*: 'The Graves of Kings'. Archaeology is not a constant in Michael's work. At times his approach to the field was overly dependent on a single archaeologist or a single site. Thus Eduard Salin dominated his understanding of Merovingian burial, while Pierre Demolon's excavation at Brebières was central to his view of settlement. For the archaeology of Anglo-Saxon England he tended to turn in later years almost exclusively to Charles Thomas and Rosemary Cramp. Yet he had astute points to make about the interpretation of archaeological material, and especially about unnecessary assumptions that underlay interpretations. Childeric's grave was something that intrigued him. So too did the burial in Mound One at Sutton Hoo. At the heart of his reading of Sutton Hoo is the question of how kingship was represented, and how that might be reflected in the archaeological record. He was sceptical of the way that the finds at Mound One were thought to be self-evidently royal. In wicked moments he would suggest in conversation that the burial could be that of a Viking, and that the grave goods were loot plundered from the East Anglian kingdom. He particularly liked to joke that, given the problem of whether there had or had not been a body in the mound, the burial could have been that of Ivarr the Boneless. The article's scepticism did not carry the day, and he knew it. He even wavered in his scepticism over the years, but he rightly republished the article in 1975, with an appendix that amounts by no means to a full retraction. Methodologically his approach is as good as any to the problem of how to read Mound One, and its doubts are too rarely heeded.

As a last piece for Manchester there was a final lecture at the Rylands, 'Gothia and Romania'. This was a parting look at the fifth-century Goths, who had played a major role in *The Barbarian West*. On this occasion he was also engaging in debate of the most civilised kind with Edward Thompson. Settlement, particularly as evidenced in place-names, attracts attention. As in his earlier writings Michael was concerned with the nature of the law in the early Germanic kingdoms. At the heart of the article, however, lies the question of the integration of the Germanic incomers. Inevitably this meant a return to the question of religion. Arianism was approached with rather more sophistication than it had been ten years earlier. The question of integration also prompted a greater emphasis on the role of bishops, with Sidonius Apollinaris, Caesarius of Arles and Avitus of Vienne coming to the fore. The first two would receive similar emphasis in later works, notably in the opening chapter of *The Frankish Church*.

In addition to the publication of 'Gothia and Romania', 1961 saw Michael's return to Oxford with his election as senior research fellow at Merton. He had never succeeded in making Manchester a true home, and was deeply grateful to Merton for finding a way to bring him back, though the loss of a professorial salary meant sacrifices. He would take on the additional task of Sub-Warden for two years from 1964. He also accepted the editorship of the *English Historical Review*. His eventual new home (from 1967), Reynolds Farm at Cassington, was a house to which he was devoted, with its medieval origins, and its traces of medieval fishponds. A manor house had been built on the site, *c*.1120, by William Clinton, treasurer to Henry I. In 1317 a licence to crenellate was granted to a resident Montacute. The leasehold was bought by Edmund Reynolds when he lost his fellowship at Michael's old college, Corpus, for popery, and it became a centre for recusants. In short, the house provided the ideal ambience for a medieval historian, and for an essentially private man. Equally important was the garden. At Cassington he could fall into a routine of an early trip into Oxford (driven in by Anne: he himself never learnt to drive), an intensive morning's work, followed ideally by a return home, work in the garden, and a return to scholarship in the evening. His passion for gardening, which he inherited from his father, was by no means confined to Cassington: Michael would take up the post of Garden Master with zeal, first at Merton and subsequently at All Souls.

The return to Oxford was almost immediately marked by the publication of *The Long-Haired Kings*, a collection of a sizeable proportion of his early articles, followed by a new, and extended essay on the Merovingians, from which the book took its name. As the title of the new essay suggests this is not a history of the Franks, but rather of their kingship, and it puts the theme of kingship firmly at the forefront of Michael's thought. It begins, necessarily, with fragmentary information. Michael still showed exemplary caution over sacral kingship, but he did introduce Woden for the first time into the picture—an indication that he was more inclined than he had once been to accept traditional interpretations of Germanic religion. After its opening section 'The Long-Haired Kings' sticks closely to individual texts, reaffirming the view that we may not know what happened, but we can discover what early medieval men thought had happened. The first major witness, inevitably, is Gregory of Tours: 'Like all good historical writing, Gregory's account of the great barbarian [Clovis] carries that kind of conviction from which the reader can never afterwards escape. Clovis is Gregory's Clovis, whether we like it or not . . .' Nevertheless, Gregory is not followed blindly: Clovis's conversion in particular prompted some searching questions and distinctions: indeed we are dealing with 'adhesion, not conversion': Christianity is merely 'an additional cult'. Over the disputed chronology of Clovis's change of religion agnosticism reigns. Less caution is expressed over the christianisation of the Franks as a whole. The picture is one of religious assimilation. Great emphasis is placed on the cultus of local saints, who are presented as the equivalent of demigods. Christ himself appears as a warrior on a gravestone from the Rhineland—an object that would again be the subject of comment in *The Frankish Church*. Assimilation is also seen in law. Cutting to the heart of a debate about the nature of the earliest Frankish code, Michael stated with accustomed concision: 'It is a waste of time to debate how narrowly "Salic", in a tribal sense, this law is.' 'Only lawyers

familiar with the practice of Vulgar Law in the West could have compiled
Lex Salica.'

While the Merovingians of the fifth and sixth centuries had to be seen
through Gregory's eyes, those of the seventh, or at least of its first half,
were observed by Fredegar. Chlothar II and Dagobert I are Fredegar's
Kings as much as Clovis had been Gregory's. A study of Frankish kingship in the second half of the seventh century and the beginning of the
eighth meant a discussion of the *rois fainéants*, and thus a return to more
fragmentary information, not least to charters. As in *The Barbarian West*
Michael was insistent that the rise of the Carolingians should not be ante-
dated. For all their weaknesses the Merovingians continued to have a
function, above all a legal function, until quite late on. Their loss first of
power and then of office had a good deal to do with shifts of allegiance
within the Frankish Church, which occurred over a considerable period
of time, and indeed some great institutions, notably St Denis, remained
loyal until remarkably late. In dealing with the eventual deposition of the
Merovingians Michael, still retaining his scepticism about sacrality, saw
nothing obviously magical about the tonsuring of Childeric II. Nor was the
anointing of Pippin and subsequently of his sons obviously a substitution
of one magic for another: rather it addressed the need to overcome the
oath-breaking involved in deposing a Merovingian.

With the publication of *The Long-Haired Kings* in 1962 Michael made
the Merovingians his own. An indication of where his future thoughts
would lie came in the same year, when he delivered his Jarrow lecture,
'Bede's Europe'. As in 'Rome and the Early English Church', the Anglo-
Saxon was placed firmly in a European context. Again Michael set the
mind of a civilised individual against an often-barbarous social reality.
Equally Bede, like other thinkers whom Michael had considered, was
treated on his own terms: 'what Bede was looking for, and what he found,
was not the unfolding of the story of Byzantine *Imperium*, nor yet, at
least directly, of the Christian *regna gentium* of western Europe: nor even
of the papacy; it was the story of the Sixth Age, the *Ecclesia Dei*'. The
approach, when adopted by other historians in the 1980s, would be
regarded as novel, but it was a lesson that Michael had learned, and had
done so long before 1962.

The Jarrow lecture was followed in print with the one scholarly piece
(on Aidan) written before 1975 not to be reprinted. Close on its heels was
a contribution to Beryl Smalley's Oxford volume on *Trends in Medieval
Political Thought*. 'The *Via Regia* of the Carolingian Age' was essentially
an extension of the subject of kingship, opened up in *The Long-Haired*

Kings. It pursued the matter through the eighth and ninth centuries, looking as usual at individuals, especially Smaragdus, Alcuin and Hincmar, the latter already a familiar figure in Michael's scholarship. It also put considerable stress on the influence of the Bible. The importance of the Old Testament, in particular, had always been acknowledged. Henceforth it was to be emphasised yet more. 'The *Via Regia* of the Carolingian Age' also sketched out much that would dominate the second half of *The Frankish Church*. From now on, indeed, Michael would more often than not be revisiting old concerns, sometimes refining a viewpoint (not always, one might think, for the better), sometimes adding, sometimes recasting, but essentially the boundaries of what interested him had been sketched. Thus 'Charlemagne and England', an article written for the massive four-volume collection, *Karl der Grosse*, showed, once again, the value of placing England in its European context. The theme would be picked up on yet later occasions, in *Early Germanic Kingship in England and on the Continent* and subsequently in *The Frankish Church*.

Even the chapter on the Visigoths which Michael added to *The Barbarian West* in 1967, and which covered new material, is in many respects a chapter on kingship. The same theme is self-evidently central to 'Gregory of Tours and Bede, their views on the personal qualities of kings'. This last article combined a study of kingship, in typical fashion, with an analysis of the attitudes of the two writers. Once again the approach was a forerunner of much that others would see as novel in subsequent decades. The paper was originally written for the 1965 Anglo-French conference held in Dijon, but was reworked for a British Council tour of several German universities in 1967, and was indeed published in *Frühmittelalterliche Studien* in the following year. The tour itself had highlighted the extent to which Michael's approach differed from that of his German peers. Nevertheless his relations with a number of those peers, among them Eugen Ewig and Peter Classen, was to become ever more cordial.

Many of the issues that concerned Michael in the late 1960s reached fruition in the 1971 Ford lectures, *Early Germanic Kingship in England and on the Continent*. His concern, admirably expressed in the preface, was, yet again to balance ideal and reality: to 'relate early medieval thinking about kingship to the practice of kings'. The preface also singles out two colleagues: Walter Ullmann, in Cambridge, whose approach to some of the material covered by Michael was rather different, and Eugen Ewig, the only scholar of the Merovingians among his contemporaries who can fairly be described as his equal. The lectures not only juxtaposed English and Continental material, but they also addressed Continental scholarship with rather unexpected directness. One might note the quiet put-down of a certain type of German scholarship that liked to classify kings 'as *Grosskönige, Heerkönige*, and *Kleinkönige*; which is as much as to say that some kings were more powerful than others. It can mark no distinction between the quality of one king and another, and possibly there was none. I therefore make no use of these classifications.' Back in 1962, in *The Long-Haired Kings* Michael had been rather more taken with such terminology. Unusually, this was a move further away from established scholarly traditions.

The first of the Ford Lectures returned once again to the matter of the Roman background to the Early Middle Ages, although here Michael drew on material that he had not discussed before. Tacitus, perhaps inevitably, is taken as the starting point for a discussion of Roman views of Germanic political structures, despite the acknowledged difficulties of so doing. In his subsequent discussions Michael is often less sceptical than he had been in earlier publications: thus the notion of sacral kingship is treated a good deal more positively, while the Scandinavian pantheon, and Woden in particular, is given more attention than had previously been the case. Perhaps in part this was the result of thinking more across the Merovingian and Carolingian periods, combining material from both. Only the issue of charisma is treated with caution equivalent to that to be found in Michael's earlier work.

With regard to other issues, old themes are combined with new examples. Æthelberht's code invites a reconsideration of the issue of legislation, which Michael had previously dealt with in the context of Merovingian legal codes. Lawgiving is presented, memorably, 'as a royal function; it is something that the emperors, through the Church, can give kings'. Law is to be read more as a guide to royal ideology than to social reality. This approach to the subject would be enormously fruitful, particularly at the hands of Michael's pupil Patrick Wormald. Yet, as before, the ideology of royal legislation is set firmly against a background of feud. Other themes would be picked up subsequently by Michael himself. The discussions of Bede, Charlemagne and Charles the Bald look forward as well as backwards. The kingship of the two Frankish monarchs had already been sketched out in 'The *Via Regia* of the Carolingian Age', and it would be discussed several times more in later work. The discussion of Alfred, meanwhile, harked back to that first *Manchester Guardian* essay.

The same year, 1971, saw one other exploration of the relations between England and the Continent in 'A background to St Boniface's mission'. It was a Festschrift piece for Dorothy Whitelock, whose help Michael had acknowledged on numerous occasions in earlier writings. A study of what the Frankish Church had achieved on its eastern border before the arrival of Boniface, it is more detailed, and more fully annotated, than much of Michael's work. To a large extent it rearranged previous scholarship to redraw the model of the christianisation of the land east of the Rhine. Unlike many of the ideas from this stage in his career, its concerns were largely new ones within Michael's oeuvre, although inevitably his conclusions would come to underpin the discussion of the same issues to be found in *The Frankish Church*.

The 1960s had essentially been years of research. In the early 1970s Michael's administrative commitments became more significant. He became a Delegate to the Oxford University Press in 1971: a task he carried out with great assiduity, as indeed he carried out all tasks to which he committed himself, for eleven years. He was also to be a Vice-President of the Royal Historical Society from 1973 to 1976. There were other developments within Oxford as well. First, Peter Brown's undergraduate teaching, and in particular his lectures on 'Society and the Supernatural from Marcus Aurelius to Mahommed', had created a pool of potential graduate students. As research fellow at Merton, Michael had not been required to teach undergraduates, although he sometimes did. Nor had he gathered many research students, although there were a few: early on in his career, notably Donald Bullough, and in the late 1960s, Patrick Wormald. Now there was something like a queue of students wishing to work on the Early Middle Ages, whose knowledge of Greek (like that of Michael himself) was such as to discourage them from working on Byzantium. To these he became the obvious supervisor—and an increasing number of postgraduates visited his rooms, full of cigar smoke, first in Merton and then in All Souls. It was not a role that he always relished, although on the whole those students who demanded most of him got most in return—overseas students, who were less in awe of the great man than were Oxford graduates, could be the most demanding. At the same time Michael was acutely aware that some research students of other universities were in difficulties, and he provided staunch support. Indeed, when called upon he could be the most supportive of mentors, both to his own students and to those of others.

The second factor that altered matters was the Chichele Chair of Modern History. When Sir Richard Southern retired from the Chair in 1969, Michael professed no interest in succeeding to it, and supported the claims of his old tutor, Geoffrey Barraclough. In 1972 he was offered, but turned down the Regius Chair in Cambridge. With the sudden retirement of Geoffrey Barraclough in 1973, however, he found himself at All Souls. As Chichele Professor Michael was not allowed to teach undergraduates, but, running a successful seminar, he was well-placed to continue and increase his supervision of research students. One final side-effect of taking up the Chichele Chair was that Michael gave up being editor of the *English Historical Review*, a post he had held since 1965.

Immediately before taking up the Chichele Chair Michael delivered the Birkbeck lectures at Trinity College, Cambridge, on the Merovingian Church—a set of lectures that were to become the first chapters of *The Frankish Church*. At least in their published form, they revisit much that Michael had already explored, although the concern is now primarily the Church rather than kings or kingship. Beginnings are grounded firmly in the Gallo-Roman Church, or rather, as he noted, Churches—in a comment that presaged a key point of Peter Brown's subsequent elaboration of the notion of 'microchristendoms'. Community indeed is a major issue in the Merovingian chapters of *The Frankish Church*. The christianisation of the countryside (so far as it went) is considered, as (and this time following Peter Brown) is the cult of relics. Against this is set Frankish paganism. Here Michael puts yet more stress on Woden than he had in previous writings, though he does not stop to justify this new emphasis. At the same time he asks starkly, and startlingly, whether Gregory of Tours, when talking of Saturn, Jupiter, Mars, Mercury should not be taken at face value. Had the Franks in their long period of residence on the borders of the Empire taken over the Roman gods? Childeric's grave is described in somewhat different terms than it had been on previous occasions: in place of 'the successful business man' we are introduced to 'a good pagan, to whom the gods have been kind'. In general the Merovingians appear as rather more sacral than they have done in earlier writings. Gregory of Tours gets perhaps the most far-reaching and nuanced appraisal that Michael ever gave him. This is certainly true of Merovingian monasticism, and the saints of the sixth and seventh centuries. Rather more of a slog is the discussion of Church councils in the Merovingian period, whereas relations with the papacy, a theme that Michael had touched on before, are eloquently treated.

The Birkbeck lectures almost mark a farewell to Michael's interests in the Merovingian period. *The Vikings in Francia* look forward. In 1971 he had already written an obituary for Frank Stenton: now in 1974 he honoured his memory with a lecture. The Vikings had made fitful appearances beforehand in discussions of Charles the Bald and Alfred, and always Michael had stressed their brutality. Now he stressed their impact on society, and in particular on monastic communities forced to migrate across France—a picture not everyone would agree with. The interpretation stems naturally from Michael's concern with authors and how they saw the world. It also takes much from his growing emphasis on paganism, and particularly on Woden, an interest that had been stimulated by the work of his student Alf Smyth. Unusually, but not uniquely among Michael's works the Stenton Lecture is a direct response to current trends in scholarship, which are mockingly described as portraying the Vikings as 'long-haired tourists who occasionally roughed up the natives'. The critique was addressed not to Michael's own pupil, Peter Sawyer, the leading English proponent of the revisionist school, but to the Belgian scholar, Albert D'Haenens. Despite the joke about tourists, the disagreement is, as ever, courteously stated.

Envisaging the brutality of early medieval life is central to much of Michael's work—which may seem strange given his horror of blood, stemming perhaps from his wartime experiences. Those experiences, on the other hand, may in part explain the need to understand the violence. The thought-world of the best of those who lived at the time, their 'nobility of mind' as he called it, is central to much of the rest of his oeuvre. In his inaugural lecture as Chichele Professor, 'Early Medieval History', he balanced the two perhaps better than in any other piece he wrote. As in the Birkbeck lectures he presents the urban communities surrounding bishops, but then moves out to the countryside (admittedly using the somewhat misleading excavation of Brebières), to communities of monks, and communities of Jews, a group which would appear more in his last works. Against this background he set a cluster of figures, none of them new to his work, but all of them reimagined: Gregory of Tours, Gregory the Great, Isidore, Julian of Toledo, before finally reaching the stars of the Carolingian Renaissance.

Brutality is part of the theme of the Prothero lecture delivered to the Royal Historical Society during the same year: 'War and Peace in the Early Middle Ages'. That Germanic kings were warleaders had never been far from Michael's assessment of kings. And in that feud was a related issue, war had often been on the near-horizon of his thought. As so often he began in Late Rome, in this instance the *De Rebus Bellicis*, adding the Bible, and then the warrior ideas of the Germanic peoples, though he was careful not to make them mere warriors rather than agriculturalists. From this beginning he looked at what might constitute an acceptable, even just, war. As ever the conclusions were nuanced, and yet they were also surprising: 'the chances of a peaceful life in the year 900 were somewhat less than in the year 500. The investment in war was greater, and its reach commonly more extensive . . . Warfare had been canalized in directions suitable to the Church, but not very efficiently.' No scholar who has specialised in the history of early medieval warfare has been more thoughtful or convincing.

The year 1976 saw a move back to noble minds: two of them, one early medieval, the other Victorian, Bede and Plummer, for the Bede centenary conference. Plummer clearly delighted Michael, not least because the two of them shared a college: but he also liked the man's mind. Plummer's Bede, a nineteenth-century divine, is carefully exposed. Equally important, more so in terms of work yet to be done, Michael sketched out what a good commentary on Bede would be like. Whether or not he already had his eye on supplying a companion volume to the Colgrave and Mynors edition of Bede's *Ecclesiastical History*, he indicated what he thought should be there. In its own way as telling was the publication history of the article itself, which appeared in the collection *Early Medieval History* before it appeared in the proceedings of the Durham conference, so that the collection might be a silver wedding anniversary present: family was at least as important as scholarship.

To Bede Michael was to return, but first there were two studies of the ninth century, and then the Carolingian half of *The Frankish Church*. First, in 1978, came the Raleigh Lecture to the British Academy on Charles the Bald, 'A Carolingian Renaissance Prince'. Michael had been elected to the Academy in 1969, and from 1977 to 1981 he was to serve as its Publications Secretary. The title of his lecture was no whim: Michael was convinced that Renaissance was an appropriate word. The detail of the argument drew largely from Rosamond McKitterick's work on the library of Charles the Bald: the overall picture returns to Michael's concerns with kingship. Out of the evidence for the king's books emerges a royal patron attempting to live up to a series of models, largely Biblical, presented to him by his clergy: Charles had tried to copy the models forced on him: Solomon, David, Constantine, Theodosius, Charlemagne. 'He was no mere warband leader. Still less was he a kind of monk or bishop. His models lay more in the Old Testament than the New.'

The next year, 1979, somewhat surprisingly, given his dislike of travelling, Michael went to Berkeley as Distinguished Visiting Professor. From there he was able to travel down to Stanford to deliver the Kates lecture, which was in fact a repeat of 'A Carolingian Renaissance Prince: Charles the Bald'. He found the visit to the United States enjoyable, but was not sure exactly what he should be doing there, and he badly missed his house at Cassington.

Two years later, in 1981, he co-edited and contributed to a Festschrift to mark the seventieth birthday of Sir Richard Southern, his predecessor but one in the Chichele Chair, who was now retiring as President of St John's College. Michael's topic was again ninth-century: 'History in the mind of archbishop Hincmar'. He had already touched on the subject nearly thirty years previously in his 'Archbishop Hincmar and the authorship of *Lex Salica*'. His emphasis on the importance of Hincmar's period at St Denis, and the influence of Hilduin, suggests that the interest may have begun even earlier, in the Lothian Prize essay of 1938. What he learnt about history from Hilduin, Hincmar used in later life, and not just in his section of the Annals of St Bertin, but through much of his writing, culminating in his *Vita Remigii*. Here, and later in *The Frankish Church*, this hagiographical piece is singled out as the work that the archbishop himself regarded most highly.

The summation of much of this work came with the publication in 1983 of *The Frankish Church*. It was Michael's longest work, and like his *Early Germanic Kingship* it was dedicated to a college: this time Merton. It had been commissioned by Henry and Owen Chadwick, who had wanted something wider, on the early medieval Church in general, but Michael had set limits to what he was prepared to cover. In some ways even the title *The Frankish Church* is a misnomer, for, as the preface announces, 'I have attempted no more than a consideration of those aspects of it that have interested me over the years'. And, quoting Amalarius of Metz, *scripsi quod sensi*. This is as much as to say that there are gaps. It is certainly not a comprehensive history of the Merovingian and Carolingian Churches (though the first is more evenly covered than the second), because large areas of Carolingian Europe get little or no consideration. Eight pages on the ninth-century missions to the pagans will strike many as too few, although the eighth-century missions fare rather better. These were, in any case, a topic that had already engaged Michael in his contribution to Dorothy Whitelock's Festschrift, and in his commentary on Bede's account of Willibrord they would engage him again later. But having said all that, the work is perhaps rather closer to a text-book than Michael would have admitted. It is built up of small sections, thumbnail sketches of individuals or of individual councils, the former perhaps getting more sensitive treatment: such sketches are indeed the building blocks of much of Michael's writing, but in a book of this length the structure is more apparent than elsewhere. It is actually a book to which one can turn to find a concise and sharp account on, for instance, Adoptionism or of the monk Gottschalk. In certain ways it is more of a handbook than it purports to be.

The first part of the book, devoted to the Merovingian Church, is essentially made up of the Birkbeck lectures of 1973–4. Thereafter *The Frankish Church* turns briefly to the reign of Pippin III, and then more substantially to those of Charlemagne, Louis the Pious and Charles the Bald. The first and the last of these three had already been the object of much study in Michael's oeuvre, Louis the Pious less so. Considerably less space is given to the older sons of Louis, and their descendants. The scale and the range of the book means that in its detail it far exceeds any of Michael's earlier works, yet the themes are often those sketched out elsewhere, and one of the chapters (on Charles the Bald) is essentially (and admittedly) a revised version of an earlier article. Indeed, while the book is called *The Frankish Church* it also has much to say about kingship. Yet, beyond the sketches of individuals who had previously not been studied in depth by Michael (Theodulf, Lupus of Ferrières, Hraban Maur, Walahfrid Strabo and Amalar to name only those subject to the most extensive treatment), one or two themes come to the fore more dramatically than in earlier work. As in the inaugural lecture a spotlight is shone on the Jews, examining them as a group both within society and at the same time challenging it. Completely new is a discussion of marriage, a difficult and fragmented subject, which concludes with the argument that Carolingians move beyond secular roots of marriage to a Christian dimension where it was good in itself. It is a discussion to which Michael refers on a number of occasions in his commentary on Bede.

The Frankish Church appeared in 1983, the year of Michael's retirement from the Chichele Chair, although he was to remain a Professor Emeritus. He was succeeded by Karl Leyser, who together with Peter Ganz was one of those friends to whom he had turned for advice on aspects of the Carolingian Renaissance. As a retirement project he had set himself a commentary on Bede's *Ecclesiastical History*, which had been commissioned by Oxford University Press. The Bede commentary was the last of Michael's work to be published, and indeed was published posthumously. It was effectively complete at the time of his death on 3 November 1985, awaiting a final revision and an introduction. It had been intended that Thomas Charles-Edwards should see it through the press were Michael to die between the completion of the commentary and its publication. There was, necessarily, some discussion as to whether it was complete enough to be published, but fortunately it was agreed, not least by his family, that it should be. In many respects commentary was the ideal form for the ruminative consideration of texts that had become increasingly central to Michael's approach. In place of an introduction 'Bede and Plummer' was added to the commentary, as were some addenda. 'Bede and Plummer' does indeed sketch out many of the issues which Michael chose to emphasise—although of course he might well have intended a very different kind of introduction, drawing together his observations on the structure of Bede's works and the issues which concerned him.

In 'Bede and Plummer' among a number of gaps he had noted in Plummer's commentary was an awareness of Bede's Eusebian sense of history, that is the extent to which he wrote an Ecclesiastical History which was concerned with salvation. So too he had commented on the lack of any reference to Gregory of Tours, that is to the Continental dimension of Bede's world, something already raised in the Jarrow lecture. These issues, of course, are much to the fore in Michael's own commentary. Time and again he draws attention to Frankish and other parallels. At times the parallels are exuberant: for instance one is drawn between the private churches described by Bede and surviving Visigothic examples, which one might guess is a reflection of a holiday he and Anne had spent visiting such monuments with his sometime pupils Roger Collins and Judith McClure. As frequent are references to the ecclesiastical nature of Bede's history. He is insistent that it is an ecclesiastical history not a history of the English Church. He stresses the extent to which Bede left unclear or omitted altogether issues that were irrelevant to his purpose. And he draws attention to the extent to which passages in Bede can be 'highly contrived'. It is an attitude towards sources that is present throughout his works—an interest in the author's purpose, rather than in a text as a store-house of fact.

The commentary is also a work which more than most of what Michael wrote reveals the range of his reading. He was not on the whole a scholar who used footnotes, sometimes admittedly because they were not required of him. By its very nature a commentary required references. What is interesting in the commentary on Bede is how much of the reference is to recent work, indeed how much is to work which had formed part of the Festschrift which had been offered to him by his pupils in 1983. Yet the commentary was also something close to a labour of love. His one-time student Michael Wood described what was to be the last meeting with his old supervisor, who remarked that he dreamed of Bede: 'He speaks to me. I feel as if I know him.' Michael was certainly committed to his task, and in many ways it suited his style more than anything else that he attempted. He could ruminate on a single mind that he found congenial.

In the preface to the Festschrift presented to Michael in 1983 Donald Bullough tried to set his old supervisor in context. His place in the tradition of Bedan scholarship is not difficult to define, and not just because of Plummer: Michael himself, in his commentary, cites several ecclesiastical historians, rather more than Anglo-Saxonists, who approached Bede in ways to which he could relate. More generally, with regard to Old English legal history he looked back to Maitland, and not just because he revered his scholarship. He regarded Maitland's style as a touchstone, and research students would be sent to read and reread *Domesday Book and Beyond* to improve their style. His own writings are all distinguished by their elegance. At times the concision leaves some ambiguity. Indeed there are passages when it is possible to wonder quite how he is interpreting the writings in front of him. It is possible to read Michael in more ways than one, and, even on rereading him, to find one's own 'new' ideas prefigured in what he wrote.

With regard to European history he is rather harder to place. On the Continent there were scholars whom he had read extensively—indeed his reviews show just how extensive that reading was. On some scholars, among them Otto Höfler, he paused for rather longer than one would now. Others, for instance Reinhard Wenskus, whom he read in a rather different way than scholars have subsequently, he was among the first to recognise. To some, notably Peter Classen and Eugen Ewig, he was deeply attached. Perhaps the latter comes closest to Michael in range and interest. Of an older generation of English scholars there were Sir Samuel Dill, O. M. Dalton and Christopher Dawson (whose *Making of Europe* was to a large extent superseded by *The Barbarian West*, although it continued to be read on the Continent, and is still worth some time). None of them looked at the Franks as he did.

There were scholars of his own generation working in England who did look across the Channel: Philip Grierson (who is frequently thanked in footnotes) and Walter Ullmann (who interpreted the Early Middle Ages rather differently) to name two. But there was no one with his precise range of interest. Indeed, to a large extent he created a subject, although it should be said that his own canvas was quite limited. He returned again and again to the same themes, constantly making subtle adjustments. In the next generation matters would be different, but that was because he and to a lesser extent Walter Ullmann had created a new tradition of early medieval scholarship in England. It has rightly been said of the two of them, 'If you seek their monument, look about you! Most of the earlier medieval historians currently working in this country are their intellectual children and grandchildren. Their influence nationally and internationally was and still is large.' Indeed, the expansion of early medieval studies in Britain has been closely associated with Michael's students. Not that he established a school, although his students learnt much from his reading of texts. To say that the Early Middle Ages look different as a result of his work is a truism. More than any other scholar he insisted that the period be taken on its own terms: brutal, yet peopled with extraordinary individuals who thought differently from us, but whose minds we could know.

IAN WOOD
University of Leeds

Note. I am profoundly grateful to Professor Andrew Wallace-Hadrill and to Mrs Anne Wallace-Hadrill for their advice and for the information they provided.

W. S. WATT

William Smith Watt
1913–2002

W. S. WATT, known to his friends as Bill, was one of the leading Latin scholars of his time. His long and energetic life makes an impressive story. To look back at it prompts reflection on the changing patterns of education and scholarship in the twentieth century.

Watt was born on 20 June 1913, the son of John Watt and his wife Agnes (née Smith). His birthplace was a moorland farm at Harthill, to the east of Glasgow, where his father was the tenant, and his mother also came of farming stock; he was always grateful to his parents for the support they gave him, but in later life showed no wish to revisit the landscape of his youth. After the local primary school he proceeded to Airdrie Academy where he was dux in 1929; as in other Scottish schools, the Latin name was given to the best scholar. Here he received a solid grounding in classics, a subject suited to stretch clever boys and girls before they are experienced enough to write original essays; such an education could then be provided in Scotland not just in the big cities but in the smaller towns, whose academies and high schools sometimes figure in the memoirs of the British Academy. Shortly before his sixteenth birthday he entered the bursary competition at Glasgow University on a trial run, and to his surprise (for he was always cautious as well as ambitious) came second out of 438 candidates. In the biographical notes that he wrote sixty years later he recorded that his bursary enabled him to take a university course without causing undue financial hardship to his parents; the fact that he could remember the exact sum (£40 for four years) shows how much he depended on the money.

Proceedings of the British Academy, **124**, 359–372. © The British Academy 2004.

In October 1929 he entered Glasgow University; he would leave home at 7.20 in the morning, walk three and a half miles to the station, and arrive in time for the 9 o'clock lecture. In each of his four years he came first in both Humanity and Greek: Humanity was the old name for Latin in the Scottish universities, a reminder of the subject's traditional place in Scottish education. Among Watt's teachers were R. G. Austin, later best known for his commentaries on Virgil, A. W. Gomme, the future commentator on Thucydides, H. D. F. Kitto, later to write books on Greek tragedy, R. G. Nisbet (the father of the present writer), expert in Latin syntax and idiom and the future commentator on Cicero's *De Domo*, and W. Rennie, part-editor of the Oxford text of Demosthenes and commentator on the *Acharnians* of Aristophanes; C. J. Fordyce, the future commentator on Catullus, who had been educated in the tradition that Watt was following, did not return to Glasgow till 1934. Watt formed a particular rapport with Austin, who was then only about thirty; his humane scholarship was less austere than Watt's, but he had a gift for encouraging talents different from his own (as he showed later when Professor of Latin at Cardiff and Liverpool). A life-long friendship developed, and in his commentary on Cicero's *Pro Caelio* (3rd edn., 1960) Austin pays tribute to Watt's 'unerring finger'.

It was the ambition of the best classical students at Glasgow (provided they were men) to win the Snell Exhibition to Balliol College, Oxford. This had been founded by John Snell[1] in 1679 with the intention that his beneficiaries should return to Scotland and preach according to the forms of the Episcopalian Church, but after protracted litigation the House of Lords permitted a laxer interpretation of the testator's wishes. The interaction of Glasgow and Oxford proved fruitful: Snell's award-holders have included Adam Smith (1740), who complained that there was too much praying at Balliol, J. G. Lockhart (1809), Scott's son-in-law and biographer, W. Y. Sellar (1842), Lewis Campbell (1850), D. B. Monro (1854), Edward Caird (1860), Andrew Lang (1864), W. P. Ker (1874), W. M. Lindsay (1877), C. J. Fordyce (1920), G. Highet (1929), R. Browning (1935), R. G. M. Nisbet (1947), F. Cairns (1961), D. N. MacCormick (1963). At Austin's suggestion Watt sat the examination in December 1931 to gain experience for the following year, but once again surprised himself, though not anybody else, by winning the award. The emoluments

---

[1] See W. Innes Addison, *The Snell Exhibitions* (Glasgow, 1901); L. Stones, 'The Life and Career of John Snell (*c*.1629–1679)', *Stair Society, Miscellany*, 2 (1984), 148–220; John Jones, *Balliol College, a History: 1263–1939* (Oxford, 1988), pp. 125–7.

(£100 for four years) were doubled by the Newlands scholarship; Watt also won the Logan medal (for the most distinguished graduate of the year in Arts) and the Ferguson scholarship[2] in classics (open to the graduates of all four Scottish universities and worth £110 for two years). These awards, which he dutifully remembered, were not just badges of honour but were to make all the difference between bare subsistence and what he called reasonable comfort.

At that time research degrees played little part in classics at Oxford, so graduates from Scotland and elsewhere undertook another undergraduate course, Classical Moderations ('Mods') on language and literature for the first five terms, and Literae Humaniores ('Greats') on philosophy and ancient history for seven terms. Mods might seem repetitive for a graduate, but Greats did not include literature till some forty years later. Watt was still only twenty, and he had studied classics for a shorter time than the products of some English schools. The course demanded a precise knowledge of Latin and Greek: thus candidates were expected to read all forty-eight books of Homer with great accuracy, so that they could remember most of the words for the rest of their lives, but not to write significant essays on the interesting problems raised. In one respect Mods went beyond anything offered at Glasgow: the questions set on some of the prepared books dealt predominantly with textual criticism. Candidates were presented with short extracts or 'gobbets' from these authors, and invited to consider the various readings with arguments for and against; to conclude that the crux was insoluble and deserving of the obelus might be taken as a sign of precocious perspicacity. The direction of scholars' studies depends on early influences more than one likes to admit, and all his life Watt was to be superb at doing gobbets, though as time went on he hit the nail on the head more expeditiously than was thought necessary in Mods.

Besides set books the staple of the Mods course was composition in Latin and Greek, not just in prose as at Glasgow, but if a candidate wished it in verse as well. Those who aspired to an academic career competed for the University scholarships, the Hertford for Latin only (which Watt won in 1935), the Craven and Ireland for Latin and Greek combined (which he won in 1934 and 1935). These examinations included quite difficult unseens and a 'Critical Paper' where essays and gobbets were set on authors outside the syllabus; old papers look fairly formidable, but as usual much depended on a tutor's understanding of what was likely to be

[2] See William Douglas, *The Ferguson Scholars 1861–1955* (Glasgow, 1956), pp. 322–3.

asked. But greater emphasis was put on composition, not just the standard exercises in prose and verse but the curiously named 'Taste Paper', where passages were set for translation into the individual style of perhaps Theocritus or Lucretius. This may seem frivolous dilettantism to many in more recent times, but it too was important for Watt's later output. Though expert textual critics are inevitably few, Britain in the last century produced more than Germany, and this sensitivity to the finer shades of language seems to have something to do with the many hours spent on proses and verses.

After his first in Mods Watt proceeded to Greats, where he was more interested in ancient history than in philosophy. In January 1937, a few months before his final examination, he was summoned to see the Master of Balliol, A. D. Lindsay (another Glasgow man); when Watt entered his study the Master looked up and said 'Ah, Watt, the fellows have been discussing arrangements for teaching Mods after Cyril Bailey retires: would you like the job?' Appointments were sometimes made like that in those distant days, without research degrees or evidence of publication, without testimonials or interviews, without interference from professors or boards, without so-called 'lecturettes' to committees of non-specialists. The procedure encouraged inbreeding, but colleges liked to appoint young scholars who could relate to undergraduates and who understood the system; suitable 'Mods dons' were hard to find, as some of the best classicists were lost to philosophy or ancient history, and colleges had every incentive to choose somebody who would be effective. After this vote of confidence Watt felt that he simply had to get a first, so he worked harder than ever; in view of the high standards expected and the quirks of an archaic marking system, even the best scholars could not allow themselves leisure to ruminate. But needless to say he got his first in Greats.

Watt had a gap year before he took up his fellowship, and it was originally planned that he should go to Munich to work on the *Thesaurus Linguae Latinae*, the indispensable lexicon that was begun in 1900 and is not yet complete. This kind of scholarship would have suited him well as he was exceptionally clear-headed and decisive: when lexicographers are confronted with an unfamiliar passage they must make their minds up without agonising too much about the possible fuzziness of language. At this juncture he received a letter from William Rennie, the Professor of Greek at Glasgow: Gomme had obtained a Leverhulme award to work on Thucydides, and Watt was invited to take his place as a lecturer for a year. He accepted with relief, for 1937 was not the best of times to go to Munich.

Watt enjoyed his return to Glasgow, where he taught Greek history as well as Greek; from his salary of £500, twice the usual rate for beginners, he was able to buy a house for his parents. He took up his fellowship at Balliol on 1 October 1938, two days after the signing of the Munich agreement and four weeks before the Oxford by-election in which A. D. Lindsay lost to Quintin Hogg. In 1938–9 he shared the Mods teaching with Cyril Bailey, well-known for his commentaries on Epicurus and later Lucretius, in 1939–40 with Roger Mynors, later to be Professor of Latin at Cambridge and then Oxford; both tutors taught both ancient languages, as was the custom before specialisation became so extreme. Their styles were complementary: while Mynors introduced his pupils to topics remote from the syllabus, Watt thought that their interests would be best served by concentration on the needs of the examination. In 1940 Mynors left for a post at the Treasury; Watt was rejected for military service because of a defective eye and continued teaching till 1941. In the meantime he was appointed keeper of the College minutes, a duty which he discharged with typical efficiency till he left Balliol; the orderliness of his mind was reflected in the tidiness of his desk, for he was never one of those scholars whose thoughts sprout from a litter of half-read offprints and half-written lectures. He was also treasurer of the Oxford Basque Children's Committee, which supported a few of the victims of the Spanish civil war; it was characteristic that he made himself useful in this practical but unostentatious way.

In May 1941 Watt joined the Inter-Services Topographical Department, then based in Oxford, as a temporary civilian officer, Admiralty; the department had been set up by Admiral J. H. Godfrey,[3] the Director of Naval Intelligence, who had been appalled by the lack of geographical information in the bungled Norwegian campaign in the spring of 1940. It was the duty of the civilian officer to coordinate and edit the data about beaches, roads, and possible airfields collected by the representatives of the three services. Watt commonly worked a twelve-hour day, and sometimes into the night as well when information was needed for plans that were not necessarily executed (perhaps they included some of Churchill's rasher inspirations). Classical scholars were thought suitable for such research as they were used to collating defective scraps of evidence, their pedantic exactitude was seen to be worthwhile when lives were at stake, and they had a reputation at that time for writing concisely and clearly;

---

[3] See Patrick Beesly, *Very Special Admiral: the Life of Admiral J. H. Godfrey* (London, 1980), p. 205.

among Watt's colleagues were such scholars as W. S. Barrett (see above, pp. 25–36), F. H. Sandbach, and A. F. Wells. Watt played a particular part in the preparation for the landings in North Africa in November 1942 ('Operation Torch'); Admiral Sir Andrew Cunningham, the naval commander, and General Eisenhower, the supreme commander, expressed their appreciation of the department's work, and Admiral Godfrey minuted to the Board of Admiralty 'I doubt if a commander of an operation has ever before been given his intelligence in so complete and so legible a form'. Later he gave Watt a testimonial saying that he possessed 'remarkable practical and intellectual ability and phenomenal staying power', qualities that his later pupils and colleagues will recognise.

In July 1944 Watt married Dorothea (Thea), daughter of R. J. Codrington Smith, the area manager of Cable and Wireless in Cyprus. She was then a junior commander in the ATS and attached to the Inter-Services Topographical Department; they first met when she disturbed him by drilling her young women outside his window. Their happy marriage was to sustain him for fifty-eight years.

In 1945 Watt resumed his position as a tutor at Balliol; in the over-crowded conditions of the post-war period he kept himself very busy, teaching up to twenty-five hours a week, sometimes even after dinner; but his load was lightened in 1948 with the appointment of a second classical tutor, K. J. Dover. Watt based his teaching on the correction of compositions and the return of 'collections' (i.e. College test-papers); essays played little part, but that was a consequence of the way the subject was examined, and at that time there were far fewer books and articles in English than was later the case. Watt was an excellent tutor, who not only instilled some of the respect for accuracy on which all deeper understanding must depend, but provided the unobtrusive encouragement that counts for more than memorable observations; Balliol had been a competitive college since the Masterships of Jenkyns and Jowett, and Watt's own career made him conscious that success in examinations might be decisive in the lives of others. He recorded with satisfaction that in the six years from 1947 to 1952 half his pupils obtained firsts in Mods; he even compiled a table showing the proportion of firsts awarded in all subjects in all colleges, a precursor of the 'Norrington Tables' that were to receive even greater attention in the quality press than prowess on the river. He could not have foreseen the enthusiasm of later politicians and educationists for weighing the imponderable and comparing the incommensurate.

Tutoring and examining (always a burden in Oxford) were so labour-intensive that Watt had relatively little time for his own researches.

Eduard Fraenkel, the Corpus Professor of Latin since 1935, had brought to Oxford some of the breadth of approach that at the beginning of the century characterised the Berlin of Wilamowitz, and through his lectures and seminars he exercised a profound influence on both 'senior members' and the best undergraduates. But he was too self-centred to be good at fostering other people's researches, and though Watt was highly regarded by him, like others he felt constricted by so dominating a presence. Nowadays, when there is pressure on young scholars to publish too much too early, it is hard to understand a time when the prevailing ethos might induce writer's block. Even so, Watt was able to prepare expert lectures on Cicero's letters; like those of his friend W. S. Barrett on Euripides, they might seem too detailed to some, but to others, and not just those who were to become professional classicists, they conveyed something of the ideals of scholarship.

In 1952 Watt was appointed Regius Professor of Humanity in the University of Aberdeen, a chair founded in 1505. At that time he had published only two short notes and a few reviews, but good Latin scholars were then hard to find, and publication was not thought important when somebody was known to be outstanding. Fraenkel wrote of him 'He is possessed of unflagging energy and a capacity for sustained hard work which I believe is uncommon. He is a born grammarian, and I have to think twice before I query any statement of his on points of language. Owing to the perfect lucidity of his mind and his severe self-discipline he is also an excellent textual critic.' That is a just assessment, and as an undergraduate I was impressed to see Fraenkel back off at one of his seminars when Watt had quietly pronounced. Fraenkel added 'If he perhaps tends every now and then to be somewhat too rational, that is, in a young man, a fault in the right direction, which will probably correct itself as he gains in experience.' There was something in this qualification, but Watt never became any less rational.

Watt's main scholarly aim at this time was to develop his work on Cicero's letters. In view of the inadequacy of L. C. Purser's Oxford text he had proposed to the University Press that he should re-edit the whole corpus, and this offer was accepted. The textual criticism of the letters is unusually difficult: the manuscripts are often unreliable, the private letters show the informality and jerkiness characteristic of the genre, prose-rhythm seldom provides the control that we find elsewhere in Cicero, there are learned literary jokes and references to obscure political and financial transactions, the scraps of Greek are persistently corrupted. The Swedish editor Sjögren had built on the work of C. Lehmann to present a convincing classification of the manuscripts, but he was much too ready to accept the transmitted reading. Watt's edition of the letters to Cicero's brother Quintus and to M. Brutus the tyrannicide was published in 1958 and set new standards of accuracy and acuteness, though only those who have studied the problems in detail will see how much thought and labour such a book required. He persuaded the Press to let him record where conjectures were first published; this is useful when a scholar gives reasons for his proposal, and it is right that we should be reminded of the contributions of the sixteenth century to the correction of the text. But for Watt precision in such matters was a duty in itself, and when I called Burman 'Burmann' he was good enough to let me know.

Watt next proceeded to the much bigger collection of Cicero's letters *Ad Atticum*. Because of his administrative responsibilities he knew that his progress was likely to be slow; so he proposed a collaboration with D. R. Shackleton Bailey, then a fellow of Jesus College, Cambridge, who had published some notable emendations to the text. The partnership failed to prosper, as both parties held firm opinions, so it was agreed that Watt should edit books 1–8 and his colleague books 9–16. When Shackleton Bailey produced a volume of *adversaria* on the subject,[4] Watt reviewed it.[5] Though some of his criticisms were justified, as was inevitable with so difficult a text, the tone of the whole was unduly combative, but this was a long-standing tradition with classical reviewers that sometimes surprises their colleagues in other disciplines. As a result the two leading experts in the field found themselves at loggerheads, though later they were to refer to each other's work with proper respect.

In 1965 Watt published his Oxford text of Cicero, *Ad Atticum* 1–8, and between 1965 and 1970 Shackleton Bailey produced in seven volumes his Cambridge edition of all sixteen books; this included a commentary that was strong on historical as well as textual details, and was made more accessible by an elegant translation. Watt was unlucky to compete with this more elaborate work: a commentary would have given greater scope for his talents than a text, for he had an impressive grasp of Latin idiom (he described the *Lateinische Grammatik* of Hofmann and Szantyr as an exciting book), he was good at noticing and coordinating relevant evidence, and Roman political history was already one of his interests. In fact both editions are indispensable, as pointed out in a judicious review

---

[4] *Towards a Text of Cicero*, Ad Atticum, Transactions of the Cambridge Philological Society, 10 (Cambridge, 1960).
[5] *Journal of Roman Studies*, 50 (1960), 278–9.

by F. R. D. Goodyear,[6] who compared Watt's text with the first volume of Shackleton Bailey. He concluded that while Watt made some good conjectures Shackleton Bailey was his superior in this respect, but that Watt had the advantage in the fullness and precision of his *apparatus criticus*.

For most of his twenty-seven years as a professor at Aberdeen Watt's talent for administration led to many calls on his time. From 1954 to 1959 he was the energetic curator of the University Library; he was resolute in the defence of his territory when he saw a point of principle, and foiled the attempt of a well-known scientific colleague to transfer the books on his subject to his own department. From 1963 to 1966 he was Dean of the Faculty of Arts, and played a major part in the great expansion of numbers that followed the Robbins report. From 1966 to 1977 he was a member of the University Court, and one of his successors noted that 'his incisive mind had obviously been applied to produce practical solutions to problems';[7] from 1969 to 1972 he was Vice-Principal of the University. He served on central bodies concerned with the training of teachers and university admissions. He was President of the Classical Association of Scotland from 1983 to 1988, and for a number of years was a member of the executive council of the Scottish National Dictionary Association. When he was convenor of the Studies Committee of Aberdeen University he set in motion the publication of the important Greig-Duncan collection of folk-songs,[8] which contains over three thousand texts and tunes; happily he was able to see the last of the eight volumes shortly before his death.

Watt became an excellent lecturer who made the right answer very clear even to the less experienced. He gave thought to the future of his best honours students, some of whom with his encouragement moved on to Oxford or Cambridge and pursued successful careers in classics or other fields. He still based his teaching on prepared books and prose composition, following the tradition that was changing in other universities; essays on Latin literature (as opposed to ancient history) were not required, but in later years he set passages for linguistic and literary comment, a form of exercise that is perhaps not practised enough. When he went to Aberdeen, Latin was in effect a compulsory subject for the ordinary degree of MA, but that was a line that he had no wish to hold even if

[6] *Gnomon*, 38 (1966), 364–71, reprinted in Goodyear's *Papers on Latin Literature*, K. M. Coleman *et al.* (eds.) (London, 1992), pp. 169–75.
[7] M. Meston, *University of Aberdeen Newsletter* (Feb. 2003), 11.
[8] Edited by Pat Shuldham-Shaw and Emily B. Lyle, published by Mercat Press for the University of Aberdeen, 1981–2002.

it had been possible. Inevitably numbers went down: Latin and Greek were disappearing in many Scottish schools with the same unfortunate results as in England, and Aberdeen was particularly dependent on its hinterland to provide competent students. In 1973 a course was started in 'classical civilisation' for those without Latin or Greek, but not surprisingly Watt did not himself teach for it. It is a matter for regret that there is no longer a classical department in the University of Aberdeen.

After his retirement in 1979 Watt had time for his own work as never before. His Oxford text of Cicero's letters *Ad Familiares* appeared in 1982; in a laudatory review F. R. D. Goodyear commented 'W.'s conjectures are usually of a high standard, being apt, neat, sensitive, and realistic . . .; many others are plausible, and were, at the lowest estimate, worth floating . . .'; at the same time he praised Watt's *apparatus criticus* as a model of brevity and precision.[9] In comparing the text with that of Shackleton Bailey,[10] which he greatly admired, he judged that in the choice of readings and conjectures honours were about equal; as he said 'it is instructive to see two exceptional scholars grappling with the same problems, sometimes problems of great subtlety'. He rightly concluded that all serious students of *Ad Familiares* need to consult both editions at all times.

Also in 1982 Watt and Philip J. Ford produced for the Aberdeen University Press a short commentary on George Buchanan's interesting *Miscellaneorum Liber*, which includes Latin poems to Henry VIII, Henry King of Scots (i.e. Lord Darnley), and Thomas Cromwell, not to mention an elegy on Calvin; his retentive memory enabled him to cite relevant classical material. In 1988 he brought out for the Teubner series a text of the minor Roman historian Velleius Paterculus (reprinted with a few improvements in 1998). The text depends on a single manuscript discovered by Beatus Rhenanus in 1515 in a Benedictine monastery in Alsace and described by him as 'tam prodigiose corruptum ut omnia restituere non foret humani ingenii'; the manuscript was later lost and its reconstruction from the first edition and other copies has generated some discussion. Watt showed his usual judgement in admitting old conjectures and added some of his own; as a result his text is much more satisfactory than the over-conservative Budé edition of J. Hellegouarc'h (Paris, 1982).

Up to his retirement Watt had published only a score of articles, mainly short notes on problems in Cicero. In the next twenty-three years

[9] *Classical Review*, NS 36 (1986), 241–3, reprinted in Goodyear's *Papers on Latin Literature* [n. 6], pp. 203–4.
[10] Cicero, *Epistulae ad Familiares*, 2 vols. (Cambridge, 1977).

he added over a hundred and twenty more; as each contained discussions on a series of passages (over sixty in one posthumous paper), the total number of conjectures was too great even for the author to count. Instead of confining himself to Cicero he now ranged over some fifty Latin writers both in prose and in verse. In 1989 at the advanced age of seventy-six he was elected a Senior Fellow of the British Academy; though usually undemonstrative, when Professor Parsons greeted him with the words 'a legendary figure', he beamed with pleasure. As he distributed his articles over some forty periodicals at home and abroad, a list will be deposited in the library of the Academy.

Work on ancient texts takes different forms and some distinctions must be drawn. On the one hand there are the palaeographers who can date a manuscript within narrow limits, identify its provenance and perhaps even the scribe, and place it in a stemma or family-tree. Unlike his tutor and early colleague Sir Roger Mynors, Watt was not an expert of this kind, though he could support his conjectures with book-learning about typical corruptions. To heal a corruption needs different skills that palaeographers do not necessarily possess; after they have laboriously collected the evidence the judgement of the textual critic may still be required. Ideally a critic should be both rational and intuitive, but one of these virtues tends to predominate: Madvig would fill a lacuna with a clear-headed assessment of what the argument required, but Heinsius could clutch the solution out of thin air without any apparent effort.[11] Here Watt belonged to the rational end of the spectrum. He could see better than others what was wrong with a passage and the traditional explanations. He would then produce a proposal that could not easily be bettered. Certainty was often impossible, particularly when he was discussing a passage with no striking qualities of style. Even so, many of his conjectures were unanswerable, and would have attracted more attention if they had been presented less modestly and had not been mixed up with others that were merely probable or reasonable.

One of the obituaries referred to Watt's admiration for Housman; though this can be taken for granted, some qualifications are needed. They may seem alike in their obsessive love of truth (what Housman called 'the faintest of the passions'), even in minor matters like the attribution of conjectures; in the same way a colleague recalls the intensity

---

[11] See A. E. Housman, *Classical Review*, 13 (1899), 173, reprinted in his *Classical Papers*, J. Diggle and F. R. D. Goodyear (eds.) (Cambridge, 1972), 2. 472; E. J. Kenney, *The Classical Text* (Berkeley, Calif., 1974), pp. 58–9; G. P. Goold, *Bulletin of the Institute of Classical Studies*, Supplement 51 (1988), 28.

with which Watt condemned editors who unthinkingly take over their predecessors' punctuation. But he did not join in the idolatry of Housman that prevailed at one time in Cambridge, where some scholars regarded him as virtually inerrant, and spoke of his texts and even his lectures as the supreme intellectual experience of their lives. When I was an undergraduate at Balliol Watt let me see that Housman on Juvenal was not necessarily right; and many years later those who attended a class on Lucan at Aberdeen were given a similar message. Watt disapproved of Housman's rhetorical presentation, which was different from his own dispassionate procedure; and though he shared Housman's intolerance of error, he learned in print at least to control his indignation. He was unhappy with the contortions of word-order that Housman was ready to posit in unsuitable authors, and with Housman's over-complicated explanations of how one word was corrupted to another (a tendency from which he himself was not immune). It remains obvious that he could not aspire to the resourcefulness of Housman at his best, particularly in his editions of Manilius.

Watt's scholarship resulted from the impact of particular educational experiences on a powerful and confident intelligence. Glasgow grammar and Oxford gobbets determined the direction of his studies, and with his unfailing realism he knew that the broader vistas were not for him; he never tried to reinvent himself, to use a modern expression that he would have liked as little as the concept. He had a Victorian belief in the written examination, which proved a more effective vehicle for social mobility than some more recent initiatives, at least as long as some schools could provide the necessary grounding. He was a man of uncompromising integrity both in his writing and his personal relationships; he did not flatter even to oil the wheels, nor could he be flattered as I found once when I tried. He followed the Aristotelian ideal of neither over-estimating nor under-estimating himself, and was critical of those whom he judged guilty of either failing. Nonsensical or pretentious articles could provoke a vigorous reaction, as when he cancelled his subscription to a periodical because he thought a contributor too self-indulgent, but there was no malice in his strictures, which were expressed with a robust humour and a deep chuckle, and sometimes enlivened with a joke from some ancient poet or an insult from Housman's prefaces.

He could seem formidable on matters of business (though his fairness was always respected), but that was only one side of a warm and sympathetic human being. Though he was a very private person, we get glimpses of him cycling with Thea near Oxford to buy furniture, energetically cultivating strawberries in his first garden at Aberdeen, lunching with congenial acquaintances at meetings of the Aberdeen Business and Professional Club (of which he was chairman in 1968), happily driving his car (a skill acquired in middle age) to visit Thea's relatives in Cornwall or his son and his son's family in Dundee, and writing friendly letters to fellow-scholars on questions of textual criticism. He could laugh at himself as well as others, as when he observed to a former colleague 'I have just written my hundredth article since my retirement, and it was very boring even for me'; but of course he was not boring to those who can still enjoy precise verbal scholarship. Few knew of his love of English as well as Latin poetry: as a young man he had learned by heart the whole of Palgrave's *Golden Treasury*, much of the anthology of longer poems known as *The English Parnassus*, and (like Macaulay) all of *Paradise Lost*, so that fifty years later when given a line he could continue; this was an astonishing achievement even for the days when learning poetry was thought to have more educational value than writing about it. In Latin he knew by heart all of Lucretius and Virgil and much else besides, which he could declaim with an exuberant feeling for the power of rhythm and poetic language; if delayed on a station platform on the way to one of his numerous committees he would recite silently to himself. This love of words must have contributed to his textual criticism, which need not be so arid an activity as is often supposed, but he seems to have thought it unprofessional to reveal his enthusiasm to the public gaze.

Even when he was well on in his eighties the flow of *adversaria* did not dry up. In spite of various infirmities and finally terminal illness he kept on writing, like the grammarian in Browning's uplifting poem. A late observation of his is characteristic: he noticed that in a line where the same word appeared twice, a copyist repeated the wrong word (a thing that can also happen with the digits of a telephone number). Most people would have left it at that, but Watt began collecting instances of the same phenomenon. He called it 'Error Wattianus',[12] not that he was ever likely to make such a mistake himself, but in the way that a perceptive clinician might perpetuate his name in a syndrome.

Watt died peacefully in Aberdeen on 23 December 2002 at the age of 89, fifty years almost to the day after his arrival in the city. He is survived by his wife and their son Robert, who is a member of the English Department

---

[12] Thus at Juvenal 9.54 'cui tot montis, tot praedia servas?' some manuscripts read 'cui praedia'. The article on the *Error Wattianus*, revised by Professor H. M. Hine, is appearing in *Classical Quarterly*, NS 54 (2004).

in the University of Dundee. He recalls how even when he was a small
boy his father treated him as grown-up and rational.

R. G. M. NISBET
Fellow of the Academy

Note. In preparing this memoir I have consulted Professor J. Delz, Sir Kenneth
Dover, J. C. B. Foster, Professor H. M. Hine, Dr D. C. Innes, T. E. V. Pearce, G. F. C.
Plowden, Professor N. Rudd, Professor D. A. Russell, R. J. C. Watt. I have also
benefited from the obituaries by Dr G. P. Edwards (*The Guardian*), Dr I. Olson (*The
Times*), and Professor Russell (*The Independent* and the *Balliol College Annual Record,
2003*).

BRUCE WERNHAM   *Sam E. P. Jerrett*

Richard Bruce Wernham
1906–1999

BRUCE WERNHAM was born on 11 October 1906 at Ashmansworth, near Newbury, Berkshire, the son of a tenant farmer. As a child he did jobs on his father's farm, and during the General Strike in 1926 he would display the skill of rolling milk churns on the platforms of Paddington Station. His grandfather's tales of village life in the 1840s and 1850s—of a time when corn was cut by hand with a scythe, and quite a lot of ploughing was done by oxen (indeed Wernham remembered the team of oxen in the farm next to his father's)—first stirred his interest in the past. At the age of eight Wernham read Anson's *Voyage Round the World*, 'a wonderful book'. He attended St Bartholomew's Grammar School, which he remembered with affection all his life, serving as Governor from 1944. In 1925 he went on to Exeter College, Oxford, and took a first in Modern History in 1928. He returned to study towards a D.Phil. There were no lectures or classes for graduate students in such matters as palaeography or diplomatic, and supervisors, Wernham later recalled, 'seldom did much to help'. His chosen theme was 'Anglo-French relations in the age of Queen Elizabeth and Henri IV', a subject that would remain at the centre of his interests for the rest of his life. After a year, he moved to London in order to work on the State Papers in the Public Record Office and the British Museum. Oxford accordingly found him a supervisor in London, Professor John Neale at University College, then preparing his classic biography of Queen Elizabeth, 'a very marked change', Wernham noted, from Oxford. Neale had recently succeeded A. F. Pollard, himself the authority on Henry VIII, who had moved on as founding director of the

Proceedings of the British Academy, **124**, 375–396. © The British Academy 2004.

Institute of Historical Research in the University of London. Pollard gave Wernham a part-time job at the Institute. 'I was now in the care of the two leading Tudor historians of the day', Wernham recalled. Much later Neale would thank Wernham 'whom I am proud to number among my pupils' for reading the proofs of *The Elizabethan House of Commons*; Wernham would in turn thank Neale (in what Neale described as 'your golden words'), 'the kindliest and most stimulating counsellor and friend since my earliest ventures into Tudor history' to whom he owed 'my deepest obligation'.

Wernham's first acquaintance with the Public Record Office in Chancery Lane came early in October 1929. He found it 'pretty terrifying'. No one had ever told him anything about sixteenth-century handwriting, and even a volume of State Papers, France, presented 'terrible problems': 'I could hardly read a word'. A kind presiding officer in the Round Room found time to help him, by showing him the basics of secretary hand and some French hands. By the end of his first day Wernham had managed to read a page or two. And evidently he quickly acquired a mastery of the records.

Such was Wernham's promise that in 1930 he was appointed to a newly created post at the Public Record Office. A. E. Stamp, Deputy Keeper of Public Records, had become concerned that the number of editors working on Record Office publications was dwindling: the output of calendars and historical publications had halved since the First World War. Stamp successfully cajoled the Treasury 'to try the experiment of offering temporary employment to a small number of young scholars, anxious to equip themselves to follow an academic career as teachers of history by acquiring through the medium of editorial work a knowledge of archives and original sources'. It was hoped that anyone appointed would, at the end of two years, be 'no mere palaeographer or laborious expert of a single class, but stand possessed of an adequate general knowledge of the various and often intricate strands from which sound history may alone be written'.[1] Wernham was the first such appointment, for two years, at a salary of £200—the basic salary laid down for successful entrants into the home civil service—which he thought by no means unreasonable at a time when 1s. 9d. (9p) could buy 'a quite palatable' three-course meal at Slater's in Holborn.

Wernham was mentored by S. C. Ratcliffe, who had an 'encyclopedic knowledge'; and two newly appointed Assistant Keepers, Charles Drew

[1] *Bulletin of the Institute of Historical Research*, 8 (1930), 90.

and Leonard Hector, and Bernard Wardle, appointed the year before, became lifelong friends, as later did two already established Keepers, J. R. Crompton and Harold Johnson. The 'new boys' lunched together in various hostelries on Chancery Lane. They went to Henry Wood Promenade Concerts in the old Queen's Hall and on several walking holidays, doing 20–25 miles a day at some 5 miles per hour (as Wernham calculated by surreptitiously timing them between milestones). His first year was spent in what he recalled as 'a most instructive sampling' of the main classes and sub-divisions of the PRO's records from Domesday Book onwards: Chancery, Exchequer, King's Bench, Common Pleas, Wardrobe, Requests, Star Chamber, Augmentations, Wards, even Papal Bulls. 'It was', Wernham recalled, 'an experience that any young historian might have envied'. Wernham felt no regret that he had abandoned his thesis: 'one of the wisest decisions I ever made': 'what would I have got comparable out of another year working for a D.Phil.?' But Wernham had already struck gold: his discovery that William Davison, though sent to the Tower as the scapegoat of Mary Queen of Scots' execution in 1587, continued for three years to share the profits of the Signet Office, led in 1931 to his first appearance in the *English Historical Review*. A year later he was invited— a remarkable recognition for a young scholar—to read a paper to the Royal Historical Society (duly published in the *Transactions* for 1932) on 'Queen Elizabeth and the siege of Rouen, 1591'. In many ways that paper set out the agenda that he was to pursue for the rest of his life: many completed theses have accomplished less.

Then Wernham gradually began to earn his keep in the PRO by calendaring Elizabethan Patent Rolls (those for 1563, eventually printed in 1960) and Wards' Feodaries surveys, doing his stint of weekly floor inspections (including checking the strong rooms to see that they were free of rats and mice), and 'writ picking' up in the Tower ('a filthier job than any I had done on my father's farm', involving trying to save what he could from sacks of rotten, powdered bundles of writs). One afternoon, Wernham recalled, he had stood in for a presiding officer in one of the search rooms: 'happily no one had any awkward questions'. From October 1931 he began to spend more and more of his time editing for the Elizabethan *Calendar of State Papers, Foreign*, so returning to the subject of his abandoned thesis. At this point the editor of the Foreign Calendars had had 'a bit of a tiff' with Neale and felt that the PRO did not support him properly: so he resigned. And then when Wernham's two-year temporary assistantship ended on 30 September 1932, at the age of twenty-six, he was appointed editor of the Foreign

Calendars, and spent the next year working in Chancery Lane wholly on the Calendars.

In the same year appeared *England under Elizabeth (1558–1603): illustrated from contemporary sources* (1932), jointly edited by Wernham and J. C. Walker, a set of printed sources for undergraduates, with a lengthy bibliography, but without any introductions to the documents. That Wernham should have compiled such a work suggests that he had university teaching in mind, even though the affectionate tones with which he recalled his full-time years in the Public Record Office and the lasting friendships that he made there suggest that he would happily have made his career there. In October 1933 Wernham was appointed to a lecturership at University College London, where Neale was professor. And soon afterwards, in April 1934, Wernham was elected a Lecturer and then a Fellow of Trinity College, Oxford. The PRO appointed him an external editor—paid at an hourly rate—of their Foreign Calendars. And from the start Trinity formally allowed him to spend a day a week in term time in the Public Record Office. So every Thursday, the day on which the rail company offered cheap day returns at 5*s.* (25p), he joined the little band of Oxford historians who made the journey—though the routes they took to get to Chancery Lane once in London diverged, Wernham and George Ramsay walking down to Lancaster Gate to take the Central Line, Pierre Chaplais taking the Bakerloo Line to Oxford Circus and changing there, and Harry Bell going by bus.[2] Wernham found the weekly day trips to London 'provided useful cover when I was getting acquainted with my future wife: the College must have been impressed by how late I seemed to be working at the PRO' as he habitually returned by the last train just after midnight. Isobel MacMillan, whom Wernham married two days after war broke out in 1939, was a Canadian of Scottish descent from Vancouver. Wernham's remarks in his obituary of his friend and colleague George Ramsay about how marriage rescued him from loneliness hint at how much his own marriage meant to him and what happiness it brought.

In March 1935 Wernham completed his first *Calendar of State Papers, Foreign*, volume xxii, diplomatic correspondence from the summer and autumn 1588, above all concerning the Netherlands. In it he provided full and detailed summaries of several hundred letters now in the Public Record Office. In his preface he offered a magisterial survey of Queen

---

[2] Pierre Chaplais did not come to Oxford until 1957: the conflation is Wernham's, see his memoir of George Ramsay, '1994 Lectures and Memoirs', *Proceedings of the British Academy*, 87 (1995), 401–14.

Elizabeth's policy towards the United Provinces. The volume appeared in 1936. By September 1939, despite his Trinity commitments (he was Senior Tutor), Wernham had prepared the next volume (and made 'quite a decent start' on the one after that), summarising, indeed often offering very nearly full transcripts of, 743 documents covering the first seven months of 1589: only the introduction covering England's relations with the Netherlands and France was not yet complete. The war, however, intervened, and it would not be till 1950 that the volume was published.

Wernham volunteered for the Royal Air Force but was not deemed medically fit for active service. On 31 December 1941 he joined the Photographic Interpretation Unit at Medmenham, Buckinghamshire, where his role was to study aerial reconaissance photographs and advise Special Operations Executive about suitable landing sites for their agents. There was some leisure for reading: he listed Garrett Mattingly's *Catherine of Aragon*, C. S. Lewis's *Screwtape Letters*, an edition of Margery Kempe ('a wearisome early 15-century mystic with semi-sexual visions and "dalliances" and frequent "weepings and wailing boisterously"'), Veale's *Frederick the Great* ('a typical and strongly-influenced by fascism whitewash and rather superficial and bogus psychological hype'). In October 1943 he was transferred to the Historical Branch of the Air Ministry in London and, alongside firewatching duties, was commissioned to prepare a history of Bomber Command from 1914. His reading in his spare time included Blunden's *Cricket Country*, Hardy's *Return of the Native*, Hayek's *Road to Serfdom*, Benjamin Franklin's *Autobiography* and Clive Bell's *Civilisation* ('a cheap smart aleck sort of book'). He aimed to restrict his smoking to five cigarettes and three pipes a day. On many days there was noisy bombing. In just over a year he produced a text of some 140,000 words, 'elegantly written and impeccably scholarly' (Noble Frankland) on *The Pre-War Evolution of Bomber Command*, dealing with the period to 1938, never published but now accessible in the PRO (PRO AIR 41/39). He was then put under pressure, and again as late as February 1949, to take his account further and produce a full history of Bomber Command during the war. But Wernham was anxious to return to teaching and to the sixteenth century. He was acutely conscious 'how rusty the war years had left me on much of what I would be teaching'. Maybe he also sensed just how difficult it would be to write an official history that was both honestly critical but remained acceptable to politicians and air chiefs. But, remarkably, he was to remain involved in a different way. One of his pupils at Trinity, Noble Frankland, who returned to Oxford after having served for two years as a navigator in Bomber

Command, went on to secure a post in the Historical Branch of the Air Ministry, and from January 1949 prepared an Oxford D.Phil. under Wernham's supervision on Bomber Command in the Second World War. In 1950 Frankland was commissioned with Sir Charles Webster to prepare the official history of what was termed the Strategic Air Offensive: Wernham would review the ensuing four volumes, published in 1961, in the *Oxford Magazine*.

Wernham's influence was indirect but considerable. Frankland warmly acknowledged his debt to Wernham's teaching. Moreover Wernham's style of teaching—regular meetings, a succession of encouraging and probing questions—allowed students to feel that they had worked out their ideas for themselves without quite grasping how far their tutor had by his questions set them well on their way. In his typescript prepared by 1945 Wernham had seen how 'Bomber Command was the supreme expression, and its operations were the first test, of an official established British belief that, for an unmilitary island power closely neighboured by great continental military states, an "independent" Air Force is an essential weapon of defence', before going on to note that 'how difficult an operation effective long range bombing on the grand scale was in fact to prove, few people had yet realised'. That was in miniature the conclusion that Webster and Frankland would reach in *The Strategic Air Offensive against Germany, 1939–45* (4 vols., 1961). Wernham explained in his review how the received view was that Bomber Command had been starved of money before the war and was consequently too small to achieve effective results, but that as it gradually expanded, it became more effective, sapped German strength and ultimately played a decisive part in the allied victory. Frankland and Webster showed that far from being a revolutionary innovation, air power was subject to the same general principles as those governing the conduct of armies and navies. For the most part the results of bombing were disappointing; not till the German fighter force was confronted and air superiority established did bombing make a decisive contribution. The idea that bomber aircraft might by destroying industries and communications and morale cripple hostile armies and fleets grew out of but was not really tested by the experiences of 1914–18; in 1944–45 they came close to doing just that. But earlier on the belief that 'the bomber will always get through' proved misguided: German fighters prevented daytime bombing; night-time bombing was wildly inaccurate; poor weather and industrial haze made navigation difficult. All that could be attempted was systematic obliteration of Germany's major cities, and even that proved difficult. But once Bomber

Command with the help of the Americans had established air superiority which they did in 1944, it was more successful. Yet instead of concentrating on focused attacks on oil targets, transport and communications, Bomber Command continued to see general area bombing as the most decisive action that it could take. With victory in sight, such destruction and terror 'became an embarrassment to the conscience', Wernham noted, concluding that Bomber Command 'for most of the time fought the way it did, not from choice, but because that was the only way it could fight at all when it alone could fight'.

At the end of the war, Wernham had been keen to return to teaching and to the sixteenth century, and to enjoy family life (Isobel and he had often been apart during the war; their daughter Joan was born in 1943). He evidently had thoughts of preparing a textbook on the Tudors and early Stuarts for Blackwells (entries in his diaries show him drafting in October 1944 and reaching chapter viii by 1949) and a course on Queen Elizabeth for Eyre and Spotiswoode, but these projects remained unfinished in what were busy years. In 1948 he served as an examiner in Finals. He completed the volume of the *Calendar of State Papers, Foreign* left unfinished in 1939, preparing a monograph-like introduction, and also published substantial related articles on the Portuguese expedition of 1590 in the *English Historical Review* in 1950. Then in July 1951 he was elected Professor of Modern History and moved to Worcester College. Inevitably, much gossip, not all of it flattering or true, attended such an appointment. It was said that Lewis Namier was being strongly supported, but also vehemently resisted. Alternatively it was suggested that A. J. P. Taylor, who had just published *The Struggle for Mastery in Europe*, and Hugh Trevor-Roper, biographer of William Laud and reporter of *The Last Days of Hitler*, were the leading contenders, but that those who supported the one absolutely refused to accept the other; then Wernham, who at that point had two *Calendars*, albeit with substantial introductions, one jointly edited collection of documents and some articles to his name emerged as a candidate who could secure a majority. Wernham held the chair for twenty-one years until his retirement in 1972.

The post, like other professorships, was in many ways an anomaly within the Oxford Modern History Faculty. Its statutory obligations were to give a limited number of lectures and classes annually, with special attention to the needs of graduate students, but the professor was not expected to take undergraduates for tutorials. At once that cut Wernham off from the daily round of college tutors and in a sense the heart of academic life in Oxford. Such a post might, however, appear to offer an opportunity to any scholar whose ambition was to devote himself to research and writing. But, as Wernham's diaries make plain, if that was the purpose underlying the position, it was not easily realised. Conscientious, not to say perfectionist, preparation of the one or two lectures or classes that Wernham gave took up several days each week in term time. As a supervisor of graduate students he was notably generous of his time, as Tom Barnes, Professor of History at the University of California at Berkeley recalls, offering weekly supervisions in which his pupil would be subjected to seemingly casual but in fact pointed interrogation. Wernham was involved in college and faculty meetings, in organising visits by distinguished historians from abroad (Braudel was a notable catch), in examining graduate students, and assessing theses for publication in the Oxford Historical Monographs series (on each of which he might spend several days), in giving occasional papers to college history societies, in serving on committees of learned bodies (such as the Wiltshire Victoria County History), in presiding over the Oxford Historical Association. Wernham meticulously recorded the time he took on tasks such as external examining—no less than 107 hours in 1962 and an astonishing 164 hours in 1963 (not counting the time spent travelling or the examiners' meetings themselves) when external examiner at Southampton. A miscellany of such activities together took up most of term. Even his Thursday trip to the PRO was often forgone. His diaries show that it was only in seventh or eighth week, once he had delivered his final lecture, that he would return to listing the State Papers or to writing his next book. Once he had taken family holidays in the vacations, that typically left him six or seven weeks in the summer for sustained work on the papers he was editing or his book. On the former he would spend perhaps four, five or six hours a day. On the latter he would write in long hand anything from 400 to 2000 words a day, mostly at the lower end of that range; returning after he had completed one chapter to re-writing the one before. No study leave was available to him in these years. When he went as Visiting Professor to the University of South Carolina in 1958 and to the University of California, Berkeley in 1965–6, both assignments involved demanding, if stimulating, teaching.

In all these years Wernham had been continuing to work on the State Papers, Foreign. But after the war Sir Hilary Jenkinson became Deputy Keeper of the PRO, and in the words of an Assistant Keeper (as Wernham wryly recalled), 'change and D.K. in all around we see'. Jenkinson wanted to reform and to cut the costs of the Calendars. In his preface to Wernham's *Calendar* published in 1950, Jenkinson announced the termination of the series. Progress with the *Calendar*, given the increasing quantity of papers in the 1590s, would inevitably be slow; and the 'swollen costs of printing' made some more economical method of publication 'urgently necessary'. Accordingly, a series of Descriptive Lists would be prepared, with indexes to 'the Subjects and to the names of all Persons and Places occurring in the Documents, even when these are not mentioned in the printed version'. The aim was 'to indicate in as condensed a form as possible all the information contained in each paper'. At first Jenkinson wanted to limit the description of each document to ten or twelve lines. Wernham thought that this would be 'disastrous'. The documents that he was studying dealt largely with matters of diplomacy, strategy and defence, 'where it is often of first importance to know not only what A said to B in general terms but what he said in detail, just how he said it, and just how B replied'. With the 'tacit connivance' of Howard Johnson, in charge of editors, Wernham 'began an exercise in damage limitation'. After a good deal of experimenting, Wernham invented what he rightly described as 'an almost completely new kind of publication', echoing to some extent the Dutch *Resolutien der Staten-Generaal*, intended to preserve the essentials of the old Calendars yet not too flagrantly to disregard Jenkinson's aims. By the time Wernham had completed the first volume in this way—amid other concerns—Jenkinson had retired and the new head of editing raised no objections. Wernham confessed that 'I sometimes feel twinges of regret for the old Calendar', but, he maintained, at least the *Lists and Analyses* give as much detailed information, if in a rather potted form. And the disaster of a complete abandonment of any publication had been staved off.

Wernham's method involved a tripartite structure. The *List* is just that: giving writer, recipient, date, length and folio numbers. There was an Index of persons, places and things. The crucial novelty is the *Analysis*. Its purpose, as Wernham explained, 'is to provide a consolidated summary, in a more or less narrative form, of all the information about any particular event or topic that is to be found in the S.P. Foreign as a whole'. These summaries were arranged in geographical sections, mostly by country. Savings of space were achieved by very brief summaries of documents giving the same information. In the first volume, the list runs from page 1 to page 90; the analysis from page 91 to page 454, in the sixth volume, printed in smaller type, the analysis goes from page 63 to page 291. Such substantial Analyses were clearly not what Jenkinson had had in mind: his proposed Descriptive Lists would have been far briefer. If Wernham had been unable to hold out for the continuation of the *Calendars*, nonetheless his *Lists and Analyses* rather subverted Jenkinson's designs.

The first of the *List and Analysis* volumes appeared in 1964, the second in 1969, the third in 1980, the fourth in 1984, the fifth in 1989, the sixth in 1993, the seventh posthumously in 2000. The labour required in preparing such analyses was immense. The first volume dealt with 1,344 papers, the second with over 1,300, the fourth with 1,192, the fifth with 1,437. The documents had to be selected, read and transcribed, précised, edited, indexed, collated. In effect the analysis amounted to a monograph in its own right. Everything, including the indexes, was Wernham's own work, except for translations of documents in Spanish and Portuguese. What would now be done—if it were done at all—by a team of researchers was here done by one man amid the various duties of college tutor or professor, or the tribulations of retirement. It is a remarkable achievement. Wernham calculated that each paper would on average take well over an hour to edit. During his career at Oxford he tried to devote some 50 or 60 days a year, say 300 hours, to the task. And that meant that a volume dealing with some 1200 to 1400 papers could hardly take less than four or five years to prepare. And how long publication then took depended on the printers—Wernham lamented the 'not always happy choice' of printers and remembered a volume that demanded repeated revises of both galleys, page proofs and even final print-offs. All that, Wernham admitted, was an apologia for his slow progress. In 1993, at the age of 87, he conceded that with some 5,600 papers to go before Elizabeth's death on 25 March 1603, his 'youthful dream' of completing the calendar for the reign would have to remain a dream. 'There is a certain limited measure of satisfaction in getting so far in the past sixty years', he noted, 'but I am not quite sure that I can see myself finishing the job!'. Nonetheless he did embark on and complete a further volume that would be published after his death.

Not everyone welcomed the *List and Analyses*. Reviewing volume ii in *Archives*, 9 (1969–70), 204–5, Geoffrey Parker praised Wernham, 'in whose high critical standards and scholarship we can place absolute confidence', but answered in the negative his question 'whether a *List and Analysis* describes its chosen documents accurately enough to allow a serious student to know whether or not any one of them contains information which he will want to know in full'. Ideally, Parker urged, we should have a full calendar; failing that, just a simple listing of documents. The uneasy compromise of the *Lists and Analyses* was not worth the expense and infinite time and trouble of preparation. Wernham would have agreed that the ideal was a full *Calendar*, but he passionately believed that the ingenious compromise that he had devised and elaborated was eminently worthwhile.

Wernham saw himself as continuing a long tradition of the editing of documents. As professor of modern history, he offered classes on what he characteristically described as Tudor handwriting (rather than palaeography) and informal lectures to new graduate students on the sources for English history, beginning with the Stuart antiquarians driven by contemporary political needs. What was crucial was the Victorian state's assumption of responsibility for publishing its records. 'The development of history as we know it would have been impossible', Wernham maintained, 'without the full and free access to records of the state'. Historical writing would have remained no more than 'a string of more or less disconnected anecdotes' all but impossible to verify. Now historians could set each document in its proper context, see it as part of an administrative process, understand why it was made; and so get a lot nearer its true meaning, to 'scientific' assessment of the evidence. 'All history is to some extent guesswork; not all evidence is recorded; but by knowing the documentary context in this way, we can reduce the proportion of guessing, we can get a higher probability.' From the late 1850s had begun what Wernham regarded as 'the great era' of official publication organised and directed by the Public Record Office. Calendars of State Papers were intended to list and to show their chief contents: some series, especially the *Letters and Papers of Henry VIII*, became much fuller (and included material from outside the PRO). Wernham rightly saw the 'sum total output of calendars since 1856'— unmatched by any other country—as 'pretty impressive'. Wernham passionately believed that such editing remained invaluable and indispensable. Why summarise documents in a printed book? Would not a serious historian go straight to the original sources, or to photocopies, or to 'those horrid microfilms'? And had not printed calendars introduced distortions of their own by making historians think them adequate substitutes for the originals? Had not such publication put the editor between the historian and the sources, 'done him out of the sensitive intuitive understanding that can only come by, as it were, laying one hand on your heart and the other on original manuscripts?' Of course he agreed that consulting originals was essential. But he was 'nil mystic about manuscripts': it did not much help to know that Elizabeth's hand appeared on one or if the spray shaken off Drake's beard stained it. And Wernham's justification for the preparation of calendars of summaries of documents was in the first place practical. Time in the archives was precious (Wernham perhaps recalling his more or less regular Thursday trips to Chancery Lane). And some sorts of questions, especially factual questions about names, dates and places—for example was anyone trying to buy Secretary Walsingham a suit of armour in the Netherlands in 1588?—can more speedily be answered if the sources are in print and supported by an index than by searching through hundreds of original folios. But Wernham also offered a larger argument. Historians need peripheral vision, not too narrow a gaze. They acquire this by browsing, perhaps in a not very concentrated way, through large quantities of not very directly relevant material. Very few scholars can afford to spend time in the archives on this 'half-throttle, half-aimless browsing': 'the sort of thing to do at the end of the day with feet up'. It was in any case hard to take in manuscripts by paragraphs. That moreover ruled out microfilm, useless when, as so often, the original documents themselves were faded or damaged, or even photocopies: you need print if you are to read fast and a lot.

In the 1960s Wernham voiced his concern at the drying up of the flow of printed calendars, lists and indexes which between the late 1850s and the outbreak of the Second World War had made the public records more accessible. The reason usually given was economic: the rising cost of editing and printing had made publication of calendars on the old scale, indeed any scale, almost impossibly costly. He had accepted that explanation and had resigned himself to hoping at best for 'just an occasional dribble of bare duplicated typescript lists'. Making a virtue of necessity, he had tried to convince himself that his predecessors had too often been corrupted by the riches of the printed resources. But detailed analysis of rates of publication suggested a rather different explanation to him. He tabulated the output of medieval calendars, modern calendars and lists and indexes, showing that in the years 1900–14 91 medieval calendars, 75 modern calendars and 34 lists and indexes were published; between 1946 and 61 the comparable figures were 19 medieval calendars, 39 modern calendars and no lists and indexes, and (as he pointed out) the comparison was misleading because many had been prepared before the war. Wernham noted that in the years 1900–9 J. L. Gairdner and R. L. Brodie published eight volumes of the *Letters and Papers of Henry VIII*; W. A. Shaw eight volumes of *Treasury Books*; Mahaffy seven of the *Irish State Papers*; J. Daniell five of the *Domestic State Papers*; A. B. Butler five of the *Foreign State Papers*; Atkinson three of the *Domestic State Papers* between 1900 and 1905; H. F. Brown three of the *Venetian Calendars* to 1905. At least as many editors must have been employed to produce the sixty-one medieval calendars. And that comparison led Wernham to conclude that the real reason for the dearth in record publications was that 'governments are not now giving the PRO the money to recruit the staff or the full-time editors to keep up an output such as the 19th century was able to afford'. (In 1968 Wernham absolved the PRO itself from blame: the PRO had to cut its coat according to the cloth 'and one suspects often the cloth will hardly turn into a mini-skirt'). And, devastatingly, Wernham went on to point out that far from being 'a simple case of government economy in hard times', the scale of publication of official histories of the First and Second World Wars and Foreign Office Documents suggested strongly that government money had been transferred to a different historical field. It was understandable: 'there was much to be said for getting our word in first'. But the time had come to 'remember that Britain's history began before 1914'.

But if Wernham was a great and ultimately prolific editor, was he, in the words of Hugh Trevor-Roper, 'an archivist not an historian'?[3] Certainly Wernham was deeply committed to the archives. And there was indeed an antiquarian streak about his interests, not least his acute sense of place, and his concern to know the local histories of places. His surviving diaries (more or less complete from the early 1930s), not reflective diaries, but much more than appointment diaries, recording as they do each day the number of tutorials he had taken, the number of lectures given, committee meetings attended, the number of essays he had marked, the number of letters that he had written, what he had read, the number of hours he had worked on the *Lists and Analyses*, the number of words of his next book that he had written—together with the maximum and minimum temperature and a brief characterisation of the weather ('cleared snow from garage but could not get car out for snow'; 'almost as bitter a day as I can remember'; 'very heavy rain and tornado near Leighton Buzzard'), as well as matters small ('stray cat had two kittens in middle of lawn') and large ('serious trouble in Korea') reveal an orderly and classifying mind. And as he himself was to observe, 'I have been a late developer as proper books go'. Was this inappropriate for an Oxford professor of history? Should he have left the task of editing and listing to junior scholars and to full-time archivists and devoted himself instead to writing? University historians living under the shadow of Research Assessment Exercises (which Wernham deplored as inimical to scholarship) are struck by how unnecessary publication was evidently felt to be in the Oxford of the 1950s and 1960s. Of course, Wernham had lost

---

[3] Hugh Trevor-Roper, personal communication to author, Feb. 2002.

vital years to the war—he was 33 when it began, and 39 when he returned to Trinity. In the early 1950s he wrote a good many entries for the *Encyclopedia Britannica*. There were several scholarly articles (significantly stimulated by invitations for special occasions, notably an essay on Thomas Wilkes's mission to the United Provinces in 1590 in the Festschrift for Hilary Jenkinson, Wernham's bête noire, a paper on Elizabethan war aims and strategy for Neale's Festschift). A great deal of Wernham's energies went into preparing lectures that were never published. A set on 'The Netherlands 1559–1715', entirely rewritten a year or two later, reveals a remarkably detailed command of Dutch history, with shrewd analysis of the disparate nature of the different provinces, of the emergence of some sense of Netherlandish community, of the international dimensions, of the internal social relationships. In retirement in 1979 at a summer school in the University of British Columbia, Vancouver, he gave a set of lectures on England under the Tudors and Stuarts 1485–1688 that reveal a talent for synthesis and clear exposition, including lectures on 'The Reformation under Henry VIII: why so little effective opposition?', 'Criticism and opposition 1585–1618', 'Charles I's "Personal Government" 1629–40'. Others have hurried into print on much less. Throughout the 1960s much labour also went into the thankless task of editing volume III covering 1559–1610 of the *New Cambridge Modern History* which eventually appeared in 1969 (a disappointingly uneven collection, but probably an impossible assignment to pull off).

A famous review that Wernham wrote in these years reveals a razor-sharp mind. He had examined Geoffrey Elton's London Ph.D. thesis in December 1948. In 1956 he wrote a devastating critique of the book into which it had been turned, *The Tudor Revolution in Government*.[4] Elton's claim seemed to Wernham 'to rest upon a rather debatable interpretation of the relationship between Cromwell's work and the developments which went before and came after him'. Elton failed 'to distinguish adequately between government and administration': the break with Rome and the dissolution of the monasteries necessarily led to an increase in bureaucratic activity. But that, Wernham insisted, 'was administration not government'. What mattered was how the state's expenditure was monitored: and here the very close involvement of Cromwell was more a matter of 'personal' than of 'bureaucratic' government. Elton had not shown that there was any fundamental change in the way the king's council operated. Many of the administrative developments after Cromwell's fall reversed

---

[4] *English Historical Review*, 71 (1956), 92–5.

rather than extended them: 'Cromwell was rather the last exponent of Henry VII's methods than the father of the Elizabethan exchequer'. And, most perceptively of all, Wernham questioned Elton's view of the relationship between Henry VIII and Cromwell. 'Because the king was not much addicted to writing—and after all, why keep a secretary and write letters yourself?—it is much too easily assumed that he was, if not a mere cipher, at least in only remote control': Wernham pointed out that Elton cited Cromwell submitting to the king 'a whole string of quite minor details' and concluded that these suggested 'that it was the minister and not the king who did as he was told'. Wernham's concluding remarks deftly but courteously summed up his scepticism. 'It is thus difficult not to feel that this book may have exaggerated the supremacy and extent of Cromwell's influence no less than the novelty and revolutionary character of the administrative changes of the time. And this, unfortunately, must leave us still in doubt as to the true significance of the developments to whose unravelling Dr Elton has devoted so much painstaking and ingenious research in so wide a range of often difficult and specialised sources.'

But Wernham disliked academic polemic. He thought the heated controversy—'the stupid family feud' between Oxford historians—over the gentry a distraction ('where have all the gentry gone?', he asked after the hue and cry had subsided). In an appreciation of Elton written when he was ninety, Wernham generously supposed that the young Elton's ambition, stimulated by Sir John Neale, had led him to exaggerate the significance of the interesting information that he had presented in his thesis—in which there is no mention of any revolution. 'Through force of circumstance his apprenticeship in Tudor history had been brief and distracted', Wernham noted: 'it is hardly surprising if in an over-eagerness to make his mark he allowed the depth and excellence of his research to tempt him a bridge too far in the conclusions he drew from it.' Where K. B. McFarlane, with whom Wernham had discussed the book, saw it as all but pernicious, Wernham thought the debates that Elton provoked his greatest contribution, given that they broadened and deepened understanding of early Tudor administration and compelled historians to look at late medieval and early modern English history as a whole. Significantly Wernham thought Elton's not being a native born Englishman, not having family roots in England partly explained his lack of interest in foreign policy or matters of national defence. Striking and characteristic here is Wernham's generosity in seeing the best in Elton's work and excusing its limitations: yet in his review he had cut right to the heart of the failings of Elton's book. Having made his point, Wernham had moved on, rather than writing his own book on the subject. Elton kept on shouting, and the *Tudor Revolution in Government* dominated the field. When Penry Williams critically reviewed Elton's Ford Lectures, *Policy and Police* (1972) in the *English Historical Review*, Elton responded, somewhat pained, that he never had much luck with the *EHR*, but at least, he assured Penry Williams, 'you are a specialist, unlike Wernham who reviewed me twenty years ago', a remark Wernham would never have made about anyone who adversely reviewed a work of his.

The best justification of Wernham's approach is that all his calendaring proved to be the groundwork for his eventual books. The first, published when he was sixty, *Before the Armada: the growth of Tudor Foreign Policy 1485–1588* (1966), did not quite clinch the point. It was a very decent superior textbook, well-written, clearly organised (it has the flavour of those older schoolbooks that had summaries in bold type indented in the text), but measured against the highest expectations, something of a disappointment—until it is re-read in the light of his subsequent books, when it appears as a necessary contextualisation of his core interest, England's relations with Spain, France and the Netherlands from the late 1580s to the late 1590s. To make sense of what was happening then, especially what was new, Wernham felt he had to begin earlier. But he did not have space to develop arguments or to offer detailed reasoning when he disagreed with other scholars, and some of his claims, especially in the first part of his period, are questionable (for example his emphasis on Henry VIII's plans for the marriage of his daughter Mary). But there was much of value, for example his development of his earlier insights 'into the effect of prevailing west winds on naval strategy: the advantages enjoyed by any invader from the south-west, and the difficulty of supplying English fleets on duty in the channel'. 'An understanding of seamanship is as desirable an attribute in diplomatic historians', C. S. L. Davies remarked, 'as the use of boots by economic ones.'

Those who did not know Wernham well might have supposed that *Before the Armada* was his swan-song, and a touch muted at that: sound and sensible, but not always exciting. In 1966, a few years before his retirement, he had bought a house in Hill Head, on the coast between Southampton and Portsmouth, (where Isobel and he had begun going for weekends from the early 1950s) with magnificent views over the Solent to the Isle of Wight (and indeed in his final year at Oxford, he lived the life of a commuter). Like many academics giving up their college rooms, he needed to get rid of books for which he would not have space at home; for some, the news that he was selling his books symbolised a wider withdrawal from scholarship. Such gossip could not have been more wrong. For on 15 July 1967, a year after the publication of *Before the Armada*, he began planning his next book, *After the Armada*, and in January 1968 he began writing: by August he had written 7312 words. In March 1969 he returned to chapter 2 and wrote 8620 words by 16 April. By September 1969 he had finished chapters 3 and 4. A year's illness halted progress until January 1971, when he was able, for once, to write during term. Nine chapters had been written by the time he retired in 1972. And once in Hill Head, he settled into a remarkable routine of active scholarship, carefully making a room on the landward side his study so that he should not be distracted from his work by the stunning views. He divided his time between work on the *Lists and Analyses* and on *After the Armada*. From 1974 he taught on a summer school in the University of British Columbia, his wife's home city. Then in 1975, Thomas Barnes, whose Oxford D.Phil. on Somerset in the 1630s he had supervised in the 1950s, invited him to give Una's Lectures in the University of Berkeley, California, published in 1980 as *The Making of Elizabethan Foreign Policy 1558–1603*. In effect these were the Ford Lectures that Wernham was (presumably) never invited to give in Oxford. Here he demonstrated his command over the sources, together with a subtle understanding of their strengths and weaknesses: 'how the abundance of incoming letters to the government, compared with the relative scarcity of outgoing, can distort our picture of the making of decisions'. Wernham also confirmed his talent as a polemicist, taking issue with Charles Wilson's Ford Lectures delivered in 1969 arguing that Queen Elizabeth's failure to intervene in the Netherlands in the late 1570s was dangerously mistaken. Elizabeth had a policy, more hers than anyone else's, even if shaped by circumstances, Wernham maintained. He believed that Wilson underestimated very seriously 'the depth of the divisions, religious, social and political, within the United Netherlands and the strength of the particularist motivation of the movement', while he overestimated William of Orange's control over the radical Calvinists in Flanders. Intervention in 1577–8 would have provoked Philip into a trade embargo at least, war at worst. Elizabeth's interventions from 1585 were, for Wernham, far more defensible: quite unexpectedly the French monarchy was close to collapse and France in danger of falling under Spanish control, with incalculable risks for England.

Lectures delivered and written up, Wernham returned to his labours on the *Lists and Analyses* and on his next book. By 1981 *After the Armada* was complete. Cape, who had published the twice-reprinted *Before the Armada*, now turned down the sequel. Fortunately Oxford University Press stepped in: they would take it if Wernham took no royalties, and cut his text by 20 per cent, which he duly and quickly did. *After the Armada: Elizabethan England and the Struggle for Western Europe 1588–1595*, published in 1984 when Wernham was 78, is by any standards a masterly book. It offers a detailed narrative, on a grand scale, of the evolution of foreign policy and of the military and naval campaigns of those years, weaving what Geoffrey Parker rightly describes as 'a single great tapestry'. The events covered were complex and various, denying their historian a simple integrative theme. Wernham's handling of such intricate and complex material is a model, compellingly readable, constantly but effortlessly relating details to larger issues. His central aim was to show the importance of the continental and military side of the war against Spain as against the more fashionable emphasis on its naval and oceanic aspects: the soldiers who served in Normandy, the Netherlands and Britanny achieved more—and cost more—than did the exploits of Hawkins and Drake. Wernham's narrative forcefully brings home the multiplicity of concerns of Elizabeth and her advisers; the hectic press of events; the limitations on her freedom of action ('the trouble in the sea war was that a sixteenth-century government lacked the power to harness this private enterprise, operating primarily for profit, to a national strategic purpose'); the difficulties of obtaining reliable information, not least on the intentions of allies, as well as those of enemies ('one of the greatest difficulties that faced all sixteenth-century governments was the difficulty of assessing accurately their intelligences about their neighbours and enemies'); the war-weariness, induced by years of heavy financial demands and impressment of men for no immediately obvious victories, seen in parliamentary reluctance to grant taxation in 1593. Queen Elizabeth emerges as the dominant force in these years, willing to embark on aggressive actions, notably the ill-fated attempt on Portugal in 1589, Willoughby's expedition in support of Henry IV later that year (which 'did more than a little to make possible Henry IV's famous victory at Ivry in March 1590'), and the despatch of the earl of Essex in support of Henry IV's siege of Rouen in 1591, until from late 1591 Elizabeth returned to a more defensive policy, in particular to prevent Spanish dominance of Brittany. 'Although her more ambitious offensive plans and enterprises came to nothing, she and her Dutch and French allies did prevent Spain from establishing its control over the whole of western Europe, from acquiring the crown of France and destroying the Dutch republic. In this defensive achievement Elizabethan England had played a very considerable part.'

Geoffrey Parker criticised Wernham's dependence on a single source: the records of Elizabeth's government, and especially its diplomatic correspondence. Wernham's account of military events would, he urged, have benefited from use of the archives of Brussels and Simancas. A question mark in Wernham's copy of Parker's review against the point that 'Parma's numerous unintercepted letters on the subject [of the raising of the siege of Rouen in April 1592] to Philip II are overlooked' suggests that Wernham was not altogether convinced. Wernham did supplement English sources by reference to some transcripts from foreign archives and some printed Spanish and Dutch sources. And such criticism prompts an obvious response—how much it is reasonable to expect any historian to cover? Wernham insisted throughout that he was not writing the history of international relations in Europe as a whole but rather giving an account of how things appeared to Elizabeth and her advisers, and for that the sources in which he had immersed himself were more than sufficient. Penry Williams's verdict was heart-felt: 'to comprehend fully the achievement of Mr Wernham in the research and writing that went to produce this splendid book, one must work . . . on the period after 1596, when we no longer have his guidance. To do that is like walking in hill country where no ordnance survey maps are available. The sense of deprivation is severe, even alarming. one can only ask, selfishly, for more.'

And that is what Wernham gave, undaunted by the death of his wife Isobel in 1986—his diaries record his daily visits to see her mostly asleep in hospital in the last year of her life after an incapacitating stroke. He was involved in the Hill Head and Stubbington Local History Society intended 'to promote interest and enjoyment of history and instigate research into local history and encourage social intercourse between persons interested in such matters', serving as its President from its inception in 1987, and supporting it financially: historians whom he invited to give lectures were astonished to find audiences of sixty or seventy. He continued to work on the *Lists and Analyses*. But his main labours were devoted to *The Return of the Armadas*, which he began on 28 October 1985 when he was 79 and completed on 25 June 1992 at the age of 86: it appeared in 1994 when he was 88.

The Return of the Armadas: The Last Years of the Elizabethan War against Spain 1595–1603 dealt with the renewed naval wars between England and Spain and with the rebellion in Ireland that threatened to give the Spanish a golden opportunity. Once more Wernham offered (in Simon Adams's words) 'a lucidly, even effortlessly, written account of military operations and diplomacy';[5] 'a carefully crafted and superbly integrated narrative which illuminated the relationship between strategic debate, diplomacy and military and naval operations' (Cliff Davies). Moreover Wernham gave special attention to the role of Robert Devereux, second earl of Essex, both in naval campaigns, especially against Cadiz in 1596 and the abortive 'armadas' of 1596 and 1597, and in a rather different role against the Irish rebels, showing the interconnectedness of foreign policy and domestic politics. His portrayal of Essex and Elizabeth is a substantial political study in its own right.

After the Armada and *The Return of the Armadas* are two monographs that would be impressive at any age: they are a remarkable achievement for an historian long in retirement. The verve and freshness of the writing vividly convey Wernham's own continuing intellectual excitement. It was not surprising that these books led to his election as a Senior Fellow of the British Academy in 1995 at the age of 88. They amount to an ample vindication of his life's commitment to his chosen field, and of the judgements of those who had long before elected him to his lectureship, fellowship and chair. If he had not been a prolific publisher while in post, in that he was typical of his time. But what was remarkable and unusual about him was the depth and sustained focus of his commitment to scholarship in the 1950s and 1960s: patient, painstaking, cumulative, and now, in long years of retirement, distilled into two volumes of grand narrative of lasting value. Nor was that all: he continued preparing a further volume of the *Lists and Analyses* and at the age of 91, a few months before his death on 17 April 1999, he wrote an essay on 'English Combined Operations during the Elizabethan War against Spain 1585–1603' for a collection edited by David Trim and Mark Fissel.

Since 1964 Wernham had regularly attended the Senior Historians Conferences at Cumberland Lodge, Windsor Great Park. In 1995 he was asked to give a short talk on 'how and why we study history'. His reflections show how his writings were the product of a larger engagement with his subject. He remembered young men going off to fight in the First World War and returning to the village injured. He came of age 'in the comparatively warm glow of the middle 1920s' and experienced 'the devastating disillusionment of the 1930s and early 1940s'. 'I have lived through all but a few years of what must be one of the bloodiest centuries in human history.' So he had not studied history 'out of any high-falutin' notion that I should thereby make the world a vastly better place': the

---

[5] *English Historical Review*, 110 (1995), 421–3.

historian was much more likely to ask 'when will they ever learn?'. Nor had he been unduly motivated by 'positions of not inconsiderable emolument'. He denied that he had a method of working and writing that could be called a method. He worked carefully through as many of the main sources of whatever he was going to write about as he could cope with, taking very full notes of all that seemed relevant and then going over and over them to piece the story together till he began to get some idea of it in its wholeness. He swelled that out with as much rather casual 'reading round' which he did with the sort of half-sleepy attention one gives to television, jotting down a note now and again of anything that particularly caught his attention. Wernham feared 'all that is very old-fashioned and ordinary, but I am no philosopher'. When he had been invited to give the talk, his first reaction had been 'what the hell can I say about that'. But his credo bears quotation:

> What has always fascinated me has been the enormous complexity and multiplicity of the subject, what Thomas Hardy rather lugubriously called 'the mournful manysidedness of things'—the way in which over a particular period of time and a particular area (in my case it has been predominantly the sixteenth century and Western Europe), how in that period, that region, a multitude of influences crisscross, interweave, interact, clash and conflict to produce a movement of change, to produce tensions that eventually burst out, often as the result of some comparatively trivial accident—that Henry III of France had a wrist that was just not strong enough to deflect the assassin's dagger . . . Some comparatively small accident that makes an eruption possible and causes the whole process to lurch off on a somewhat different course. The attraction and the challenge of history to me is to try to see all that as a whole, and to see also not only what people of the time saw in the main area of their vision but also what they saw out of the tail of their eye, in their peripheral vision—to see all that in its wholeness, 'to grasp the scheme of things entire'—that is for me the appeal and challenge of history.

That explained why almost all Wernham wrote was in narrative form: 'that I find so far—maybe some day I'll discover a better way—is the best, indeed I might say the only way of trying to convey this sense of wholeness, of simultaneous multiplicity producing movement and change. Even by narrative you can of course never really convey that wholeness fully—you still have to take things one at a time—but it is enormous fun trying to do it and you can in the narrative way convey a real idea of movement and some idea of wholeness.'

Wernham's experience of writing a narrative of Bomber Command had strengthened such sentiments. In some ways that and his historical interests interacted more broadly. In an unpublished talk on 'Elizabethan Sea Power and 20th century Air Power', Wernham reflected on the similarities in the ways that men thought about them. The rulers of the realm faced similar revolutions in matters of national defence, showed similar foresight in planning novel ways of dealing with them, but also similar lack of foresight in applying novel methods and in realistically assessing their likely effectiveness.

On Bomber Command, on Elton's Tudor Revolution, on the merits of Elizabeth's foreign policy, Wernham was bold and incisive in his interpretations. But without hiding his views or pulling his punches in his books and reviews, he nonetheless managed to avoid the rancorous exchanges that so characterised so many early modern historians. Indeed in conversation he was remarkably generous about other scholars' work and never spoke ill of other historians, above all never questioning their motives. He unhesitatingly offered both Geoffrey Elton and Charles Wilson hospitality when they gave the Ford Lectures in Oxford. Michael Maclagan, the medievalist at Trinity, remembered him as 'the most kindly and agreeable friend and colleague for whom a man could wish'. Wernham appreciated his good fortune. If he had been called up at once when he volunteered for service in 1941—his commission was delayed on medical grounds—he would have been on a ship that reached Singapore just in time to be captured by the Japanese and spent the war in a prison camp. If he had stayed just a few minutes later when visiting his wife in Royal Berkshire Hospital, Reading a few days after his daughter Joan had been born in 1943, he would have fallen victim to German bombs when walking through the town centre. He was grateful for the opportunities that he had been given—the post in the PRO, the fellowship at Trinity, the professorship of Modern History—and never envious of the successes and honours of others. Throughout his long life he took an intense and simple pleasure in his learning, teaching and writing. And he was delighted when at the age of 88 he was elected to the Academy in 1995.

G. W. BERNARD
University of Southampton

Note: I should wish especially to thank Bruce Wernham's daughter and son-in-law, Joan and Sam Jerrett, for allowing me access to unpublished papers, notes and diaries, from which quotations and information in the text above have been taken, and for their generous hospitality. I should also wish to thank those who have shared their impressions of Bruce Wernham with me, including James Campbell, the late Michael Maclagan, Noble Frankland, John Fraser, Thomas Barnes, David Trim, Cliff Davies, Penry Williams, Kevin Sharpe, the late Hugh Trevor-Roper and Geoffrey Parker.